THE DOMESTIC SOURCES
OF
AMERICAN FOREIGN POLICY

Insights and Evidence

THE DOMESTIC SOURCES
OF
AMERICAN FOREIGN POLICY

Insights and Evidence

Edited by

Charles W. Kegley, Jr.
University of South Carolina

Eugene R. Wittkopf
Louisiana State University

St. Martin's Press
New York

Library of Congress Number:87-060560

For information, write:
St. Martin's Press, Inc.
175 Fifth Avenue
New York, NY 10010

Graphics: G&H Soho
Cover Design: Tom McKeveny

ISBN: 0-312-01142-3

ACKNOWLEDGMENTS

"Breakdown: The Impact of Domestic Politics on American Foreign Policy" by I. M. Destler, Leslie H. Gelb, and Anthony Lake. Copyright © 1984 by I. M. Destler, Leslie H. Gelb and Anthony Lake. Reprinted by permission of Simon & Schuster, Inc.

"A Leadership Divided: The Foreign Policy Beliefs of American Leaders, 1976–1984" by Ole R. Holsti and James N. Rosenau. This article was written especially for this book. Copyright © 1987 by Ole R. Holsti and James N. Rosenau.

"America's State of Mind: Trends in Public Attitudes Toward Foreign Policy" by John E. Reilly. Reprinted with permission from Foreign Policy 66 (Spring 1987). Copyright 1987 by the Carnegie Endowment for International Peace.

"The Influence of Ethnic Interest Groups on American Middle East Policy" by Mitchell Bard. This article was written especially for this book.

"The Iron Triangle: Inside the Defense Policy Process" by Gordon Adams. Copyright © 1987 by Gordon Adams. This article was written especially for this book.

"Playing the Government's Game: The Mass Media and American Foreign Policy" by William A. Dorman. Reprinted by permission of the Bulletin of the Atomic Scientists, a magazine of science and world affairs. Copyright © 1985 by the Educational Foundation for Nuclear Science.

"The Electoral Cycle and the Conduct of American Foreign Policy" by William B. Quandt. Reprinted with permission from Political Science Quarterly 101, no. 5 (1986): 825–37.

Acknowledgments and copyrights continue at the back of the book on p. 288, which constitutes an extension of the copyright page.

In memory of my father and my mother
                                    CWK

For my mother and in memory of my father
                                    ERW

PREFACE

This book focuses on the domestic sources of American foreign policy. To many foreign policy analysts schooled in the logic of political realism, that emphasis may seem misplaced. During the past decade, however, American foreign policy has become increasingly politicized, to the point, as we note in our introductory essay, that the old aphorism "politics stops at the water's edge" now seems little more than a quaint historical cliché. As the internationalization of American politics proceeds at an accelerating pace, the nexus between what happens abroad and what happens at home demands attention.

The book is organized into three parts adapted from the analytical framework elaborated in our *American Foreign Policy: Pattern and Process* (St. Martin's Press, 1987). The first part focuses on the societal environment of American foreign policy-making, the second on the institutional structures within which decisions are framed, and the third on the individual policymakers who make choices for the nation and on the policy-making positions they occupy. Throughout, we have sought to provide essays that are informed theoretically and empirically, and are as up-to-date as possible.

We gratefully acknowledge the help William A. Clark provided in bringing this collection together and the continuing support of our friends at St. Martin's Press, and especially Larry Swanson, Richard Steins, and Beverly Hinton. We also wish to thank Russel Bova, Dickinson College; John H. Esterline, California State Polytechnic, Pomona; and Ole R. Holsti, Duke University, for their comments in reviewing this material.

Charles W. Kegley, Jr.
Eugene R. Wittkopf

CONTENTS

The Domestic Sources of American Foreign Policy:
An Introduction
CHARLES W. KEGLEY, JR., AND EUGENE R. WITTKOPF   1

PART I   THE SOCIETAL ENVIRONMENT   11

1 Breakdown: The Impact of Domestic Politics on American
   Foreign Policy
   I. M. DESTLER, LESLIE H. GELB, AND ANTHONY LAKE   17

2 A Leadership Divided: The Foreign Policy Beliefs of American
   Leaders, 1976–1984
   OLE R. HOLSTI AND JAMES N. ROSENAU   30

3 America's State of Mind: Trends in Public Attitudes Toward
   Foreign Policy
   JOHN E. RIELLY   45

4 The Influence of Ethnic Interest Groups on American Middle
   East Policy
   MITCHELL BARD   57

5 The Iron Triangle: Inside the Defense Policy Process
   GORDON ADAMS   70

6 Playing the Government's Game: The Mass Media and
   American Foreign Policy
   WILLIAM A. DORMAN   79

7 The Electoral Cycle and the Conduct of American Foreign Policy
   WILLIAM B. QUANDT   87

PART II   THE INSTITUTIONAL SETTING   99

8 The President and the Management of Foreign Policy: Styles and
   Models
   ALEXANDER L. GEORGE   107

9 The Presidency and the Imperial Temptation
   ARTHUR M. SCHLESINGER, JR.   127

10   Reagan's Junta: The Institutional Sources of the Iran-*Contra*
     Affair
     THEODORE DRAPER   131

11   Why State Can't Lead
     DUNCAN L. CLARKE   142

12   President, Congress, and American Foreign Policy
     THOMAS E. CRONIN   149

13   Politics Over Promise: Domestic Impediments to Arms Control
     STEVEN E. MILLER   166

14   The President, "Intermestic" Issues, and the Risks of Policy
     Leadership
     RYAN J. BARILLEAUX   178

PART III   DECISION MAKERS AND THEIR POLICY-
                MAKING POSITIONS   189

15   What's Wrong With Our Defense Establishment
     DAVID C. JONES   195

16   How Could Vietnam Happen? An Autopsy
     JAMES C. THOMSON, JR.   205

17   Are Bureaucracies Important? A Re-examination of Accounts of
     the Cuban Missile Crisis
     STEPHEN D. KRASNER   215

18   The Divided Decision-Maker: American Domestic Politics and
     the Cuban Crises
     FEN OSLER HAMPSON   227

19   New Foreign Policy Problems and Old Bureaucratic
     Organizations
     CHARLES F. HERMANN   248

20   The Role of Leaders and Leadership in the Making of American
     Foreign Policy
     MARGARET G. HERMANN   266

About the Editors and Contributors   285

THE DOMESTIC SOURCES
OF
AMERICAN FOREIGN POLICY

Insights and Evidence

THE DOMESTIC SOURCES OF AMERICAN FOREIGN POLICY: AN INTRODUCTION

Charles W. Kegley, Jr., and Eugene R. Wittkopf

Understanding the goals of American foreign policy and the means through which they have been pursued poses intellectual challenges to the thoughtful observer. The assumptions that have guided American foreign policy during the past five decades have persisted in spite of momentous global changes and often rapidly unfolding international events. Five themes capture the assumptions underlying the principal ends and means of post–World War II American foreign policy: globalism, anticommunism, containment, military might, and interventionism.[1] Each has proven remarkably resilient. How do we make sense of this? How can we explain the remarkable durability in the foreign policy orientation of the United States and its apparent policy inertia in the face of complex changes occurring in world politics?

Change, not continuity, also seems to characterize American foreign policy. From the perspective of daily newspaper headlines and the electronic media, American foreign policy recurrently appears to dart first this way and then that in response to episodic developments abroad. What explains these perturbations? And how should they be interpreted against the background of the apparent permanence of the assumptions underlying postwar American foreign policy?

There is a third characteristic of contemporary American foreign policy: a disturbingly recurrent record of failure. When faced with crisis, American foreign policy often has appeared to fall into chaotic disarray, outside the control of the government, and unable to cope successfully. It is this proclivity that stimulated the authors of one assessment to title their revealing diagnosis *Our Own Worst Enemy: The Unmaking of American Foreign Policy.*[2] How does one explain the inability of the United States to frame a coherent response to emergent opportunities and threats emanating from beyond the nation's borders?

To answer these questions, we must look at the multiple sources from which American foreign policy derives. The durability, discontinuity, and disarray exhibited in American foreign policy cannot be traced simply to the turbulent international environment that renders ours an age of crisis, or even to the profusion of issues populating the global agenda which today strain the ability of even the most efficient governments to cope.[3] American foreign policy must also be traced to the influence of conditions internal to the United States and to the characteristics peculiar to those responsible for the nation's behaviors abroad. For American foreign policy is shaped in part by the domestic needs and political demands articulated from within the American political system, by the processes through which American foreign policy is formulated, and by those who aspire to manage and direct them.

The Domestic Sources of American Foreign Policy addresses these dimensions of American foreign policy-making. While acknowledging that American foreign policy springs from external as well as internal factors, this book focuses on those factors that endow the world's largest and oldest democracy with peculiar and sometimes unique characteristics which distinguish it from others in the community of nations, and which, correspondingly, may give its foreign policy a peculiar and unique cast. Similarly, just as domestic factors may account for American foreign policy today, the future course of the nation's orientation toward the world may also be shaped by the force of those influences.

INTERNAL CONDITIONS AND EXTERNAL BEHAVIOR

The proposition that domestic stimuli are a source of foreign policy is not novel. In ancient Greece, for instance, Thucydides observed how the external behavior of the Greek city-states was often shaped less by what each was doing toward the others than by what was occurring within them. He added that often the behavior leaders emitted toward other city-states was undertaken to affect, not relations with the targets of the action, but instead the political climate within the leaders' own city-states.

To acknowledge the existence of this same linkage in today's world is to challenge the conventional interpretation of the determinants of relations among nations. To most observers, the international system resembles a billiard table, and the units of the system—states—are likened to billiard balls whose reactions are determined exclusively by the impact of each unit on the others as they collide in an endless action-reaction sequence of events. What occurs *inside* the balls, and how that might propel them to move in one direction or another, is beyond the purview of the "billiard ball" model of international politics. To look at the domestic sources of foreign policy, then, is to look at conditions and activities within the state, instead of only conditions outside it. Such a focus implies that we abandon the assumption that all states are unitary actors, as suggested by the billiard ball metaphor within which societal cleavages and the political disputes they engender are presumed to have no effect on foreign behavior. Instead, the domestic-sources perspective conforms to the view that the "foreign policy of governments is more than simply a series of responses to international stimuli, that forces at work within a society can also contribute to the quality and contents of its external behavior."[4]

This perspective is particularly applicable in efforts to understand contemporary American foreign policy and the sources from which it derives. American society is relentlessly pluralistic; its democratic form of government encourages the active involvement of the American people in determining what the government does; and its institutional structures invite debate among the officials selected to govern. American "exceptionalism" and the American experiment in governance undeniably create a situation where domestic influences on foreign policy are especially—perhaps uniquely—strong.

Developments in world politics also demand that attention be given to the internal roots of external behavior. The world has changed in many ways since the United States first emerged a superpower following World War II. Today, it is a truism that the world has shrunk dramatically as the web of global interdependence among nations has progressively tightened. Ironically, the internationalization of the global political economy has expanded domestic pressures on the formulation of governments' foreign policies. That trend has reduced the significance of borders, compromised the sovereign autonomy of the nation-state, blurred the distinction between foreign and domestic politics, expanded the number and scope of issues on nations' foreign policy agendas, heightened the saliency of welfare issues, aroused the efforts of private groups to modify national policies, and elevated the participation of domestically oriented government agencies in the foreign policy-making process.[5] At the same time, national security issues have gained increased urgency as the capacity for nuclear destruction has grown geometrically. Faced with the threat of catastrophic war, citizens in many different countries have mobilized to restrain their governments from pursuing policies believed to enhance, not deter, the prospects of a nuclear apocalypse.

Let us elaborate on this perspective as it applies to the United States by taking a closer look at the sources of American foreign policy and the factors that combine to give it shape and direction.

THE NEXUS BETWEEN DOMESTIC INFLUENCES AND POLICY OUTCOMES

Political commentators and analysts often share similar views about the dominant goals of postwar American foreign policy. But they differ widely in their explanations of its causes. Disagreement exists because the sources of American foreign policy are difficult to trace.

Analytically, we can take an important step toward tracing causation by taking cognizance of the existence of a number of simultaneously powerful influences. Broadly speaking, perceptions about the multitude of domestic influences on American foreign policy-making can be grouped into three basic categories: (1) the *societal* environment of the nation; (2) its *institutional* setting; and (3) the individual characteristics of the nation's *decision makers* and the *policy-making positions* they occupy. It is in reference to these three basic categories of internal sources of foreign policy that more discrete explanatory variables can be logically sorted and grouped.

The relationship between the basic categories and American foreign policy-making and their interrelationships among one another are depicted in Figure 1.[6] The figure posits that domestic policy influences are *inputs* to the foreign policy-making process that act as conditioning factors in the policy-making game and that collectively shape the decision-making process that converts policy inputs into foreign policy. In this context, we can think of foreign policy as the goals that the nation's officials seek to realize abroad, the values that give rise to those goals, and the means or instruments through which they are pursued. Conceptualized as the *outputs* of the process that converts domestic

Figure 1. The Domestic Sources of American Foreign Policy: Three Layers of Influence

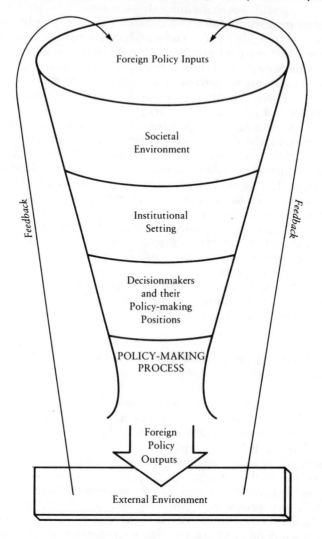

influences into goals and means, foreign policy (or, perhaps preferably, policies) is typically multifaceted, ranging from discrete behaviors linked to specific issues to recurring patterns of behavior that define the continuous efforts of the United States to cope with the environment beyond its borders. Importantly, however, neither discrete events nor broad policy patterns are likely to be accounted for adequately by reference to only one explanatory factor.

Many of the discrete variables that make up the categories that define the domestic sources of American foreign policy are easily identified, but the lines between the categories themselves are not always clear-cut. To help draw these larger distinctions as well as explicate the smaller ones, it is useful to think of the explanatory categories in terms of layers of complexity and size.

At the broadest level is the *societal environment*. The political culture of the

United States—the basic needs, values, beliefs, and self-images widely shared by Americans about their political system—stands out as a primary societal source of American foreign policy. Minimally, those beliefs find expression in the kinds of values and political institutions American policymakers have sought to export to others in the postwar period. Included is a preference not only for democracy over authoritarianism and totalitarianism, but also for capitalism over socialism. From the viewpoint of the American *liberal tradition*—captured in preferences for limited government, individual liberty, due process of law, self-determination, free enterprise, inalienable (natural) rights, the equality of citizens before the law, majority rule, minority rights, federalism, and the separation of powers—fear of Communism, a persistent pattern in postwar American foreign policy, is clearly understandable. It inheres in Americans' views of themselves, their government, and their leaders.

While it is unassailable that American political culture colors what the nation's political leaders want and (usually, at least) how they go about getting it, the liberal tradition is an amorphous guide to action. Public opinion may be a more meaningful guide to which political leaders turn when weighing public preferences. Here, two traditions stand out. One, the *elitist* tradition, maintains that the only opinions that matter are those embraced by the small group of corporate, financial, legal, and university professionals who are in positions to "call the shots." Once known as "The Establishment," these influential Americans are believed to have the ability to shape the opinions of the mass of the American public so as to support policies that fit the interests and values of the elites. The mass media are often viewed as a key cog in the elitist machine, since it is through the media that the elite is often assumed to manipulate the mass. Government decisions, from this viewpoint, are little more than expressions of elite preferences. Indeed, decision makers themselves, while sometimes members of the elite, are often little more than "proximate policymakers" who merely express elite preferences in such things as acts of Congress.

The other tradition is *pluralism*. Here public policy flows upward rather than downward, as in the elitist model. Mass public opinion is accorded greater weight in this model, and it finds expression through interest groups, which seek to pressure government for policies consonant with the preferences of "average" Americans. National security issues, especially during times of crisis, are normally thought to be beyond the purview of interest group activity, but there is some evidence that challenges that traditional view.[7] Beyond dispute is the increased ability of interest groups to pressure government in an environment where the distinction between foreign and domestic policy is increasingly blurred, as has come to be the case given the growing economic interdependence of the United States with the rest of the world. From a pluralist perspective, laws passed by Congress not only embody public policy; they also register the balance of contending forces within American society at any particular point in time.

The media appear less conspiratorial in the pluralist than in the elitist model, but their role is potent nonetheless. Indeed, to some the media *are* public opinion. Minimally, the media help to set the agenda for public discussion and often lay out for the American people the range of interpretations about foreign policy issues from which they might choose. Thus the media help to aggregate the interests of more discrete groups in American society.

Political parties also aggregate interests. In the two-party system of the

United States political parties are broad coalitions of ethnic, religious, economic, educational, professional, working-class, and other kinds of groups. One of the most important functions these broad coalitions serve is the selection of personnel to key policy-making positions. They also have the capacity to serve as referenda on past policy performance. What role foreign policy attitudes and opinions play in shaping citizens' choices on these broad issues is difficult to determine. On the one hand, most citizens are motivated not by foreign policy issues but by domestic ones. Their electoral choices seem to reflect those preferences. On the other hand, foreign and national security policy issues also often figure uppermost in Americans' minds; for some they are critical when they enter the voting booth. In an environment where a few thousands of votes in a few electoral precincts can mean the difference between a candidate's victory or defeat, foreign policy is not so easily dismissed.

The elitist and pluralist models are ideal types—caricatures, perhaps. But they help identify key elements of the societal setting as an explanation of American foreign policy: political culture; the foreign policy beliefs and preferences of leaders and masses; and the role of the media, interest groups, and elections as expressions of (or of the absence of, as the case may be) political attitudes and preferences. These ideas will be explored in the essays in Part I.

As we peel away the societal environment as a source of American foreign policy, a second category is revealed: the *institutional setting,* consisting of the various branches of government and the departments and agencies assigned responsibility for decision making and management. The category incorporates as a source of American foreign policy those diverse properties related to the structure of the United States government that limit or enhance the foreign policy choices made by decision makers and affect the ways in which those choices are implemented. Underlying the notion of institutional influences on foreign policy is the compelling assumption that a relationship exists between the substance of policy and the process by which it is made.

The structure of the American "foreign affairs government" encompasses a cluster of variables and organizational actors which influence, directly and indirectly, what the United States does—or does not do—abroad. Most striking in this regard is the division of authority and responsibility for foreign policy-making between Congress and the president. The Constitution of the United States embraces the eighteenth-century belief that the abuse of political power is best controlled, not through its centralization, but through its fragmentation in a system of checks and balances. Because authority and responsibility for the making and implementation of foreign policy are divided, the separation of powers between the legislative and executive branches is an "invitation to struggle."[8]

The struggle for control over foreign policy-making is not confined to the executive and legislative branches. American foreign policy is formulated through the activities of many executive-branch departments and agencies which have proliferated in size and grown in number as the United States has assumed a "globalist" foreign policy. The growing interdependence of the United States with the global political economy has reinforced these trends as a number of executive-branch departments oriented primarily toward domestic affairs have increased their stake in the foreign policy game.

With growth has come fragmentation of authority over policy-making, a characterization that takes on special meaning when the often overlapping roles performed by the White House and National Security Council staffs, the State Department, the Defense Department, the Treasury Department, the Central Intelligence Agency, and other decision-making units with a role in the policy-making process are observed. As more agencies have established a presence in the foreign affairs government, and as the clout of these competing institutions has expanded, the management of policy-making by the president, whose role in the conduct of foreign affairs is preeminent, has become more difficult. To many, blame for the incoherence and inconsistency sometimes exhibited in American foreign policy lies here.

Ironically, efforts to enhance presidential control of foreign policy-making by centralizing it in the White House have exacerbated rather than diminished incoherence and inconsistency. That conclusion emerges from an examination of the apparently perpetual contest that has emerged between the president's adviser for national security affairs and the secretary of state. Whereas many believe that the secretary of state should be the primary voice in making and executing American foreign policy, and that the national security adviser should be little more than a coordinator and facilitator of the policy process, the record of the past two-and-a-half decades demonstrates otherwise. The national security adviser has often played the role of a second secretary of state, with the inevitable conflicts that implies. In the extreme, members of the National Security Council, headed by the president's national security adviser, have even undertaken covert operational responsibilities apparently beyond the control not only of the secretary of state but of the president himself. That is the clear message of the Tower Commission Report on the Reagan administration's National Security Council system, whose purpose was to investigate the Iran-*contra* arms-for-hostages deal pursued by NSC staffers in 1985 and 1986.

If disagreements between the White House and the established departments responsible for foreign policy are a source of policy inconsistency and incoherence, the sheer size of the foreign affairs government and its bureaucratization tend to promote policy compromise and persistence, not policy innovation and revision. Thus the institutional setting of American foreign policy-making and the nature of democratic institutions generally inhibit the ability of the United States to adaptively alter its course in world affairs. The French sociologist Alexis de Tocqueville predicted as much over 150 years ago when he observed that "Foreign politics demand scarcely any of those qualities which a democracy possesses; they require, on the contrary, the perfect use of almost all those faculties in which it is deficient."

Looking to the institutional setting as a source of American foreign policy thus requires an examination of the responsibilities of a number of institutions and their relations with one another: the institutionalized presidency, with particular attention to the National Security Council and the national security adviser and his staff; the cabinet-level departments and the other agencies with foreign affairs responsibilities; and Congress.

When we peel away the institutional setting as a domestic source of American foreign policy, the people who make the policies can be brought into the picture more directly. Here the focus is on *decision makers* and their *policy-making positions*. The underlying proposition is that the personalities, psychological predispositions, perceptions, and role responsibilities of the people recruited into positions of power and responsibility for the making of American foreign policy make a difference. Indeed, the individual *decision maker* is the ultimate source of influence on policy, the final mediating force in the causal chain linking the other domestic forces to the ends and means of American foreign policy.

There are a number of ways in which personality and perceptional factors may impinge upon foreign policy-making. Ideas about Communism and the Soviet Union instilled early in life, for example, may subsequently affect the attitudes and behavior of those responsible for negotiating with Soviet leaders.[9] Similarly, policymakers' orientations toward decision making may profoundly affect the nation's foreign policy strategies. It has been suggested, for example, that American decision makers in the twentieth century can be characterized as either *crusaders* or *pragmatists*.[10] The hallmark of the crusader is a "missionary zeal to make the world better. The crusader tends to make decisions based on a preconceived idea rather than on the basis of experience. Even though there are alternatives, he usually does not see them." The pragmatist, on the other hand, "is guided by the facts and his experience in a given situation, not by wishes or unexamined preconceptions. . . . Always flexible, he does not get locked into a losing policy. He can change direction and try again, without inflicting damage to his self-esteem."[11] Woodrow Wilson has been described as the preeminent crusader, while Harry Truman has been described as the personification of the pragmatist.

Personality factors also help explain how presidents will choose to manage the conduct of foreign affairs. A president's psychological approach to information processing, known as his cognitive style, his orientation toward political conflict, and his sense of political efficacy are all important in understanding how he will structure his policy-making system and how he will deal with those around him.[12] In this case personal predispositions form a bridge between the institutional setting of American foreign policy-making and the process of decision making itself.

Presidents sometimes make foreign policy decisions not for their effect on the external environment but for purposes of influencing domestic politics. Foreign policy can be used to mobilize popular support at home, to increase authority through appeals to patriotism, and to enhance prospects for reelection. Nothing better illustrates the connection between domestic politics and foreign policy.

Although policymakers doubtless use foreign policy for domestic purposes, it is unclear whether they do so because of who they are or because of the positions they occupy. Given the apparent frequency with which policymakers in the United States and other countries alike engage in this type of behavior, it would appear that politicians' *role requirements*, not their personal predilections, explain this behavior. Policymakers' positions thus appear to stimulate certain predictable patterns of behavior. Conversely, the position an individual holds may constrain the impact of personality on policy-making behavior. Institutional roles thus reduce the influence of idiosyncratic factors on policy performance.

Individuals do, of course, have the capacity to interpret the roles they occupy, a fact that blurs the distinction between decision makers and their policy positions as competing rather than complementary explanations of American foreign policy. Clearly, however, policy-making positions, or roles, severely circumscribe the freedom and autonomy of the particular individuals who occupy them, and thus diminish the range of politically feasible choices. Hence, the relationship between the person and the position, and between the impact of decision makers and their roles on policy outcomes, is important to understand as a source of American foreign policy. That conclusion is illustrated nowhere more clearly than with a simple aphorism drawn from our understanding of the impact of bureaucratic politics on policy outcomes: where you stand depends on where you sit.

In sum, a focus on decision makers and their policy positions as a category of domestic influences on American foreign policy draws attention to the capacity of individuals to place their personal imprints on the nation's conduct abroad, while simultaneously alerting us to the need to examine the forces that constrain individual initiative. Principal among these are the role-induced constraints that occur within organizational settings. Because the making and execution of American foreign policy is fundamentally a group, or organizational, enterprise, we can surmise that these constraints are considerable. Part III will focus on these and on the capacity of individuals to transcend them.

THE DOMESTIC CONTEXT OF AMERICAN FOREIGN POLICY AND THE SOURCES OF AMERICAN FOREIGN POLICY

The categories described above, which organize our examination of the domestic sources of American foreign policy, encourage a systematic examination of the linkages between what happens at home and what happens abroad. But what happens abroad is also a function of the behavior of other nations and of extranational forces over which no nation, no matter how powerful, exerts control. A complete understanding of American foreign policy thus requires sensitivity to external as well as internal influences on American foreign policy.

A focus on the domestic sources of American foreign policy is warranted nonetheless. During the past decade, American foreign policy has become increasingly politicized, to the point that the old aphorism "politics stops at the water's edge" now seems little more than a quaint historical cliché. The boundaries separating developments at home and abroad, whether in matters of national security, economic well-being, or social welfare, are often blurred and seemingly nonexistent. As the internationalization of American politics proceeds at an accelerating pace, the nexus between domestic politics and foreign policy demands increasing attention.

NOTES

1. For a book-length analysis of these themes and the forces that sustain them, see Charles W. Kegley, Jr., and Eugene R. Wittkopf, *American Foreign Policy: Pattern and Process*, 3rd ed. (New York: St. Martin's, 1987).
2. I. M. Destler, Leslie H. Gelb, and Anthony Lake, *Our Own Worst Enemy: The Unmaking of American Foreign Policy* (New York: Simon and Schuster, 1984). A portion of the book is reprinted below in Part I.
3. See Charles W. Kegley, Jr., and Eugene R. Wittkopf, eds., *The Global Agenda: Issues and Perspectives*, 2nd ed. (New York: Random House, 1988).
4. James N. Rosenau, "Introduction," in James N. Rosenau, ed., *The Domestic Sources of Foreign Policy* (New York: Free Press, 1967), p. 2.
5. Robert O. Keohane and Joseph S. Nye, *Power and Interdependence: World Politics in Transition* (Boston: Little, Brown, 1977).

6. Both the figure and the analysis that follows are adapted from Charles W. Kegley, Jr., and Eugene R. Wittkopf, *American Foreign Policy: Pattern and Process*, 3rd ed. (New York: St. Martin's, 1987), in which the authors use a pretheoretical framework consisting of five source categories to organize analysis of American foreign policy. As described in detail there, the five source categories are the external, societal, governmental, role, and individual categories. For purposes of the analysis in this book, which focuses exclusively on domestic sources of American foreign policy, the external source category is not treated, and the four remaining categories are regrouped and renamed somewhat to refer to the societal environment, the institutional setting, and decision makers and their policy-making positions. By combining the role and individual categories into a single category, we in effect take two competing explanations—one which sees the characteristics of the individuals who make policy as the key explanation, the other which focuses on individuals not because of who they are but because of the roles they occupy in the policy-making system—and inquire not only into their separate effects but also into their potentially reinforcing interactions as an explanation of American foreign policy.

7. See, e.g., Bernard C. Cohen, "The Influence of Special-Interest Groups and Mass Media on Security Policy in the United States," pp. 222–241 in Charles W. Kegley, Jr., and Eugene R. Wittkopf, eds., *Perspectives on American Foreign Policy* (New York: St. Martin's, 1983), and Fen Osler Hampson, "The Divided Decision-Maker: American Domestic Politics and the Cuban Crises," *International Security* 9 (Winter 1984–1985), 130–165. Hampson's article is reprinted in Part III of this book.

8. Edwin S. Corwin, *The President: Office and Power* (New York: New York University Press, 1940), p. 200.

9. The classic study of this phenomenon is Ole R. Holsti's study of Secretary of State John Foster Dulles. See Ole R. Holsti, "The Belief System and National Images: A Case Study," *Journal of Conflict Resolution* 6 (September 1962), 244–252.

10. John G. Stoessinger, "Crusaders and Pragmatists: Two Types of Foreign Policy Makers," pp. 448–465 in Charles W. Kegley, Jr., and Eugene R. Wittkopf, eds., *Perspectives on American Foreign Policy* (New York: St. Martin's, 1983).

11. *Ibid.*, pp. 448–449.

12. Alexander L. George, *Presidential Decisionmaking in Foreign Policy: The Effective Use of Information and Advice* (Boulder, Colo.: Westview Press, 1980). A portion of George's book, with an epilogue on the Reagan administration written especially for this book, is reprinted in Part II.

Part I: The Societal Environment

Consensus. Bipartisanship. The Establishment. All three terms relate in one way or another to the belief that foreign policy is somehow "above politics." According to this belief, national interests are put ahead of partisan and personal interests in the formulation and execution of American foreign policy. The international strategic situation, not domestic considerations, is what matters. It is this viewpoint that undergirds Americans' long-standing belief that politics "stops at the water's edge."

That simple aphorism may once have been true, but, as suggested in the introduction to this book, it no longer is. It may always have been the case that the choices made by American policymakers are the result of internal, and not just international, considerations. The neccessity of maintaining a power base, the pragmatic desire to preserve the freedom to maneuver in the future, and the political need to remain popular with voters are political motivations not confined to the present or the recent past. If these considerations have gained special prominence as we try to understand American foreign policy today, their roots can be traced to the 1970s, and to the Vietnam tragedy in particular.

Any number of "lessons" can be drawn from the long and unhappy involvement of the United States in Indochina, which spanned some two decades from the 1950s to the 1970s. Principal among them are the conclusions that American military power by itself cannot achieve the objectives of American foreign policy, and that defense policy is not a substitute for foreign policy. Those convictions lay at the heart of the so-called Vietnam syndrome, a confluence of beliefs that led American policymakers in the years following United States withdrawal from Vietnam in 1973 to the conclusion that neither the American people nor their representatives in Congress would support U.S. intervention overseas—at least not protracted intervention—as a way of advancing the nation's interests and globalist foreign policy objectives. If American society had once supported the nation's role as global policeman, no longer was that true.

Other developments during the 1970s contributed to the growing politicization of American foreign policy. Détente was one. As a pattern and process designed to relax tensions with the Soviet Union, détente called into question the wisdom and assumptions of containment, the strategy—widely supported at home—that had served as the cornerstone of American policy abroad for more than two decades. Watergate was another. Recall that the burglary of Democratic national headquarters at the Watergate hotel complex in 1972 was carried out by a gang of former CIA "operatives" whose initial creation was motivated by foreign policy considerations, specifically a desire by the Nixon administration to quell Vietnam War dissidents in the name of national security. With the ignominious resignation of Richard Nixon as president of the United States in August 1974, Watergate challenged Americans' faith in their political institutions and their belief that a presidency preeminent in foreign policy continued to be a necessity in the post–Cold War era.

Vietnam, détente, and Watergate stand out as events illuminating how societal factors have come to impinge upon American foreign policy-making in unprecedented ways. To these might be added OPEC. In the winter of 1973–1974, the Organization of Petroleum Exporting Countries was able to increase fourfold the price of oil traded internationally at precisely the time the United States was becoming increasingly, and some thought, dangerously, dependent on imported oil. Overnight, it seemed, the United States and its allies in the industrialized world who enjoyed seemingly unparalleled military might found themselves subject to the whims of fourth-rate military powers who commanded little more than commodity power. Conventional definitions of "national security" and how best to secure it no longer seemed relevant. As new definitions were sought, those taking cognizance of the emerging complex global interdependence in which the United States and the other Western democracies now found themselves entangled worried about their growing vulnerability to the new global realities. As these changes and challenges percolated through American consciousness, new opportunities permitting societal forces to influence the content and conduct of American foreign policy emerged as well.

The essays that follow in Part I employ many of these ideas to examine the ways attributes of American society and the behavior of domestic actors influence the formulation of American foreign policy. Collectively, they focus attention on the interplay of American society with the larger community of nations of which it is a part, to illuminate how the process of policy-making at home is affected by politics abroad, and how both internal and external expectations and actions ultimately combine to influence the character and content of American foreign policy. The essays place special emphasis on the beliefs and preferences of Americans in leadership positions and of the American people in general regarding the appropriate role of the United States in world affairs. They also examine interest groups, the media, and elections, some of the societal channels through which those beliefs and preferences are asssumed to exert an impact on American foreign policy.

The Societal Environment as an Influence on American Foreign Policy. We begin the examination of the societal environment as a source of American foreign policy with a broad-ranging assessment of what's wrong with contemporary American foreign policy, and why. The essay is premised on the belief that inconsistency and incoherence have become endemic to American foreign policy, and is motivated by a desire to diagnose the causes. The afflictions are lodged, argue I. M. Destler, Leslie H. Gelb, and Anthony Lake, in their essay "Breakdown: The Impact of Domestic Politics on American Foreign Policy," in the changing beliefs of American elites and the mass public and in the foreign policy roles played by "The Establishment," the media, Congress, and others.

The authors contend that the domestic context of American foreign policy today has become dysfunctional to the effective pursuit of foreign policy because it has become more partisan and ideological. Simply put, it is now more political.

We noted earlier that the domestic divisions growing out of the involvement of the United States in the war in Vietnam relate intimately to the growing partisanship and ideological divisions over foreign policy issues apparent in recent years. Ole R. Holsti and James N. Rosenau provide systematic evidence to support the proposition that Vietnam was a dramatic event that fundamentally altered the foreign policy beliefs of influential segments of the American populace. Their article, "A Leadership Divided: The Foreign Policy Beliefs of American Leaders, 1976–1984," which draws on a series of systematic inquiries into the attitudes and beliefs of American elites, describes three distinct strands of thinking that emerged among American leaders in the wake of Vietnam, as described by the terms Cold War internationalism, post–Cold War internationalism, and semi-isolationism. Holsti and Rosenau demonstrate that despite the profound challenges to American foreign policy and the changes that have occurred in world politics since Vietnam, the divisions in the foreign policy beliefs of American leaders remain. Thus the impact of the Vietnam tragedy, which appears to have been responsible for a fundamental fragmentation of the postwar foreign policy consensus that had been based on a broad agreement among leaders about the nature of the Soviet threat, about the appropriateness of the containment strategy, and, more generally, about the globalist role of the United States in world affairs, persists. The consensus that once described elite attitudes toward the ends and means of American foreign policy no longer exists.

The elitist model of foreign policy-making described in the introduction to this book implies that a study of public attitudes toward American foreign policy could stop here. That is, if elites rule, once the foreign policy beliefs of American leaders have been described, there is no reason to probe public opinion further. The pluralist model, on the other hand, demands that attention be given to mass public opinion as well. Interestingly, available evidence indicates that the fundamental foreign policy beliefs of elites and the mass public, as described by systematic evidence gathered during the post-Vietnam decade, are remarkably similar.[1] On particular issues of the day, however, elites and masses are likely to differ substantially. Our third selection in Part I, "America's State of Mind: Trends in Public Attitudes Toward Foreign Policy," demonstrates that. Written by John E. Rielly, president of the Chicago Council on Foreign Relations, and based on an important and influential series of public opinion surveys undertaken since the mid-1970s to determine elite and mass attitudes on foreign policy issues, the chapter identifies the simultaneous existence of important temporal continuities as well as divergences in the opinions of leaders and masses.

The Chicago Council's surveys also reveal important trends in the foreign policy attitudes of the American people generally. Perhaps most striking is their "growing appreciation of the importance of foreign affairs . . . combined with a desire for a larger U.S. world role." The shift reflects a decline in the perceived importance of the domestic issues that dominated the attention of Americans in the 1970s, and a corresponding increase in concern for America's role in the world. Interesting in this respect is Rielly's conclusion that "foreign-policy problems have more than doubled in importance for the American people in the last 8 years." The "inward-looking" attitudes that characterized the American people in the wake of the Vietnam tragedy appear to have receded.

The pluralist model, which implicitly underlies the work of the Chicago Council on Foreign Relations, maintains that "average" Americans are able to express their views and to pressure the government, through interest groups, to heed them. Despite the ubiquitous presence of interest groups, their ability to influence policy is uncertain. If there is one interest group that is believed to be successful, it is the so-called Jewish lobby. It is often claimed, for example, that the decision of the Truman administration to recognize the state of Israel within minutes of its declared independence in 1947 was largely a response to the influence of Jewish people in America. Similarly, continued U.S. support of the state of Israel in the face of often overwhelming international opprobrium is believed by many to be a consequence of the domestic influence of the Jewish lobby.

Mitchell Bard subjects these seemingly self-evident conclusions to scrutiny and finds them wanting. The Jewish lobby is more aptly described as an Israeli lobby, he cautions, and even on issues that pertain directly to Israel it is often not clear whether U.S. support for Israeli foreign policy positions is attributable to the Israeli lobby or to other factors. Noteworthy is his observation that the lobby typically frames its position in terms of the national interest *of the United States,* and, most importantly, his conclusion that the mere exercise of pressure does not demonstrate its success; where there is activity there is not necessarily influence.

Gordon Adams also examines the relationship between societal actors and the government, this time in the area of national security policy. Whereas Bard's discussion of the Jewish lobby conforms to the pluralist model of policy-making, Adams's point of view, as described in his "The Iron Triangle: Inside the Defense Policy Process," is more akin to the elitist tradition, as he seeks to explain the reasons underlying defense budget policy decisions.

Adams largely dismisses the national security and bureaucratic politics explanations for defense budget decisions, and focuses instead on the "highly political arena in which defense contractors, defense bureaucrats, and the Congress are linked" so as to form a kind of subgovernment—an *iron triangle*—that has grown into an incredibly powerful domestic political force. The basis of its political clout is the tremendous resources appropriated by Congress for national defense since World War II, which have fostered "a close intimacy among the Pentagon, its defense industry clients, and members of Congress with a special interest in the defense section of the federal budget." As these groups interact to promote policies that protect the subgovernment, it has a tendency to become "iron" as it becomes increasingly isolated from other policy arenas, from Congress as a whole, and from the public. Given the bureaucratic momentum underlying defense contracting, neither congressional nor presidential oversight is able to control the immense power of this massive military-industrial establishment.

In addition to interest groups, we drew attention, in the introduction, to the mass media. Elitists and pluralists alike believe the media play an important role in the process whereby societal forces shape American foreign policy. How that role should be viewed normatively (whether as a constructive or destructive force) is less certain. William A. Dorman gives us pause for concern in his essay "Playing the Government's Game: The Mass Media and American Foreign Policy." The title conveys the message: In Dorman's words, "the dominant journalistic paradigm remains one that tends to share the state's fixations rather than to question them." The implication is that the media characteristically serve less as an independent critic of what the government is doing than as a supporter of the government's activity, in an incestuous game, with the result that "the media have moved further and further away from the watchdog role democratic theory assumed they would play in affairs of state where national defense and foreign policy are concerned." Thus, when the media tell us what to think about, and often what to think, the message frequently conforms to what the government has in mind.

Democratic theory promises that the voice of the people is ultimately expressed through the ballot box. If our political leaders do not perform up to expectations, or if they pursue unpopular policies, elections provide the means to remove them from office. As noted earlier, however, it is difficult to determine the extent to which electoral behavior is motivated by foreign policy issues and concerns. Because most elections involve a variety of different and often overlapping issues, it is difficult to ascertain whether voters cast their ballots for a candidate because of, or in spite of, his or her stand on a particular issue. Political leaders pay special attention to the effects of their behavior on the judgments of voters nonetheless—to a point, in fact, that may have untoward effects on the nation's foreign policy.

William B. Quandt explores the connection between elections and foreign policy behavior in "The Electoral Cycle and the Conduct of American Foreign Policy." Noting the constitutional requirement that congressional elections be held every two years and presidential elections every four, Quandt concludes that "presidents have little time during their incumbency when they have both the experience and the power needed for sensible and effective conduct of foreign policy." His theme echoes many of the judgments made in other essays included in Part I, and thus serves as a fitting conclusion to our consideration of the societal environment of American foreign policy-making: "The price we pay [for the structure of the electoral cycle] is a foreign policy excessively geared to short-term calculations, in which narrow domestic political considerations often outweigh sound strategic thinking, and where turnover in high positions is so frequent that consistency and coherence are lost."

NOTES

1. For evidence, see Eugene R. Wittkopf, "On the Foreign Policy Beliefs of the American People: A Critique and Some Evidence," *International Studies Quarterly* 30 (December 1986): 425–445; and Eugene R. Wittkopf, "Elites and Masses: Another Look at Attitudes Toward America's World Role," *International Studies Quarterly* 31 (June 1987):131–159.

1. BREAKDOWN: THE IMPACT OF DOMESTIC POLITICS ON AMERICAN FOREIGN POLICY

I.M. Destler, Leslie H. Gelb, and Anthony Lake

In Washington, daily news stories and cocktail-party confessionals; in editorials and classrooms across the country; in the banalities and profundities of officials, diplomats, columnists and scholars—we hear the same lament: Something is wrong with American foreign policy. Debates rage over the reasons for our inability to come to terms with the world, or bring the world to terms with us. Who now argues that nothing is wrong?

There is no doubt that the world has changed. It has become more complicated, more dangerous, less susceptible to American influence. This is well known. It is time that Americans also recognize the ways in which we ourselves have changed when it comes to making our foreign policies.

. . . [F]or two decades now, not only our government but our whole society has been undergoing a systemic breakdown when attempting to fashion a coherent and consistent approach to the world. The signs of the breakdown can be found in public attitudes and politicians' promises; in the behavior of the Congress, the press, and the foreign policy establishment; and within the offices of the White House, the State and Defense Departments, and other foreign policy agencies. And the breakdown has produced policies with a peculiar blend of self-righteousness and self-doubt.

At home, policy makers devour one another in a game that approaches a national blood sport, as White House aides and Cabinet officers do daily battle behind the scenes and through the press. Congress and the President play pin-the-tail-on-the-donkey (or -elephant) over who has the responsibility for foreign policy and who gets the blame for foreign failure. Political play acting is better rewarded than hard work; political speechmaking passes as serious policy making. Our debates give more weight to ideological "certainties" than to the ambiguities of reality. Tolerance and trust, the essential ingredients of a healthy democratic system, are always sought for oneself but rarely given to others.

The result is policies that speak more for the vagaries of our own politics than to the conditions of the world in which we must live. In January 1977, Jimmy Carter proclaimed a new American foreign policy that would set right

Note: Superscripts have been added to the text and the footnoting style changed to permit the use of numbered endnotes.

the sins of his predecessors. Four years later, Ronald Reagan said he would reject and reverse the international course of Jimmy Carter. To a foreigner unversed in our ways, such erratic behavior by so powerful a nation can only seem bizarre, if not dangerous. But to most Americans, it seems perfectly understandable, for we have become all too acccustomed to giving our own partisan struggles priority over consistency or coherence in our foreign policies.

By most measures, the United States is still the strongest power in the world and will remain so for many years to come. And our foreign-policy problems are by no means unmanageable. But we are taken less and less seriously by our friends as well as our adversaries. World problems and conflicts that could be tempered by competent and consistent American leadership are left to fester. We seem unable either to flow with change in the developing world or prevent change contrary to our interests. Our relations with the Soviet Union have been torn into shreds, and together with Moscow we have put ourselves in deadly straits—a situation in which peace hinges on the mutual terror of nuclear war, with little else to create restraint and moderation.

We have lost a coherent sense of United States national interests, the enduring purposes of policy that flow from values, geography, and our place in the hierarchy of world power. In almost all other nations, it takes a revolution to redefine these basic purposes. For the last two decades in the United States, it has required only a Presidential election or the prospect of one. In May 1983, former West German Chancellor Helmut Schmidt went public with a widely shared lament:

> As Chancellor I worked under four presidents, and it's quite an experience, I can tell you. . . . First Carter sent his vice-president to tell us almost everything done by his predecessors was wrong and implied that our cooperation was in vain and something different had to start. Then, along comes Reagan and tells us the same thing.[1]

"The alliance needs continuity," Schmidt tells us. "We've put all our eggs in your basket."

But the American basket is badly frayed. The political bodies of Presidents and Secretaries of State are strewn all over the place. Ronald Reagan's four immediate predecessors all were felled, and foreign policy played a major role. Each, save Richard M. Nixon in 1972, faced a serious renomination challenge in the primaries, and each challenge exposed deep ideological cleavages on foreign affairs. And at Cabinet level and below, the foreign-policy stage has come to resemble the final gory scene of *Hamlet,* played in gray flannel and pinstripes.

Why do we act this way? The heart of the problem, it seems to us, is this:

> For two decades, the making of American foreign policy has been growing far more political—or more precisely, far more partisan and ideological. The White House has succumbed, as former Secretary of State Alexander Haig recently put it, to "the impulse to view the presidency as a public relations opportunity and to regard Government as a campaign for reelection."[2] And in less exalted locations, we Americans—politicians and experts alike—have been spending more time, energy and passion in fighting ourselves than we have in trying, as a nation, to understand and deal with a rapidly changing world.

Some Americans have come to live with our condition by seeing it as readily curable; others by dismissing it as hopeless; and many by adjusting to it and believing that it is no worse than it has been before.

The easy cure is usually sought in an attractive fantasy: We need only find a Prince Charming whose kiss can awaken the Sleeping Beauty of an effective foreign policy. The problem can be put in order simply by putting the right man or woman in the right job. Thus, the sighs of satisfaction could be heard throughout most of Washington in the summer of 1982, when President Reagan replaced Secretary of State Alexander Haig with George P. Shultz. "Let George do it!" became a rallying cry in the White House and among the capitol's *cognoscenti*. But in Washington, even the most powerful fairy tale has a short half-life. And when Sleeping Beauty fails to stir after repeated embraces, many of those who were first to proclaim Prince Charming come to condemn him as the frog. Still, many hope that another Prince, perhaps a Henry Kissinger, could perform the necessary feats of magic.

For others, there is hope in bureaucratic engineering, in a search for organizational means to restore the Secretary of State to his "rightful place" and put the national-security adviser back in his. Such schemes have risen to prominence in the first and last months of every administration for the last dozen years. But in between they are mostly forgotten, for such schemes are neither as easy nor as crucial as they are portrayed. Bureaucratic fixes can help, but they will not produce grand results. Foreign policy is not merely the product of bureaucratic maneuver; it flows from our larger political system. Ideas and ideology are as important as the organization tables of the government. Yet often in academic circles, students of foreign policy are taught to think about the federal bureaucracy first and national politics second.

Then, there are those—often scholars—who conclude that the maladies are beyond correction. To them, the problem lies not so much in ourselves as in our stars, beyond our reach. It is in the malaise and bureaucratization of postindustrial societies, or in the inevitable fragmentation of power attendant on modern government and the collapse of traditional values. The world is simply too complex to be managed much better than it is. Certainly, there is some truth to all of this, and there is wisdom in understanding the limits imposed by forces larger than ourselves. Yet, hope and effort are too easily abandoned in the sweep of such analyses.

Finally, some take solace in the belief that the way we make our foreign policy today is not really so different from what it was in the first two decades after World War II. There have always been a left and a right, rivalries between White House courtiers and departmental barons, abrupt shifts in policy, deception, and people playing politics with the national interest. Today's vices may be proportioned somewhat differently, but the net result, so this argument goes, is the same.

It is our contention that this last judgment is profoundly wrong; that the ways in which we have made our foreign policy in the last twenty years are worse, even far worse in many respects, than in the two decades following World War II. And still more important is the fact that to whatever degree things are worse, we can far less afford such policy disarray. We no longer have the cushion of military and economic preponderance that we had in the 1950s and 1960s. We are no longer so strong; others are not so weak. The mistakes hurt more, and the wounds are not so easily healed. And in a nuclear age, the risks are ever more immense. . . .

How *is* American foreign-policy making different from the way it was in the first twenty years after World War II? What was there about policy and politics that served us well then—and does not now?

There was certainly much to deplore about our behavior during that period. We succumbed to the redbaiting and McCarthyism that not only destroyed the careers of honorable and talented men, but postponed the day when more than a handful of politicians could dare to suggest moves to improve relations with Moscow. We failed in the late 1950s and early 1960s to exploit the emerging deep split between China and Russia. We did not see that Ho Chi Minh might be a nationalist as well as a Communist. And there was the awful case of President Kennedy's fearing to call off the Bay of Pigs invasion that had been planned under his predecessor. One should not view this period through rose-tinted glasses. Nor do we argue that Americans can—or should—go back to the days of almost unchallenged Presidential supremacy, Congressional passivity, and a press as well as a public who, for the most part, took the President's pronouncements on trust.

Still, the years after 1945 were years of considerable policy creativity. The policies and programs put together under President Truman, virtually all of them continued under President Eisenhower, were a creative triumph—the Marshall Plan to rebuild the shattered European economies and stabilize their political systems; the North Atlantic Treaty Organization to defend the West; successful programs to bring our former blood enemies, Germany and Japan, into the democratic community; a substantial military-aid effort to bolster friends abroad under attack; encouragement of our European allies to grant independence to their colonies in Asia and Africa. These efforts had coherence and purposefulness. A central goal was to contain the spread of Soviet influence. At the same time, there was willingness to develop non-American centers of strength in Europe. Whatever the shortcomings of these programs in understanding or level of effort, they represented the most generous and far-reaching of any great power in history. To be sure, the United States benefited. But it also sacrificed, and others benefited as well.

Truman and Eisenhower, and Kennedy to a lesser extent, were also prepared to make politically unpopular decisions, often the hallmark of a keen sense of the national interest. Conservatives put a great deal of heat on Mr. Truman to do something to prevent a Communist victory in China prior to 1949. But almost without exception, those who knew the situation in China believed that providing more aid to the Nationalist anti-Communist forces would be throwing good money after bad and that the Nationalists were corrupt and divided beyond hope. For the former Senator from Missouri it would have been far easier to ask Congress for additional funds than to step aside from the civil war in China as he did. And Truman was to pay a high political price for accepting the advice of almost all his military and political experts in limiting the use of American force in the Korean War.

Eisenhower also took leadership stands that were probably unwise on political grounds. This was so in 1956, when he opposed the British, French, and Israeli invasion of Egypt under Gamal Abdel Nasser. Nasser was ranked high on the hit list of the American public. But Eisenhower believed strongly that the United States had to uphold the principle that attacks by sovereign states against other sovereign states could not be condoned. And like his predecessor, the former World War II military hero kept in check enormous pressures for vast increases in military spending. Both Truman and Eisenhower understood the national-security value of a sound American economy, and neither was panicked into seeing the Soviet military machine as ten feet tall.

There is a strong tendency to attribute the successes of these first fifteen years after the war to "politics stopping at the water's edge." These were said to be the halcyon days of bipartisanship or nonpartisanship, of Democrats and Republicans putting national interests above party interests. But such a description has always been more myth than reality. Conservatives and liberals were at one another's throat constantly. There was never a time when Truman was not besieged. The Korean War and rolling back Soviet influence in Europe were major campaign themes for Eisenhower in 1952 against Adlai E. Stevenson, the Democratic candidate. Stevenson tried to make foreign policy a key issue in the 1956 campaign, and Mr. Kennedy succeeded in doing so in 1960.

But while politics was never in short supply, it was moderated by a near-consensus in elite and general public opinion. The leadership in the Executive Branch and the Congress each knew where the other stood, and both were ready to make deals that fit both the national interest and party interests. The prevailing anti-Communist ideology, though thoroughly ingrained in what was commonly called a consensus, did not preclude the practical. The doctrinaire quality of the consensus was finally to produce disaster in Vietnam and the destruction of the consensus itself. But it was also true, paradoxically, that the existence of the consensus created room for maneuver and doing sensible things. Supports for generous aid levels and anticolonialism, while necessarily justified in terms of meeting the Communist threat, was generally considered to be politically acceptable and even statesmanlike.

Take the case of Senator Arthur H. Vandenberg, Republican of Michigan. As chairman of the Senate Foreign Relations Committee from 1947 to 1949, the former isolationist joined hands with the administration and brought the country into a new and unprecedented era of internationalism. But this wily old politician had his own reasons for reaching out. Despite his subsequent canonization as the patron saint of bipartisanship, Vandenberg was as much a partisan as a statesman.

Reflecting on the limits of cooperation, he wrote that "When and where it is possible, in clearly channeled and clearly defined projects, for the legislature, the executive and the two major parties to proceed from the beginning to the end of a specific adventure, so that all are consulted in respect to all phases of the undertaking, I think it is a tremendously useful thing." But, he added, "to think that can be done as an everyday practice in regard to all of the multiple problems of international import which now descend upon the State Department every day, in my opinion is totally out of the question."

The Senator knew that he *had* to cooperate on the central, European issues of the day: "The Republican Party has this dilemma: if it does not cooperate in the world, it will be blamed for destroying the peace, as in 1920. If it cooperates too much with the Democratic administration, it will be charged with having no policy of its own." His answer was to back Mr. Truman's European policy where "we could lose everything," and attack on Asian policy where "there is no solution I can think of anyway."

There were enough Republicans like Vandenberg and enough Democratic conservatives to ensure Presidents Truman, Eisenhower, Kennedy, and, for a while, Lyndon B. Johnson of a workable and steady majority to back most of their foreign ventures. From 1945 to 1965, Presidents had what might better be labeled a solid majorityship than a free bipartisan ride.

As long as Presidents stayed in the political center with a moderate kind of anti-Communism, they could navigate between the ideological extremists. The left was singularly unpowerful. Truman could get elected in 1948 even after the defection of the left led by former Vice-President Henry Wallace. The right was larger, vocal, far more powerful than the left. But when Senator Joe McCarthy fell, moderates could see that the right was far from invincible.

Power was in the political center, and the foreign-policy center was owned by the Establishment, a relatively homogeneous group of bankers, lawyers, and Foreign Service officers, largely from the northeastern part of the United States, largely pragmatic and centrist in beliefs.

The anti-Communist-policy consensus was at the heart of centrism and majorityship, and gave it steadiness and direction. But it led to rigidity as well, and in this rigidity lay the seeds of the center's destruction. The doctrines at the heart of the consensus, and their political force, called for American intervention in Vietnam. Yet these doctrines retained their appeal only so long as the United States did not have to endure a prolonged crisis, and as long as no extended sacrifice of blood or treasure was required. The iron triangle of consensus, centrism, and majorityship could survive brief failures and setbacks—the loss of China, ruptures in the Western alliance with Britain and France over their attack on the Suez Canal in 1956, the Bay of Pigs fiasco in 1961, and even the trauma of not going all out to win during the Korean War—but it did not survive Vietnam.

The endless and seemingly hopeless agony of the Vietnam War destroyed the consensus, sprayed power out from the center toward the political extremes, and made the forging of majorities a trying affair. Moderates and liberals joined with the inheritors of the Henry Wallace tradition in a coalition of the left that, for the first time, enjoyed real political power. This coalition began to question the basic principles of postwar American foreign policy as rigidly ill-suited to the new and far more pluralistic world and ill-equipped to understand the limits of American power in such a world. Those liberals, conservatives and rightists who remained supporters of the war regarded the liberal-moderate defection as nothing short of betrayal. Their sentiments did not go unrequited, as the new left coalition roundly pilloried them as Cold Warriors and warmongers.

By 1965, the systemic breakdown in the American foreign-policy system had begun, and five years later it was well advanced. The center, the ballast for majorityship and consensus, was shattered. The extremes now had the preponderance of power. For being doctrinaire, the center was torn apart by the left in the 1960s over Vietnam. Then, because of the center's advocacy of détente and arms control with Moscow, the right rapped it for weakness. In time, the center came to stand for nothing. Centrists seemed to represent a geography, not a philosophy. Their position was defined solely by placement precisely between the extremes, wherever they might be. What they failed and refused to recognize was that the extremes were not simply engaged in a typical joust for power; by the late 1970s they were aiming at the defeat of the centrists as well as each other.

The making of American foreign policy had entered a new and far more ideological and political phase. The effects could be seen throughout our system of foreign-policy making: Public opinion was split, and with it our political parties. Ideological struggles within parties became as intense as those between them. Presidents became increasingly vulnerable and made themselves more so as they promised new foreign ideological triumphs that failed to materialize. The Establishment, which once helped keep things together, was now replaced by foreign-policy activists who ferociously tore the fabric apart. Battles for power among Presidential courtiers and departmental barons became a national spectacle. Congress and the news media tugged at the seams of what remained. Each of these changes reinforced the others, and all became rooted in new patterns of public opinion.

Ten years ago, political scientist John E. Mueller developed an influential model of public opinion. It held that up until the late 1960s public opinion on foreign policy fell into three categories: a leadership stratum of small numbers with shared views on ends and means; an attentive and educated group who "followed" Presidential and elite leadership in their internationalism and Cold War interventionist policies; and a noninternationalist mass public that knew and cared little for foreign affairs and generally backed a two-track policy of peace and strength.

By William Schneider's recent perceptive analysis, this pattern began to come apart in the late 1960s, because of ideological polarization within the leadership stratum. "Counter-elites emerged on both the right and the left to challenge the supremacy of the old foreign-policy establishment,"[3] writes Schneider. This, in turn, split the attentive followers and destroyed the consensus. The mass public, in its turn, became more activist and difficult to lead, in part due to the intrusion of television news on foreign affairs into their living rooms. More than before, the public wanted it both ways: no American military involvement and no Communist gains.

To make political calculations trickier still, in recent years the swings in public opinion on key issues have become wider and more frequent. In the space of a decade, the polls have shown the public calling for big defense cuts, then major increases, and then—once again—cutbacks in planned military spending. Clearly, the public had become less patient and less predictable.

Reflecting and reinforcing public opinion, party politics and beliefs have also fractured. Just as Barry Goldwater in 1964 took the Republican nomination away from Nelson Rockefeller and wrested control of the party from its liberal Eastern Establishment, Eugene McCarthy's followers in 1968 initiated a fundamental challenge to the Democratic party's powers that were. In the 1970s, Presidential primaries became ever more important, and ideological activists in both parties extended their sway. There is no doubt that today liberal Republicans and conservative Democrats play a sharply limited role in their Presidential conventions, compared to the pre-1965 years. In 1960, both parties in their platforms praised bipartisanship, called for more military strength and more aid, and approved the search for arms control with the Soviet Union—all in strikingly similar language. By 1980, the two parties took sharply divergent stands on dealing with Moscow, human rights, and most Third World questions.

Presidents themselves bore heavy responsibility for the fissures. If Presidential conduct of foreign policy up to 1964 can be described as "imperial," it is not stretching reality too far to see it thereafter as irresponsible. Before the breakdown, Presidents derived much of their power and authority over national-security matters from the belief that they stood above politics, that they would sacrifice short-term political gains for long-term goals, and that they somehow embodied the enduring national interest. Too many times since 1964 they have used foreign policy to enhance their personal positions, thus personalizing, politicizing and sometimes even trivializing the content and conduct of foreign affairs.

In so doing, they become almost like any other politician, and their words, facts, motives and actions became ever more subject to scrutiny and doubt. They thus squandered their own authority to construct steady majorities. By coming down into the political pits, they legitimized opposition on political grounds.

Presidents, especially from John F. Kennedy on, trapped themselves. By promising everything in their campaigns—to stay out of war and to stop Communist expansion—they set expectations that could not be met and that could lead only to public disillusionment.

It is inevitable that politics and policy come together. Democratic debate is more likely than doctrine to produce sensible foreign-policy decisions. There neither can nor should be a return to the days of doctrinaire consensus. The question, rather, is how responsibly we use the foreign-policy institutions that have become more open, more democratic. Will they be used to fashion mature policies of consistency and coherence, or will they be exploited for short-term political advantage? Too often the motivating force for our Presidents in making key decisions during the past two decades has been either gaining short-term political advantage—keeping political adversaries at bay, diverting attention from domestic problems, and scoring political points—or satisfying some set of values that bore little relation to reality but pleased political ideologues. (An ideologue can be defined as one who knows the answers before he knows the facts.)

What were some of the most egregious examples?

John F. Kennedy went ahead with the Bay of Pigs invasion in 1961 (even though it would have been clear, if properly examined, that it would fail) in part because of his campaign rhetoric and fear of being accused of being too soft. He told people privately that the war in Vietnam was hopeless, but did nothing to disengage or reduce American stakes—in fact, he heightened them with his own rhetoric and stepped up American military involvement.

Lyndon B. Johnson allowed the Vietnam problem to fester during the campaign of 1964, while he misled the public about where the logic of his rhetorical commitments and beliefs was taking the nation. Thereafter, he failed to make hard choices about the war. He refused to call up the reserves, which limited the military manpower available but kept some critics quiet: and he put off proposals to raise taxes to pay for the war, producing virulent inflation in subsequent years but postponing the painful immediate costs.

Richard M. Nixon oversold, along with Henry Kissinger, the idea that détente with the Soviet Union meant "a stable structure of peace" and "an era of negotiation not confrontation," when they both fully realized that serious problems were inherent in relations with Moscow. This helped to repel the challenge from his left and win the 1972 election, but standards were set for Soviet behavior that they knew Moscow would never meet.

Nixon and Kissinger also left a number of serious ambiguities in the text of the SALT I offensive-arms agreement of 1972, so as not to leave the Moscow summit empty-handed. Later, when Moscow exploited these ambiguities, they were almost forced to accuse the Soviets of cheating. Again, they ended up casting doubt on their own creation.

Gerald Ford decided against consummating the SALT II negotiations—although Kissinger and others felt that that was possible—for fear of giving political ammunition to his challenger for the Republican party nomination, Ronald Reagan. Later, Ford and others reckoned that this hesitancy may have cost him the Presidency in his race against Jimmy Carter. Not only arms control but his own political fortunes suffered.

Jimmy Carter carried his human-rights rhetoric and efforts to prevent the spread of nuclear-weapons capabilities to points where he succeeded in gratuitously alienating our allies. He exploited Iran's holding dozens of Americans hostage by playing on the crisis as a way of neutralizing Senator Edward M. Kennedy's challenge to him in the Democratic primaries. The same issue then helped to destroy him, as did his unsuccessful effort to pose as a latter-day Cold Warrior against Reagan's charges of softness.

Ronald Reagan, for clearly political reasons, lifted the grain embargo that Carter had placed on the Soviets in the wake of their invasion of Afghanistan, even as he pressed our allies not to sell industrial products to Moscow. That pleased the American farmer, but made no sense to our allies. Nor did it make much sense later when he invoked trade penalties against any ally selling certain oil and gas equipment to Moscow, when virtually all his advisers told him there was no chance the allies would refrain from selling.

In Lebanon, home of religious and factional rivalries dating from Biblical days, Reagan also shifted back and forth between ideology and political expediency. Singling out the East-West dimension of the conflict, he insisted that any retreat from support of the crumbling government of President Amin Gemayel would destroy American credibility worldwide. But then, with the Presidential election fast approaching at home, he reversed course and ordered the withdrawal of United States marines, a course he has previously dismissed as an unthinkable "surrender."

Reagan also became the first post–World War II President, as opposed to Presidential candidate, to maintain that the United States was militarily inferior to the Soviet Union. It is one thing to make the case that military trends are adverse and that defense spending needs to be increased. But it is quite another for a President to proclaim a presumed inferiority to the world, which can only discourage friends and embolden adversaries. Continued reference to American inferiority might have been grist for the party faithful, but it was dubious diplomacy.

. . . [T]hese . . . words and deeds made no sense on foreign-policy grounds. Nor were they the acts of stupid people, acting carelessly and without information or without the benefit of other points of view. From all evidence, they were calculated, driven by politics and ideology.

This is not to say that Presidents for the last twenty years did not make defensible and sensible decisions. But such decisions were in shorter supply than those made by their predecessors. Of equal importance, the good that they did was often colored, even overwhelmed, by the irresponsible. Lyndon Johnson's creditable efforts in Europe and the Third World were ignored because of Vietnam. Richard Nixon's policy of détente with Moscow and the opening to China were weighed down by his divisive rhetoric, by prolonging the war in Vietnam, by invading Cambodia, and by helping to "destabilize" a democratically elected government in Chile. Gerald Ford's steadiness in his first year paled beside his later walking away from his own policies under pressure from Mr. Reagan. Jimmy Carter's fine performances in achieving the Camp David accords, and gaining Senate approval of the Panama Canal Treaties—contributing to a greater sense of identity between the United States and developing nations—lost their luster in the political maneuvers of 1980. Ronald Reagan's success in establishing greater respect for American power was undermined by early anti-arms-control statements and his failure to deal sensibly with the Soviets.

But the breakdown is not just in Presidency and Presidents. It is in our political system as a whole. It is, as Thomas L. Hughes has written, a case of the collective irresponsibility "when repeated failures produce no discernible correction in basic behavior patterns or institutions."[4] Presidential irresponsibility has been accompanied by the growing irresponsibility of our elites, Congress, and the news media. They have fed on each other and spread the disorders.

We have irresponsible elites, who often seem more dedicated to demolishing one another's world visions and careers than to undertaking the hard, slogging work of putting together a sustainable line of policy action. The old Establishment of relatively homogeneous, part-time, pragmatic and mostly bipartisan Northeasterners has been subsumed by a much larger, more diverse elite of full-time foreign-policy professionals. Their diversity and expertise are valuable. But they also are far more political and ideological than their predecessors.

The Establishment, for all its shortcomings and tendency toward being doctrinaire, served as a brake on politics. It stood for common sense, a willingness to hear out and accommodate other views within a certain range, and a sense of responsibility and proportion about policies and institutions. Today's foreign-policy elites help to drive policy into domestic politics and push debates toward the extremes. They are no longer a steady source of broad support for national policies; they support only those Presidents they actually serve—and not always then.

We have an irresponsible Congress, which often in the last two decades has posed obstacles to coherent Presidential policies without offering real alternatives. Members of Congress have grabbed headlines and sometimes power. But while making it harder for Presidents to exercise their responsibilities, Congress has not accepted its own attendant responsibility to share in tough decisions or propose serious alternatives.

To be sure, Presidents Johnson and Nixon did a lot to provoke Senators and Representatives of all political persuasions. Secret wars, double bookkeeping and duplicity are bound to generate Congressional reaction. So, in the 1970s legislators put more and more laws on the books to make themselves a part of the policy process. Yet, views in Congress itself were so diverse and power so dispersed that Congress was forever pulling in several directions at the same time.

As with Presidents, Congress did some commendable things. At its best, Congress probed and questioned administrations, and forced them to justify important and dubious acts. Congress properly would not take at face value the various schemes offered by the Carter and Reagan administrations for basing the new MX missile. Congress properly has a role to play in determining whether or not American forces should go to war. But for the most part,

Congress has failed either to implement its laws or, preferably, to work with the Executive to make them succeed.

Just as Congress was emboldened by the Vietnam and Watergate experiences to assert itself, so were the national news media. Investigative journalism, necessary for ferreting out the abuses of those years, became the model. The news media generally, and television in particular, do not do well in dealing with ideas and institutions. They are more at home portraying personalities and headlining extreme statements. So, in an era of more politics and more ideology, the media have consistently amplified the worst features of the system and thus quickened the breakdown.

The price we are paying for the breakdown is very large indeed. At precisely the moment when we need to husband our strength and use it more efficiently; at a time when there is no choice but involvement in world affairs; in an era when others look to us for maturity and sophistication in dealing with international problems of growing complexity—at that moment we are taken less seriously than at any time since World War II.

In December 1981, in the Israeli Knesset (or Parliament), it was the night when Prime Minister Menachem Begin's government announced the annexation of the Golan Heights, Syrian territory. Ever since the 1967 Arab-Israeli war, when Israel captured that stretch of high ground from Syria, it had been a major element of American policy to prevent the Golan issue from permanently blocking Syrian-Israeli talks. An American correspondent asked a member of the Knesset if there would not be trouble with Washington over the annexation. "For two days, maybe," came the reply. "But we have seen that you can get over your problems with us very quickly."

In Saudi Arabia in 1982, during a trip to that country by Defense Secretary Caspar Weinberger (who was a well-known friend of the Saudis), a Saudi general was asked by an American reporter what his government had promised the Americans in return for the advanced arms just offered. It was clear to all that the Administration was facing mountainous opposition in obtaining Congressional approval of such sales. But the contempt in the answer from the Saudi was as plain as the disdain in Jerusalem—"Your are just arms merchants and we pay cash."

For years, Western European diplomats have regularly clutched at the lapels of their American colleagues to plead, "Where is your government going in its defense planning? On arms control? Toward China? On the neutron bomb, human rights, nuclear non-proliferation? What are your priorities? What will they be a year from now?"

African diplomats too are left to wonder about American directions. Do we believe that closer ties to the South African government can actually help encourage an end to apartheid, as suggested by the Nixon, Ford and Reagan administrations? Or does the United States propose to distance itself from South Africa's whites so long as the blacks there are denied their rights, as was the trend under Johnson and Carter?

Nations cannot afford to disregard us, and they do not. American power remains enormous, and Washington is a factor in almost every world issue. But what can the United States accomplish in the Middle East, for example, when Israeli leaders know that because of American politics they have little to fear from flouting American interests and when Saudi leaders think we care more for cash than for policy? And why should Europeans follow us when they cannot predict where we shall lead tomorrow? That is what it means to be taken increasingly less seriously, or at the very least, less seriously than we should be.

The cost is substantial. For it is only when a great power such as ours can bring its weight to bear steadily over time that we have a chance of breaking some international deadlocks. The persistence and the weight are the greatest weapons in diplomacy. But such consistency and patience comes only with a widely accepted popular view of our national interests.

When a nation's conduct abroad is governed so much by the whims of politics and the dictates of ideology, by who the leadership happens to be every four years, it has no such definitions. To be sure, other countries alter and shade their policies. But, by contrast to the United States, they are almost all models of stability.

For them (as for us in the years after World War II), policy has been guided in the main by an enduring and consistent set of values, by geography, by certain economic needs, and by purposes shared among elites. These have carried over from government to government in almost all countries, whether the leaders were Conservatives or Socialists. The foreign policies of West Germany changed in no essential when Mr. Schmidt's Social Democratic party was replaced by the Christian Democrats under Helmut Kohl; nor France's by virtue of Socialist François Mitterrand's succeeding the more conservative Valéry Giscard d'Estaing; nor the Soviet Union's when Leonid I. Brezhnev died and Yuri V. Andropov succeeded him.

For most nations, only war and revolution have overturned centuries of national interest. That happened in the Russian revolution of 1917; in Mao Tse-tung's revolution in China after World War II; in Fidel Castro's takeover of Cuba in 1959; when the Ayatollah Khomeini overthrew the Shah of Iran in 1979; and when the nations of Africa gained their independence. For others, it took fundamental changes; for us, merely an election or a change in political imperatives, bringing a call for sweeping new designs.

The United States was always different, as the French observer Alexis de Tocqueville noticed more than a century ago. So pragmatic and stable in our internal politics we were, yet so ideological and quixotic in foreign affairs. Other nations were deemed to be so decadent that we would not go near them, or so sinful that we had to redeem them.

For more than a century, we could afford this. We could live in isolation from the political wars in Europe, then go forth to impose our ideals, and then retreat again behind the ocean and our wealth. After World War II, we could not afford the isolationist illusion. And it seemed to others that our country understood this, understood that its well-being was now inextricably bound with the outside world, understood that international life was complicated and ambiguous. We had learned the lesson that we had to cooperate as well as compete with our adversaries and that in the nuclear age we could not safely keep the peace by strength alone. Participation in the United Nations, the Marshall Plan, foreign aid, international banking institutions, NATO—all were demonstrations of a new maturity.

For at the heart of the creative burst after World War II was a mature internationalism, which recognized that America's interests were served, in the long run, by seeking common purpose and mutual advantage with other nations. Hence the importance of helping Europe and Japan recover their strength, not only in opposition to the Soviet Union but also for the sake of a strengthened world economy.

The post-World War II leaders took the world for what it was, a place filled with enduring conflicts. They sought not to remake it in our image, but to act within the realm of the possible, to dampen those forces that threatened world conflagration, to nurture those that built cooperation through enlightened self-interest.

Then something happened. Perhaps in part from the shock and humiliation of Vietnam, America began to turn from this internationalist view of its interests to new forms of nationalism. This turn was later reinforced by the frustration of the Iran hostage crisis. It was not a return to the nationalistic isolationism of the 1920s and 1930s. The isolationist impulse had been beaten back. It was a new, more complex form of nationalism.

For many conservatives, it was and is a rejection of accommodation with allies or adversaries for the sake of mutual gain—the belief that with a new assertion of national will and military strength, the United States could somehow impose its way on the world. For the first time in decades, it was on the right in America that one found the most important assaults on our European alliance.

On the left, the new nationalism took the form of a doctrinaire insistence on the universal applicability of our ideals, whatever the cultural and political realities of other societies. While Cyrus Vance, an internationalist of the old school, spoke of promoting human rights with pragmatism and flexibility, his President was portraying the same policy in terms of a moral crusade. In this, Carter was repeating the mistake of Woodrow Wilson, who had failed to sell his vision of a postwar world because he put it in terms of an almost personal morality. Both seemed more concerned with the purity of their vision than with gaining the cooperation necessary—at home and abroad—for its fulfillment.

And for many liberal politicians who had an eye on the labor vote, there was an emerging economic nationalism in their support for protection against foreign competition.

The new nationalisms of both right and left recalled some earlier American attitudes. They played on a lack of knowledge about the world. Americans speak few foreign languages, and language is the only way into the bloodstream of another culture. And the new nationalisms reflected a traditional American impatience with the intractability of international problems.

Ideologues on the left and the right of our political system exploited these attitudes, promised solutions where there were only enduring problems, and withheld their support from any effort to manage those problems if it did not conform entirely to their own philosophies. Our system went into shock, into a systemic breakdown. . . .

NOTES

1. *Washington Post*, May 5, 1983.
2. *Time*, April 9, 1984, p. 67.
3. William Schneider, "Public Opinion," in Joseph S. Nye, Jr., ed., *The Making of America's Soviet Policy* (New Haven: Yale University Press [for the Council on Foreign Relations], 1984).
4. Thomas L. Hughes, "The Crack-Up: The Price of Collective Irresponsibility," *Foreign Policy*, No. 40 (Fall 1980), p. 35.

2. A LEADERSHIP DIVIDED: THE FOREIGN POLICY BELIEFS OF AMERICAN LEADERS, 1976–1984

Ole R. Holsti
James N. Rosenau

During the two decades following the end of World War II, most Americans accepted a number of basic principles about foreign affairs and the role of the nation in the world, including the following:

- The United States had the responsibility and capabilities to be actively involved in efforts to create a just and stable world order. There were, to be sure, some prominent isolationists—for example, former President Herbert Hoover—who argued that such efforts would ultimately bankrupt the country. Moreover, even the internationalists disagreed on priorities (Europe versus the Far East, for example) or on details of implementation. Nevertheless, a substantial majority of American leaders appeared to have become convinced that the 1930s had demonstrated the bankruptcy of isolationism.

- The United States should be actively involved in a broad range of international organizations. The fact that certain people hoped and believed that the United Nations might be the forerunner of some type of world federation (for example, the United World Federalists), whereas others were much more skeptical (like former Secretary of State Dean Acheson), does not undermine the proposition.

- The United States should not only join, but should take a lead in creating peacetime alliances. Formation of NATO in 1949, followed by a flurry of alliance activity during the following decade, represented a sharp departure from practice during the first century and a half of U.S. independence. During the period between World War I and World War II many were persuaded that the nation would be dragged into unnecessary wars by reckless allies; after World War II, however, most leaders emphasized the deterrent and collective-security benefits of alliances.

- Liberalization of foreign trade was necessary to avoid destructive trade wars that would not only hurt all nations but would also contribute to political instability. Once again, the dominant view appeared to have been drawn significantly from the "lessons of the 1930s," which witnessed trade wars, a worldwide depression, and the collapse of democratic government in Germany and other parts of Europe. The result was broad support for the Bretton Woods arrangements, the General Agreement on Tariffs and Trade, and the like.

- Foreign aid programs, both economic and military, were not only an obligation for the richest nation in the world, they were also a hardheaded expression of U.S. national interests.

- Containment, rather than "roll-back" or preventive war (or a retreat into isolation), represented the most effective means of meeting the challenge of Soviet expansion. There were differences of emphasis and detail even within the majority supporting containment. For example, George F. Kennan, the intellectual father of containment, had serious reservations about the open-ended quality of President Truman's address to the Congress on March 12, 1947, as Truman appeared to place few limits on possible American efforts to protect other nations from Soviet imperialism. John Foster Dulles engaged in some rhetorical excesses in condemning containment as a static rather than dynamic policy during the 1952 campaign and, in a symbolic effort to demonstrate a break with past policies, he forced Kennan into retirement in 1953. However, Dulles's policies were essentially a continuation of containment, and containment itself was widely accepted as the proper response to the Soviet challenge.

As a consequence of the widespread acceptance of these principles, the Truman, Eisenhower, and Kennedy administrations could generally count upon a favorable response from the Congress, the media, other leaders, and the informed public when they pursued policies based on the above premises.

The foreign policy consensus of the 1945–1965 period was shattered by the Vietnam War. The post-Vietnam period has been marked not merely by disagreements about specific applications of basic principles or details of implementation, but also by a lack of consensus on fundamental beliefs about the international system, the proper American role in it, and appropriate strategies for pursuing the national interest. At least three quite different ways of thinking about international affairs have emerged among American leaders.

THREE PERSPECTIVES ON FOREIGN AFFAIRS[1]

Cold War Internationalism[2]

Cold War internationalists are oriented toward the state of relations between East and West, locating along that axis the most fundamental challenges to a just and stable international order. Without denying that the international system has undergone some change since the 1950s, they nevertheless see a fundamental continuity in the structure of the system, the sources of threats to peace and stability, the appropriate international role for the United States, and the most effective instruments of external policy. They perceive a world of conflict in which the primary cleavages are those dividing the United States and its allies from the Soviet empire and in which most, if not all, of the most salient issues and conflicts are closely linked to each other and to that fault line. A quintessential statement of this outlook on world affairs may be found in Ronald Reagan's assertion, "Let's not delude ourselves. The Soviet Union underlies all the unrest that is going on. If they weren't engaged in this game of dominoes, there wouldn't be any hot spots in the world" (House, 1980: 1). In a system thus structured, disturbances in one region will reverberate throughout the international area, and the consequences of failures in one area will be not unlike those predicted by the "domino theory" that was so frequently invoked during the Vietnam period. Within that system the United States faces an ambitious, often aggressive, but always patient, coalition of adversaries led by Moscow. Cold War internationalists depict the Soviet Union as an expansionist power that, under the guise of "peaceful coexistence" or détente, is lulling and gulling the United States into policies that bear a disturbing resemblance to those of Britain and France during the 1930s.

Whatever delusions Americans may have had about détente, the Soviet Union has continued, often not even in a subtle fashion, a relentless Cold War against the West. In that conflict the Soviet arsenal of methods ranges from terrorism and subversion to Third World interventions by Cuban proxies. The basic errors have been to assume that the Soviet Union has only sought acknowledgment that it has reached a status of parity with the United States, and to believe that, having reached superpower status, the USSR is now a conservative, status quo force in world affairs. In fact, the Soviet Union is not just another great power whose goals and methods may at times bring it into conflict with its lesser neighbors or with other major powers. Moscow harbors quite different global aspirations, and far broader global ambitions, whether pursued by the dour and brutal Joseph Stalin or the smiling and sophisticated Mikhail Gorbachev.

The overarching reality of the global system, according to Cold War internationalists, remains the confrontation between an expansionist Soviet Union and its allies, on the one hand, and the noncommunist nations on the other. And with respect to this fundamental fact of international life, changes during the past two decades are the occasion for neither congratulations nor complacency. Citing trends in Soviet defense spending during the past two decades, as well as recent adventures in Angola, Ethiopia, Yemen, Afghanistan, Vietnam, Nicaragua, Grenada, and elsewhere, the Cold War internationalists argue that the balance of power—or what Soviet theoreticians call "the correlation of forces"—has swung so far in favor of the USSR that at best the international system is unstable, and at worst it may be headed for war.

The dangerous military asymmetry between the two superpowers has two dimensions. One is the imbalance of strategic and conventional forces; the other is the sharp difference that characterizes American and Soviet thinking about the role of force. Whereas the Americans are concerned with containment and deterrence, the Soviets are also thinking about the political implications of strategic forces and about winning a war, should it break out. As a consequence, the Cold War internationalists fear that the Soviets may gain their expansionist goals through nuclear coercion and blackmail. To avoid being faced with a "surrender or suicide" choice, the United States must immediately come to grips with the gaps both in strategic hardware and in realistic thinking about how to win a nuclear war as well as how to avoid one. The Reagan administration's military buildup only meets the minimal requirements of national security, and thus it must not be reversed or slowed down by budgetary or domestic political constraints.

The basic problem for the United States is, therefore, to maintain the territorial and political integrity of the noncommunist parts of the world in the face of a highly armed, expansionist power that harbors an unchanging commitment to achieving a position of global hegemony. Even if some Cold War internationalists accept the proposition that the contemporary international system is more complex than the world that faced Metternich or Bismarck, they do not agree that the prudent, time-tested axioms of international intercourse—the realpolitik "rules of the game"—have been rendered obsolete; one of the central myths of American foreign policy is that there is an alternative to realpolitik. Some may agree that the game is more complex than dominoes, but few are prepared to dismiss the metaphor of the chessboard, of a game with a well-defined hierarchy based on power, in which position is a critical factor and which is basically zero-sum (your gain is my loss, and vice versa) in nature. The prescription is thus clear and unequivocal: The United States must accept the responsibilities and burdens of its leadership position within the noncommunist sector and, at minimum, it must restore a balance of power sufficient to convince the Soviet leadership that aggrandizement will not pay. To charges that such policies will merely revive the Cold War, advocates of Cold War internationalism usually reply that it never ended; détente and arms control were merely ploys by which the Soviets continued the conflict while the United States slept.

Expressions of deep concern about recent trends in American foreign and defense policies abound among Cold War internationalists. As a source of danger to national survival, running a close second behind self-generated delusions about détente, they see Washington's obsession with arms control, and especially with what they perceive as its most notorious products—the SALT I and II agreements. To those who warn of an uncontrollable arms race in a SALT-free world, they reply that the United States long ago opted out of the competition, leaving the USSR as the lone entrant in the race. The Reagan administration's decision in 1986 to "break out" of the informal agreement between the United States and the USSR to abide by the unratified SALT II treaty was widely applauded by Cold War internationalists as a long overdue step.

Although Cold War internationalists may disagree among themselves on the fine details of how to cope with the "present danger," two shared themes unite them. First, the United States must undertake substantial increases in military spending. It is now clear many Cold War internationalists within and outside the Reagan administration believe that even projected defense expenditures of $2 trillion would be totally inadequate, and that far greater defense outlays are necessary to restore American credibility and the genuine war-fighting capability that they believe to be the only effective deterrent to the Soviet challenge. They tend to support preservation of the triad concept through deployment of the MX land-based mobile missile program, and revival of the B-1 bomber; and this is by no means a complete shopping list, for it touches only upon strategic forces. Above all, Cold War internationalists support the Strategic Defense Initiative (SDI) program initiated by President Reagan in 1983 with the goal of rendering nuclear weapons "impotent and obsolete."

But perhaps even more than imbalances in military capabilities, the Cold War internationalists emphasize a second point, what they diagnose as an imbalancce in resolution and willingness to use power, if necessary, to preserve vital national interests. A number of them have already written off Western Europe as hopelessly caught in a web of neutralism, pacifism, and defeatism, and they regard the United States of the détente era as only a few steps behind in the process. The "Reagan Doctrine" of military support to anticommunist forces in Nicaragua, Afghanistan and Angola, along with the military buildup and SDI, are necessary to demonstrate that the "collapse of Western will" during the 1970s has been reversed.

Post–Cold War Internationalism[3]

Post–Cold War internationalists are not unaware of East-West tensions, if only out of recognition that therein lies the major danger of nuclear holocaust, but their conceptual map is more strongly oriented toward issues that tend to divide the world along a North-South line. At the center of their worldview is a series of closely related propositions concerning the international system, its key actors, and America's proper role within it. The growing list of serious threats to a stable and just world order has created an international system of such complexity and interdependence as to render totally obsolete the premises that informed American foreign policy during the two decades following the end of World War II. Whereas the Cold War internationalists perceive an essentially bipolar structure that dominates most critical issues, the post–Cold War internationalists see a far richer and more varied menu of both threats to, and opportunities for, creation of a viable world order. Dangers arising from strategic/military issues remain real, but the roots of future international conflict are to be located not merely in military imbalances—real or perceived—but also in problems arising from poverty, inequitable distribution of resources, unfulfilled demands for self-determination, regional antagonisms, population pressures, technology that outpaces the political means for controlling its consequences, and the like. Whereas the Cold War internationalists maintain that the chessboard remains a valid metaphor of the global system, the post–Cold War internationalists perceive a multidimensional game in which the logic of the situation will ultimately reward cooperation more handsomely, and in which outcomes are more often than not non–zero-sum.

Not only has the age of bipolarity passed (if, indeed, it ever existed), but it is both futile and dangerous to believe that it may be replaced by resurrecting a classical balance-of-power system. Put most simply, unprecedented changes relating to actors, objectives, values, and, indeed, the very nature of power itself, have rendered the balance of power a wholly inadequate model for world order. The primary task, then, is to create, nurture, and sustain new structures and processes for dealing effectively and equitably with a range of issues that goes well beyond traditionally defined security concerns. At the core of this worldview is the premise that one cannot effectively cope with the problems and opportunities arising from "complex interdependence" save by means of international cooperation on an unprecedented scale; a crucial lesson of Vietnam is that no nation, not even one as powerful as the United States, can alone shape a just and stable world order.

The post–Cold War internationalist image of the Soviet Union varies sharply from that of the Cold War internationalists. The latter emphasize that the monolithic nature of the Soviet system gives rise to a uniformity of foreign policy goals, whereas the former place stress on the complexity of both Soviet structures and external motivation; typically they regard the USSR as a traditional great power rather than as a revolutionary, inherently expansionist one.

Soviet foreign policy motivations can therefore be understood, if not admired, as a mixture of security concerns and aspirations for recognition as the equal of the United States. Thus, whereas Cold War internationalists interpret Soviet actions in Afghanistan and elsewhere as part of a master plan to gain control of strategic areas—for example, as stepping-stones toward control of the Persian Gulf oil fields—the post–Cold War internationalists usually interpret such actions more benignly, as motivated by local conditions, defensive consider-ations, temptations to take advantage of low-risk gains that few major powers could resist, or efforts to score points in the continuing conflict with China. Although they do not applaud such actions as the invasion of Afghanistan, they are at least as likely to be critical of American "overreactions" to these episodes as the Cold War internationalists are to condemn Washington's complacency.

Because the post–Cold War internationalists are less than awed by the Soviet Union, they are prepared to explore various forms of accommodation with Moscow, and they acknowledge that success will require flexibility by both of the superpowers. For example, the *New York Times* editorialized that, "Like the United States, the Soviet Union is becoming a mostly conservative force in world affairs, restrained by the fear of nuclear war and burdened with defense of far-flung political and economic interests." As a consequence, "The central axiom of Soviet-American relations today is that the interests of the two na-tions will periodically coincide and produce collaboration to try to preserve stability in unstable lands and so to avert a superpower conflict" (*New York Times*, 1979: A20). Far more than the Cold War internationalists, they are inclined to see merit in reviving détente by exploring various tension-reducing initiatives put forward by Chairman Gorbachev, if only because failure to do so will, at best, give him a propaganda victory by default.

On no issue is there perceived to be a clearer conjunction of interests than on arms control. Whereas the Cold War internationalists insist upon tight connec-tions between SALT and other issues, the post–Cold War internationalists are skeptical of efforts to create such linkages. They are especially critical of tying arms-control negotiations to satisfactory Soviet-American relations on such is-sues as Third World conflicts. Only by separating that inherently difficult rela-tionship into its component parts is there any real prospect of achieving progress on any of them. The Cold War internationalists regarded both the rate of growth in Soviet defense spending and external adventures in Africa, Central America, and the Middle East, as well as terms of the agreement itself, as ample reason for rejection of the SALT II Treaty; the post–Cold War internationalists—many of whom have questioned whether the Soviet Union has even matched, much less surpassed, American force levels—almost uniformly supported the treaty as inherently equitable, as a barrier against even greater Soviet military spending, and as the centerpiece of any effort to stabilize relations between the superpow-ers. Moreover, not a few post–Cold War internationalists suggest that the alarm-ist claims of The Committee on the Present Danger and others are no more justified than were cries about a "missile gap" during the closing months of the Eisenhower administration. And even if the claims of Soviet military superiority were valid, they question whether such capabilities could be translated into political advantage, especially in light of Soviet defense needs arising from the Sino-Soviet dispute, the probable unreliability of the Soviets' Eastern European allies, and other difficulties. Although some post–Cold War internationalists criticized the far-ranging arms-control proposals tabled by President Reagan at the 1986 Iceland summit meeting because they were poorly thought out and had not been discussed with NATO allies, they also disputed the wisdom of the president's decision to reject any agreement that would restrict the SDI program.

Consistent with these interpretations, the post–Cold War internationalists believe that an active American role in creating an equitable and stable world order is indispensable, not only because mankind is denied the luxury of procrastination in dealing with many world-order issues, but also because to do otherwise may be to leave the field to those whose goals and values may be less benign. This is not to say that they are uncritical of American policies or institutions. Indeed, some of them hold views—for example, "The disposition toward repression in American foreign policy is mainly a matter of structure, not will" (Falk, 1976:99)—that are strikingly similar to the Cold War internationalists' Manichaean image of the USSR. The United States has both the obligation, especially in relations with the less-developed nations, and the capabilities to contribute toward creation of the institutions and processes necessary to deal effectively and in a timely fashion with the broad agenda, by no means limited to the purely geopolitical and strategic, of critical international issues. Withdrawal from an active international role, as suggested by the isolationists, is neither morally acceptable nor, in any case, a realistic option for the United States.

As a result, some of the notable differences between the Cold War internationalists and post–Cold War internationalists revolve around their conceptions of the Third World. The former view the less-developed nations largely in strategic terms, as one of several sites of a global East-West conflict. In contrast, the post–Cold War internationalists tend to view the Third World as the hapless victims of nature (the uneven distribution of such vital resources as oil or arable land, or unfavorable climatic conditions) or of their colonial heritages. Post-liberation exploitation by the rich industrial nations of the West and, above all, by the multinational corporations, is an added burden. These conditions are regarded as necessary, and usually sufficient, to explain everything from populations that grow faster than gross national products to highly repressive regimes. It thus follows that there are both prudential and moral reasons for the industrial democracies to undertake massive programs of resource transfers as part of a "New International Economic Order": prudential because only such undertakings can promote international stability and ultimately avert a North-South conflict; moral because justice and retribution for past sins require a more equitable distribution of the globe's goods and services. If the Cold War internationalists rarely exhibit excessive sensitivity to repressive governments of the right, many post–Cold War internationalists are equally tolerant of the most authoritarian left-wing governments, for whose excesses blame can usually be assigned elsewhere.

It was noted earlier that the Cold War internationalists demand some significant changes in recent American foreign and defense policies. The post–Cold War internationalists are, for very different reasons, equally critical of those policies. A necessary, if not sufficient, condition for success in implementing their proposals is a dramatic reorientation of America's international role. Stanley Hoffmann (1978) poses the alternatives in the title of his book, *Primacy or World Order*. To opts for the former means a continuation of excessive concern for military strategy; interventions to support unworthy regimes in areas where vital interests are, at best, marginally at stake; and neglect of global problems that ultimately offer a far greater threat to American security than many of those that have recently obsessed Washington. That choice assures for this country, and the global community as well, a future of confrontation, conflict, crises, and chaos—and the certainty of ultimate failure to achieve either primacy or world order. To choose the course of world order, on the other hand, requires a significant reexamination of some deeply ingrained American pretensions, premises, patterns of thought, and policies. At minimum, the politics of negotiation, compromise, and cooperation—what Hoffmann calls "moderation plus"—must replace the politics of confrontation and crisis.

Semi-Isolationism[4]

Unlike the two internationalist schools of thought on contemporary international affairs, semi-isolationists are concerned primarily with domestic problems, which they see arising at least in part from excessive, if not obsessive, concern with both East-West and North-South issues. Much of their criticism of recent diplomacy is directed at premises that an activist foreign policy can create, either through balance-of-power manipulations or through pursuit of utopian schemes, a world order that is more congenial to American security, interests, or values. Viewing the international environment as fundamentally intractable, if not inherently anarchic, they regard the premise that this nation can create a just or stable world order as a dangerous, but typically American, exercise in hubris. At worst it leads to dangerous and futile crusades to "make the world safe for democracy" or some other equally elusive goal; at best it can only lead to cynicism and despair when, as is inevitable, the utopian plans are not fulfilled.

For the semi-isolationists, the cardinal rules that should guide this nation's concerns are, "Know thy limits" and "Heal thyself first." George McGovern's plea, "Come home, America," although clearly not a formula upon which to ride into the White House in 1972, nevertheless struck a responsive chord among a not insignificant element in the United States. George Kennan's assertion, "I think that I am a semi-isolationist" (Kennan, 1978:125), George Meany's proclamation that "free trade is a sham," and the appeal of "project independence" to many once confirmed internationalists, indicate that isolationism has achieved a degree of respectability and support unknown since before Pearl Harbor.

Semi-isolationists share with the post–Cold War internationalists several key propositions about contemporary international relations. They agree that the era of bipolarity has passed, in large part because the Soviet Union has been transformed from an aggressive revolutionary state into a conservative great power, governed by a cautious leadership whose memories of the destruction wrought by World War II far outweigh their zeal for high-risk international adventures. Thus, what the Cold War internationalists perceive as a military superpower, confident that a dramatic change in the "correlation of forces" is opening up an era of unprecedented opportunities for Soviet expansion, the semi-isolationists diagnose as a great power beset with intractable domestic problems, ranging from rampant alcoholism and an inefficient agricultural sector to potential ethnic conflicts. Additionally, they see a Kremlin with an agenda full of international difficulties, including, but not confined to, the

China problem and threats of nationalism within its Eastern European empire. And, whereas the Cold War internationalists see in the fast-rising Soviet arms budget a clear indication of ultimate Soviet intentions—and thus an unprecedented threat to Western civilization—the semi-isolationists are inclined to attribute the Soviet side of the arms race to a mixture of genuine fears of a two-front war, bureaucratic momentum, and strategic irrationalities that are not the monopoly of the leadership in the Kremlin. Most importantly, the record of Soviet efforts must not be exaggerated by alarmists; it is one on which the abysmal failures in China, Yugoslavia, Egypt, Sudan, and elsewhere far outweigh the few successes in such lesser countries as Yemen, Angola, Ethiopia, and Vietnam.

In some respects the semi-isolationist diagnosis of Soviet-American relations goes further. With their emphasis on the fact that the real problems and threats faced by both the superpowers are largely domestic in origin, the semi-isolationists are inclined to deny that there are any genuine conflicts of interest between them. The danger, then, is not so much that either poses an insuperable threat to the vital interests of the other but, rather, that fear, miscalculation, and misperception will drive them into a conflict that can only result in their mutual destruction, if not that of all mankind. The arms race plays a central role in this dangerous situation. It denies both sides resources that could be used to deal with vital domestic issues. More dangerously, the propensity to adduce aggressive foreign policy motivations from arms budgets and deployments drives the arms race in an action-reaction cycle that can only lead to a disastrous outcome.

But the semi-isolationists are not inclined to give much greater credence to either the direst fears or the fondest hopes of the post–Cold War internationalists. For starters, they tend to regard the term "complex interdependence" as descriptively inaccurate for the most part, and a fact to be deplored rather than celebrated where in fact it does exist. As Kennan has put it, "To what extent this interdependence really exists and constitutes a commanding reality of our time, I cannot say. I will only say that however much there is of it, as a feature of the situation of the United States, I wish there were less" (Kennan, 1977:50). The hope and expectation that interdependence provide both the imperative and the opportunity for long-overdue structural changes in the international system are dismissed as chimerical and utopian. The progeny of interdependence are more likely to be intervention and conflict than cooperation and progress.

The semi-isolationist diagnosis of the contemporary international situation thus differs radically from that of the other two internationalist viewpoints described earlier. Its primary elements may be summarized in a set of three propositions. First, the USSR does indeed possess the capabilities to rain great destruction on the United States and the other Western democracies, but it lacks the slightest intention of doing so.

Second, many Third World nations do indeed envy and oppose the industrial democracies—often successfully exploiting wholly irrational guilt complexes in the West—but, save for a few isolated instances, they lack totally the capabilities for threatening the vital interests of the United States. There are thus few, if any, compelling reasons for taking seriously some of the more strident demands from the Third World for "reparations" or other types of massive resource transfers. Where the power to threaten such national interests in fact exists, notably with respect to oil, it is largely the consequence of a short-sighted, mad American rush to place our head in the noose by failing to exercise sufficient discipline in the use of resources and thus to avoid becoming the eager hostages of OPEC. There are stark differences between the post–Cold War internationalists and the semi-isolationists on the Third World, for the former are often inclined to insist that the United States cannot, either morally or practically, be indifferent to the claims of the poor nations. The semi-isolationist response rejects the moral argument and asserts that economic and political development can only arise from self-reliance; they cannot be imposed or implemented from abroad, and the effort to do so may, in fact, hinder rather than assist the development process.

Third, the real threats to a just and humane social order in this country are largely to be found within its own borders rather than abroad. Decaying cities, inflation, unemployment, cultural decadence, illiteracy, crime, drugs, unprecedented budget deficits that more than doubled the national debt between 1980 and 1986, loss of economic competitiveness, a crisis in the farm belt, unresolved racial issues, environmental depredation, and other familiar problems pose, according to the semi-isolationists, a far greater threat to the quality of American institutions and lives than do the ambitions of the men in the Kremlin or the strident and generally unjustified demands of Third World leaders for a new international order. Indeed, many semi-isolationists share with their intellectual forefathers a conviction that an activist foreign policy is incompatible with a stable and progressive domestic order—and perhaps is not even compatible with the maintenance of democratic institutions. The semi-isolationist argument is thus sustained not only by a pessimistic estimate of Washington's ability to solve pressing international problems. It is perhaps even more fundamentally grounded in a fear that the United States will lose its soul by excessive international involvement, whether to play the realpolitik game prescribed by the Cold War internationalists, or the "complex interdependence" game favored by the post–Cold War internationalists. *"The inescapable lesson common to both Vietnam and Watergate is that the ultimate trade-off is between internationalist foreign policies and the integrity of our constitution. We cannot maintain both"* (Ravenal, 1975:91. Italics in the original).

Consistent with these diagnoses, the semi-isolationist "grand design" for American foreign policy differs sharply from those of both internationalist schools of thought. The semi-isolationists recognize the existence of conflicts along both North-South and East-West axes, but they tend to dismiss as a dangerous delusion the notion, widely accepted in the United States during the decades following the end of World War II, that there is any compelling practical or ethical imperative for this nation to be centrally involved in the amelioration of the world's ills. Especially discriminating selectivity should be exercised in limiting defense commitments to an indispensable minimum. Most importantly, there must be an awareness that just as every international problem is not caused by Americans, so, too, it does not necessarily have a unique or effective American solution.

More specifically, the semi-isolationist prescription includes several main points. The United States should place high priority on negotiating outstanding differences with the Soviet Union, with the minimal goals of slowing down or reversing the arms race and thereby reducing the threat of unintended or unwanted conflict. The semi-isolationists differ sharply from both varieties of internationalism with respect to appropriate policies toward the Third World. The Cold War internationalists regard the less-developed nations as a crucial battleground between the two major blocs, and the post–Cold War internationalists view them as the victim of neglect, if not exploitation, by the rich nations. The semi-isolationists reject both of these diagnoses, the first because it can lead only to endless American interventions in volatile areas that do not threaten or even seriously engage vital American interests, and the second because it fails to recognize that self-reliance rather than external assistance offers the only effective path to development. Hence the prescription that the United States should deal with the Third World nations only on the basis of genuinely shared interests—which are likely to be quite limited in scope— rather than on the basis of guilt for conditions that are not of America's making, or of romantic visions about what those interests might be. For the semi-isolationists, the central lesson of Vietnam is that the United States cannot provide security for those who are incapable or unwilling to make the necessary sacrifices; nor can it provide the means of material, political, or spiritual improvements for those who are indifferent to such problems.

Semi-isolationists believe that the United States should also initiate a process of disengagement from external alliances and military commitments, until the security perimeter has reached a clearly defensible position. Some would define such a position as including Western Europe, Japan, and Israel; others would support a perimeter that is even more circumscribed. The Soviets or Chinese might choose to take advantage of such a narrowly defined perimeter by embarking upon external adventures in the Third World. However, such actions would rarely infringe upon vital American interests.

Finally, if the United States is to have a salutary influence on the rest of the world, it will come about largely through a demonstrated capacity to solve its own pressing domestic problems. In a large sense, then, acccording to semi-isolationists, America's abillity to contribute to a solution of many global issues—be it human rights or democratic development—is limited to the power of example. It therefore behooves this nation to achieve a satisfactory resolution of these problems at home before turning its attention and energies to preaching to or materially helping others.

WHO ARE THE ADHERENTS OF THE THREE FOREIGN POLICY BELIEF SYSTEMS?

More systematic evidence, drawn from a nationwide leadership survey in 1976, demonstrated the existence of the three foreign policy belief systems described in the previous section. The 2,282 participants in the survey included military officers, business executives, foreign service officers, media leaders, clergy, labor leaders, public officials, and lawyers, among others. There has been a good deal of speculation about the sources of the foreign policy cleavages that arose in the post-Vietnam era. For example, according to some observers, the divisions were essentially generational in origin, pitting the "hard-line" views of the older "World War II" generation against the "dovish" and isolationist beliefs of those constituting the "Vietnam generation." The 1976 leadership survey provides an opportunity to assess the validity of this and other generalizations about societal divisions on international affairs. Leaders taking part in this survey were initially ranked by their responses to thirty-two questions. Further analyses were then undertaken to identify characteristics that may be associated with the three perspectives (see Table 1).

The results may be summarized briefly. The continuing impact of the Vietnam War on leadership beliefs is demonstrated in the finding that a *Vietnam policy position* is the best predictor of foreign policy beliefs; leaders participating in this survey were classified according to their policy preferences (whether they sought to achieve a complete victory, to withdraw completely, to follow a policy in between victory and withdrawal, or were not sure) in both the early and late stages of the war (Holsti and Rosenau, 1979). Those consistently seeking victory were classified as supporters; critics favored a complete withdrawal at both times; and five other groups were formed on the basis of various combinations of responses. The category *ideology* shared with a Vietnam policy position the top rank as the most potent predictor of foreign policy beliefs; conservatives favored Cold War internationalism, and liberals were stronger advocates of the other two perspectives on international affairs. Differences between *occupations* were also quite pronounced; for example, media leaders, clergy, and educators tended to adhere to views labeled as post–Cold War internationalist, while military officers predominated among Cold War internationalists, and labor leaders were substantially more pronounced in their support for semi-isolationalism than any other occupational group. *Political party* preferences were also related to foreign policy beliefs, but those relationships largely disappeared if ideology was held constant; for example, liberal Republicans tended to respond as liberals rather than as members of the GOP, and conservative Democrats also shared more views with conservatives than with other Democrats. *Military service* proved to be a rather weak predictor of foreign policy beliefs; it was especially weak after controlling for occupation, thereby permitting a distinction between career military officers and leaders who had experienced a limited service in the armed forces. Finally, age and gender differences were especially weak explanatory factors; the most pronounced divisions cut within rather than across generations, and, in most respects, women and men responded very similarly to a broad range of foreign policy issues.

In summary, the 1976 survey revealed an American leadership divided on some fundamental aspects of international affairs. The cleavages appear to have originated in the decade-long war in Vietnam and to have been reinforced by both psychological (ideology) and sociological (occupation) factors.

FOREIGN POLICY BELIEFS, 1976–1984: CONTINUITY OR CHANGE?

The previous section summarized data collected in 1976, within a year of the final American withdrawal from Vietnam. During the next several years, different foreign policy leaders, other issues, and new crises came to dominate America's external relations. Have these, combined with the passing of time, eroded the impact of Vietnam? Have they served to forge a new consensus, as Vietnam receded into the past, and as Americans found their newspapers, evening news, and political debates centering on the price and availability of imported oil, trade balances and the value of the dollar, the Panama Canal, human rights

Table 1. Who are the Adherents of the Three Foreign Policy Belief Systems?: The Relationship Between Leader Attributes and Foreign Policy Belief Systems in the 1976, 1980, and 1984 Surveys of American Leaders[a]

Attributes of Leaders	YEAR	Groups Highest on Cold War Internationalism[b]	Groups Highest on Post–Cold War Internationalism[b]	Groups highest on Semi-Isolationism[b]
VIETNAM POLICY POSITION	1976	Supporters	Critics	Critics
(7 categories, Critics to Supporters)	1980	Supporters	Critics	Critics
	1984	Supporters	Critics	Critics
IDEOLOGY	1976	Most conservative	Most liberal	Most liberal
(5 categories, Most conservative to	1980	Most conservative	Most liberal	Most liberal
most liberal)	1984	Most conservative	Most liberal	Most liberal
OCCUPATION	1976	Military officers	Clergy	Labor leaders
(10 categories)		Business executives	Educators	Media leaders
	1980	Business executives	Clergy	Labor leaders
		Military officers	Labor leaders	Clergy
	1984	Military officers	Clergy	Clergy
		Business executives	Labor leaders	Labor leaders
POLITICAL PARTY	1976	Republicans	Democrats	Democrats
(3 categories, including indepen-	1980	Republicans	Democrats	Democrats
dents)	1984	Republicans	Democrats	Democrats
GENERATION	1976	——	——	——
(4 categories, based on year of	1980	——	——	——
birth)	1984	——	——	——
MILITARY SERVICE	1976	Veterans	——	Non-veterans
(2 categories, veterans and	1980	——	——	——
non-veterans)	1984	——	——	——
GENDER	1976	——	——	——
	1980	——	——	——
	1984	——	——	——

[a]In 1976, 2,282 leaders filled out and returned questionnaires; the comparable figures for 1980 and 1984 are 2,502 and 2,515.

[b]Groups that are highest on each of the three belief system scales are listed if: (1) differences among them are statistically significant (.001 level) *and* (2) the correlation between the attribute and foreign policy beliefs is at least .20. Dashes indicate that differences among the categories do not satisfy *both* criteria.

abroad, Cubans in Angola and Ethiopia, hostages in Iran, Russians in Afghanistan, civil wars in Central America and Lebanon, the Camp David accords, the
intricacies of SALT, MX basing modes, SDI and the deterioration of détente?
As a consequence, have spokesmen for the Carter and Reagan administrations,
who agree on little else, been correct in asserting that these events have erased
the last traces of the "Vietnam syndrome," while bringing Americans together
in a new, post-Vietnam consensus? In short, have the external features and
internal structure of American leadership beliefs, circa 1976, been "overtaken
by events?"

A second foreign policy leadership survey was conducted in 1980, a few
weeks after the start of the hostage crisis in Iran and the Soviet invasion of
Afghanistan. The second survey involved 2,502 American leaders and provided
a substantial body of evidence about foreign policy beliefs in the wake of
turmoil in and near the Persian Gulf area. A number of questions compared
responses in the 1976 and 1980 surveys and assessed the degree of change in
foreign policy beliefs during the intervening years. Each effort yielded similar
and reinforcing results: changes were not wholly absent, but they represented a
relatively minor theme in an overall pattern of striking continuity. Not only did
the 1976 and 1980 samples of leaders respond in very similar ways to ninety-
three foreign policy questions that appeared in both questionnaires, but the
pattern of group responses summarized in Table 1 remained virtually intact.
Deep cleavages on many fundamental issues persisted, and they tended to
reflect differences on the Vietnam War, ideology, and occupation, rather than
such other attributes as sex, generation, or military services.

The results of a third survey, in 1984, once again reveal a pattern of greater
continuity than change in the foreign policy beliefs of American leaders. As
revealed in the right-hand column of Table 1, background attributes associated
with the competing belief systems among the 2,515 respondents resembled
those of 1976 and 1980.

Against a background of domestic and international stability, these results
might not seem especially noteworthy, but on any list of adjectives that might
be attached to the 1976–1984 period, "tranquil" is among the least appropriate. The earliest survey was initiated with a recently installed and popular
Gerald Ford in the White House. Jimmy Carter was among the longer shots in
a crowded list of Democratic presidential hopefuls, and Ronald Reagan's falter-
ing campaign for the GOP nomination appeared to be the last hurrah in his
political career. The Shah of Iran, a pillar of American security policy in the
Persian Gulf region, was firmly on the Peacock Throne, and Afghanistan might
as well have been located on the back side of the moon for all the interest or
knowledge most Americans had in that obscure Southwest Asian nation.

Four years later, President Carter was waging a desperate battle to win his
own party's presidential nomination, while Ronald Reagan, who would defeat
Carter in the general election, was well on his way to an easy victory in the
Republican primaries. The Shah had gone into exile and was dying. His successors in Teheran had triggered a 444-day crisis by invading the American embassy and taking its personnel hostage. Soon thereafter, Afghanistan was the
victim of a brutal invasion by the Soviets, casting a distinct chill in relations
between Washington and Moscow, if not bringing on an outright renewal of
the Cold War. Even had the rest of the world remained free from conflict and
change—evidence from virtually every region clearly proved that it had not—
the period in question was undeniably characterized by tumult and turmoil.

The next four years witnessed growing conflict in Central America and the Middle East, the outbreak of war between Iran and Iraq, several changes in Soviet leadership, and an accelerating global arms race. A very popular President Reagan would win re-election by a landslide, but even his supporters agreed that the 1980 "defense consensus" was being washed away by a flood of red ink.

Against such a background, the major findings of the 1980 and 1984 leadership surveys—the foreign policy beliefs of American leaders remained quite stable—is of more than passing interest, whether one's concern is with substantive, theoretical, or policy-oriented aspects of American foreign policy.[5]

NOTES

1. The first two sections of this article draw extensively upon Holsti (1979); the third and fourth draw in part on Holsti and Rosenau (1984).
2. A representative sample of the literature of this genre includes: Schlesinger (1977) and Podhoretz (1980); most foreign policy articles in *Commentary* and *National Review*, editorials in the *Wall Street Journal*; columns by George Will, Roland Evans, and Robert Novak; publications of The Committee on the Present Danger, the National Strategy Information Center, the Heritage Foundation, the Ethics and Public Policy Center at Georgetown University, and The Committee for the Free World; and various writings of Paul Nitze, Walter Laqueur, Edward N. Luttwak, Ben J. Wattenberg, Carl Gershman, Eugene Rostow, W. W. Rostow, Fred Iklé, Colin Gray, Daniel O. Graham, Albert Wohlstetter, Herbert Stein, and Irving Kristol.
3. This viewpoint is effectively represented by Hoffmann (1978), Keohane and Nye (1977), and Brown (1974); articles in *Nation* and *Progressive*; columns by Arthur Schlesinger, Jr., Tom Wicker, and Anthony Lewis; editorials in the *New York Times* and *Washington Post*; and the foreign policy writings of James Chace, Harlan Cleveland, Elliott L. Richardson, Jean Meyer, Robert Levgold, Robert McNamara, Richard Barnet, Richard Falk, Paul C. Warnke, Les Aspin, Morton Kondracke, Jan M. Lodal, Adam Yarmolinsky, Richard H. Ullman, and Thomas Hughes.
4. Among the most articulate statements of the semi-isolationist position are Kennan (1977) and Ravenal (1975). Both of these prolific authors have also developed their positions in many other writings during the past half-decade. Aspects of the semi-isolationist viewpoint may also be found in materials from various labor leaders, some industrialists, and several spokesmen for the Libertarian party.
5. A further development of these points may be found in Holsti and Rosenau (1984).

REFERENCES

Brown, Seyom. (1974). *New Forces in World Politics*. Washington: The Brookings Institution.
Falk, Richard A. (1976). "Beyond Internationalism," *Foreign Policy*, 24 (Fall):65–113.
Hoffmann, Stanley. (1978). *Primacy or World Order*. New York: McGraw-Hill.
Holsti, Ole R. (1979). "The Three Headed Eagle: The United States System and Change," *International Studies Quarterly*, 23 (September):339–359.
Holsti, Ole R., and James N. Rosenau. (1979). "Vietnam, Consensus, and the Belief Systems of American Leaders," *World Politics*, 23 (October):1–56.
———. (1984). *American Leadership in World Affairs: Vietnam and the Breakdown of Consensus*. London and Boston: Allen and Unwin.
House, Karen Elliott. (1980). "Reagan's World: Republican Policies Stress Arms Buildup, a Firm Line to Soviet," *Wall Street Journal* (June 3):1, 25.
Kennan, George F. (1978). "An Appeal for Thought," *New York Times Magazine* (May 7):43.
———. (1977). *The Cloud of Danger*. Boston: Little, Brown.
Keohane, Robert O. and Joseph Nye. (1977). *Power and Interdependence*. Boston: Little, Brown.
New York Times. (1979). "A Rhomboid of Rhetoric" (January 11):A20.
Podhoretz, Norman. (1980). *The Present Danger*. New York: Basic Books.
Ravenal, Earl C. (1975). "Who Needs It?" *Foreign Policy*, 18 (Spring):80–91.
Schlesinger, James R., et al. (1977). *Defending America*. New York: Basic Books.

3. AMERICA'S STATE OF MIND: TRENDS IN PUBLIC ATTITUDES TOWARD FOREIGN POLICY

John E. Rielly

Throughout the 1970s, public-opinion surveys sponsored by the Chicago Council on Foreign Relations (CCFR) confirmed that the American public had developed a preoccupation with such issues as inflation, unemployment, and energy. It was inclined to withdraw from international responsibility and harbored a feeling of military weakness and insecurity.

Concern over these issues has now receded. A growing appreciation of the importance of foreign affairs is evident, combined with a desire for a larger U.S. world role. Both the American public and its leaders now believe that a favorable military balance has been restored with the Soviet Union and that the United States plays a more important role in the world. But while Americans now feel more secure, their support for increased defense spending is diminishing. Even so, most Americans are prepared to continue defense efforts at their current level.

One consequence of these perceptions and feelings is continued support for arms control and slightly increased support for certain measures associated with détente with the Soviet Union. But in contrast to their support for the Reagan administration's defense build-up, most Americans do not support some of the more aggressive elements of its foreign policy, including its military intervention abroad, its active promotion of democracy, and its implementation of the Reagan Doctrine through covert action against communist-oriented regimes in Afghanistan, Angola, and Nicaragua.

Despite growing friction between the United States and its principal partners in the Organization for Economic Cooperation and Development over trade and financial issues, the public's highly favorable attitude toward Western Europe and Japan continues; in the case of Japan, somewhat surprisingly, it even improves. However, since the beginning of this decade American interest in and sympathy toward the Middle East has declined substantially. Public willingness to commit troops in crises involving Western Europe and Japan is greater than ever, but the reluctance to commit troops in other areas of the world, including Central America, continues unchanged.

Americans remain self-interested, a fact brought out by the 1986 polling. The desire to protect American jobs or to secure access to energy still takes priority over such altruistic objectives as promoting democracy, defending human rights, or improving other countries' standards of living.

Large gaps continue between public and leadership attitudes and, on many issues, between the views of the public and the leadership and those expressed by Reagan administration officials. The attitudes of outside leaders and government officials are closer to one another than to the general public. But an interesting development is the emergence of notable gaps between the views of administration officials and those of labor, media, educational, and religious leaders.

These are the principal findings of the survey sponsored by the CCFR and conducted by the Gallup Organization between October 20 and November 12, 1986. During this period, just before news of the U.S. arms sales to Iran broke, 1,585 men and women were interviewed in person. In addition, 343 leaders were interviewed, either in person or by telephone, between mid-September and mid-November. The leadership group comprised officials from the Reagan administration, Congress, international business, labor, the media, academe, religious institutions, private foreign-policy organizations, and special-interest groups.

This is the fourth CCFR study of the foreign-policy attitudes of Americans. The first was conducted in December 1974, following the resignation of President Richard Nixon. The second, conducted in November and December 1978, fell almost midway in the presidency of Jimmy Carter—shortly before the fall of the shah of Iran—and during a period of sharp inflation. The third, completed exactly 4 years later, occurred at the end of the second year of the Reagan administration, when the country was in deep economic recession.

In the three earlier studies, the preoccupation with domestic economic issues displayed by those surveyed reversed public-opinion trends from 1940 to 1973. In a series of Gallup polls taken during that 33-year period, American leaders and the public, in ranking the "most important problems facing the country," almost always assigned highest priority to foreign-policy and security issues. The surveys taken in the 10 years after 1973 revealed a shift to domestic issues—especially inflation and unemployment and access to energy supplies. Now a return to a greater sensitivity to foreign affairs has occurred. As a result, the public's concern for foreign policy, as opposed to domestic economic and social issues, is more evenly balanced. Twenty-six per cent of the problems the public selected when asked to identify the "biggest problems facing the country" concerned foreign policy—with arms control, U.S.-Soviet relations, and terrorism heading the list. The comparable figure for 1982 was 15 per cent, and for 1978, 11 per cent. Stated differently, foreign-policy problems have more than doubled in importance for the American people in the last 8 years. The same trend holds for American leaders: In 1986, 42 per cent of the "biggest problems" identified by leaders dealt with foreign policy, compared with 23 per cent in 1978. In 1978, inflation was clearly the biggest problem in the eyes of 67 per cent of the public and 85 per cent of the leaders. Unemployment was the top problem in 1982 for 64 per cent of the public and 53 per cent of the leaders. But with the sharp drop in inflation from 1978 to 1986 and an easing of unemployment from 1982 to 1986, both issues have lost prominence.

Also receding is the "inward-looking" attitude that characterized the American people throughout the 1970s. The leadership group has remained virtually unanimous over the past decade that the United States should play an active world role. Among the public, those who said that the United States should play "a more active role in the world" rose from 54 per cent in 1982 to 64 per

U.S. Foreign-Policy Problems

"What are the two or three biggest foreign-policy problems facing the U.S. today?"

	Public			Leaders		
	1986	1982	1978	1986	1982	1978
War/Arms race with USSR	31%	29%	20%	39%	39%	29%
Terrorism	13	0	0	5	0	0
General foreign policy	15	23	22	15	18	18
U.S. economy	13	13	17	13	9	13
Latin America	7	3	4	12	8	3
Middle East	5	13	13	6	15	18
South Africa	3	1	2	5	1	6
Europe	2	5	1	3	6	2
Asia	0	1	2	1	2	8
Miscellaneous/Don't know	11	12	19	4	2	3

U.S.-Soviet Relations——1986

	Public	Leaders
Favor negotiating arms control agreements	80%	95%
Favor resuming cultural and educational exchanges	78	98
Favor increasing grain sales	57	82
Oppose restricting trade	52	73
Oppose prohibiting exchanges of scientists	53	83
Oppose limiting sales of advanced U.S. computers	33	20
Favor sharing technical information about defending against missile attacks	23	—*

* Dash means "not asked."

cent in 1986. The proportion of the population very interested in news about other countries or about U.S. relations with other countries also has shown a steady rise. Indeed, news concerning America's relations with other countries now ranks second in importance after local news, having overtaken national news.

There has been an interesting and significant shift in the way that both the public and U.S. leaders now perceive America's place in the world. Asked whether the United States plays a more important and powerful role as a world leader today than it played 10 years ago, 41 per cent of the public said that it does. The 1982 figure was 27 per cent. In that year, 44 per cent of the public stated that the United States played a "less important" role in the world. But only 26 per cent chose that option in 1986. An even larger shift occurred among the leaders. Ten per cent of the leaders believed in 1982 that the United States played a more important role in the world. By 1986 that figure had climbed to 33 per cent. In 1982, 52 per cent of the leaders thought that the United States played a less important role. By 1986 that figure had fallen to 27 per cent. This shift in how both the American public and the leaders see America's role in the world is perhaps the most important change that has occurred in the Reagan years.

This change is undoubtedly influenced by the way Americans view the U.S.-Soviet military balance. Both the public and the leaders believe that the U.S. military position with respect to the Soviet Union has improved substantially. Among the public, 28 per cent now say that the United States is militarily stronger, as compared with 21 per cent in 1982. And 48 per cent believe that both are about equal, compared with 42 per cent in 1982. An even greater shift has occurred since 1978. Then, 56 per cent of the public believed that the United States was falling behind the Soviet Union militarily.

Even among American leaders who never judged the military balance to be as weighted against the United States as did the public, a substantial shift has occurred. In 1978, 39 per cent of American leaders believed that the United States was falling behind the Soviet Union. In 1982, 15 per cent judged the Soviet Union to be stronger. That figure is now 11 per cent. Twenty-eight per cent of the leaders now believe the United States is stronger militarily, again up 8 points from 1982. Fifty-nine per cent state that the two sides are about equal.

A more confident view of America's role in the world and of the U.S.-Soviet military balance reduces the sense of urgency about additional steps to shore up American military power. Consequently, support for increased defense spending is continuing to decline at both the public and the leadership levels. The shift has been under way since early 1981, reversing the previous trend of 1974–1978, when there was an increase of 19 per cent in favor of higher defense spending. By 1982 the number favoring greater defense spending dropped by 11 per cent, while the number favoring cuts increased by 8 per cent. Over the past 4 years these trends have continued. In brief, the larger defense budgets currently favored by Reagan and Secretary of Defense Caspar Weinberger do not enjoy support from either the American public or its leaders.

Americans continue to see relations with the Soviet Union as the biggest foreign-policy problem facing the United States. Yet because of the greater sense of military security, support for measures associated with détente continues and in some cases has expanded slightly. There is both greater concern about issues of war and peace and strong support for measures of cooperation with the Soviet Union. When asked about seven specific areas of possible cooperation with the Soviet Union, the public responded strongly in favor of most such efforts. Significant majorities favor negotiating arms control agreements, educational and cultural agreements, selling grain to the Soviet Union, and easing the restriction on U.S.-Soviet trade. Only on selling computers to the Soviet Union and sharing technological information on the Strategic Defense Initiative does the public strongly prefer restrictions. Elite support for

The Perceived Military Balance

	Public			Leaders		
	1986	1982	1979	1986	1982	1979
U.S. stronger	28	21	33	28	20	—
USSR stronger	17	29	32	11	15	—
About equal	48	42	26	59	63	—
Don't know	7	8	9	2	3	—

NOTE: Dash means "not asked."

cooperative measures is even higher, as is its opposition to the sale of advanced computers.

Clearly, the early Reagan administration's harsh rhetoric and the president's failure to reach agreement on an arms control breakthrough at the November 1986 Reykjavík summit did not slow down the desire for increased cooperation. Coming to power as a determined opponent of détente, Reagan has gained an unintended success: In restoring a perception of a military balance more favorable to the United States, he has increased support for détente. Not that the American people have altered their basically negative view of the Soviet Union: The Soviet Union once again emerges next to last in a preference rating of 24 countries. Interestingly, Soviet leader Mikhail Gorbachev does somewhat better than his country, registering fourth from the bottom on a list of world leaders, or slightly higher than then Soviet leader Leonid Brezhnev did 4 years ago.

Although U.S. relations with Western Europe and Japan have been the subject of much controversy in recent years, U.S. attitudes have remained consistently positive. Both leaders and the public believe that the United States has a "vital interest" in both areas. They also see vital interests in the Western

Attitude Toward America's Vital Interest Around the World——The Public & Leaders

| Country | Does Have Vital Interest | | | |
| | Public | Leaders | Public | Leaders |
	1986		1982	
Great Britain	83%	94%	80%	97%
Canada	78	96	82	95
Japan	78	98	82	97
West Germany	77	98	76	98
Saudi Arabia	77	88	77	93
Israel	76	86	75	92
Mexico	74	96	74	98
The Philippines	73	81	—	—
Egypt	61	—	66	90
China	61	89	64	87
Nicaragua	60	63	—	—
South Africa	59	63	38	54
South Korea	58	80	43	66
France	56	82	58	84
Taiwan	53	48	51	44
Iran	50	—	51	60
Syria	48	—	36	46
Brazil	44	63	45	80
Italy	41	—	35	79
India	36	55	30	57
Poland	35	—	43	47
Nigeria	31	—	32	53

NOTE: Dash means "not asked."

Hemisphere and in the Middle East, specifically in Egypt, Israel, and Saudi Arabia.

Over the past decade, and again in 1986, Canada, Great Britain, the Federal Republic of Germany, Japan, and Saudi Arabia ranked again in the top five countries, with Mexico near the same level. Most of these same countries also evoked the warmest responses in a preference rating by Americans. And the Federal Republic and Japan have consistently enjoyed a high ranking from both the public and the elite in terms of the country's vital interests. Their places in the ratings improved even more in this survey. Especially surprising is the eight-point jump in the preference poll by Japan, which has been the target over the past 4 years of repeated harsh criticisms by American congressional, industrial, and union leaders.

Continuing the level of support of 4 years ago, 70 per cent of the public and 85 per cent of the American leaders believe that the United States should either increase the commitment to NATO or keep it at the same level. Similarly, when asked to choose between leaving American troops in Europe for the time being or withdrawing over the next 5 years and letting the Europeans provide for their own nuclear and conventional defense, 82 per cent of the leaders responding favored the status quo.

A series of questions targeted for the leadership sample indicates no substan-

Thermometer Ratings for Countries——The Public

Country	Mean Temperature (degrees)		
	1986	1982	1978
Canada	77	74	72
Great Britain	73	68	67
West Germany	62	59	57
Japan	61	53	56
Mexico	59	60	58
Israel	59	55	61
The Philippines	59	—	—
France	58	60	62
Italy	58	55	56
Brazil	54	54	52
Poland	53	52	50
China	53	47	44
Taiwan	52	49	51
South Korea	50	44	48
Saudi Arabia	50	52	48
Egypt	49	52	53
India	48	48	49
South Africa	47	45	46
Nigeria	46	44	47
Nicaragua	46	—	—
Syria	34	42	—
Soviet Union	31	26	34
Iran	22	28	50

NOTE: Dash means "not asked."

Attitudes on Use of U.S. Troops Overseas——1986

Situation:	Favor Sending Troops		Oppose Sending Troops		Don't Know	
	Public	Leaders	Public	Leaders	Public	Leaders
1. Soviets invade Western Europe	68%	93%	24%	5%	8%	2%
2. Soviets invade Japan	53	82	36	12	11	6
3. Nicaragua allows Soviets to set up missile base	45	67	42	27	13	6
4. Arabs cut off oil to U.S.	36	—	51	—	13	—
5. Arabs invade Israel	32	57	54	38	14	5
6. Soviets invade China	27	14	61	78	12	8
7. Iran invades Saudi Arabia	26	—	59	—	15	—
8. El Salvador government losing to leftist rebels	25	—	56	—	19	—
9. Nicaragua invades Honduras to destroy contra bases	24	17	60	74	16	9
10. North Korea invades South Korea	24	64	64	32	12	4
11. China invades Taiwan	19	—	64	—	17	—

NOTE: Dash means "not asked."

tial shift in priorities from Europe to Asia, a possibility that has worried European observers. When asked which is more important to the United States, 46 per cent of American leaders chose Europe and 18 per cent chose Asia. Thirty-four per cent indicated that Europe and Asia are equally important. Similarly, American leaders overwhelmingly chose Europe (69 per cent) over Asia (15 per cent) as an area for postgraduate study for a son or daughter. With regard to language preferences, Spanish (34 per cent) and French (22 per cent) ranked first and second, well above Japanese (16 per cent) and Chinese (12 per cent). But there is a significant difference between the congressional attitude and that of administration leaders concerning the priority to be given Europe as opposed to Asia. Ten per cent more congressional leaders than administration figures favored the first alternative of leaving American troops in Europe for the time being as opposed to withdrawing them over a 5-year period. Perhaps related are differences between congressional and administration leaders over the preferred site of graduate study: 69 per cent of the congressional leaders favored Europe, compared with 46 per cent of the administration leaders.

The same preference for Europe is evident in public and elite attitudes about the use of troops in crises. Asked where they would support the use of American troops, both the public and the leaders gave their strongest support to the use of U.S. troops to repel a Soviet invasion of Western Europe. The public response (68 per cent) represents a small increase (3 per cent) over 1982 and a substantial increase (14 per cent) over 1978. The leadership response (93 per cent), however, is virtually unchanged over the last decade. Using troops to defend Japan ranked second. But the gap between use of troops for Europe and for Japan is substantial. Fifty-three per cent of the public would support the use of U.S. troops if Japan were invaded by the Soviet Union. Eighty-two per cent of American leaders shared this view. The high degree of elite support concerning the defense of Japan has remained constant over the past decade.

Another priority area, the Middle East, is declining in perceived importance. Fewer Americans consider the region one of the country's most important foreign-policy problems, nor are as many willing to support use of American troops in the area. Yet Israel's place in the preference poll has risen in the last 4 years; Israel remains one of the top six countries where Americans believe the country has a vital interest. Saudi Arabia also ranks high from the standpoint of vital interest, but it does not rate a high place in the preference poll. Iran is at the bottom of the list of countries.

Concern about unemployment and inflation—indeed, about economic issues generally—is receding. Most Americans continue to view foreign economic policy through the lens of self-interest, but they believe that the impact of foreign policy on the U.S. economy has declined substantially during the last 4 years. While a majority of Americans still see foreign policy as having a major impact on the U.S. economy generally—for example, on gasoline prices, on the value of the dollar abroad, and on unemployment—there has been a substantial drop (10 per cent to 14 per cent) in the level of this perception. Notwithstanding the oil glut, public concern with energy supplies remains high, and Saudi Arabia is still perceived as one of the top countries of vital interest to the United States.

Despite the massive trade deficit, the last 4 years saw a measurable decline in popular support for protectionist measures, as well as a modest increase in support for economic aid to other countries. The leadership sample strongly supports free trade: Two-thirds favor eliminating tariffs on imported goods and fewer than one-third believe that tariffs are necessary. Continuing a trend of more than a decade, public sentiment is the reverse. Fifty-three per cent believe tariffs and trade restrictions necessary; only 28 per cent favor eliminating them. The longstanding gap between the public and the leadership views on this issue, however, has been narrowed by 15 percentage points over the last 8 years—with leaders slightly more protectionist and the public slightly less so. It is noteworthy that this decline in support for protectionism took place at a time when the political leadership of the country, especially in Congress, was increasingly disposed to urge protectionist measures.

On another controversial foreign-policy issue, South Africa, 57 per cent of the public and 79 per cent of the leaders favor sanctions designed to pressure the South African government to modify its system of apartheid. Presented with alternatives on sanctions the public divided three ways: one-third favored no action, one-third favored limited economic sanctions (the current policy of the Reagan administration), and one-third favored stringent economic sanctions.

Along with an increase in willingness to use troops to defend Western Europe and Japan, there is continued resistance to their use elsewhere. Nearly one-fourth of the public would support the use of U.S. troops if the Salvadoran

Differences Between Leaders and the Public——1986

	Public	Leaders	Gap (Leaders minus public)
1. Best to take an active part in world affairs	71%	99%	+ 28%
2. Tariffs are necessary	66	31	− 35
3. Goal of protecting Americas' jobs very important	79	44	− 35
4. Favor using U.S. troops if: N. Korea invaded S. Korea	28	67	+ 39
USSR invaded Japan	60	87	+ 27
Arabs invaded Israel	38	60	+ 22
5. Vietnam War was not wrong or immoral	29	57	+ 28
6. Favor foreign military aid	36	78	+ 42
7. Favor military and economic aid to rebels against communist-supported governments	24	52	+ 28
8. Believe U.S. military aid to Central America is not likely to lead to U.S. military involvement	20	52	+ 32
9. Favor aid for foreign economic development and technical assistance	60	93	+ 33
10. Goal of strengthening U.N. very important	49	23	− 26
11. Favor exchanging scientists with the USSR	59	86	+ 27
12. Favor using military force to fight illegal drug trafficking without countries' permission	29	7	− 22

government were losing to leftist rebels, if Nicaragua invaded Honduras, or if North Korea invaded South Korea. Yet a plurality of the public and more than two-thirds of the leaders would support the use of troops if "Nicaragua allow[ed] the Soviets to set up a missile base." This strong response to a military move similar to the Soviet Union's effort to deploy missiles in Cuba in the early 1960s is consistent with public and leadership support for a strong response to direct Soviet military involvement in the hemisphere. It contrasts sharply, however, with the low priority given to Central America overall and with the strong opposition to U.S. involvement there.

The public also displays limited enthusiasm for the Reagan Doctrine. Two-thirds of the public favors giving either no aid or economic aid only to rebel groups fighting communist-supported governments in places like Afghanistan and Angola. Only 24 per cent of the public favors both military and economic aid, which is firmly supported by almost 52 per cent of the leaders. Forty-two per cent of the public is opposed to any aid. The public's concern that such actions will involve the country militarily in places like Central America has led to a distinct lack of enthusiasm for the Reagan Doctrine. At the same time, the Reagan administration's military intervention in Grenada and Libya received support from a majority of the public. Evidently the public is not averse

Foreign-Policy Goals for the United States——1986

	(Per Cent "Very Important")	
	Public	Leaders
1. Protecting the jobs of American workers	78	43
2. Ensuring adequate supplies of energy	69	72
3. Worldwide arms control	69	83
4. Combating world hunger	63	60
5. Reducing our trade deficit with foreign countries	62	—*
6. Containing communism	57	43
7. Defending our allies' security	56	78
8. Matching Soviet military power	53	59
9. Strengthening the United Nations	46	22
10. Protecting the interests of American business abroad	43	32
11. Promoting and defending human rights in other countries	42	44
12. Helping to improve the standard of living of less developed nations	37	46
13. Protecting weaker nations against foreign aggression	32	29
14. Helping to bring a democratic form of government to other nations	30	29

* Dash means "not asked."

to taking the risks involved in military action, provided the action is short-lived and the results are quickly apparent. It remains strongly opposed to involvement over a long period of time.

A substantial gap continues to exist between the views of leaders and the public on a wide variety of foreign-policy issues. Leaders continue to favor a more active U.S. role in the world and are more interventionist and more supportive of the Reagan Doctrine. Leaders continue to be strong supporters of free trade and support military and economic aid. Leaders give a higher priority to defending allies' security as a foreign-policy goal, and a lower priority to strengthening the United Nations. They are less concerned about protecting American jobs at home or promoting American business abroad.

Leaders continue to be much more (20 per cent to 30 per cent) inclined to support the use of U.S. troops in various crises—for example, A Soviet invasion of Western Europe or Japan, a North Korean invasion of South Korea, an Arab invasion of Israel, or the establishment of a Soviet missile base in Nicaragua. However, their views are closer to the negative attitudes of the public with respect to the use of American troops if Nicaragua were to invade Honduras or if the Soviet Union were to invade the People's Republic of China. Leaders are less inclined than the public to endorse the goal of "containing Communism," but are more inclined to consider as a "great threat" the coming to power of a communist government in specific countries such as France, Mexico, or Saudi Arabia. By large margins (40 per cent) leaders support military aid to other countries and are considerably less worried that military aid to Central America may lead to U.S. military involvement there. Leaders are overwhelmingly opposed to negotiating with terrorists (74 per cent) but are less inclined than

Major Differences Between Opinions of Administration Officials and Other Leaders——1986

	Administration Officials (n = 22)	Other Leaders (n = 321)	Gap (% Administration minus % others)
Congress is too strong	77%	28%	+ 49%
Tariffs should be eliminated	100	67	+ 33
Favor mutual nuclear freeze	40	82	− 43
Goal of containing communism very important	86	40	+ 46
Vietnam War was wrong and immoral	5	45	− 40
Goal of matching Soviet power very important	91	56	+ 35
Favor expanding spending on national defense	43	10	+ 33
U.S. is militarily stronger than USSR	9	30	− 21
Favor military and economic aid to rebels against communist-supported governments	100	48	+ 52
Europe more important than Asia	27	49	− 22
Would send son or daughter to Europe rather than Asia	46	76	− 20
Sympathize more with Israel (than with Arab nations) or "don't know"	32	63	− 31
U.S. efforts to overthrow the leftist government of Nicaragua were excellent or good	70	15	+ 55
Goal of promoting democratic governments abroad very important	55	27	+ 28
Agree that we must support some military dictators because they oppose communists	82	60	+ 22
Favor negotiating with terrorists	0	23	− 23

the public to favor the use of military force against terrorist groups or the assassination of terrorists. Administration officials were unanimously opposed to negotiating with terrorists.

Leader's preferences are more in agreement with the policies of the Reagan administration on trade and military and economic aid. Although less than a majority, they are substantially more supportive of the Reagan Doctrine. But both leaders and the public continue to assign a higher priority to cooperation with the Soviet Union than does the administration. In this regard, the fact that the administration now is paying more attention to achieving arms control agreements with the Soviet Union and is tempering the earlier confrontational rhetoric has moderated the gap between the public and the administration on these issues since 1982.

One area where the views of both public and leaders were more in accord with the administration in November 1986 (before the Iran crisis broke) than in 1982 was the role of Congress. The number who felt that the congressional role is too weak declined substantially among both the public and the leaders. The number who felt that Congress's role is too strong went up, slightly among the public and substantially among the leaders. A similar shift occurred in both public and leadership attitudes on whether the CIA should be encouraged to work covertly to weaken or to overthrow governments unfriendly to the United States. A substantial (13 points) change occurred among leaders in favor of greater support for the covert role by the CIA, and there was an equally sharp drop in those opposed. A smaller change in the same direction occurred among the public.

Within the leadership group itself, there are important differences of view. On such questions as the defense budget, the Reagan Doctrine, and the covert role of the CIA, large differences (30 per cent or more) occur between leaders from the administration on the one hand and other leaders, especially from labor, the media, education, and religion, on the other. By an overwhelming gap of 49 per cent, more administration leaders than other leaders sampled believe that the foreign-policy role of Congress is too strong. Other large gaps (more than 30 per cent) exist between administration leaders and the rest of the leadership in support of the elimination of tariffs, the invasion of Grenada, the bombing of Libya, increased defense spending, and covert aid under the Reagan Doctrine.

Yet despite strong disagreements with the Reagan administration on specific foreign-policy issues, most of the public and leaders in November 1986 are more hopeful about the world than they were 6 years earlier. There is more public support for a more active U.S. role in the world. The turnaround is not massive, however, and could be reversed because the change largely reflects a perceived favorable shift in the U.S.-Soviet military balance of power and a higher estimation of the U.S. role in the world at the end of 1986. Responding to better economic conditions and perceiving an improvement in the military balance with the Soviet Union, Americans now look more favorably on foreign countries generally than in earlier years. The erosion of support for a more active American role that had been under way for more than a decade has been halted, at least temporarily. Whether the weakening of the American presidency and of the Reagan administration by the Iran crisis will undermine this trend is not clear now.

4. THE INFLUENCE OF ETHNIC INTEREST GROUPS ON AMERICAN MIDDLE EAST POLICY

Mitchell Bard

In the three most commonly used models of foreign policy decision making, the rational-actor, organizational-process, and bureaucratic-politics models, there is little or no consideration given to the role played by interest groups in influencing policy outcomes. The only decision-making model that places domestic politics at the center of its analysis is the pluralist model, and that model has been only tangentially applied to foreign policy-making.

If the bureaucratic-politics model is best described by the aphorism, "Where you stand depends on where you sit," then the pluralist model might be summarized as, "Which way you lean depends on who's pushing you." Pluralism refers to the existence of a variety of relatively independent organizations competing in the political marketplace.

The critics of the pluralist model tend to define it in laissez-faire economic terms; that is, public policy can best be understood as the product of the free play of group pressures and that an "invisible hand" working through competing interests yields an outcome that is beneficial to society. The model is defined this way in order to level the same type of critique against the concept of a free market of political ideas that is used against notions of the free economic market; that is, no real competition exists because of monopolies, oligopolies, and iron triangles, so political outcomes are inefficient, create inequalities, and undermine the national interest. These critics have done little more than construct a straw man to knock down, however, since the model never claimed that a "free market" exists in politics. Pluralism does not require that interest groups be equal or that political power be evenly distributed. On the contrary, it is far more likely that one or more interest groups will dominate a particular policy debate.

A good example of the application of the pluralist model is the competition between the Arab and Israeli lobbies in the making of foreign policy. In this case, there is no presumption of equality: the Israeli lobby is clearly dominant. Nevertheless, it does not necessarily follow that this advantage in the balance of lobbying power enables the Israeli lobby to influence policy.

DEFINING THE LOBBIES

One of the most commonly held notions in American politics is that Jews have a great deal of influence on U.S. foreign policy. In the view of some people "Jewish-Americans" *control* U.S. policy in the Middle East to the detriment of the national interest. This attitude is typified by former Senator James Abourezk, who has called the Israeli lobby "the most powerful and pervasive foreign influence in American politics today."[1]

Such critics persistently charge that American Jews have pervasive influence. The truth, however, is that the Israeli lobby is unable to affect major foreign policy decisions and is actually capable of influencing only a narrow range of policies that benefit Israel.

Most people are familiar with business and professional lobbies which try to influence policy. These lobbies usually hire one or more people, lobbyists, to try to persuade government officials to support their interests. American Jews are represented by such lobbyists, who use direct efforts to influence policymakers. But other, less formal efforts are also used to influence policy.

The organization that is registered as a lobby is the American Israel Public Affairs Committee (AIPAC). This organization and others that attempt to directly influence policymakers may be designated the *formal lobby*. There are also organizations that do not engage in direct lobbying (e.g., B'nai B'rith and Hadassah), but do disseminate information and encourage their members to become involved in the political process. In addition, there is a large component of Jewish political influence that is unorganized—Jewish voting behavior and public opinion. These indirect means of influence may be designated the *informal lobby*.

All of the above are generally referred to as the "Jewish lobby"; however, this label is inaccurate because a large proportion of the Israeli lobby is composed of non-Jews. The "Israeli lobby" can be defined as *those individuals and organizations that directly and indirectly influence American policy to support Israel.*

The Israeli lobby does not have the field to itself; there is a competing interest group—the "Arab lobby." The National Association of Arab-Americans (NAAA), like AIPAC, is a registered domestic lobby that forms the core of the formal lobby. There is also an informal lobby that exerts indirect influence. Just as the Israeli lobby is not exclusively composed of Jews, the Arab lobby is not composed entirely of Arabs; nevertheless the label is appropriate in this case because it refers to those *formal and informal actors that attempt to influence U.S. foreign policy to support the interests of the Arab states in the Middle East.*

THE INFORMAL LOBBY

American Jews recognize the importance of support for Israel because of the dire consequences that could follow from the alternative. The perceived threat to Israel is not military defeat, it is annihilation. At the same time, American Jews are frightened of what might happen in this country if they do not have political power. As a consequence, Jews have devoted themselves to politics with almost religious fervor. This is reflected in the fact that Jews have the highest percentage voter turnout of any ethnic group. The Jewish population in the United States is under six million, roughly three percent of the total population, but 89 percent live in twelve key electoral college states. These states alone have enough electoral votes to elect the president. If you add the non-Jews shown by opinion polls to be as pro-Israel as Jews, it is clear that Israel has the support of one of the largest veto groups in the country.

The disproportionate influence of the American Jewish population is in direct contrast with the electoral involvement of Arab-Americans. There are less than three million Arabs in the United States, and roughly 80 percent of them are Lebanese Christians who tend to be unsympathetic to the Arab lobby's goals. This reflects another major problem for the Arab lobby—inter-Arab disunity. This disunity is reinforced by the general discord of the Arab world, which has twenty-one states with competing interests. The Arab lobby is thus precluded from representing "the Arabs."

The political activism of Jews forces representatives with presidential ambitions to consider what a mixed voting record on Israel-related issues may mean in the political future. There are no benefits to candidates taking an openly anti-Israel stance, and considerable costs in both loss of campaign contributions and votes from Jews and non-Jews alike. Potential candidates, therefore, have an incentive to be pro-Israel; this reinforces support for Israel in Congress. Actual candidates must be particularly sensitive to the concerns of Jewish voters; it follows that the successful candidate's foreign policy will be influenced, though not bound, by the promises that had to be made during the campaign.

Political campaign contributions are also considered an important means of influence; typically, Jews have been major benefactors. It is difficult to assess the influence of campaign contributions on legislative outcomes, particularly with regard to Israel-related issues where support or opposition may be a consequence of nonmonetary factors. In addition, one does not know if a candidate is pro-Israel because of receiving a contribution or receives a donation as a result of taking a position in support of Israel. In the past, Jewish contributions were less structured and targeted than those of other interest groups, but this has changed dramatically as Israel-related political action committees (PACs) have proliferated.

The first pro-Israel PAC was formed in 1978, but there was little activity until 1982, when thirty-three pro-Israel PACs contributed $1.87 million to congressional candidates. Like donations from other PACs, most of this money was given to incumbents, and because of the long association of Jews with the Democratic party, nearly 80 percent went to Democrats. The number of PACs more than doubled in 1984, as did their contributions. It was estimated that over seventy pro-Israel PACs spent nearly $3.6 million in 1984.[2]

On the Arab lobby side there are only three PACs, which spent a trivial sum in 1984. The lobby did take a more active and visible role than ever before, however, in that election. The most obvious example was the Arab lobby's efforts to defeat Clarence Long (D-Md.), one of the driving forces behind increasing aid to Israel, in a deliberate effort to demonstrate that lobby's ability to punish Israel's friends on Capitol Hill.

As in the visible campaign undertaken in 1982 by the Israeli lobby to defeat pro-Arab congressman Paul Findley of Illinois, the Arab lobby claimed victory when Long was defeated. As was the case in the Findley campaign, the reasons for Long's defeat were rooted in politics unrelated to the Middle East. In Long's case, redistricting took away a large percentage of his constituency and, after a narrow victory in 1982, he became a high priority target of the Republican National Committee.

PUBLIC OPINION

The absence of a large voting bloc requires the Arab lobby to develop sympathies among the general public if it is to use public opinion or the electoral process as a means of influencing U.S. policy. The lobby has tried to support sympathetic American groups such as Third World organizations, and to cultivate friendships in the academic and business realms, but, as opinion polls have consistently shown, there is relatively little popular support for the Arab cause. In the last sixteen years, polls have found that sympathy for Israel varied between 35 percent and 56 percent, while sympathy for the Arabs has oscillated between 1 and 14 percent. Recent polls show that support for Israel still exceeds that of the Arabs by about four to one. Even though there has been a slight increase in support for the Arabs in the last several years, this change has not affected sympathies toward Israel.

THE FORMAL ISRAELI LOBBY

The organization that directly lobbies Congress on behalf of the Israeli lobby is AIPAC. The lobby was founded by I.L. Kenen in 1951, when Israel's supporters decided to appeal directly to Congress for legislation to provide aid to Israel to circumvent State Department opposition. Up until 1973, Kenen was AIPAC's only lobbyist. Today, there are four lobbyists, a staff of eighty, and a budget of nearly $5 million. The current director is Tom Dine, a former legislative aide to Senators Church and Muskie. The director of AIPAC is generally considered one of the most influential men in Washington, and Dine is no exception.

AIPAC was not the first domestic lobby to concern itself with foreign affairs, but it is regarded as the most powerful. The lobby strives to remain nonpartisan and thereby keep friends in both parties. By framing the issues in terms of the national interest, AIPAC is able to attract broader support than could ever be possible if it were perceived to represent only the interests of Israel. This does not mean AIPAC does not have a close relationship with Israeli officials: it does, albeit unofficially. Even so, there are times when the lobby comes into conflict with the Israeli government. Despite such disagreements, the Israeli lobby tends to reflect Israeli government policy fairly closely.

Lobbyists usually roam the halls of Congress trying to get the attention of legislators so they can explain their positions. AIPAC has the luxury of being able to call its allies in Congress to pass along information and then leaving much of the work of writing bills and gathering cosponsors to the legislative staffs. The lobbyists themselves are mostly Capitol Hill veterans who know how to operate the levers of power.

Since it does not use stereotypical lobbying tactics, the Israeli lobby depends on the network it has developed to galvanize the Jewish community to take some form of political action. The network comprises at least seventy-five different organizations that in one way or another support Israel. Most cannot legally engage in lobbying, but are represented on the board of directors of AIPAC so that they are able to provide input into the lobby's decision-making process. Equally important is the bureaucratic machinery of these organizations, which enables them to disseminate information to their members and facilitate a rapid response to legislative activity.

A second coordinating body is the Conference of Presidents of Major American Jewish Organizations. It is composed of leaders of thirty-eight different organizations, and is responsible for formulating and articulating the "Jewish position" on most foreign policy matters. The Conference allows the lobby to speak with one voice in a way its opponents cannot. The Conference is the main contact between the Jewish community and the executive branch, while AIPAC tends to be the conduit to the legislative branch.

Even with the Jewish population concentrated in key states, there are still only a total of six million Jews; therefore, the Israeli lobby is dependent on the support of non-Jewish groups, and actively works to form coalitions with broad segments of American society. The lobby has successfully built coalitions comprising unions, entertainers, clergymen, scholars, and black leaders. These coalitions allow the lobby to demonstrate a broad public consensus for a pro-Israel policy.

THE FORMAL ARAB LOBBY

There had always been an Arab lobby in the United States, composed of what I.L. Kenen called the petro-diplomatic complex, and consisting of the oil industry, missionaries, diplomats, and CIA agents. According to Kenen, there was no need for an "Arab" lobby because the petro-diplomatic complex did the Arabs' work for them.[3]

The Arab lobby became an official, active, and visible advocate of the Arab cause in the wake of the oil embargo. "The day of the Arab-American is here," boasted Richard Shadyac; "the reason is oil."[4] From the beginning, the Arab lobby has faced a disadvantage not only in electoral politics but also in organization. There are several politically oriented groups, but many of these are solo operations with little financial or popular support. Some of the larger, more representative groups include the Middle East Research and Information Project; the Middle East Affairs Council; Americans for Near East Refugee Aid; and the American Palestine Committee.

The National Association of Arab-Americans (NAAA) is a registered domestic lobby, patterned after AIPAC, that was founded in 1972 by Richard Shadyac. He believed the power and wealth of the Arab countries stemming from their oil reserves would allow the Arab lobby to take advantage of the political process in the same way the Jews have been thought to.

Like AIPAC, the NAAA makes its case on the basis of U.S. national interests, arguing that a pro-Israel policy harms those interests. Aid to Israel is criticized as a waste of taxpayers' money, and the potential benefits of a closer relationship with the Arab states is emphasized. In 1977, after Anwar Sadat's historic visit to Jerusalem, the Arab lobby made its displeasure over U.S. support for the initiative known to President Carter, who wrote in his diary: "They [Arab-Americans] have given all the staff, Brzezinski, Warren Christopher, and others, a hard time."[5] Although the lobby's concerns have begun to reach the highest levels of government, there have been no perceptible changes in U.S. policy.

Most of the nation's major corporations have not supported the Arab lobby; in fact, prior to the 1981 AWACS sale, oil companies were about the only corporations willing to openly identify with Arab interests. The reason for this is that most corporations prefer to stay out of foreign policy debates; moreover, corporations may feel constrained by the implicit threat of some form of retaliation by the Israeli lobby. The major oil companies feel no such constraints. According to Steven Emerson, the four companies that comprise the Arabian American Oil Company (ARAMCO)—Exxon, Standard Oil of California, Mobil, and Texaco—have "conducted a surreptitious multimillion-dollar campaign to manipulate public opinion and foreign policy on the Middle East" for the last fifteen years.[6] Participation in the public-relations campaign amounted to the price of doing business in the oil-producing nations.

The campaign began after the 1967 war when ARAMCO established a fund to help present the Arab side of the conflict. That campaign took on greater urgency in 1973 after the chairman of the board of ARAMCO met with Saudi King Faisal and was pressured to take a more active role in creating a sympathetic attitude toward the Arab nations. A month later Mobil published its first advertisement/editorial in the *New York Times*. Since 1973, ARAMCO has maintained its public-relations campaign and become involved in occasional legislative fights such as that over the AWACS sale, but, on the whole, the campaign has had no observable impact on U.S. policy.

There are other nonoil companies that are involved in the Arab lobby, the most well-known being Bechtel, and an increasing number can be expected to be willing to participate as Arab investment in the United States grows. Estimates of current Arab investment range from $50 billion to $200 billion, and Arab investors (nations and individuals) have bought shares and controlling interests in a wide range of American companies, creating the potential for expanding Arab political influence.

CONTRASTS

There are at least two major differences between the Arab and Israeli lobbies. First, the Arab lobby almost always lobbies negatively; i.e., *against* pro-Israel legislation rather than *for* pro-Arab legislation. The NAAA's legislative initiatives, for example, rarely relate to the Arab world. Most of their time is spent trying to generate opposition to Israel's "occupation" of the West Bank, Golan Heights, and Gaza Strip as well as its alleged violations of human rights; attempting to cut U.S. aid to Israel and block its use for settlements on the West Bank; and pleading for the recognition of the PLO and the need for a Palestinian state. This agenda contrasts with that of the Israeli lobby which, with the exception of opposing arms sales to Arab states hostile toward Israel, directs its activities toward promoting a pro-Israel rather than anti-Arab foreign policy.

The other major difference between the two lobbies is the use of paid foreign agents by the Arab lobby. Pro-Arab U.S. government officials can look forward to lucrative positions as lobbyists, spokesmen, and consultants for the Arab cause. For example, the outspoken critic of the Israeli lobby, former Senate Foreign Relations Committee Chair J. William Fulbright, was hired by the Saudis and the United Arab Emirates, and a former assistant secretary for legislative affairs and special assistant to President Kennedy, Fred Dutton, was hired as the agent for Saudi Arabia who spearheaded the AWACS campaign and reputedly conceived the "Reagan vs. Begin" angle.

INFLUENCE

There is a kind of Cartesian mentality latent in the literature on interest groups that seems to suggest that interest groups exist and therefore must have influence. In the case of the groups under investigation here, this view is too simplistic. For example, if we examine the agenda of the NAAA, it is clear the Arab lobby has lost on every issue relating to Israel. There is no formal opposition to Israel's policies in the occupied territories, and U.S. aid to Israel has continued to rise, with increasingly favorable terms being given regarding the balance of grants and loans. There has been no move toward recognition of the PLO, and a recent American peace proposal, the 1982 Reagan Plan, specifically opposed a Palestinian state.

Perhaps the best example of the Arab lobby's relative weakness was seen in 1981, when AIPAC persuaded a majority of Congress to sign a letter opposing the AWACS sale. The NAAA tried to obtain support for a congressional resolution condemning violence in the Middle East and calling for a suspension of arms deliveries to Israel after its attack on Beirut. The NAAA recruited only seven sponsors in the House.

Similarly, the existence of an Israeli lobby does not prove that it influences U.S. policy. Senator Charles Mathias, a man who has been subject to lobby pressure, suggested that it does influence policy. He wrote that, "as a result of the activities of the [Israeli] lobby, congressional conviction has been measurably reinforced by the knowledge that political sanctions will be applied to any who fail to deliver."[7]

This is actually a fairly recent phenomenon. Congress did not take an active role in Middle East policy until after the 1967 Six-Day War. Afterwards, in 1968, 1970, and 1971, Congress pushed the administration into selling fighter planes to Israel by appropriating arms-sales credits before the president had decided to sell the planes.

It is difficult to explain why the Israeli lobby was unable to get more support for Israel before 1967. One reason was the United States' perception that Israel was strong enough to defend itself without direct American assistance. Alternatively, Israel was not yet considered a strategic asset, and Iran was being groomed as the West's police force for the region. There was also the State Department's omnipresent fear that aid to Israel would antagonize the Arabs and threaten U.S. interests in the area. Finally, the Israeli lobby did not become organized to the extent it is now until after 1967. Before then, much of the lobbying activity was conducted by individual Jews who enjoyed access to decision makers as a result of personal relationships.

The situation changed dramatically after the October 1973 war began. In the first twelve days of the war, the United States airlifted $825 million worth of military supplies to Israel. President Nixon told Congress the resupply was necessary to offset the resupply of Syria and Egypt by the Russians. Congress then approved $2.2 billion in emergency assistance.

Between 1946 and 1971, Israel received a total of $1.5 billion in aid, but since 1974 total aid has exceeded $20 billion. The shift in U.S. policy was a result of several factors, including a desire to ease Israel's economic burden, the belief that rearming Israel would convince the Arabs to abandon the war option, and the hope that the U.S.-Israel aid relationship could be used in negotiations with the Arabs as evidence of American leverage over the Israelis. Also, by demonstrating the military superiority of Israel, given U.S. arms, Secretary of State Henry Kissinger hoped to woo the Arabs into the American camp. What is significant about this policy is that it was consistent with Israeli lobby interests, but was formulated independent of lobby input.

The Israeli lobby has successfully persuaded Congress to increase aid levels above administration requests several times. For example, in 1982, despite the U.S. recession, unhappiness over the Israeli operation in Lebanon, and administration opposition, Congress still voted to increase aid to Israel. Congressional increases may be influenced by direct lobbying, but administration requests and the general support for aid to Israel are more likely products of independent calculations of the national interest. It is unlikely, however, that similar aid levels would be proposed in the absence of an organized Israeli lobby. Nevertheless, it is difficult to assess influence when the administration, Congress, and the Israeli lobby all agree on a policy, as is usually the case with foreign aid. It is therefore necessary to look at legislation that is either opposed by some important interest or that would not be considered in the absence of an Israeli lobby.

LEGISLATIVE INNOVATION

There are several examples of legislation that would not have been introduced without Israeli lobby pressure: a resolution to re-examine U.S. membership in the United Nations if Israel were expelled; the prohibition of payments to UNESCO because of Arab-sponsored resolutions condemning Israel; the reduction of funding for the International Atomic Energy Agency because of the illegal rejection of Israel's credentials; the reduction of funding for the United Nations Relief and Works Agency because UNRWA camps were used, in violation of U.S. law, to train PLO terrorists; and a measure ending the automatic granting of visas to PLO members. These bills were relatively noncontroversial; the same cannot be said for legislation regarding Soviet emigration and the Arab boycott.

In 1973, Senator Henry Jackson and Representative Charles Vanik introduced resolutions to amend the Trade Reform Act to "deny tariff benefits to any 'non-market,' i.e., totalitarian, country barring free emigration of its citizens." It was designed to help Russia's three million Jews gain the opportunity to emigrate. The Nixon administration actively campaigned against the amendment, and Kissinger warned that Jewish intransigence on the issue imperiled détente and endangered world peace. While corporations anxious to trade with the Soviets lobbied against the amendment, AIPAC recruited cosponsors for the bill. In the end, the amendment passed by lopsided margins in both Houses, in what was seen as a victory for the Israeli lobby.

The other major piece of legislation illustrative of Israeli lobby influence is the anti-boycott bill (proposed in 1976) which prohibits American firms from cooperating with the Arab boycott of Israel. *Candidate* Jimmy Carter had said, in an apparent appeal for Jewish votes during the foreign policy debate with President Ford, that the boycott was a disgrace and that he would do everything he could as president to stop it.

President Carter saw the situation a little differently; however, fearing that legislation that was too strong might endanger his Mideast peace efforts and cause OPEC to raise oil prices. American corporations, fearing a reduction in trade, vigorously opposed the bill. "Although American principles and ideals were at stake in the boycott controversy," *Congressional Quarterly* wrote, "the issue has been pursued almost exclusively by the nation's Jewish community."[8]

In 1976, both houses of Congress voted overwhelmingly for an anti-boycott bill, but President Ford was able to defeat it through an end-of-session parliamentary maneuver. The business lobby recognized that some form of legislation would be adopted with the ascension of Jimmy Carter to power, so, in 1977, negotiations ensued between the Business Roundtable and representatives of the Israeli lobby which resulted in a compromise agreement that was adopted verbatim by the Congress.

Like the Jackson-Vanik Amendment, the anti-boycott bill demonstrated Israeli lobby influence. In both cases, however, Congress was solidly behind the lobby's position. A more accurate test may be to look at cases where the lobby is at odds with not only the administration and "big business," but also with a large proportion of Congress. The proposed arms sales to Saudi Arabia in 1978 and 1981 offer two such cases.

THE SAUDIS GET F-15 JETS

Congressional review of arms sales has given the Israeli lobby access to the decision makers, and it has taken advantage of this access by trying to stop arms sales to hostile Arab states. The lobby's argument, in brief, is that arms sales to the Arabs endanger Israel, threaten the stability of the Middle East, and perpetuate the arms race. These arguments have generally been accepted by a majority of representatives, and were used to force President Ford to modify his proposal to sell mobile HAWK antiaircraft missiles to Jordan in 1975. Ford eventually agreed to sell Jordan only immobile missile batteries. Similarly, in 1976, Ford wanted to sell air-to-ground missiles to Saudi Arabia; in order to head off a possible veto of the sale, he had to compromise by cutting the number of missiles to be sold from 1,500 to 650. A far more difficult fight arose over the proposed sale of F-15 fighter planes to Saudi Arabia. The Israeli lobby mobilized its supporters to try to kill the sale; simultaneously, the largely dormant Arab lobby came to life.

The Arab lobby had been active from its inception, but it was not until the 1978 proposal to sell F-15s to Saudi Arabia that its presence was felt on Capitol Hill. There are several possible explanations for the lobby's sudden emergence. The best explanation is probably that this arms sale brought the first major congressional fight for something of vital interest to an Arab state. Previous arms sales had been for smaller quantities of less sophisticated weapons, which the Israeli lobby had tried to reduce in quantity rather than obstruct. The F-15 sale was the first all-out effort by the Israeli lobby to block a sale to the Arabs, and the Arab lobby knew it would have to fight to get the sale approved.

Proponents of the sale argued that Saudi Arabia is a moderate Arab state that needs support if a peace settlement is to be achieved in the Middle East. They also expressed a desire to maintain a "balanced" relationship in the region as well as to insure U.S. oil interests. As in any arms sale, there was the threat the Arabs would go elsewhere to buy the weapons. There was also the omnipresent Soviet threat to the region. Israel's supporters had a different outlook, summed up by Senator Moynihan, who called the sale "a rationalization of American nervelessness in the area of international economic policy as well as political and military policy."[9]

The opponents of the sale forced a compromise: the F-15s were to be based beyond the range of Israel, and would not be equipped with bomb racks or air-to-air missiles. These concessions won over some of the undecided, but did not dampen the Israeli lobby's resolve to block the sale. In what was described as a "litmus test" for future support from Jews, the Senate voted to allow the sale.

The NAAA declared victory and celebrated the end of the Israeli lobby's "veto" over American Middle East policy. The Israeli lobby had taken on the administration, the petro-diplomatic complex, and much of the Senate, including some traditional supporters, and lost the battle. The F-15 vote illustrated the limits of the Israeli lobby's influence; but as subsequent events have shown, it did not signal a change in U.S. policy, as witnessed by the fact that the sale included fifteen F-15s and seventy-five F-16s for Israel as well. This was only a skirmish, however, compared to the lobbying war that would be waged over the proposed sale of AWACS to Saudi Arabia.

THE BATTLE OVER AWACS

The compromise on the F-15 sale—that the planes would not include bomb racks or carry missiles—was resented by the Saudis, who persistently asked for the additional equipment. In 1980, President Carter was forced to reject these requests after receiving a letter signed by sixty-eight senators (mobilized by AIPAC) opposing such a sale. In 1981, President Reagan decided to sell the Saudis not only the enhancement equipment, but also highly sophisticated AWACS radar planes.

The Israeli lobby immediately went to work collecting signatures on a letter opposing the sale, and by August AIPAC had lined up a majority of Congress against it. After the House disapproved the sale, the Arab lobby launched an intense campaign to persuade senators considered "vulnerable" to vote for it.

As one would expect, the oil and defense industries lobbied hard for the sale. By far the biggest lobbying effort, however, was orchestrated by Boeing—the main contractor for AWACS—and United Technologies, which alone had $100 million at stake. The presidents of Boeing and UT sent out more than 6,500 telegrams to subsidiaries, subcontractors, and distributors all over the country urging them to support the sale. Support from those directly involved should come as no surprise; what made this issue unique, however, was the involvement of many businesses and organizations, such as the Florist Insurance Company, which had no direct interest in the debate.

What was probably more important than the Arab lobby campaign, however, was the decision of the single most powerful foreign policy lobbyist to throw his full weight behind the sale. On October 1, President Reagan held a press conference in which his statements of support for the sale were seen as a direct challenge to the Israeli lobby. "While we must always take into account the vital interests of our allies," Reagan said, "American security interests must remain our internal responsibility." Then, in what was obviously a reference to Israel, he added: "It is not the business of other nations to make American foreign policy.... I suppose what really is the most important thing is a perception that other countries not get the perception that we are being unduly influenced one way or the other with regard to foreign policy." In the following three weeks, Reagan succeeded in changing the minds of eight senators who had cosponsored the resolution of disapproval, and the sale was allowed to proceed.

The turning point came when the president began to make his case personally to the senators. Several senators announced they were supporting the president after receiving "top secret" assurances regarding Israel's security. Others were given more tangible reasons to switch their votes, such as promises to support appropriations for projects in their home states. One of the best examples was Republican Roger Jepsen of Iowa, who was seen as the key senator needed for the sale's approval. According to one White House official, "We just beat his brains out." The White House generated calls and letters from Jepsen's constituents and threatened to stop cooperating with him in the future. As the official said, "We stood him up in front of an open grave and said he could jump in if he wanted to."[10] Jepsen chose not to jump, and switched his vote to support the sale.

This time the Israeli lobby had been opposed by the president, big business, and many of the leaders of the Senate. The loss was a narrow one, however, and the lobby not only succeeded in forcing the administration to place a variety of restrictions on the sale, but was also able to persuade the administration to compensate Israel with additional aid and weapons. Moreover, the Congress has not approved any arms sale to an Arab state since 1981. For example, when Reagan attempted to sell arms to Jordan in 1984, Congress stipulated that Jordan enter the peace process first; when King Hussein refused to do so, the sale was dropped. More recently, in 1986, the administration proposed the sale of Stinger missiles to Saudi Arabia and, for the first time in history, the sale was vetoed by the Congress.

LIMITS TO LOBBY POWER

The inability of the Israeli lobby to stop the F-15 and AWACS sales demonstrates that the power of the lobby is limited. Support for the lobby's interests is by no means automatic, as critics would have us believe. In fact, one can find a number of policy decisions that were opposed by the Israeli lobby and others that were not made even under lobby pressure for them. This becomes even clearer when major diplomatic and military decisions are considered; for example, the Sinai disengagement agreements, the Syrian-Israeli agreement, and the Camp David peace treaty were made with little or no input from the Israeli lobby.

The most blatant example of the United States acting independent of Israeli lobby interests occurred in 1956, when the United States sided diplomatically with the Soviet Union against Israel, Great Britain, and France in the Suez War. Perhaps the lobby's biggest failure persists to this day: the United States' refusal to recognize Jerusalem as Israel's capital.

Overall, the Arab lobby's influence is negligible, except in those rare instances where its interests coincide with those of the administration, key legislators, and a broad segment of the business community. The pressure to support pro-Arab policies is likely to increase, however, because of the potential economic gain or threat of loss. In January, 1983, the ambassador to Kuwait told the U.S.-Arab Chamber of Commerce in San Francisco bluntly: "American businessmen must understand that their success in the Mideast hinges on how the U.S. deals with Israel."[11]

At the moment, the balance of lobbying power remains clearly in favor of the Israeli lobby, but Arab economic power will make it possible for the Arab lobby to obtain greater access to the political process than ever before; nevertheless, unless a large number of Arabs immigrate to the United States and public opinion changes radically, the Israeli lobby should still prevail in the marketplace of political ideas.

CONCLUSION

In most of the interest group literature, there has been an emphasis placed on the description of group formation and maintenance, and relatively little investigation of influence. The main reason for this is that influence is frequently taken for granted. Reference to interest group influence on foreign policy tends to contradict this conventional wisdom, however, because there is said to be little or no interest group influence over foreign policy. This is sometimes explained in terms of the absence of any direct impact of most foreign policies on a segment of the public. The case of the Israeli lobby is frequently cited as an exception, but it really is only the most obvious example of an interest group that is concerned with foreign policy on the basis of nontangible, suprapersonal interests in a particular policy.

The Israeli lobby is generally considered to be the most powerful foreign policy interest group, so I would not expect other interest groups to enjoy the same degree of success in reaching their foreign policy objectives; nevertheless, the pluralist forces described in this chapter should apply to other groups concerned with different foreign policy areas. Thus, for example, an analysis of the balance of lobbying power between Americans of Greek and Turkish descent should help explain the direction of U.S. policy in the Mediterranean. The balance shifts according to the relative access, resources, cohesion, size, social status, and leadership of the competing groups. To these factors must be added the informal components of voting behavior and public opinion. The ability to build coalitions with other groups can shift the balance one way or the other.

The preceding analysis demonstrates that the Israeli lobby enjoys the balance of lobbying power; ceteris paribus, the lobby should achieve its objectives whenever the president supports it and will tip the balance in the direction of the legislature when the president opposes it. Whether the lobby will prevail in the latter case will largely depend on policy content and the locus of decision.

If the locus of decision is the executive branch, then the president's position will always prevail; however, decisions made in the legislative branch will be subject to far greater influence from nonexecutive actors, and the generally sympathetic Congress will sometimes support the Israeli lobby over presidential opposition, as it did in the Jackson-Vanik and anti-boycott cases. The lobby's ability to overcome presidential opposition also varies according to policy content, with the lobby enjoying far greater success on economic issues such as foreign aid than on security-related issues such as arms sales.[12]

Pluralism alone, as the other chapters in this book demonstrate, does not explain foreign policy decision making, but this chapter illustrates why interest group influence should not be excluded from any analysis of American foreign policy.

NOTES

1. Peggy Strain, "Abourezk Rips Israel-Lobby Power as 'Dangerous,' " *Palestine Digest*, (April 1977), p. 9.

2. John Fialka and Brooks Johnson, "Jewish PACs Emerge as a Powerful Force in U.S. Election Races," *Wall Street Journal*, (Feb. 26, 1985), p. 1.

3. I.L. Kenen, *Israel's Defense Line*, (New York: Prometheus, 1981), p. 114.

4. Congressional Quarterly, *The Washington Lobby*, (Washington, D.C.: Congressional Quarterly, 1974), p. 117.

5. Jimmy Carter, *Keeping Faith*, (New York: Bantam Books, 1982), p. 299.

6. Steven Emerson, "The ARAMCO Connection," *The New Republic*, (May 19, 1982, reprint), p. 3.

7. Charles Mathias, Jr., "Ethnic Groups and Foreign Policy," *Foreign Affairs*, (Summer 1981), p. 994.

8. Congressional Quarterly, "Carter Moves Cautiously on Anti-Boycott Proposals," *Weekly Report*, (March 12, 1977), p. 437.

9. Congressional Quarterly *Almanac*, (Washington, D.C.: Congressional Quarterly, 1978), pp. 410–411.

10. John Hyde, "How White House Won Jepsen's AWACS Vote," *The Des Moines Register*, (Oct. 29, 1981), p. 1ff.

11. Harre W. Demoro, "Kuwait Envoy Talks Tough on US, Israel," *San Francisco Chronicle*, (Jan. 29, 1983), p. 7.

12. Mitchell Bard, "The Water's Edge And Beyond: Defining the Limits of Domestic Influence on U.S. Middle East Policy," Unpublished Ph.D. Dissertation, University of California at Los Angeles, 1987.

5. THE IRON TRIANGLE: INSIDE THE DEFENSE POLICY PROCESS

Gordon Adams

Between 1981 and 1987, the Reagan administration budgeted $1.8 trillion for national defense, the highest seven years in peacetime defense budget history. By fiscal year 1988, the Pentagon plans to spend as much money for national defense, after inflation, as it has spent in any year since 1946. Only peak spending for Korea (1953) and Vietnam (1968) will have surpassed this level.

This massive military buildup is restocking and modernizing the entire U.S. arsenal, from offensive strategic weapons to conventional forces. A whole new generation of strategic systems is entering the arsenal: the MX, Trident II, Pershing II, and air-, sea-, and ground-launched cruise missiles, along with the B-1B bomber. Conventional forces are receiving whole new generations of tanks, ships, aircraft, and missiles.

Through 1985, the tide of rising spending seemed irreversible, with large public approval and congressional willingness to provide 95 percent of every defense dollar requested by the administration. Public and Congress alike seemed caught up in the administration's desire to "re-arm America" and "catch up with the Russians."

Under pressure from rapidly rising federal deficits, Congress passed the Gramm-Rudman-Hollings law in 1985 and brought the defense budget explosion to a halt. Even then, so large a volume of resources had been poured into defense that the Pentagon found it unnecessary to cancel major weapons programs. The weight of accumulated appropriations still being spent on weapons kept defense spending levels high, even though new budgets slowed down.[1]

The primary public rationale for such spending is traditionally to be found in the rhetoric of "natural security." Realities, myths, and assumptions about national security are important ingredients in defining the framework within which debates about defense spending priorities take place.

National security rhetoric holds that the defense budget grows logically out of a process which starts with an assessment of the threats to the United States. From the threat, the theory goes, defense planners come to conclusions about the need for military force, the role of the armed forces, and the actual forces and equipment needed. From this perspective, national security needs define the size and contents of the defense budget.[2]

Most Americans are familiar and comfortable with national security as the framework within which they debate defense issues. Yet national security, cloaked in secrecy as it is, can provide both a legitimate explanation for defense policy and at the same time a cloak of expertise and credibility behind which other explanations of defense budgets might be found. As current policy debates suggest, not all national security rationales are totally convincing, in and of themselves. Critics of defense policy have noted, for example, that current policy exaggerates the "threats" to the United States and that the defense buildup has been based on a series of myths: the myth that the Soviet Union outspent the United States on defense in the 1970s; that U.S. forces are, as a result, "vulnerable"; and that the Warsaw Pact dramatically dominates the forces of NATO.[3]

Moreover, it is not always clear that there is a direct link between increased spending and new weapons on the one hand and greater military security on the other. For example, the new U.S. offensive and defensive strategic nuclear weapons appear to have been an incentive to the Soviets to increase their own strategic spending. Expanding capabilities for U.S. military action in Third World countries appears to have encouraged the use of American troops in Grenada, Honduras, and Lebanon, with mixed results for national security.

The national security rationale does not always provide an adequate explanation for specific defense budget and policy decisions. Behind this rationale lurks a second explanation for such decisions: the bureaucratic processes of the Defense Department. Defense budgets, spending decisions, wasteful contracting, and weapons that won't die despite their questionable contribution to national security are all linked, in part, to the way the Pentagon does its business day to day.

This bureaucratic explanation for the defense budget includes the tendency of Pentagon officials to defend and promote the interests of their agency; a fascination inside the military services with the next generation of military technology; the rivalry or mutual logrolling among services, leading to wasteful duplication and higher budgets; and a contracting process that builds in high rates of spending on weapons.[4]

The Army, Navy, and Air Force, for example, compete for defense budget funds, often for weapons that duplicate each other. The Air Force is buying an F-15 and F-16 fighter while the Navy buys an entirely separate pair, the F-14 and F-18. In the 1990s, the Air Force and Navy each plan a separate new fighter, despite efforts to create a joint program. Joint programs, such as the new Army tactical ballistic missile or the earlier F-111 fighter/bomber, are usually terminated or end up in the hands of one service alone while the other service goes its own way.

Inside each service, moreover, officials become attached to a weapon, in part because the next weapon ensures that the service continues to have a specific military mission in the future. Although the B-52 bomber could survive until the year 2000 as a carrier for air-launched cruise missiles, for example, the Strategic Air Command (SAC) insists on having a new bomber—the B-1. Without the B-1, SAC's only significant mission after 2000 would be to manage land-based strategic missiles and in-flight refueling of tactical fighters.[5]

The way the defense bureaucracy negotiates and administers its contracts has also had a direct impact on costs and on the defense budget. In 1981, David Stockman, then Director of the Office of Management and Budget, described the Department of Defense as a "swamp of waste" containing some $10–$30 billion in excessive spending that could be eliminated with no risks for American national security.[6] In 1983, the President's Grace Commission, appointed to explore waste in federal spending, also pointed to roughly $30 billion a year in unnecessary Pentagon spending.[7]

Bureaucratic infighting, self-protection, and inefficiency also help keep defense spending levels high, have a direct effect on procurement choices, and make doing defense business attractive to private-sector companies. In the end, however, both national security and bureaucratic explanations for defense budgets and policies miss a crucial piece of the process, the political "black box," within which defense decisions are made. The activities that keep defense spending high, that protect new weapons, and that inhibit discussion of alternative national security policies are all played out in a highly political arena in which defense contractors, defense bureaucrats, and the Congress are linked. This arena can be described as an "Iron Triangle," linking the three sectors.

This triangle grows out of a deep-rooted and historical intimacy linking the Defense Department and its corporate suppliers of weapons and services. Intimacy between government and business, of course, is anathema to traditional American political ideology, which suggests that business and government are antagonistic. In reality, a cooperative set of relations has developed between business and government in the twentieth century, especially in the arena of defense spending. This relationship began during World War I, when business executives planned virtually all sectors of U.S. industrial production for the war and a new military industry began to grow in America.

The relationship developed into a permanent one during and after World War II. The Defense Department, which, as the War Department, had subsidized construction of a vast military production base during the war, continued a clear policy of maintaining that base in the private sector. The U.S. commitment to a global foreign policy provided a justification and focus for continuous defense planning, a large military force, and massive arms procurement.

This constant interaction has expanded and deepened since the 1950s. All three participants benefit: Defense Department officials, defending their missions, find useful allies among contractors committed to remaining in defense business. Both seek the active participation of a third major actor—the Congress. Through Congress, the Defense Department acquires the funding that enables the relationship to continue; therefore, the Congress must be brought into the relationship as an active participant. The result is a close intimacy among the Pentagon, its defense industry clients, and members of Congress with a special interest in the defense section of the federal budget (the Armed Services Committees, the Defense Appropriations Subcommittees, and members from districts and states that have military bases or defense contractors within their boundaries).

This triangle has several features. First, there is a close working relationship and an intimate interpenetration between the corners of the triangle. Policymakers and administrators move freely between industry and government. Policy issues tend to be discussed and resolved among the participants, who develop and share common values, interests, and perceptions. As the industry and government officials interact, they share policy-making authority; often private-sector participants become policymakers and administrators without ever entering public service. Defense Department power and private industry power become indistinguishable.

Second, this triangle has emerged slowly over time. It was not willfully created in a single moment, but came into being as a result of constant interaction among its participants. Defense Department bureaucrats help nurture and maintain the industry. Industry has pursued policies and procedures it desires from the Defense Department, and works to maintain the triangle as circumstances change. Both work hard to build and maintain support in Congress. Shared interests develop between bureaucrats and industry, and disagreements must be reconciled over time through constant interaction.

Third, the triangle has become "iron." Through the years, it has become isolated from other areas of policy, from many in the Congress, and especially from the public. Strenuous efforts have been exerted by the participants to keep it isolated and protected. As a result of this isolation, outsiders and their perspectives on policy alternatives are shut out and have no credibility inside the triangle. Defense Department officials and industry planners share the assumption that they act not only in their own interests but in the "public interest" as well. Behind the veil of national security, the triangle has developed unique political power.

The essential ingredients of power inside this "iron triangle" are information, access, influence, and money. The defense contractors seek access to the bureaucracy and Congress in order both to influence decisions and to gain information. The information they provide to the Congress and the Defense Department influences the decisions of both.

Defense contractors are the most crucial actors in this process. They are highly self-conscious about the link between the political arena and their business success. Defense is big business: the Defense Department contract market amounts to over $150 billion per year. It is also a concentrated and stable business: most of the leading contractors to the Defense Department have been in the business for over forty years, and the top twenty-five receive 50 percent of all of the contract dollars the Defense Department awards. Finally, it is important business: many of the leading contracting companies do well over 50 percent of their sales with the federal government.[8]

Inside this closed world of defense decision making the process begins with the awarding of research and development (R&D) contracts. Here, removed from public view and congressional oversight, industry and the Defense Department devise the weapons systems of the future. Today's multiple independently targetable nuclear warheads and laser-guided missiles were once small items buried deep in the R&D budget.

A review of the research and development contracts awarded to the nation's eight leading defense contractors (Boeing, General Dynamics, Grumman, Lockheed, McDonnell Douglas, Northrop, Rockwell International, and United Technologies) shows that they received $23 billion from the Defense Department and the National Aeronautics and Space Administration in the 1970s, and considerably more in the 1980s. In addition, between 1973 and 1978 (the only data publicly revealed), these eight companies were reimbursed for another $1.3 billion of corporate R&D investments through a little-known program called Independent Research and Development/Bids and Proposals (IR&D/B&P).[9]

This program enables contractors to develop weapons that will ultimately be sold to the Defense Department, without risking their own money. In other words, ideas for new weapons originate with the firms that stand to gain if these weapons are produced. At this crucial early stage, ideas are freely exchanged between industry and governments, giving contractors ample opportunity to influence decisions. As one defense industry official described the process in the late 1960s: "Your ultimate goal is actually to write the R.F.P. [Request for Proposal], and this happens more often than you might think."[10]

Major contractors are well represented on the roughly fifty mixed government/nongovernment committees and hundreds of subcommittees that advise the Defense Department or NASA—most notably the Defense Science Board and the scientific advisory groups of each branch of the military. Access to these key committees gives the contractors a further chance to affect new weapons policies long before the public or Congress have even heard of them.[11]

The close ties between industry and government are reinforced by a steady flow of employees back and forth. In the 1950s, congressional studies revealed that more than 1,000 retired military personnel had taken jobs in the defense industry. In the 1960s, this number rose to about 2,000. Between 1969 and 1974, the figure reached 2,000 for the top 100 Pentagon contractors. For the eight leading contractors noted above, 2,000 of their employees transferred either from industry to the government or from government to the firm in the 1970s. Of the nearly 500 civilians in this group who moved in either direction during this period, 34 percent worked in the key R&D offices in the services and the office of the Secretary of Defense.[12] Continuing this traffic in the 1980s, roughly 2,000 military retirees have been moving each year from the Pentagon to the contracting industry.

Many individuals circulate at the highest levels of industry and government. General Alexander Haig, for example, moved from the Army to the presidency of United Technologies, then to the position of secretary of state. The first Weinberger deputy for R&D, Richard DeLauer, had been a vice president at TRW, a major defense contractor. James Wade, chief of acquisition policy under Secretary Weinberger, left the Pentagon in the 1980s for an R&D contracter, System Planning Corp.

The examples are legion. Thomas Jones, a former deputy program manager for Boeing, became staff assistant to the Defense Department delegation for the SALT talks in 1971, returned to Boeing in 1974 as a program and products evaluation manager, was back in the Defense Department working on strategic policy in 1981, and then returned again to Boeing in a research position. Seymour Zeiberg, deputy undersecretary of defense for strategic and space systems in 1977, joined Martin Marietta in 1981 as a vice president for research. Walter LaBerge, deputy undersecretary of defense for research and engineering in the 1970s, became executive assistant to the president of Lockheed Missiles and Space Company.

This movement and the close familiarity it breeds provides contractors with unique access to the defense policy-making process. *The Wall Street Journal* reported on February 29, 1980, that Boeing had obtained information about plans for a land-based nuclear missile from a Boeing employee "on leave to work in the Pentagon's Weapons Research and Development Office." Once this employee had read a key report, he telexed its substance to a former Pentagon employee working at Boeing's headquarters in Seattle. The *Journal* concluded: "The movement of weaponry experts between industry and government jobs, frequently on the same project, facilitates the easy flow of information and tends to blur the distinction between national security and corporate goals."

The end result of this familiarity and special access is that competitive bidding for defense contracts falls by the wayside. In the 1980s, for example, only 10 percent of all Pentagon contracts, in dollar value, are awarded as a result of public advertisement and sealed, competitive bids. The vast bulk of contracts are awarded as a result of negotiations, many of them with one sole-source contractor.

Once a research and development contract has been awarded, it becomes increasingly difficult for the government to consider cancellation, even if the program is not performing adequately. Defense contractors use significant lobbying resources to protect their contracts, with the Washington, D.C., office serving as the nerve center of the effort. From 1977 through 1979, for example, the eight leading contractors noted above employed 200 people in their Washington offices, including 48 registered lobbyists.[13]

It is difficult to verify the expense of such activity, since contractor records are considered proprietary, not public, information. According to audits released by the Defense Contract Audit Agency in 1981, however, Boeing, General Dynamics, Grumman, Lockheed, and Rockwell International spent $16.8 million on their Washington offices in 1974 and 1975, or an average of $1.6 million per year each. Rockwell alone spent $7 million from 1973 though 1975 on its Washington office.[14]

A contractor's Washington office performs many functions, including keeping track of program developments in the Pentagon and NASA, following the progress of legislation, lobbying on Capitol Hill, handling public relations, funneling information back to the company, and handling negotiations with foreign buyers. Virtually all of the nonentertainment expenditures of these offices, including lobbying activities (until 1982) have been billed to defense contracts as administrative expenses. The Defense Department made this practice slightly more difficult in 1982 with a regulation that prohibited billing lobbying expenses to contracts, but enforcement of this regulation has been relatively weak.

Defense contractors also use political action committees (PACs) as part of their influence strategy. PACs, permitted by law since 1974, are ostensibly independent entities which gather voluntary campaign funds from corporate employees and distribute them to candidates for public office. According to Professor Edwin Epstein of the University of California, defense contractors operate some of the largest PACs in America.[15]

PACs of the eight leading contractors were especially active in the 1970s and 1980s, channeling well over $4 million into federal election campaigns. The bulk of their contributions went to members of Congress representing states where the companies operate, or to members of the key defense policy and appropriations committees in both houses of Congress. Such current or former senators as Strom Thurmond (R-S.C.), John Tower (R-Tex.), John Warner (R-Va.), Sam Nunn (D-Ga.), all on the Senate Armed Services Committee, have been especially important recipients of large defense contractor PAC contributions.

Occasionally, different aspects of Iron Triangle operations flow together. Former Representative Bob Wilson (R-Calif.), for example, was a major recipient of defense contractor contributions in the 1970s, while he was ranking Republican on the House Armed Services Committee. After his retirement, he joined a lobbying firm in Washington that represented, among others, Rockwell International.

The Iron Triangle does not use inside Washington resources alone. Contractors reach outside Washington into their own grass roots in the hinterlands. Defense contractors' employees, stockholders, subcontractors, and suppliers are all part of the network and may, indeed, depend upon it for their livelihood. Leading unions such as the United Auto Workers and the Machinists have large memberships in defense companies, and locals of those unions often respond to the company's call to support a particular weapons program in Washington.

In the mid-1970s, for example, Rockwell International mounted a grassroots effort on behalf of the struggling B-1 bomber program, which was on the brink of cancellation. The company urged its 114,000 employees and the holders of its 35 million shares of stock to write their member of Congress. More than 3,000 subcontractors and suppliers in forty-eight states were also asked to tell Congress about the adverse impact scrapping the B-1 would have on specific states and congressional districts. Rockwell acknowledged that it spent more that $1.35 million on such efforts from 1975 through 1977. Moreover, although B-1 production was cancelled by President Carter in 1977, R&D funding kept a testing program alive until 1981, when President Reagan revived the production program. By 1989, the Air Force will have purchased 100 B-1B bombers, as a living testimonial to the Iron Triangle.

The interlocking ties within the Triangle and the steady flow of personnel, resources, information, and influence through it, create a community of interest in which it becomes almost impossible to tell who is in charge. Over time, participants inside the Triangle become prisoners of their own isolation, identifying corporate gain with the pursuit of national security.

In the Congress, members of defense-related committees jealously guard their power over legislation and appropriations, criticizing nonspecialist members for their interference in defense-related decisions. This tension was especially noticeable in the 1980s, for example, with hearings on defense-contractor performance carried out by the House Energy Committee under Chair John Dingell (D-Mich.). Over the past three decades, other committees—Banking, Joint Economic, and Government Operations—have expressed interest in defense issues, but find legislative access difficult.

Within the executive branch, the power of the Iron Triangle is real. There are few other government agencies that can counterbalance the political clout of the Defense Department, which is the largest source of employment (with over 3 million employees) and the purchaser of 75 percent of all goods and services bought by the federal government. In the Reagan era, moreover, the authority of the Defense Department has extended well into the domain of arms-control policy, generally overseen by the State Department and the Arms Control and Disarmament Agency.

Even the president's own Office of Management and Budget found it difficult to resist the power of the Pentagon. In the early 1980s OMB Director David Stockman made several efforts to cut back on large Pentagon budget requests, but failed totally in those efforts. As Phillip Hughes, former deputy director of OMB's predecessor (the Bureau of the Budget), put it:

> The most relevant consideration is, in blunt terms, sheer power—where the muscle is—and this is a very power-conscious town, and the Secretary of Defense and the defense establishment are a different group to deal with, whether the Congress is dealing with them or whether the Budget Bureau is dealing with them.[16]

The growth of the Iron Triangle substantially changes our perception of the distinction between government and industry. Echoing President Eisenhower's concern about the military/industrial complex, economist Murray Weidenbaum, later chairman of the Reagan Council of Economic Advisers, recognized this risk as early as the 1960s:

> The close, continuing relationship between the Defense Department and its major suppliers is resulting in convergence between the two, which is blurring and reducing much of the distinction between public and private activities in an important branch of the American economy.[17]

With the advantage of historically unprecedented defense budgets, the interpenetration of industry and government—the Iron Triangle—in the defense sector has only grown stronger. Informed and effective debate over defense policies and new weapons programs was all but abandoned in an unrestrained burst of defense spending between 1981 and 1985. Even with the deficit-induced pressures to hold down the level of defense budget growth, the fiscal base on which the Iron Triangle rests grew to twice the size it had been in 1981. Effective cost control has become difficult, as tales of contractor waste and abuse testify.

The power of the Iron Triangle must be restrained. A case can be made that companies whose very existence depends directly on public tax expenditures should not have such influence over the spending of those funds, and that they have a duty to be more than normally forthcoming about their spending practices. There are some, such as economist John Kenneth Galbraith, who argue that since the public/private distinction has already been substantially blurred, major defense contractors should simply be nationalized. The precedent exists for such a policy: Before World War II, public ownership of defense production facilities was common, especially in shipbuilding and ammunition. Some will argue that public ownership is no greater guarantee of production efficiency and is politically unrealistic, though it might make contractor performance more directly accountable to the source of its funds—the Congress and the public.

Short of this solution, since the subcontracting, stockholding, lobbying, and personnel characteristics of these companies are part of the process by which the Iron Triangle is reinforced, public regulation and greater disclosure of information would provide the groundwork for greater public accountability and debate over this policy process.

A truly open national security apparatus is urgently needed, one that is concerned not only with bureaucratic survival and corporate gain, but with an open debate over real national security requirements.

NOTES

1. Budgets, or "budget authority," are monies voted for the Defense Department each year. Because a substantial share of these budget appropriations are spent over several years, however (it takes up to seven years to build an aircraft carrier), actual Pentagon spending ("outlays") lags behind appropriations. Each year's actual spending includes some funds that were appropriated for that year (largely for military and civilian personnel) and some funds that grew out of earlier year budgets (largely for weapons).

2. Each Defense Department annual report by Secretary of Defense Caspar Weinberger has had this tone. See, for example, Department of Defense, *Report of the Secretary of Defense*, for Fiscal Years 1983 and 1984.

3. See, for background, Franklyn Holzman, "Are the Soviets Really Outspending the U.S. on Defense?" *International Security*, Vol. 4, No. 4, Spring, 1980, pp. 86–104; Holzman, "Soviet Military Spending: Assessing the Numbers Game," *International Security*, Vol. 6, No. 4, Spring, 1982, pp. 78–101; Holzman, "Are We Falling Behind the Soviets?" *Atlantic*, July, 1983, pp. 10–18; Richard Stubbing, "The Imaginary Defense Gap: We Already Outspend Them," *Washington Post*, February 14, 1982, p. C-1; Federation of American Scientists, *Public Interest Report*, September, 1982; John Collins, *U.S.-Soviet Military Balance: Concepts and Capabilities, 1960–1980*, (New York, McGraw-Hill, 1980); and Senator Carl Levin, *The Other Side of the Story*, monograph, May, 1983.

4. See Morton J. Peck and Frederick M. Scherer, *The Weapons Acquisition Process: An Economic Analysis*, Boston: Harvard School of Business Administration, 1962; J. Ronald Fox, *Arming America: How the U.S. Buys Weapons*, Boston: Harvard School of Business Administration, 1974; Harvey M. Sapolsky, *The Polaris System Development: Bureaucratic and Programmatic Success in Government*, Boston: Harvard University Press, 1972; A. Ernest Fitzgerald, *The High Priests of Waste*, New York: Norton, 1972; and Richard Stubbing, *The Defense Game*, (New York: Harper & Row, 1986).

5. The Air Force is currently funding a next-generation bomber, the "advanced technology bomber", to succeed the B-1B. See Gordon Adams, *The B-1 Bomber: An Analysis of Its Strategic Utility, Cost, Constituency and Economic Impact*, New York: Council on Economic Priorities, 1976; Gordon Adams, "A Bomber for All Seasons," *Newsletter*, New York, Council on Economic Priorities, February, 1982.

6. Quoted in an article by William Grieder, *Atlantic*, December, 1981.

7. President's Private Sector Survey on Cost Control ("Grace Commission"), *Task Force Report on the Office of the Secretary of Defense, Task Force Report on the Department of the Army, Task Force Report on the Department of the Air Force*, Washington, D.C., July, 1983.

8. This is particularly true of General Dynamics, Grumman, Lockheed, McDonnell Douglas, and Northrop, who are usually among the top ten contractors with the Defense Department.

9. See Gordon Adams and Christopher Paine, "The R&D Slush Fund," *The Nation*, January 26, 1980.

10. A North American Aviation official quoted in David Sims, "Spoon Feeding the Military: How New Weapons Come to Be," in Leonard Rodberg and Derek Shearer (eds.), *The Pentagon Watchers*, (Garden City, N.Y.: Doubleday, 1970), p.249.

11. See Gordon Adams, *The Politics of Defense Contracting: The Iron Triangle*, (New Brunswick, N.J.: Transaction Press, 1982), Chapter 11. See also the report of the Defense Department Inspector General's office, 1983, on the interrelationship of industry and the Defense Department in the Defense Science Board, as reprinted in the *Congressional Record*, July 22, 1983, pp. S 10663–S 10677.

12. See Adams, *op.cit.*, Chapter 6, and Council on Economic Priorities, *Military Maneuvers*, (New York: CEP, 1975).

13. See *Armed Forces Journal*, June and July 1980.

14. See Adams, *op.cit.*, Chapter. 9, reviewing these DCAA audits.

15. See Edwin M. Epstein, "The Emergence of Political Action Committees," in Herbert E. Alexander (ed.), *Political Finance*, Sage Electoral Studies Yearbook, Vol. 5, (Beverly Hills: Sage Publications, 1979), pp. 159–97, and Adams, *op.cit.*, Chapter 8.

16. Quoted in Richard Kaufmann, *The War Profiteers*, (Garden City, N.Y.: Doubleday, 1972), p.180. This view of Pentagon clout is reinforced by another former OMB official, Richard Stubbing, in *The Defense Game, op. cit.*

17. Murray Weidenbaum, "Arms and The American Economy: A Domestic Convergence Hypothesis," *American Economic Review*, Vol. 58, No. 2, (May 1968), p.428.

6. PLAYING THE GOVERNMENT'S GAME: THE MASS MEDIA AND AMERICAN FOREIGN POLICY

William A. Dorman

No democratic institution struggling under the weight of the nuclear age has undergone a more troubling and profound transformation than the news media. Before the atomic bomb, journalism never hesitated to march off to war, but the news media usually were eager to demobilize once victory seemed at hand—not unlike American society as a whole.

In many significant ways, however, the return to peacetime assumptions and practices did not occur after 1945. Instead, the mass media came to embrace the nuclear confrontation's fundamental assumption that the United States now faced a permanent, ruthless, and intractable enemy. Given such a presupposition, not surprisingly, the mainstream news media—those print and broadcast organizations considered the dominant sources of information for the general public—have performed during the Cold War as they always have during hot ones.

What has taken shape 40 years after Hiroshima, therefore, can best be described as a journalism of deference to the national-security state. The free marketplace of ideas, if it ever existed, has given way to an arena of limited popular discourse, whose parameters are set in the "national interest" as defined by official Washington. Seemingly absent in post-World War II society is even the possibility of a forum for robust debate over foreign policy and defense issues. As a result, for nearly four decades political elites have been permitted to indulge their global fantasies without serious challenge.

The sense of permanent crisis that grips most Americans and makes possible a continuing obsession with nuclear weapons is, to be sure, not wholly the doing of mainstream journalism. However, the news media have played a decidedly necessary if not sufficient role. For the pictures about foreign affairs in the heads of most Americans are largely put there by the news media, and these pictures throughout the Cold War have been neither reassuring nor substantively at odds with official Washington's dark vision of the world. As a result of living in a mental garrison state that feeds on the media's stark imagery of the forces arrayed against us, most Americans have been only too willing to turn over large parts of their good fortune to preparations for war in general and nuclear war in particular.

Note: Some footnotes have been deleted, and others have been renumbered to appear in consecutive order.

Certainly, there are journalists working for specialized publications or in the alternative and opinion media who exercise independent judgment about U.S. defense policy. And there are guerrilla-types within the mainstream who, despite obstacles and at risk to their reputations for "objectivity" question and challenge the statist perspective on the nuclear story. But their work, hopeful as it may be, is more an indication of what might and could be done than representative of what is done routinely. Patterns and not exceptions, finally, are what matter, and the dominant journalistic paradigm remains one that tends to share the state's fixations rather than to question them.

The nuclear obsession, of course, is bound up almost wholly with the Soviet Union: when Americans think of nuclear war, they have only one enemy in mind. It is with the representation of the Soviet Union, then—its motives, behavior, and intentions—that the U.S. media have most effectively and devastatingly served the logic of the nuclear regime. This service has been rendered not through lies, but rather through the routine interpretations of demonstrable truths in relentlessly negative terms. In this regard, the media have not so much created hostile images of the Soviets out of whole cloth as they have tailored them according to a pattern cut in Washington.

There is compelling evidence that the news media have consistently gone along with Washington's overstatements of Soviet strength and military spending, generally supported increases in U.S. military spending, and usually questioned the deployment of new weapons systems only on the basis of whether they are sound investments. Soviet leadership is routinely portrayed in the darkest of terms, and the bleakest motives are habitually ascribed to Soviet behavior. There is also ample evidence of the media's reluctance to dispute U.S. interventions abroad until *after* significant elites begin to defect from a policy consensus—which usually is far too late. Finally, the news media have invariably interpreted the particulars of arms negotiations in ways that are favorable to official Washington and decidedly hostile to the Soviet Union.

This record has prompted George Kennan, the architect of containment, to write of the news media's "endless series of distortions and oversimplifications," "systematic dehumanization of the leadership of another great country," and the "monotonous misrepresentation of the nature and attitudes of another great people." According to Kennan, "the view of the Soviet Union that prevails today in large portions of our governmental and journalistic establishments [is] so extreme, so subjective, so far removed from what any sober scrutiny of external reality would reveal, that it is not only ineffective but dangerous as a guide to political action."[1]

While the news media's frightening picture of the external threat significantly contributes to the difficulty of organizing a sustained challenge to the nuclear regime, their portrayal of internal political dissent from official U.S. policy frequently makes such a task nearly impossible. At best, those who have questioned the state's assumptions and policies have been depicted by the mainstream media as naive romantics, while at worst they have been portrayed as dupes or subversives. Moreover, the media have done little to oppose the suppression of dissent during periodic "red scares," more often than not adding to the fires instead of dousing them. Here again, journalism has too often enforced the limits on public discourse established by the state rather than extended them.

Press behavior since 1945 is probably best understood within the context of the general psychological revolution that has been a major feature of the atomic age. Since Hiroshima, journalism, like most other aspects of society, has been held in nuclear thrall. The prospect of absolute warfare against the homeland (and species) created the national-security state, and journalism has proved no more independent of it than national government, education, the church, or business. Yet it is the news media that should sound the alarm at abuses of state power. Aside from an occasional atavistic twitch, like the Pentagon Papers affair, the media have moved further and further away from the watchdog role democratic theory assumed they would play in affairs of state where national defense and foreign policy are concerned.

The journalistic response to a sense of permanent emergency developed, over a period of years, in ways parallel to the state's. Foreign and defense policy came to be seen only through the lens of superpower confrontation. Statist concerns for containment, deterrence, and credibility crowded out traditional democratic and journalistic assumptions about open politics and the dangers of secrecy. In this latter regard, even when the news media publicize matters the nuclear regime would prefer kept from public view, journalism usually justifies its performance by arguing that the material is not really secret within the *state's* definition of the term.

For instance, as William M. Arkin has pointed out, the *Washington Post* editorially answered critics in late 1984 by arguing that virtually all of the information it had published about a space shuttle carrying a new military intelligence satellite had been "unclassified" by the government.[2]

A similar case in early 1985 involved publication in the *New York Times* of information that the United States had unilaterally devised wartime contingency plans to deploy nuclear depth charges in Canada, among other places, news which had already appeared in newspapers abroad. As it turned out, the *Times* story had been prepared with the help of a State Department official whose assistance had been authorized by the head of the National Security Council. It is a reasonable assumption that such cooperation was forthcoming in the hope of exerting damage control on the story.

The tactic appears to have worked: according to the newspaper's national security correspondent Leslie H. Gelb, who wrote the piece, "The *Times* editors and I were concerned about genuine national security as well as news. Therefore, we agreed at the outset to limit the story to those four countries where the contingency plans had already been publicly disclosed." And even though Gelb said he had more sensitive information in his possession, such information has not been made public.[3] It bears mention that Gelb formerly held high posts in the State and Defense Departments.

Gradually, then, the U.S. mainstream news media have psychologized and routinized the needs and strategies of the national security state in permanent emergency. The result has been a vastly diminished *civil* voice in journalism. Editor and journalist Robert Karl Manoff, in his landmark discussion of the subject, has defined such a voice as one "with proud recourse to moral authority, dependence on unmediated expression, respect for individual opinion and independent journalistic judgment."[4] In its place has emerged the *statist* voice, with its reliance on official sources, its preoccupation with Washington policy debates, and its acceptance of the terms in which these debates are couched. Even when journalists have seemed to soften their view of the Soviet Union— during the détente years of Nixon and Kissinger, for example—or in the spring of 1985 and the ascendancy to power of Mikhail Gorbachev, the shifts in perspective have originated in Washington, not as a result of a change in the judgments of reporters.

Nowhere are the consequences of a predominantly statist voice clearer than in the media's seeming passivity in covering the specific strategic policies that govern the development, deployment, and use of the nuclear arsenal. Nuclear strategy for the past four decades has received little more than perfunctory attention, with the boundaries of debate being set in Washington instead of in newsrooms. Too, such reporting as there has been on strategic doctrine has largely accepted policy declarations at face value. Coverage has tended to ignore the fact that declared policy represents only the façade of a complex strategic agenda.

Perhaps the news media are at the height of their statism in covering the process of nuclear arms negotiations, when they reflexively assume the posture of the U.S. government. Again to cite Manoff: "The press may reflect and give vent to domestic differences over negotiating strategies, but when it comes to discussing the details and rationales of the other side's position, independent reporting stops at the water's edge."[5]

The willingness of the news media to defer to the national security state is not limited to nuclear matters. Mixed in with nuclear anxiety since World War II has been national ambition to achieve what publisher Henry Luce labeled "the American Century," a time when the United States would be dominant and the world would be a better place for it. In this regard, throughout the Cold War, the news media have usually allowed Washington to define political situations abroad. Too, mainstream journalism has tended to accept uncritically the notion that Third World countries cannot have politics, only fates, and it is best for all concerned if the United States ultimately determines what those fates are to be.

This acquiescence has led the news media to withhold information about U.S. interventions, sometimes knowingly, as was the case in the Bay of Pigs; or, more frequently, to interpret them favorably, as with the interventions in the Congo, Dominican Republic, and Grenada, while routinely lending support to the contention that the world's problems, such as they are, usually result only from Soviet subversion.[6]

Journalism's consistent willingness to suspend independent judgment and to accept Washington's frames, labels, and assessments has had predictable consequences. Thus Cuban involvement in Angola received sustained media attention while U.S. involvement was downplayed; the absence of popular support for Polish martial law was made plain, but the illegitimacy of the Shah of Iran went unnoticed; a pronouncement by the Philippines' Ferdinand Marcos two years ago [1983] that antigovernment agitators and publishers who allowed their facilities to print "propaganda" could be executed received only passing mention in the national news. It is not difficult to imagine the tone and scope of press coverage if a similar statement were to be made by the Sandinista government in Nicaragua.

Vietnam, it should be noted, was not the grand exception to the media's statist inclination, as many observers have assumed. This reality has been confirmed by several prominent journalists, whose retrospective comments suggest that the journalistic establishment was at odds with Washington more because of concern over how effectively the war was being fought than with whether it should have been fought at all.[7]

The reasons for media behavior are far more complex and subtle than those usually advanced by critics of the statist orientation. Cronyism, careerism, sheer ignorance, or unconscionable pursuit of profit all play their roles. But nothing that is said here should be interpreted to mean that journalists are part of a planned conspiracy, or that their editors act on instructions directly received from the State Department or the Pentagon. Rather, my argument is that the process by which journalism generally tends to reflect official policies is a function of both the media *system's* ideological orientation and Cold War conditioning. It is reflexive instead of deliberate.

Such behavior is deeply rooted in nuclear anxiety, but it also stems from acceptance of the idea of a paramount Soviet threat, plus the profound suspicion that mature capitalist entities hold for Third World revolutions, which involve people instead of technology. Finally this behavior incorporates an intuitive assumption that for corporate journalism to reach a mass audience, it must rule out taking a strong adversary stand against the state.

Most mainstream journalists, of course, reject out of hand the notion that the news media serve as an instrument of the state. Steeped in the ethical rhetoric of a democratic press, they genuinely see themselves as tough-minded practitioners of a well-defined craft, with clearcut rules to eliminate personal bias. To the extent that they see a problem, they perceive it largely as the result of government lies, half-truths, and official deceptions, or of having to cope with the impersonal economic realities of the marketplace. In this latter regard, the journalistic fraternity engages in a form of intellectual plea bargaining. Rather than admit operating under the influence of ideology—a felony—journalists cop a plea and admit only the pursuit of profit, which in American society is a misdemeanor at worst.

In their personal beliefs, most journalists see themselves as being deeply worried about nuclear catastrophe, like anyone else. A late-1983 Gallup survey of journalistic convictions, indeed, revealed that 81 percent of the journalists polled favored an agreement between the United States and the Soviet Union for an immediate and verifiable freeze on the testing, production, and deployment of nuclear weapons. However, only 4 percent of the same journalists answered "the nuclear arms race" when asked what they thought was the most important problem facing the country. And they split down the middle when asked which of two courses of action would be most likely to increase the likelihood of nuclear war: 49 percent replied that continuing the arms race would be more likely to do so; 45 percent that "falling behind the Soviet Union in nuclear weaponry" was more likely to cause a conflict.

Finally and most important, because journalists know they do not consciously lie, they assume they have written or spoken the truth. They believe devoutly in the first tenet of the journalistic faith: the U.S. news media are nonideological. Thus many journalists are alternatively bewildered and outraged when critics assert that they are serving the national security state. They tend to interpret such criticism as slander, an attack on their personal integrity, and dismiss it as the mean-spirited work of ideologues who can face neither the truth about the Soviet Union nor the nature of a world hostile to U.S. interests. Their self-image, in short, is well protected.

A major clue to understanding the journalistic mindset can be found in the media's professional model. American journalism prides itself on having developed a fairly rigid set of conventions and rules to guide performance. These rules are believed to produce objectivity, being predicated on the notion that if verifiable truths are reported even-handedly, objectivity will result. These rules also put a high premium on passivity. At a national conference on war, peace, and the news media, Judith Miller of the *New York Times* argued: "Our job is not to make the news, or to put forth controversial ideas that will affect the news. Our mission is to cover those ideas and events as they come up."[8]

In particular, the basic tenets of journalism are strongly biased toward established authority, since the authority itself can be readily verified, if not the information it provides. A charmed circle of "credible" news sources which is difficult to break into results, particularly in the area of nuclear arms. . . .

Secure in the belief that their personal partisan biases are firmly under control, many journalists conclude that they are nonideological. Yet what matters in a discussion of a dominant ideology—here defined as well-ordered world view shaped by the requirements of the national security state—are shared biases, not individual opinions. To be sure, a journalist's personal opinions may not correspond to society's dominant ideology, but the orientation of the system in which journalists work certainly does. And as with work in any industrial bureaucracy, the individual reporter's preference is not likely to prevail. More important, it is precisely because a worldview is so widely shared inside and outside the journalistic system that it appears nonprejudicial. As one former correspondent remarked, "Is a fish aware of water?" Thus, the major ideological hurdle for journalists to overcome is the belief that they are nonideological.

However, proper emphasis should not be on individual journalists but rather on the system in which they operate. In the United States, most of the dominant frames for defense issues are established by the prestige print media of the Washington-New York axis, including the *New York Times,* the *Washington Post,* the *Wall Street Journal,* and others. Together with the wire services, they provide a sort of trickle-down journalism for the rest of the country.

Such media are mature, highly capitalized corporations whose main product happens to be perceptions. Ownership in the industry as a whole is among the most concentrated in the United States. The owners and decision-makers are important members of what journalist and author Sidney Zion, cited in *Harper's* magazine, termed the "League of Gentlemen," his phrase for the establishment. According to Zion: "Even when the press attacks a particular administration, its owners and managers still belong to that League of Gentlemen, and still consider the government to be basically right." In agreeing with Zion about the "League" and its nature, columnist Tom Wicker, an associate editor of the *New York Times,* added in the same issue: "Sure, someone could write a two-line memo tomorrow and change the news policy of the [*Times*] to be more skeptical and challenging of established institutions. But they won't do it, not because they don't have the power to do it, but because they don't want to suffer more than the minimal necessary disapproval of the League of Gentlemen."[9]

Beyond a range of pressures to conform ideologically that can be exerted on a reporter by a complex set of bureaucratic checks and balances, there is also the reality that the profit-oriented news media find independent journalism "costly." While there is no evidence to indicate that media profits and a nonconfrontational relationship with the Soviets are incompatible, it remains that specialists are expensive, generalists less so. In this sense, to leave the conventional Washington wisdom unchallenged happens also to be economical for contemporary bottom-line journalism. . . .

One final force at work on the news media demands mention. In the past five years, a major campaign from the political right has been directed against them. The right argues that the media are antidefense, soft on the Soviet Union, and antinuclear. While these conservatives say that they are interested in an open press, their analysis can only lead to a more closed system, in which the statist perspective is *totally* dominant. . . .

Besides the possibility of intimidating the media into an even less objective stance than it usually takes, such a campaign works to the detriment of antistatist critics in two other equally significant, if more subtle, ways:

- The right's criticism tends to reinforce the journalists' self-image of being independent from the state. How could journalism be serving the interests of the nuclear regime, such reasoning goes, if the political right is upset? But this view fails to comprehend that the right's basic quarrel with the media, in addition to being based on a fantasy view of Cold War history, is more an argument over degree than kind. That is to say, the mainstream media usually tend to conclude that the United States ought to use less force to pursue its aims than the political right believes necessary. There is no fundamental disagreement, however, about the United States' role in the world.

- The current wave of conservative criticism makes it appear to the thoughtful observer that the question of media performance is merely a right-versus-left argument, when instead the debate ought to focus on what journalistic model best serves an open society.[10]

Because of the onslaught from the pronuclear right, it is all the more imperative that those concerned about the nuclear dilemma begin to pay careful and sustained attention to the role the media play, and can play, in the crisis at hand. . . .

The central fact remains that there is an undeniable need, some 40 years after Hiroshima, to reinvent American journalism, a task for which the media seem unprepared, unwilling, or both. . . .

NOTES

1. George F. Kennan, "On Nuclear War," *New York Review of Books* (Jan. 21, 1982), pp. 21–22.

2. William M. Arkin, "Waging Secrecy," *Bulletin* (March 1985), pp. 5–6.

3. Gerald M. Boyd, "White House Role in Article is Cited," *New York Times* (March 3, 1985), p. 3.

4. Robert K. Manoff, "Covering the Bomb: Press and State in the Shadow of Nuclear War," in *War, Peace and the News Media:* Proceedings, David Rubin and Ann Marie Cunningham, eds. (New York: Department of Journalism and Mass Communication, New York University, 1983), p. 202.

5. Robert K. Manoff, "The Media's Nuclear War," *PSR* [Physicians for Social Responsibility] *Newsletter* (Fall 1984), p. 2.

6. See Jonathan Kwitny, *Endless Enemies* (New York: Congdon and Weed, 1984).

7. Phillip Knightley, *The First Casualty* (New York: Harcourt Brace Jovanovich, 1975), pp. 380–381.

8. Rubin and Cunningham, op. cit., p. 193.

9. "Can the Press Tell the Truth," *Harper's* (Jan. 1985), pp. 48, 50.

10. For the most comprehensive analysis available of the political right's attack on the news media, see Walter Schneir and Miriam Schneir, "Beyond Westmoreland: The Right's Attack on the Press," *The Nation* (March 30, 1985), pp. 361–367.

7. THE ELECTORAL CYCLE AND THE CONDUCT OF AMERICAN FOREIGN POLICY

William B. Quandt

Two-hundred years ago, when the Constitution was taking shape, the conduct of the new nation's foreign affairs was not central to the concerns of the Founders. Once independence was achieved, it was widely believed, the United States would be able to remain comparatively uninvolved with the rest of the world. A wide ocean separated it from the messy politics of Europe and permitted the first president to imagine the United States could remain unentangled in the affairs of the rest of the world.

The Founders did, of course, make passing reference to the division of powers between the executive and the legislature in such matters as negotiating and ratifying treaties with foreign powers and with raising an army and a navy and directing them in time of war. As elsewhere in the Constitution, on these matters one sees the determination to prevent too much power from being concentrated in any one part of the federal government.[1] Divided responsibility was the key to avoiding abuses of power, and in the domestic arena the wisdom of this philosophical bent has been widely applauded. In the conduct of foreign policy, however, it is much more difficult to argue that the virtues of divided responsibility enhance the common defense or promote the general welfare.

Still, even the most ardent proponent of strong presidential leadership in foreign policy would have a difficult time arguing that the specific provisions of the Constitution regarding foreign policy are at the root of our contemporary problems in world affairs. . . .

[T]he Constitution does not cripple the president in the conduct of foreign policy, at least not because of the definition of powers. These are defined sufficiently broadly and ambiguously so that a strong and popular president can provide effective leadership, while a relatively weak and unpopular one will have a difficult time. That is pretty close to what one imagines the intent of the Founders must have been.

THE PROBLEM OF THE ELECTORAL CYCLE

But there is still a constitutionally rooted problem that seriously affects the conduct of foreign policy. It derives from the structure of the electoral cycle.

Note: Some footnotes have been deleted, and others have been renumbered to appear in consecutive order.

Here there is no ambiguity at all in the Constitution. Presidential elections take place every four years; congressional elections every two years; and since the passage of the twenty-second amendment, a president can only be elected twice. In practice, this often means that presidents have little time during their incumbency when they have both the experience and the power needed for sensible and effective conduct of foreign policy. The price we pay is a foreign policy excessively geared to short-term calculations, in which narrow domestic political considerations often outweigh sound strategic thinking, and where turnover in high positions is so frequent that consistency and coherence are lost. . . .

The electoral arrangements for the presidency and Congress have rarely been justified by the contribution they make to sound foreign policy. The rationale is almost entirely domestic. Representatives are supposed to remain closely tied to the wishes of their constituents; hence the two-year term. Senators are expected to take a broader view and thus are given six-year terms. The Senate is supposed to embody a degree of continuity, and, therefore, only one-third of its membership is up for election at any given moment. Presidents fall in between, having to renew their mandate after four years and being obliged to retire at the end of a second term. A pervasive distrust of presidential power can be detected in these arrangements, a distrust that is historically understandable, but which also can have debilitating effects on foreign policy.

In domestic policy it is probably wise to structure the federal system so that presidential authority is limited. After all, the country has so many diverse interests that it is hard to imagine the system working well unless there are strong incentives for compromise and moderation. A certain amount of inconsistency, of vacillation, of changing the calculus of winners and losers is needed to keep this heterogeneous country together. The federal structure and the electoral cycle are all part of the system that allows domestic political issues to be resolved with a minimum of conflict and violence.

Foreign policy is different. Washington speaks for the country as a whole in foreign policy. The president is supposed to be the commander-in-chief of the armed forces. And in the modern world he literally holds the power of life and death, since he has the ultimate authority to decide on the use of nuclear weapons. Such decisions might have to be made in a matter of minutes, and extraordinary measures are taken to be sure that the president is always in a position to act on the basis of the best information available. In the nuclear era there might not be time to consult with Congress, to await declarations of war, or to cultivate public understanding. An enormous responsibility rests with the president, and presumably it is in everyone's interest that matters affecting the nation's welfare and security be handled with skill, expertise, and intelligence. The present electoral arrangements do not contribute to that goal.

THE NATURE OF THE PROBLEM

Ideally, one would like to see a president bring wisdom and experience in foreign affairs to the Oval Office. Once there, one could hope that he or she would have the time, the power, and the authority to deal with problems of national security and foreign policy in ways that promote the national interest.

But to list these desirable circumstances is to be reminded of how far they are from the recent historical record.

Wisdom is something that a president either has or lacks, and the electoral cycle cannot be held responsible. But experience and power, as well as the time and inclination to deal with foreign affairs, are tied to the rhythms of the electoral cycle. Simply stated, a newly elected president may well have the authority, the power, and the inclination to address foreign policy issues, but he rarely has the experience necessary to form sound judgments. Thus, it is common for serious errors to be made in the first year of a presidential term. During the second, and part of the third year, there may be a happy coincidence of sufficient power, experience, and time to deal with the complexities of world affairs. But during the last year or more of a typical first term, a president is drawn into the politics of reelection and rarely has much time or inclination to deal with foreign policy issues unless they seem to hold out the promise of winning votes, which is rarely the case.

A reelected president in his second term faces a somewhat different problem. Experience and authority are likely to be available, but after the mid-term elections the "lame-duck" problem is very likely to set in, making it difficult for a president to conduct foreign policy. Leaders abroad will begin to ask themselves why they should bother to deal with this president, when someone else will be in the Oval Office before long, perhaps bringing a change of policy with him. The opposition party has little incentive to help the outgoing president win any foreign policy victories, and within his own party the struggle for succession may weaken his normal base of support. In normal times it would be surprising to find major foreign policy successes in the last phase of a two-term president's incumbency.

This simple descriptive model should not be seen as an absolute guide for how a president will fare in the conduct of foreign policy at different moments of his term. Crises can radically change the normal political calculus, enhancing presidential power and forging a bipartisan base of support. But if a crisis turns into a prolonged, indecisive, costly commitment—as in Vietnam and Lebanon—domestic political considerations are likely to come to the fore again and force a president's hand.

None of this would matter so much if presidents did not really have much to say about foreign policy. In theory, policy might be carried out by the experienced professionals in the bureaucracy on a nonpartisan basis. Or a grand bipartisan consensus might develop that would establish the broad lines of policy, leaving the president relatively free from domestic political considerations as long as he operated within that consensus. Those who used to proclaim that "politics stops at the water's edge" were expressing the hope that a nonpartisan foreign policy could be found. But certainly since the mid-1960s and the trauma of Vietnam, there has been no consensus on foreign policy that could insulate a president from the impact of domestic politics and the electoral cycle.

FIRST-TERM PRESIDENTS: THE TYPICAL PATTERN

A president's assessment of risks and opportunities is generally a product of his experience in office and where he stands with respect to the electoral cycle. For analytical purposes and at the risk of some distortion of a more complex reality, it is useful to distinguish among patterns in the first year of a presidential term, the second year, the third, and the fourth.

These categories are useful for understanding the typical evolution of policy over a four-year cycle. They alert the observer to the changing weight of domestic political considerations as a presidential term unfolds. The time when a president decides to do something is heavily influenced by this cycle, unless he is reacting to a foreign policy crisis.

If a president and his advisers are inattentive to the political cycle, they are apt to make serious mistakes. A learning process seems invariably to take place in the course of a four-year term. By the end, most presidents recognize that some of what they tried early in their term was unrealistic; they have become more familiar with the limits on their power; they aim lower and pay more attention to the timing of their major moves.

A skillful president will make use of the political cycle to enhance the chances of success in his foreign policy. A careless one will probably pay a high price for ignoring domestic realities. Events, of course, can get out of control, as they did for Jimmy Carter with the Iranian hostage crisis in 1979. It was particularly bad luck for him that this happened just as an election year was beginning. By contrast, Ronald Reagan managed to terminate the controversial American military presence in Lebanon just before his reelection campaign began in 1984, and the issue seemed to do him no political harm at the polls. Luck and skill go hand in hand in successful political careers.

Looking back on their time in office, presidents and their advisers usually decry the intrusion of domestic politics so heavily into the foreign policy arena. Former Secretary of State Cyrus Vance has argued that the only solution to the problem is to elect a president for one term of six years.

> From experience in the making of foreign policy in several administrations, I have concluded that a four-year presidential term has serious drawbacks, especially when it comes to foreign affairs. It takes each new president from six to nine months to learn his job and to feel comfortable in the formulation and execution of foreign policy. For the next eighteen months the president can operate with assurance. But during the last year or so, he is running for reelection and is forced to divert much of his attention to campaigning. As a result, many issues are ignored and important decisions are deferred. Sometimes bad decisions are made under the pressures of months of primary elections. And at home and overseas, we are frequently seen as inconsistent and unstable.[2]

Others have tried to address the problem by pleading for bipartisanship, the removal of foreign policy from the domestic political agenda. Zbigniew Brzezinski, President Carter's national security adviser, has written:

> Every Administration goes through a period of an ecstatic emancipation from the past, then a discovery of continuity, and finally a growing preoccupation with Presidential reelection. As a result, the learning curve in the area of foreign policy tends to be highly compressed. Each Administration tends to expend an enormous amount of energy coping with the unintended, untoward consequences of its initial, sometimes excessive, impulses to innovate, to redeem promises, and to harbor illusions. In time, preconceptions give way to reality, disjointedness to intellectual coherence, and vision to pragmatism. But by the time this happens, the Presidential

cycle is usually coming to an end. That the four-year election process has a perni-
cious influence on foreign policy is evident, but it is also clear that this structural
handicap is not likely to be undone.[3]

The Pattern of the First Year

A president and his advisers often begin their term with relatively little background in foreign policy issues. This lack of background is especially important
if the president has been a Washington outsider and if there has been a change
of the party in control of the White House. But even in the case of a Washington insider, such as a senator with experience on the Foreign Relations Committee or a vice president moving up to the presidency, there is little reason to
expect more than the faintest familiarity with most foreign policy issues.

Presidents are not allowed the luxury of taking no position on issues until
they have learned enough to make sensible judgments. Instead, on issues that
evoke strong public interest, such as the Middle East or arms control, candidates for the presidency will be expected to have a position and may even
devote a major speech to the topic.

These first definitions of a president's position, often taken in the midst of
the campaign, are typically of considerable importance in setting the administration's initial course. They are likely to reflect general foreign policy predispositions—a tough policy toward the Soviets, for example—and will generally
imply that the previous administration was on the wrong track and that things
will soon be put straight. (This, of course, assumes that the presidency is
passing from one party to the other.) In addition to defining a course of action
by contrasting it with one's predecessor in office, a newly-elected president will
have to decide what priority to attach to the main foreign policy issues on the
agenda. Not all issues can be dealt with at once, and a signal of presidential
interest or disinterest may be more important in setting the administration's
policy than the substantive position papers that inevitably begin to flow to the
White House from the bureaucracy.

If an issue is treated as important, and if presidential predispositions are
reflected in the charting of the initial course, the early months of the new term
are likely to be marked by activism. Having just won a national election, the
president will probably be optimistic about his ability to use the office to
achieve great results in foreign and domestic policy. If initiatives are decided
upon, they tend to be ambitious. It takes time to recognize what will work and
what will not.

It also takes time for a president and his advisers to develop a comfortable
working style. A high degree of confusion is not unusual in the early days.
Public statements may have to be retracted, and it will take time to know who
really speaks for the president among the many claimants to the role. In addition, it will take time for the president and the new secretary of state to develop
contacts with various foreign leaders. These encounters will eventually add to
their education, but at the outset there is usually only a faint understanding of
the foreign players, their agendas, and their strengths and weaknesses.

What all of this adds up to is a first year that is often somewhat experimental, where policy objectives are set in ambitious terms, where predispositions
and campaign rhetoric still count for something, and where international realities are only dimly appreciated. Typically, toward the end of the first year it

becomes clear that the policy agreed upon in January or February has lost momentum or is on the wrong track. Reassessments are then likely, but not until considerable time and energy have been invested in pursuing false leads and indulging in wishful thinking.

The Pattern of the Second Year

Despite the frequent disappointments of dealing with foreign policy issues in the first year, presidents rarely decide to turn their attention away from the international arena in their second year. If recent experience is a guide, year two is likely to be marked with considerably greater success, either in promoting international agreement through negotiations or in the skillful management of a crisis.

The difference between the first and the second year shows that experience can be a good teacher. Policies in the second year are often more in tune with reality. There is less of an ideological overlay in policy deliberations. At the same time, goals are likely to be less ambitious. Plans for comprehensive solutions may be replaced by attempts at more modest partial agreements.

By the second year, some of the intrabureaucratic feuding and backbiting is likely to have subsided, or at least a president has had the chance to put it to an end if he so chooses. The gap between the political appointees and the foreign service professionals has also narrowed, and more regional expertise is typically being taken into account during policy discussions. If a senior bureaucrat has survived into the second year, he is no longer seen as the enemy and has often been judged a team player. In any case, the failures of year one tend to make the president's men less contemptuous of the knowledge of the professionals.

During the second year, presidents also begin to realize that mishandling of foreign policy issues, especially in the Middle East or concerning U.S.-Soviet relations, can be costly. Congressional elections are scheduled for November, and in most cases the party in power has to expect some losses. Such losses make it more difficult for the president to govern, and thus he has a strong interest in minimizing them. This is no time for controversial initiatives. If initiatives are to be taken, there is a high premium on the appearance of success. The mood in the White House is much less experimental than in the first year. Practical criteria come to the fore. Success may require compromises with principle. This is the year in which presidents realize that the slogan of politics being "the art of the possible" is applicable to foreign as well as domestic policy.

The Pattern of the Third Year

During the third year of a typical presidential term, foreign policy issues are likely to be assessed at the White House in terms of whether or not they can help advance the incumbent's reelection bid. The tendency, therefore, is to try for an apparent success if an initiative is underway, even if the result leaves something to be desired. The administration will even be prepared on occasions to pay heavily with concessions or with promises of aid and arms to get an agreement.

If the prospects for an agreement do not look good during the third year, the tendency is to cut one's losses and to disengage the president from the diplomatic effort. Above all, the president does not want to be seen as responsible for a foreign policy failure as the election year approaches. And certainly by the end of the third year, if not considerably earlier, the pre-election season is likely to be underway.

The rush for success, along with the tendency to abandon controversial and costly policies, means that mistakes are often made in the third year. Opportunities may be lost through carelessness. The price of agreement may become very high as the parties to negotiations realize how badly Washington wants a success. Political considerations tend to override the requirements of steady, purposeful diplomacy. Nonetheless, this is sometimes a year in which genuine achievements are possible, especially if the groundwork in the second year has been good.

The Pattern of the Fourth Year

Most presidents go to great lengths to deny that electoral considerations are allowed to influence their conduct of foreign policy. But as political realists, they all know that they must take politics into account. If nothing else, the extraordinary demands on a presidential candidate mean that little time is left for consideration of complex foreign policy problems, for meeting with visiting heads of state, or for fighting great battles with Congress over aid or arms sales. Added to this is the desire not to lose the support of constituencies that have particularly strong feelings about specific foreign policy issues. This can be important in terms of votes as well as in terms of financial contributions to the party and to congressional candidates.

The guidelines for the fourth year with respect to potentially controversial foreign policy issues are thus fairly simple. Try to avoid taking a position. Steer clear of new initiatives. Stick with safe themes and patriotic rhetoric. Attack your opponent as inexperienced, ill-informed, possibly reckless. If crises are forced upon you, they must of course be dealt with, and even in election years presidents have considerable authority in emergencies.

In brief, most presidents recognize that they can hope to achieve little in foreign policy in the midst of an election campaign. Even if a president were prepared to take some bold initiative, foreign leaders would be reluctant to respond positively out of a concern that the president might not be in office the following January. Statesmen are likely to want to know who will be in the White House for the next four years before they take major decisions. This weakens the influence of the president in his fourth year even when he is not up for reelection.

THE PATTERN OF THE SECOND TERM

For a president in his second term, the four-year pattern changes significantly. The first year and a half may be the best time for taking foreign policy initiatives. The president knows as much about substance as he ever will. The reelection has provided the proof he may feel he needed that the public is behind him.

Late in the second year, however, domestic considerations begin to intrude on foreign policy concerns. Midterm elections are likely to be of special importance, for they will determine to a large extent how much power the president has in his last two years. If he loses control over one or both houses of Congress, his legislative agenda will be in jeopardy. Any significant loss for his party may speed up the succession struggle and can embolden his opponents in Congress. The idea that a president who does not have to face reelection will be free to act in a statesmanlike manner in his last two years misses the point. He may be free, but he is unlikely to be taken very seriously as he reaches the end of his term. At some point in the third or fourth year, the "lame duck" phenomenon is bound to affect the president.

SOME ILLUSTRATIVE EXAMPLES

In the post–World War II era, only two men, Dwight Eisenhower and Richard Nixon, assumed the office of president with some measure of expertise in world affairs. Even for these two, however, there were vast gaps in their knowledge and a period of on-the-job training was essential. All other presidents—Harry Truman, John Kennedy, Lyndon Johnson, Gerald Ford, Jimmy Carter, and Ronald Reagan—had relatively little experience with world affairs by the time they assumed office.

If we leave aside the cases of Truman, who became president in the midst of a war, and of Eisenhower, who had to deal with the Korean war in his first year, we can look for typical errors of inexperience especially in 1961, 1977, and 1981. These are the purest examples of a relatively inexperienced man coming to the Oval Office after having campaigned against the previous incumbent.

Whatever one may think of the brief Kennedy presidency, its first year was not its finest hour. In the spring of 1961 Kennedy stumbled into the Bay of Pigs fiasco. In addition, having campaigned on the basis of a nonexistent missile gap, he had to reverse course and adapt to new realities, but not before he had set in motion a new phase of the arms race.

For Carter, his first year was marked by excessive ambition and awkwardness. He tried to move abruptly away from the arms control guidelines that Gerald Ford and Leonid Brezhnev had laid out at Vladivostok, calling instead for deep cuts in strategic weaponry. The Soviets rejected this new proposal and precious time was lost before arms negotiations could get back on track. In the Middle East, Carter launched an ambitious peace initiative, but compromised its success by some of his clumsy public diplomacy and by mishandling the surrounding dialogue with the Soviet Union. By fall 1977, he felt that he was paying a heavy domestic political price for his Middle East efforts and told Egypt's President Anwar Sadat that there was little more that he could do. At that point Sadat, perceiving Carter's weakness, set off on his own to deal with Israel directly.

Reagan's first-year errors were in part a product of inexperience. In the Middle East, for example, he lent his weight to a policy of building strategic consensus against the Soviet Union. From this perspective, regional problems such as the crisis in Lebanon and the Arab-Israeli conflict were relatively unimportant. Countries such as Israel, Egypt, and Saudi Arabia, all strongly anti-Soviet, would be encouraged to drop their local quarrels and cooperate in pursuit of anti-Soviet policies. Needless to say, strategic consensus was illusory, and neglecting the problems of Lebanon and the Palestinians set the stage for the explosion that came the following year.

Presidents in the second year have presumably learned something of value from their on-the-job experience. This is a time to look for initiatives that are rooted in realism and crisis management marked by some skill and self-confidence. For Kennedy, the Cuban missile crisis came in the second year and his handling of it won him high marks as a tough but flexible statesman. Nixon's deft management of the Jordan crisis, particularly the mobilization of Israeli power to help deter the Syrians, came in his second year. Carter's Camp David success was similarly timed. Finally, Reagan's well-conceived but poorly executed Middle East peace initiative also came late in his second year.

Third years are difficult to characterize. On the one hand, presidents have the power and the experience to do well, but they may feel the need to rush for success or to drop controversial issues before the election year is upon them. Particularly in recent years the reelection campaign seems to begin about mid-way through the third year. Eisenhower may have been somewhat affected by these considerations in the way he handled the Soviet Union in 1955. Here was a mixture of conciliation—the spirit of Geneva—and confusion—the response to the Soviet arms deal with Egypt. On this latter point, Eisenhower wavered between trying to win Egypt's President Gamal Abdel Nasser away from the Soviets with offers of economic aid for the Aswan High Dam and punishing him for refusing to make peace with Israel and for flirting with the Soviets. Not surprisingly, as the election year arrived, the decision was to punish Nasser. The Aswan offer was abruptly withdrawn; Nasser responded by nationalizing the Suez Canal; and before long Eisenhower faced a full-scale international crisis on the eve of elections.

Kennedy's third year is difficult to judge. He seems to have been on the way toward dealing effectively with the Soviets on arms control. Where he was heading with his policy toward Southeast Asia is difficult to determine.

Carter's third year was a mixed one in foreign policy. It began with the collapse of the Shah's regime in Iran, which caused great confusion in Washington. About the same time, however, Carter threw himself into the final negotiations for [an] Egyptian-Israeli peace treaty and was successful. He also pushed SALT II through to signature. But he dropped the Middle East issue when the Palestinian autonomy negotiations were getting underway, thus insuring their failure, and he was unable to win Senate ratification for SALT II.

Election years rarely witness great success in foreign policy. Carter struggled in frustration with the Iranian hostage crisis. Reagan withdrew ignominiously from Lebanon after more than 250 Marines had died. The great exception to this pattern, of course, was Nixon in 1972. Nixon was an unusual president in many ways. He had served as vice president under Eisenhower for eight years, and thus came to the Oval Office with much more knowledge of world affairs than other presidents. He also had a shrewd sense for timing in politics and seemed to realize that his reelection prospects would be helped if he could demonstrate his skill in foreign policy in the election year. Most other presidents have shied away from foreign policy initiatives as the election drew close. Nixon, however, prepared his biggest moves in near secrecy over the previous years. Then in 1972 he brought the American involvement in Vietnam to an end, he traveled to China, and he signed the SALT I agreement in Moscow. All this took place in the space of several months and in an election year. His

Democratic challenger, who had been painting Nixon as a reckless warmonger, never had a chance. Many voters, who felt little personal regard for Nixon, nonetheless had to admit that he was a master at the game of nations. His electoral victory was complete.

CONCLUSION

The American political system was not designed with the conduct of foreign policy in mind. Checks and balances, frequent elections, and the concept of popular sovereignty were all meant to limit abuses of power, not to make it easy for a president to govern. In foreign policy the constraints are often less than in the domestic arena. But in modern times even foreign policy has become highly controversial, and thus subject to all the political forces that limit the power of a president.

To understand how American foreign policy is made, one needs to look carefully at the views of key decision makers, especially the president and his top advisers. The individuals do matter. But they operate within a political context that has some very regular features. Therefore, if they are to leave their imprint on policy, they will have to understand what the broader constitutional system allows. And they will have to learn much about the world as well.

Presidents do have great power at their disposal. It is often most usable in the midst of crises, when the normal restraints of political life are suspended, at least for a little while. Presidents can also usually count on a fairly wide latitude in the conduct of foreign policy in their first two years. But in time the need to appeal to the electorate, to have congressional support, and to prepare for reelection appears to dominate thinking at the White House, regardless of who is the incumbent.

This means that the United States is structurally at a disadvantage in trying to develop and sustain policies that require a mastery of complex issues and call for consistency and a long-term vision to enhance the prospects of success. It is hard for presidents to look beyond the next few months. Consistency is often sacrificed for political expediency. Turnover of personnel in top positions erodes the prospects for continuity.

At the same time, the United States, for these very reasons, rarely pursues a strongly ideological foreign policy for long. There are pressures to pursue a course that has broad popular support, eschewing extremes of left or right. Pragmatic criteria are a common part of policy debates. Thus, if one course of action has clearly failed, another can be tried. This may be hard on the nerves of other world leaders, but sometimes this experimental approach is needed if a viable policy is to be found. . . .

Realizing the full potential of the office of the presidency is probably the best practical solution to the problems posed for the conduct of foreign policy by the constitutionally-designed electoral cycle. But that requires that the American people elect statesmen as presidents, and that cannot be expected in the television era. Thus, we will probably have to live with a system that weakens the ability to conduct an effective foreign policy. Understanding that reality may be small consolation, but it may serve to temper the grandiose notion that the United States, as a great power, can reshape the world in its image. Neither the realities of the world nor those of our own political system will allow that.

NOTES

1. See James MacGregor Burns, *The Deadlock of Democracy: Four-Party Politics in America* (Englewood Cliffs, N.J.: Prentice Hall, 1963), 8–23, on Madison's concept of checks and balances.

2. See Cyrus Vance, *Hard Choices: Critical Years in America's Foreign Policy* (New York: Simon and Schuster, 1983), 13.

3. See Zbigniew Brzezinski, *Power and Principle: Memoirs of the National Security Adviser, 1977–1981* (New York: Farrar, Straus, Giroux, 1983), 544.

Part II: The Institutional Setting

Foreign policy is a product of the actions officials take on behalf of the nation-state they lead. Because of this, it can be argued that the way a government is structured for purposes of policy-making will affect the conduct and content of foreign affairs as well. In other words, a relationship can be hypothesized to exist between the substance of policy and the institutional setting from which it derives. The proposition is particularly compelling if attention is focused, not on the kinds of foreign policy *goals* the nation's leaders select, but on the *means* they choose to satisfy particular objectives.

In the United States, the salient feature of the foreign policy-making institutional setting is that the president and the institutionalized presidency—the latter consisting of the president's personal staff and the Executive Office of the President—are preeminent in the foreign policy-making process. This preeminence derives in part from the authority granted the president in the Constitution and in part from the combination of judicial interpretation, legislative acquiescence, personal assertiveness, and custom and tradition that has transformed one branch of the U.S. federal government into the most powerful office in the world. The very nature of the postwar world could be added to the list, for the crisis-ridden atmosphere that has pervaded most of the post–World War II period contributed to the enhancement of presidential authority by encouraging the president to act energetically and decisively when dealing with global challenges. The widely shared consensus that the international environment demanded an active American world role, which existed among American leaders and the majority of the American people, also contributed to the feeling that strong presidential leadership in foreign policy was needed. Although some (notably in Congress) questioned this proposition in the immediate aftermath of Vietnam, the need for strong presidential leadership in foreign affairs appears to have been a widely accepted viewpoint throughout most of the postwar period.

Because of the president's key role in foreign policy-making, it is useful to consider the institutional arrangements as a series of concentric circles which in effect alter the standard government organization chart so as to draw attention to the core, or most immediate source, of the action. Thus the innermost circle in the policy-making process consists of the president, his immediate personal advisers, and such important political appointees as the secretaries of state and

Figure 1. The Institutional Setting: The Concentric Circles of Policy Making

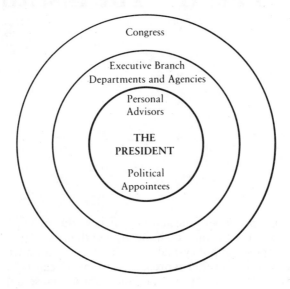

Congress

Executive Branch
Departments and Agencies

Personal
Advisors

**THE
PRESIDENT**

Political
Appointees

defense, the director of central intelligence, and various under and assistant secretaries who bear responsibility for carrying out policy decisions. The most important decisions involving the fate of the nation are made, in principle, at this level.

The second concentric circle contains the various departments and agencies of the executive branch. If we exclude from that circle the politically appointed heads of agencies and their immediate subordinates, whom we have already placed in the innermost circle, we can think of the individuals within the second circle as the career bureaucrats who provide continuity in the implementation of policy from one administration to the next. Their primary tasks—in theory—are to provide top-level policy makers with the information necessary for making decisions and to then carry out those decisions when they are reached.

As noted in the introduction to this volume, the involvement of the United States in a complex webwork of interdependent ties with other nations in the world has led to the involvement in foreign affairs of a number of organizations whose primary tasks are oriented toward the domestic environment, such as the Agriculture, Commerce, and Treasury departments. Still, the State and Defense departments and the Central Intelligence Agency (CIA) command center stage among the dozens of executive-branch departments and agencies now involved in foreign affairs. The State Department's role derives from being the only department charged (in theory, at least) with responsibility for the totality of America's relations with other nations. The Defense Department and the CIA, on the other hand, have derived their importance from the threatening and often crisis-ridden atmosphere of the postwar years, in which they seemed to have had ready alternatives from which top-level policymakers could choose when the more passive means of diplomacy and negotiation seemed destined to fail.

Moving beyond the departments and agencies of the executive branch, the third concentric circle consists of Congress. A single institutional entity, Congress often appears to embrace many different centers of power and authority—ranging from the House and Senate leadership to the various coalitions operative in the legislative branch, and from the various committees and subcommittees in which the real work of Congress is done to the individual senators and congressmen who often vie with one another for publicity as well as power. Placing Congress in the outermost circle underscores the fact that, of all the institutions involved in foreign policy-making, it is least involved in the day-to-day conduct of the nation's foreign relations.

THE INSTITUTIONAL SETTING AS AN INFLUENCE ON AMERICAN FOREIGN POLICY

The conceptualization described above was suggested some years ago in *To Move a Nation* by Roger Hilsman, who is both a perceptive student of American foreign relations as well as a former participant in the policy-making process. Interestingly, Hilsman argues in his book that while the institutional setting may affect the form and flow of policy, the politicking inherent in the process by no means conforms to neatly compartmentalized paths. Thus what the nation chooses to do abroad is the product of an often intense political struggle among all the pertinent players in the policy-making process and is affected not only by institutional structures but also by the policy-making positions occupied by decision makers and by the characteristics of the individuals who act out the roles embodied in them.

Alexander L. George discusses the interaction between individuals and institutions in his essay, "The President and the Management of Foreign Policy: Styles and Models." As George notes, information, competence, and influence over policy are widely dispersed throughout the government, and this "imposes on the president and his assistants the task of mobilizing available information, expertise, and analytical resources for effective policymaking." George describes three different approaches presidents have evolved for managing these tasks: the "formalistic," "competitive," and "collegial" models. What approach a president will choose and how it will be permitted to operate in practice will itself be shaped by the president's personality, that is, by his cognitive style (analogous to worldview), by his sense of efficacy and competence, and by his general orientation toward political conflict. By using these concepts, George is able to build an insightful portrait of the whys and hows of presidential approaches to control and coordination of policy analysis, and of policy implementation from Roosevelt to Reagan.

One of the struggles that seems to have become endemic to the policy-making process is that between the head of the National Security Council staff, the president's assistant for national security affairs, and other key participants in the process, notably the secretary of state. The struggle grows out of a basic decision every new president must make as he contemplates the management tasks he faces: whether to give his secretary of state the primary role in the foreign policy-making system or to centralize and manage that system from the White House, often with the aid of an assertive adviser for national security affairs. The record since the 1960s reveals a clear preference for White House dominance. Henry Kissinger's rise to prominence during the Nixon and Ford presidencies began from his White House base. Similarly, Zbigniew Brzezinski, Jimmy Carter's national security adviser, eventually emerged as a key figure in the Carter administration's foreign policy-making apparatus. And Alexander Haig's resignation as Ronald Reagan's first secretary of state appears to have been caused at least in part by a conflict between the secretary and his own former assistant, William P. Clark, whom Reagan had appointed as national security adviser in early 1982.

Clark was the second in a string of Reagan administration national security advisers that included Richard V. Allen, Robert C. (Bud) McFarlane, John M. Poindexter, and Frank Carlucci. None possessed the credentials that would permit him to assume the role of "resident intellectual," as had Kissinger and Brzezinski, and none achieved the dominance these two men had, so as to permit him to become the Reagan administration's chief policy spokesman and negotiator with other nations. At least two, however—McFarlane and Poindexter, both of whom were aided by another staff member, Lt. Colonel Oliver L. North—undertook covert operational activities designed to trade arms to the Iranian government in return for the release of American hostages held in Lebanon, with the profits from the sale of arms allegedly to be channeled to the *Contras* fighting the Sandinista regime in Nicaragua, in apparent contravention of congressional prohibitions. The whole bizarre episode conjured up reminiscences of the Vietnam debacle, which had led the distinguished historian Arthur M. Schlesinger, Jr., to write of the "Imperial Presidency"[1]—a label implying an abuse of presidential power that perhaps threatened the very system of checks and balances the Founding Fathers had intended when they framed the Constitution two centuries ago.

Schlesinger reminds us of the meaning of the imperial presidency in his essay "The Presidency and the Imperial Temptation." Although the immediate context of the essay is the arms-for-hostages affair that embroiled the Reagan presidency and threatened to paralyze its final years in the White House, Schlesinger probes beyond specific events to inquire into the conditions that tempt the imperial urge in the first place and into what executive usurpation of power portends. Several conclusions stand out. That the presidency will survive is certainly the comforting message. That the "imperial temptation is the consequence of a global and messianic foreign policy," and that the "imperial presidency, once a transient wartime phenomenon, has become to a degree institutionalized," are more disquieting. The unsettling implication is that we may not have seen the last imperial challenge.

Theodore Draper continues the inquiry into the meaning of the arms-for-hostages deal in "Reagan's Junta: The Institutional Sources of the Iran-*Contra* Affair." Picking up on Schlesinger's imperial presidency theme, Draper suggests that the crisis of the Reagan presidency relates not only to what a president can do, but also to what those around him can do by acting in his name. The roots of the predicament, Draper argues, can be found in the growing centralization of control over foreign policy-making in the White House, which has often freed presidents from constitutional restraints. The national security adviser and his staff have been the mechanisms through which this institutional development has been accelerated. The consequence of presidential decision making and management through a "junta" rather than through the existing structures of government, Draper suggests, may ultimately challenge American democracy itself, because it substitutes the will of the president and those around him for the "popular will."

In developing his thesis, Draper usefully describes how and why the national security adviser has grown in importance—to the point, as we noted in our introduction, that he now rivals the secretary of state in prestige and influence. Interestingly, however, there is widespread agreement among both practitioners and scholars that the national security adviser's role should be confined to that of facilitator and coordinator, not that of resident intellectual and chief spokesman and negotiator, and certainly not that of covert intelligence agent. Why, then, do presidents persist in their efforts to control policy analysis and implementation from the White House, with the national security adviser, operating under the aegis of the National Security Council, as the principal institutional as well as personal instrument for doing so? Specifically, why do presidents not choose the alternative of giving the secretary of state and the Department of State primary responsibility for managing American foreign policy?

In part the answer to these questions is that historically the State Department has often been viewed as "the problem." The nature of "the problem" and the other factors that militate against a greater State Department role are examined by Duncan L. Clarke in his essay, "Why State Can't Lead." Although some secretaries of state have played a leading role in formulating and directing foreign policy, Clarke notes, the State Department rarely does, because of "the gap between what presidents want and expect and what they come to believe State can or will give them." Presidents "expect loyalty, responsiveness to their needs and directives, an opportunity to exercise foreign-policy leadership, and sensitivity to their domestic political requirements. No recent president has found the department able or willing to perform as expected." When presidents find the State Department unable to meet their needs, they turn elsewhere, notably to their own personal staff members.

The State Department also "encounters vehement resistance from other departments when the policy issues it tries to control affect their areas of jurisdictional responsibility and interest." Yet it is at a competitive disadvantage in dealing with them. Unlike the Department of Defense and unlike other primarily domestically oriented organizations such as the Agriculture, Commerce, Treasury, and Labor departments, the State Department has few domestic clientele groups (supporters of bureaucratic agencies who are served by or receive benefits from the organizations) to defend and support it. Because its principal focus is on foreign countries, it speaks by definition to a broad but weak *national* constituency rather than to particular, specialized interests. In contrast, the other departments and agencies have linkages with domestic political groups that give them important political influence in an environment where policy-making is politics. Furthermore, because of its relatively small size, the State Department often lacks bureaucratic muscle in dealing with other organizations and thus finds itself bargaining from a position of weakness rather than strength.

Congress is often a participant in the jockeying for power and influence that occurs among bureaucratic agencies, as well as a focal point of interest-group efforts to lobby the government for particular policies and programs. Our next three essays provide insight into how these intensely political processes are played out.

We begin with an essay by Thomas E. Cronin, a leading presidential scholar, entitled "President, Congress, and American Foreign Policy." Cronin addresses the constitutional provisions relating to the role of the Congress and the president in foreign policy-making and the way the abuse of power by many recent presidents has stimulated Congress to define a more assertive role in foreign policy-making. Interestingly, Cronin notes that many of these efforts amount more to constraints on presidential behavior than to means to define a larger congressional role. Congressional war powers and efforts to oversee the CIA are among the specific policy areas examined, and the reasons underlying the rise and subsequent decline of the Reagan presidency's influence over Congress are given attention.

Cronin concludes his examination of the political tug-of-war between Congress and the president with the observation that Congress is ill-equipped to play a national leadership role: "Assuredly, Congress is a splendid forum that represents and registers the diversity of America. But that very virtue makes it difficult for Congress to provide leadership and difficult for it to challenge and bargain effectively with presidents. . . . Congress has regained some of its lost power, and it has tried to curb the misuse and abuse of power—but it has not really weakened the presidency." Cronin adds the admonition that "Both the president and Congress have to recognize they are not supposed to be two sides out to 'win' but two parts of the same government, both elected to pursue together the interests of the American people."

Congressional restrictions on presidential power are often viewed as efforts to redress the balance of power over foreign policy-making by giving Congress a greater voice. In fact, the Constitution lodges considerable authority over foreign policy in the Congress. In addition to general legislative powers that grant Congress nearly limitless authority to affect the flow and form of foreign relations, Congress is authorized constitutionally to deal with the regulation of international commerce, the punishment of piracies and felonies committed on the high seas and of offenses against the law of nations, and declarations of war. Congressional power to appropriate funds from the Treasury and to tax and spend for the common defense and the general welfare are also powerfully important to the conduct of foreign affairs. Thus, while the president bears primary responsibility for the conduct of foreign affairs, Congress has the capacity to subtly affect presidential behavior.

The ability of Congress to place its imprint on the nation's foreign policy is enhanced when the president decides to formalize relations with a foreign power in the form of a treaty. Senate approval is then required—which gives a minority of only thirty-four senators power to veto a presidential initiative.

In "Politics over Promise: Domestic Impediments to Arms Control," Steven E. Miller includes consideration of "the politics of ratification" in his examination of the domestic impediments to achieving arms-control agreements with other nations. He begins his inquiry with a useful discussion of the long history of U.S. efforts to negotiate arms-limitation agreements with others, concluding, however, that "arms control has not lived up to its promise." Domestic politics, he argues, is the primary culprit.

In addition to the politics of ratification, Miller concludes that the number of players in the game (each of whom has important bureaucratic stakes in the issue, and therefore bargains intensely to influence the outcome), the disruptions caused by the electoral cycle, and public attitudes toward arms control all shape the domestic political climate in which arms-control efforts must be hammered out. His conclusion will not please advocates of arms control: "Any agreement that successfully runs the gauntlet of impediments will necessarily be modest in impact—otherwise it would not have survived."

We conclude Part II with a focus on congressional-executive interactions in the area of foreign economic policy-making. Using the concept of "intermestic issues," which refers "to those matters of international relations which . . . closely involve the domestic economy," Ryan J. Barilleaux examines—in his essay "The President, 'Intermestic' Issues, and the Risks of Policy Leadership"—two instances of economic policy-making—the Trade Expansion Act of 1962, and the Trade Act of 1970—in an effort to determine the factors that influence successful presidential policy-making. His conclusion from these cases is that the domestic political environment will powerfully affect outcomes. The risks a president faces will also affect outcomes, and these, argues Barilleaux, will be greater in intermestic than in traditional foreign policy issues, because the interests affected are not only foreign but also domestic. In examining these interests, with all the risks—and, indeed, opportunities—they present presidents, Barilleaux provides important insight into the politics of policy-making in an issue area that has assumed increased importance in the United States in recent years, and thereby illuminates the ways in which American foreign policy often springs from domestic sources.

NOTES

1. Arthur M. Schlesinger, Jr., *The Imperial Presidency* (Boston: Houghton Mifflin, 1973).

8. THE PRESIDENT AND THE MANAGEMENT OF FOREIGN POLICY: STYLES AND MODELS

Alexander L. George

Every new president faces the task of deciding how to structure and manage high-level foreign-policymaking in his administration. The task is a formidable one since responsibility for different aspects of national security and foreign policy is distributed over a number of departments and agencies. Relevant information, competence, and influence over policy is widely dispersed within the executive branch as well as outside of it. This imposes on the president and his assistants the task of mobilizing available information, expertise, and analytical resources for effective policymaking. In addition, the president and his closest associates have the responsibility for providing policy initiative and coherence throughout the executive branch.

To discharge these tasks effectively requires internal coordination within the government. Those parts of the executive branch that have some responsibility for and/or contribution to make to a particular policy problem must be encouraged to interact with each other in appropriate ways. Left to themselves, these various agencies, of course, would interact voluntarily and achieve some measure of "lateral coordination" in formulating policy. But it is essential for the president (and each department or agency head) to ensure lateral coordination by institution of various procedures and mechanisms, such as ad hoc or standing interdepartmental committees, policy conferences, liaison arrangements, a system of clearances for policy or position papers, etc.

However important lateral coordination is, it cannot be counted upon to produce the caliber of policy analysis, the level of consensus, and the procedures for implementation required for an effective and coherent foreign policy.

Moreover, lateral coordination may be weakened and distorted by patterns of organizational behavior and the phenomenon of "bureaucratic politics" that create impediments to and malfunctions of the policy-making process. Accordingly, all presidents have found it necessary to impose mechanisms for control and coordination of policy analysis and implementation from above—either from the White House itself or from the NSC—or have fixed responsibility for achieving control and coordination with the State Department; or have adopted a combination of these mechanisms.

Note: Some footnotes have been deleted, and others have been renumbered to appear in consecutive order.

The traditional practice for seeking improvement in the performance of the foreign-policymaking system was to undertake *structural reorganization* of the agencies and the mechanisms for achieving their coordination and cooperation. Periodically—indeed, at least once in each presidential administration—the foreign-policymaking system was reorganized. But the results of reorganizations have been so disappointing that the "organizational tinkering" approach has fallen into general disrepute. Instead, greater attention is being given to the *design and management of the processes* of policymaking. . . .

. . . [T]he first and foremost task that a new president faces is to learn to define his own role in the policy-making system; only then can he structure and manage the roles and relationships within the policy-making system of his secretary of state, the special assistant for national security affairs, the secretary of defense, and other cabinet and agency heads with responsibilities for the formulation and implementation of foreign policy.

The president's basic choice is whether to give his secretary of state the primary role in the foreign-policymaking system or to centralize and manage that system from the White House itself. Still another model is that of a relatively decentralized system that is coordinated from the White House for the president by his special assistant for national security affairs.

A new president may receive advice on these matters from specialists in organization or in foreign policy, but in the last analysis his choices in these matters will be shaped by preferences of his own that stem from previous experience (if any) in executive roles and the extent to which he regards himself as knowledgeable and competent in foreign policy and national security matters. Finally, as all president-watchers have emphasized, the incumbent's personality will shape the formal structure of the policy-making system that he creates around himself and, even more, it will influence the ways in which he encourages and permits that formal structure to operate in practice. As a result, each president is likely to develop a policy-making system and a management style that contain distinctive and idiosyncratic elements.

Detailed comparison of past presidents from this standpoint suggests that a variety of personality characteristics are important, of which three can be briefly noted. The first of these personality dimensions is *"cognitive style."* Cognitive psychologists have found it useful to view the human mind as a complex system for information processing. Every individual develops ways of storing, retrieving, evaluating, and using information. At the same time the individual develops a set of beliefs about the environment, about the attributes of other actors, and about various presumed causal relationships that help the person to explain and predict, as best he can (correctly or incorrectly), events of interest to him. Beliefs of this kind structure, order, and simplify the individual's world; they serve as models of "reality." Such mental constructs play an important role in the individual's perception of what is occurring in his environment, in the acquisition and interpretation of new information, and in the formulation and evaluation of responses to new situations.

. . . For present purposes, the term is used to refer to the way in which an executive such as the president defines his informational needs for purposes of making decisions. "Cognitive style" also refers to his preferred ways of acquiring information from those around him and making use of that information, and to his preferences regarding advisers and ways of using them in making his decisions. . . .

A second personality dimension that influences a president's choice of a policy-making system is *his sense of efficacy and competence* as it relates to management and decisionmaking tasks. In other words, the types of skills that he possesses and the types of tasks that he feels particularly adept at doing and those that he feels poorly equipped to do will influence the way in which he defines his executive role.

A third personality dimension that will influence the president's selection of a policy-making model is his general *orientation toward political conflict* and, related to this, toward interpersonal conflict over policy among his advisers. Individuals occupying the White House have varied on this personality dimension, too. Thus, we find that some chief executives have viewed politics as a necessary, useful, and perhaps even enjoyable game while other presidents have regarded it as a dirty business that must be discouraged or at least ignored. The personal attitude toward conflict that a president brings into office is likely to determine his orientation to the phenomena of "cabinet politics" and "bureaucratic politics" within his administration as well as to the larger, often interlinked, game of politics surrounding the executive branch. Individuals with a pronounced distaste for "dirty politics" and for being exposed to face-to-face disagreements among advisers are likely to favor policy-making systems that attempt to curb these phenomena or at least shield them from direct exposure. They also are likely to prefer staff and advisory systems in which teamwork or formal analytical procedures are emphasized in lieu of partisan advocacy and debate.

Cognitive style, sense of efficacy, and orientation toward conflict (and, of course, the nature of any prior experience in executive roles and the level of personal competence and interest in foreign policy and national security affairs)—all these combine to determine how a new president will structure the policymaking system around him and how he will define his own role and that of others in it.

Three management models have been identified that characterize at least in general terms the approaches displayed by different presidents in recent times.[1] These are the "formalistic," "competitive," and "collegial" models. The formalistic model is characterized by an orderly policymaking structure, one that provides well-defined procedures, hierarchical lines of communication, and a structured staff system. While the formalistic model seeks to benefit from the diverse views and judgments of participants in policymaking, it also discourages open conflict and bargaining among them.

The competitive model, in contrast, places a premium on encouraging a more open and uninhibited expression of diverse opinions, analysis, and advice. To this end the competitive model not only tolerates but may actually encourage organizational ambiguity, overlapping jurisdictions, and multiple channels of communication to and from the president.

The collegial model, in turn, attempts to achieve the essential advantages of each of the other two while avoiding their pitfalls. To this end, the president attempts to create a team of staff members and advisers who will work together to identify, analyze, and solve policy problems in ways that will incorporate and synthesize as much as possible divergent points of view. The collegial model attempts to benefit from diversity and competition within the policymaking system, but it also attempts to avoid narrow parochialism by encouraging cabinet officers and advisers to identify at least partly with the presidential perspective. And by encouraging collegial participation in group problem-solving efforts, this approach attempts to avoid the worst excesses of infighting, bargaining, and compromise associated with the competitive model.

Truman, Eisenhower, and Nixon employed one or another variant of the formalistic approach. Franklin D. Roosevelt employed the competitive model, and John F. Kennedy the collegial one. As for Lyndon B. Johnson, he began by trying to emulate Franklin Roosevelt's style and gradually moved toward a formalistic approach but one that exhibited idiosyncratic features.

Let us begin with Franklin D. Roosevelt, whose unusual policy-making system is the prototype for the competitive management model. A dominant feature of FDR's personality was his strong sense of political efficacy. He felt entirely at home in the presidency, acting in the belief that there was close to a perfect fit between his competence and skills and some of the most demanding role requirements of the office. Then, too, FDR viewed politics and the games that go with it as a useful and enjoyable game and not, as others before him (for example, Taft and Hoover) as an unsavory, distasteful business to be discouraged or avoided. FDR not only felt comfortable in the presence of conflict and disagreement around him; he saw that, properly managed, it could serve his informational and political needs. Instead of trying, as his predecessor had, to take the politics out of the policy-making process, Roosevelt deliberately exacerbated the competitive and conflicting aspects of cabinet politics and bureaucratic politics. He sought to increase both structural and functional ambiguities within the executive branch in order to better preside over it. . . . Roosevelt did not attempt to create a formal, centralized model of the policy-making process (as advocated, for example, in later Hoover Commission proposals for reorganization of governmental agencies); rather, he deliberately created "fuzzy lines of responsibility, no clear chains of command, overlapping jurisdictions" in order to promote " 'stimulating' interdepartmental conflict which could and did eventually land in his own lap."[2]

At the risk of simplification, it is possible to delineate some features of the distinctive communication network or patterns associated with FDR's competitive model[3] (see Figure 1).

The following are characteristic features of the competitive model (FDR): (1) the president deliberately encourages competition and conflict among advisers and cabinet heads by giving them overlapping assignments and ambiguous, conflicting jurisdictions in given policy areas; (2) there is relatively little communication or collaboration among advisers; (3) the president reaches down on occasion to communicate directly with subordinates of cabinet heads to get independent advice and information; (4) relevant information on important policy problems is forced up through the network to the president himself; competing advisers are forced to bring important policy problems to the president for resolution and decision; but (5) the president avoids the risk of becoming overloaded or involved by operating this system selectively; on occasions (not depicted on the chart), he encourages and insists that subordinate officials settle things themselves and refuses to become identified with their policies or pet projects.

Harry Truman adopted a different strategy for coping with the complex morass that governmental structure had become as a result of Roosevelt's style and administrative practices and the wartime expansion of agencies. Initially, Truman tried to tidy up the mess by clarifying and dividing up the jurisdictions.

Figure 1. The Competitive Model (FDR)

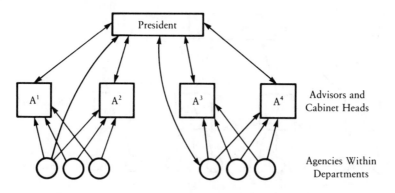

He also established the NSC in 1947 as a vehicle for providing orderly, balanced participation in foreign-policymaking deliberations. Truman tried to weaken the game of bureaucratic politics by strengthening each department head's control over his particular domain and by delegating presidential responsibility to him. New in the office, Truman took special pride in his ability to delegate responsibility and to back up those he trusted. He learned through experience, however, that to delegate too much or to delegate responsibility without providing clear guidance was to jeopardize the performance of his own responsibilities.

When faced with larger policy issues that required the participation of heads of several departments, Truman attempted to deal with them by playing the role of chairman of the board, hearing sundry expert opinions on each aspect of the problem, then making a synthesis of them and announcing the decision. Truman not only accepted the responsibility of making difficult decisions, he liked doing so for it enabled him to satisfy himself—and, he hoped, others—that he had the personal qualities needed in the presidency. His sense of efficacy expressed itself in a willingness to make difficult decisions without experiencing without undue stress. A modest man in many ways, Truman adjusted to the awesome responsibilities of the presidency suddenly thrust upon him by respecting the office and determining to become a good role player. By honoring the office and doing credit to it, he would do credit to himself. Included in this role conception was Truman's desire to put aside personal and political considerations as much as possible in the search for quality decisions that were in the national interest. He was willing to accept the political costs both to himself and to his party entailed in making controversial decisions, such as his policy of disengaging the United States from the Chinese Nationalists in 1949, his refusal to escalate the Korean War after the Chinese Communist intervention, his firing of General MacArthur, and his refusal to dismiss his loyal secretary of state, Dean Acheson, when he came under continuing attack.

Truman's variant of the formalistic model may be depicted, again in simplified terms, as in Figure 2.

The following are characteristic features of the formalistic model (Truman): (1) specialized information and advice flows to the president from each of his cabinet heads and advisers; (2) the president tends to define the role of each cabinet head as a functional expert on some aspect of national security or

Figure 2. The Formalistic Model (Truman)

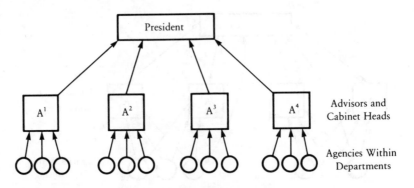

foreign policy; each official briefs the president authoritatively on that aspect of a policy problem for which he has jurisdiction; (3) each adviser receives information and advice from his subordinate units; (4) the president does not encourage his advisers to communicate with each other or to engage in joint efforts at policy analysis and problem solving; (5) the president sticks to channels and seldom reaches down to bypass a cabinet head to get independent information or advice from one of his subordinates; and (6) the president takes responsibility for intellectual synthesis of specialized inputs on a policy problem received from his advisers.

Dwight D. Eisenhower avoided personal involvement as much as possible in the bureaucratic politics aspects of policymaking within the executive branch and in less savory aspects of politics generally. At the same time, however, Eisenhower recognized that conflict and politics are inevitable and adapted to them by defining his own role as that of someone who could stand "above politics," moderate conflict, and promote unity. In doing so, Eisenhower expressed his special sense of efficacy that led him (and others) to believe that he could make a distinctive and unique contribution by seeming to remain "above politics" and by emphasizing the shared values and virtues that should guide governmental affairs. This did not prevent Eisenhower, however, from engaging in political maneuvers of his own when he perceived that his interest required it.[4]

Eisenhower did not attempt (as Nixon was to later) to depoliticize and rationalize the formal policy-making process completely. Rather, Eisenhower's variant of the formalistic model encompassed advocacy and disagreement at lower levels of the policy-making system, even though he wanted subordinates eventually to achieve agreement, if possible, on recommendations for his consideration. Moreover, formal meetings of the large NSC were often preceded by less formal "warm-up" sessions with a smaller group of advisers that provided opportunities for genuine policy debate. . . .

. . . [T]he visible structure of [Eisenhower's] formalistic model differed from Truman's. This can be seen by comparing the chart for Truman's system with that presented here of Eisenhower's (see Figure 3).

The following are characteristic features of the formalistic model (Eisenhower); it is similar to Truman's variant of the formalistic model with two important exceptions: (1) a "chief of staff" position is created to be utilized,

Figure 3. The Formalistic Model (Eisenhower)

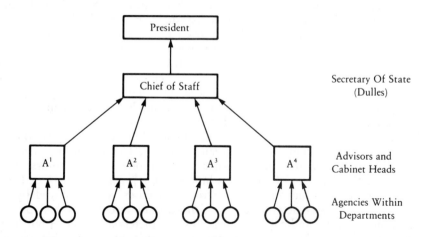

when the president wishes, as a buffer between himself and cabinet heads and to arrange for preparation of formal recommendations to the president (Sherman Adams performed this role for Eisenhower on domestic policy matters; in practice, Secretary of State John Foster Dulles came to assume a similar, though informal, role for Eisenhower in foreign policy, though not in defense matters); and (2) again, unlike Truman's version of the formalistic model, in this one the president attempts to protect himself from being overloaded by urging advisers and cabinet heads to analyze problems and resolve policy differences wherever possible at lower levels.

Richard Nixon, too, strongly favored a formalistic model. As a number of observers have noted, several of Nixon's well-defined personality characteristics shaped his management style and approach to decisionmaking. During his early years, Nixon had developed a cognitive style that enabled him to cope with deeply rooted personal insecurities by adopting an extremely conscientious approach to decisionmaking. As described so well in his book, *Six Crises,* the whole business of acquiring information, weighing alternatives, and deciding among them was experienced by him as extremely stressful, requiring great self-control, hard work, and reliance upon himself. Dealing with difficult situations posed the necessity but also offered an opportunity for Nixon to prove himself over and over again. He experienced his greatest sense of self and of his efficacy when he had to confront and master difficult situations in which a great deal was at stake.

Nixon's pronounced sense of aloneness and privacy, his thin-skinned sensitivity and vulnerability were not conducive to developing the kind of interpersonal relationships associated with a collegial model of management. Rather, as Richard T. Johnson notes, "Nixon, the private man with a preference for working alone, wanted machinery to staff out the options but provide plenty of time for reflection. . . ." Similarly, "with his penchant for order," Nixon inevitably "favored men who offered order," who acceded to his demand for loyalty and shared his sense of banding together to help him cope with a hostile environment.[5]

Nixon's preference for a highly formalistic system was reinforced by other personality characteristics. He was an extreme "conflict avoider"; somewhat paradoxically, although quite at home with political conflict in the broader public arena, Nixon had a pronounced distaste for being exposed to it face-to-face. Early in his administration, Nixon tried a version of multiple advocacy in which leading advisers would debate issues in his presence. But he quickly abandoned the experiment and turned to structuring his staff to avoid overt manifestations of disagreement and to avoid being personally drawn into the squabbles of his staff, hence, Nixon's need for a few staff aides immediately around him who were to serve as buffers and enable him to distance himself from the wear and tear of policymaking.

It is interesting that Eisenhower's "chief of staff" concept was carried much farther in Nixon's variant of the formalistic model. The foreign-policymaking system that Kissinger, the special assistant for national security affairs, developed during the first year of Nixon's administration is generally regarded as by far the most centralized and highly structured model yet employed by any president. Nixon was determined even more than Eisenhower had been to abolish bureaucratic and cabinet politics as completely as possible; but, more so than Eisenhower, Nixon also wanted to enhance and protect his personal control over high policy. To this end, a novel system of six special committees was set up operating out of the NSC, each of which was chaired by Kissinger. These included the Vietnam Special Studies Group, the Washington Special Actions Group (to deal with international crises), the Defense Programs Review Committee, the Verification Panel (to deal with strategic arms talks), the 40 Committee (to deal with covert actions), and the Senior Review Group (which dealt with all other types of policy issues).

Reporting to the Senior Review Group were six lower-level interdepartmental groups that were set up on a regional basis (Middle East, Far East, Latin America, Africa, Europe, and Political-Military Affairs), each of which was headed by an assistant secretary of state. In addition, Kissinger could set up ad hoc working groups composed of specialists from various agencies and run by his own top staff aides.

Thus, not only did Kissinger's committee structure reach down into the departments and agencies, absorbing key personnel into various committees controlled by Kissinger or his staff aides, but other committees created on an interdepartmental basis, though chaired by assistant secretaries of state, were given their assignments by Kissinger and reported to the Senior Review Group chaired by Kissinger. As a result, a novel, unconventional policy-making structure was created and superimposed upon the departments and largely superseded the traditional hierarchical policy-making system. Striking differences with Eisenhower's formalistic model can be noted (see Figure 4).

John F. Kennedy felt much more at ease with the conflictual aspects of politics and policymaking than his predecessor Dwight Eisenhower; his sense of efficacy included confidence in his ability to manage and shape the interpersonal relations of those around him in a constructive fashion, and his cognitive style led him to participate much more actively and directly in the policy-making process than Eisenhower had or Nixon would later on. These personality characteristics contributed to forging a collegial style of policymaking based on teamwork and shared responsibility among talented advisers. Kennedy recognized the value of diversity and give-and-take among advisers, and he encouraged it. But Kennedy stopped well short of the extreme measures for stimulat-

Figure 4. The Formalistic Model (Nixon)

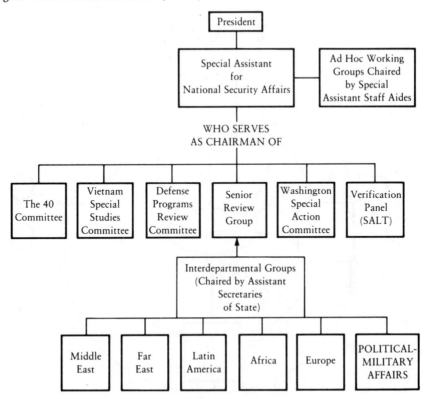

ing competition that Roosevelt had employed. Rather than risk introducing disorder and strife into the policy-making system, Kennedy used other strategies for keeping himself informed, properly advised, and "on top." He did not find personally congenial the highly formal procedures, the large meetings, and the relatively aloof presidential role characteristic of Eisenhower's system. Particularly after the failure of the Bay of Pigs invasion of Cuba, Kennedy employed a variety of devices for counteracting the narrowness of perspective of leading members of individual departments and agencies and for protecting himself from the risks of bureaucratic politics. . . .

The kind of teamwork and group approach to problem solving that Kennedy strove to create—and achieved with notable success in the Cuban missile crisis (1962) at least—is often referred to as the "collegial" model to distinguish it both from the more competitive and more formal system of his predecessors. The sharp contrasts between Kennedy's collegial system and the competitive and formalistic models emerge by comparing Figure 5 with Figures 1–4.

The following are characteristic features of the collegial model (JFK): (1) president is at the center of a wheel with spokes connecting to individual advisers and cabinet heads; (2) advisers form a "collegial team" and engage in group problem-solving; (3) information flows into the collegial team from various points lower in the bureaucracy; (4) advisers do not perform as individual filters

Figure 5. The Collegial Model (JFK)

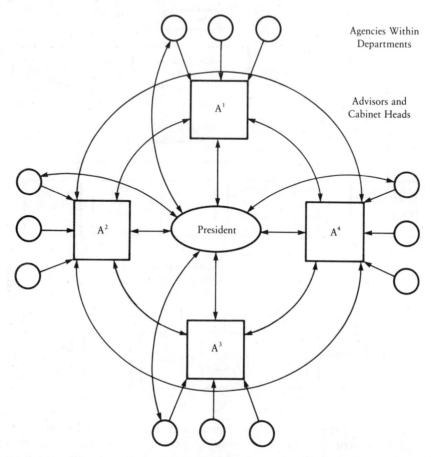

Agencies Within
Departments

Advisors and
Cabinet Heads

to the president; rather, the group of advisers functions as a "debate team" that considers information and policy options from the multiple, conflicting perspectives of the group members in an effort to obtain cross-fertilization and creative problem solving; (5) advisers are encouraged to act as generalists, concerned with all aspects of the policy problem, rather than as experts or functional specialists on only one part of the policy problem; (6) discussion procedures are kept informal enough to encourage frank expression of views and judgments and to avoid impediments to information processing generated by status and power differences among members; and (7) the president occasionally gives overlapping assignments and occasionally reaches down to communicate directly with subordinates of cabinet heads in order to get more information and independent advice.

As for Jimmy Carter, his management style is perhaps aptly characterized as embracing elements of both the collegial and bureaucratic models. As one observer reported, Carter's national security policymaking system [was] "an amalgamation selectively drawn from the experiences of his predecessors."[6] As in Kennedy's case, Carter initially rejected a "chief of staff" system for organizing his work and contacts with others. (Hamilton Jordan was appointed chief of staff in mid-1979.) Instead, Carter clearly preferred a communications structure in which he was at the center of the wheel with opportunity for direct contact with a number of officials and advisers. Further, again like Kennedy, Carter preferred to be actively involved in the policy-making process and at earlier stages before the system produced options or a single recommended policy for his consideration.

At the same time, Carter differed from Kennedy in preferring a formally structured NSC system and retained elements of the "formal options" system developed by Kissinger for Nixon. Carter restored the prestige of the NSC staff following the brief eclipse that occurred during the Ford years (1974–1977) when Kissinger was secretary of state, and he relied on its studies for help in making decisions. Carter's preference for underpinning the collegial features of his management model with formalistic structure and procedures was not surprising given his training and experience as an engineer. Carter brought with him to the White House a cognitive style and sense of personal efficacy that gave him confidence in the possibility of mastering difficult problems and of finding comprehensive "solutions" for them.[7] In his somewhat technocratic approach to policymaking, experts and orderly study procedures played an essential role, and so the features of the collegial model that Carter valued had necessarily to be blended somehow with features of a formalistic model.

In this mixed system, policymaking was not as highly centralized as in the Nixon administration. Carter not only allowed relatively liberal access to the Oval Office, he also had a more decentralized advisory system than did Nixon. This reflected not only his personality and management style, but also the lessons that he and others drew from the experience of his predecessors in that office. Carter's main concern was to set up his foreign-policy machinery in a way that would avoid the extreme centralization of power that Kissinger, as special assistant for national security affairs, had acquired during Nixon's first term and that led him to replace for all practical purposes the secretary of state. . . .

Although Carter succeeded in avoiding a highly centralized, "closed" system of foreign-policymaking, it must also be said that he was much less successful in avoiding the potential difficulties of the mixed formalistic-collegial model that he preferred. A number of weaknesses became evident in the Carter system that seriously affected its performance. The collegial model requires close contact and continuing interaction between the president, his secretary of state, and the assistant for national security affairs. This they achieved, at least for a time, but their respective roles remained highly fluid and not well defined. There was, for example, no clear arrangement for policy specialization and division of labor among these three principals. (In contrast, the secretary of defense's role appears to have been well enough understood by all concerned so that his participation on policymaking was relatively free of serious ambiguities or conflicts with others.) In the absence of role definition and specialization, all three—the president, his secretary of state, and the national security assistant—can and do interest themselves in any important policy problem. A shared interest in all major policy problems is to be expected in a collegial system, but some understandings must also be developed to regulate initiative, consultation, the articulation of disagreements, and the formulation of collective judgment. Carter evidently counted on the fact that the three men knew and respected each other prior to his election to the presidency to make his collegial approach work. And, to be sure, on the surface it genuinely seemed to be the case that the three men got along well. More than cordiality, however, is needed for effective policymaking in a collegial system.

Collegiality entails certain risks, and its preservation may exact a price. Some evidence indicates that the preservation of cordiality was accompanied, at least in the first part of Carter's administration, with a perhaps partly unconscious tendency to subordinate disagreements over policy among the three men that should have been articulated, confronted, and dealt with in a timely fashion. One of the problems was Carter himself. He had a habit of suddenly taking the initiative or intervening in an important foreign-policy matter, as in the case of his human rights initiative, leaving Vance and Brzezinski with the embarrassing and difficult task of making the best of it or of trying to modify the policy.

Another weakness of Carter's system quickly developed and proved difficult to cope with. Foreign policy became badly fragmented in the first year of Carter's administration. It was characterized by (1) overactivism—the floating of many specific policy initiatives within a relatively short period of time; (2) a tendency to initiate attractive, desirable policies without sufficient attention to their feasibility; (3) poor conceptualization of overall foreign policy, and, related to this, a failure to recognize that individual policies conflicted with each other; (4) a poor sense of strategy and tactics; (5) a badly designed and managed policy-making system.

These flaws cannot be attributed merely or even primarily to Carter's inexperience in foreign policy. After all, his administration included various high-level officials who were experts on foreign policy. Part of the explanation had to do with important aspects of his personality, which are attractive in and of themselves. Carter was a man of high moral principles, as exemplified by his sincere commitment to human rights. He wanted to imbue American foreign policy with renewed moral purpose; he was an activist in this respect, and therefore took genuine pleasure that his administration could launch so many worthwhile policy initiatives so quickly. He could see no harm in pushing ahead simultaneously with so many good initiatives.

What was needed to safeguard against an overloading of the foreign policy agenda and the fragmentation of foreign policy was a strong policy planning and coordinating mechanism, one that would alert Carter to this problem and assist him in dealing with difficult trade-offs among conflicting policy initiatives by establishing priorities, and generally to better integrate the various strands of overall foreign policy. Such a policy planning and coordinating mechanism, however, was lacking. The need to develop it somehow fell between the two stools of Carter's mixed collegial-formalistic model. Thus, neither the formalistic nor the collegial components of Carter's system provided the necessary planning-coordinating mechanism and procedures. . . .

Another problem was that Vance and Brzezinski did have important disagreements over policy, particularly on matters having to do with assessment of Soviet intentions and the best strategy and tactics for dealing with the Soviet Union. The effort to preserve collegiality in the first eighteen months of the administration may have led both men to paper over their disagreements and to avoid the difficult but necessary task of coming to grips with these fundamental policy questions. But these matters could not be avoided indefinitely, and after jockeying and competing with each other to influence Carter's position on these issues, first one way and then the other, the controversy between Vance and Brzezinski spilled out into the open—with Brzezinski aggressively speaking out to undermine the positions taken by the secretary of state. Among other things, Brzezinski wanted the administration to exploit the Sino-Soviet conflict, "play the China card," in order to exert pressure on the Soviets. . . . Ultimately, of course, Vance left the administration in 1980 because of his disagreement with Carter's decision, supported by Brzezinski, to attempt a military rescue of American diplomatic personnel held hostage in Iran.

But the roots of the problem lie deeper. It has to do with the question whether an expert on foreign policy, someone who wants to influence foreign policy, should be put into the position of assistant for national security affairs. . . . Until Kennedy became president, the person who served as assistant for national security affairs was not an adviser on policy; rather, he was supposed to confine himself exclusively to being a neutral, efficient, sophisticated manager of the process and the flow of work. Since then, the assistant, while retaining the role of custodian-manager of the process, has gradually acquired important new roles—that of a major policy adviser himself, that of public spokesman for and defender of the administration's foreign policy, and that of an operator actively engaged in the conduct of diplomacy.

This development came to a head with Kissinger, who as Nixon's national security assistant, acquired and tried to perform *all* of these roles. The result was not only that he was overloaded, but also that he experienced serious conflict among these various roles. The most important role conflict was that Kissinger's roles as the major policy adviser and operator undermined his incentive to serve as the *neutral* custodian-manager of the process. Instead, being only human and quite self-confident regarding his own judgment in foreign policy, Kissinger succumbed to the temptation of using his control of the many NSC committees and over the policy-making process in order to enhance his influence with Nixon at the expense of others in the system who may have had different views. It was predictable that Brzezinski would experience similar temptations.

There were other weaknesses in the management of Carter's foreign-policy system. Under Brzezinski, and given the character of his staff, the NSC did not function effectively to help coordinate the various strands of foreign policy and to help Carter with his difficult task of managing the various contradictions and trade-offs between different foreign-policy objectives. Neither Brzezinski himself nor his deputy, David Aaron, earned a reputation in their positions for being good administrators or for defining their roles as high-level staff rather than as activists in making policy. In fact, both appear to have been much more interested in influencing policy rather than in managing the policymaking process in a neutral, efficient manner. Moreover, many of the people Brzezinski brought into the NSC staff to work with him were also eager to influence policy as best they could from the vantage point of the White House.

As a result, the fragmentation of foreign policy at the conceptual level, to which many critics called attention, was reinforced by the failure to develop an effective central coordinating mechanism for the organization and management of the policy-making process. Beginning in the second year of his administration, Carter turned increasingly to the creation of special task forces for each major policy issue in order to centralize authority in the White House and to improve coordination of agency and department officials on behalf of presidential policy. Following the successful use of ad hoc task forces to direct efforts to secure ratification of the Panama Canal Treaty and to deal with other major issues, in late 1978 Carter established an executive committee headed by Vice President Mondale to be responsible for dealing with the president's agenda and priorities. This committee endorsed a plan for forming task forces for all major presidential issues for 1979. Task forces were established on a dozen issues of high priority, including domestic as well as foreign-policy issues.

Each of these three management models tends to have certain advantages and to incur certain risks. These are discussed in some detail by Richard T. Johnson with respect to each of the six presidents he studied (see Table 1)[8]. . . .

Table 1. Three Management Methods

Formalistic Approach

Benefits	Costs
Orderly decision process enforces more thorough analysis.	The hierarchy which screens information may also distort it. Tendency of the screening process to wash out or distort political pressures and public sentiments.
Conserves the decisionmaker's time and attention for the big decision.	
Emphasizes the optimal.	Tendency to respond slowly or inappropriately in crisis.

Competitive Approach

Places the decisionmaker in the mainstream of the information network.	Places large demands on decisionmaker's time and attention.
Tends to generate solutions that are politically feasible and bureaucratically doable.	Exposes decisionmaker to partial or biased information. Decision process may overly sacrifice optimality for doability.
Generates creative ideas, partially as a result of the "stimulus" of competition, but also because this unstructured kind of information network is more open to ideas from the outside.	Tendency to aggravate staff competition with the risk that aides may pursue their own interests at the expense of the decisionmaker.
	Wear and tear on aides fosters attrition and high turnover.

Collegial Approach

Seeks to achieve both optimality and doability.	Places substantial demands on the decisionmaker's time and attention.
Involves the decisionmaker in the information network but somewhat eases the demands upon him by stressing teamwork over competition.	Requires unusual interpersonal skill in dealing with subordinates, mediating differences, and maintaining teamwork among colleagues.
	Risk that "teamwork" will degenerate into a closed system of mutual support.

Source: Richard T. Johnson, *Managing the White House* (New York: Harper and Row, 1974). Reproduced with minor changes and additions in *The Stanford Business School Alumni Bulletin,* Fall 1973.

Over the years, as the foreign-policy activities in which the U.S. government is engaged have multiplied, the organizational arrangements for dealing with them within the executive branch have proliferated. To some extent, the sheer magnitude and complexity of the foreign-policy enterprise forces every modern president to rely at least to some extent on formalistic procedures. It would be difficult in the modern era for even so gifted a politician and leader as Franklin Roosevelt to rely heavily on a competitive model. Of particular importance, therefore, are . . . variants of formalistic models that . . . attempt to make use of elements of the competitive and/or collegial models as well. . . .

POSTSCRIPT: THE REAGAN ADMINISTRATION

Even before Ronald Reagan took office in January 1981 he indicated that he would reduce the scope and functions of the office of the assistant for national security affairs in order to avoid a repetition of the damaging competitive relationship that had developed between Brzezinski and Secretary of State Vance in the Carter administration. . . .

It was also evident, even before he appointed Alexander Haig as secretary of state, that President Reagan wished to create a foreign-policymaking system centered in the State Department rather than in the White House, and that he would select a strong, dominant specialist in foreign affairs for that position. The appointment of Richard Allen as assistant for national security affairs and the public characterization of the role he would play seemed entirely consistent with this objective. Although knowledgeable in foreign affairs, Allen did not enter office with the intellectual stature of Kissinger or Brzezinski. . . . The basis for a renewal of conflict between the secretary of state and the assistant for national security affairs in the new administration seemed to have been removed both by the sharp downgrading of the special assistant's role and by the nature of the appointments made to fill the two positions.

However, for various reasons, many of them of a quite unexpected nature, Reagan's State Department-centered foreign policy system did not work as effectively and smoothly as expected. . . . Haig did have the confidence and respect of the president, but he lacked the close association and long-standing friendship that was enjoyed by such long-time Reagan advisers as Edwin Meese, who had been appointed to the key position of counselor to the president, and Michael Deaver, who was serving as assistant to the president and deputy chief of staff. Meese and Deaver, along with James Baker, stood closest to the president in the White House. (Baker, appointed as chief of staff, had joined Reagan's inner circle after working for George Bush in his 1980 presidential campaign.) Haig's undisguised presidential ambitions (he had tested the water in the early stages of the 1980 contest for the Republican nomination) could hardly have encouraged a sanguine view on the part of the Meese-Deaver-Baker troika concerning the wisdom of allowing the secretary to put himself squarely astride the foreign-policymaking system in a way that might have overshadowed the White House. In the months that followed the inauguration, indications of conflict between Haig and Allen and their staffs began to appear in the media.

That conflict should develop among Reagan's foreign policy team was not surprising or unexpected. Reagan had entered the White House without a well-developed set of position papers on security matters and foreign policy, such as challengers for office usually prepare during their presidential campaigns. Indeed, his campaign advisers had decided not to attempt to articulate specific positions in order not to expose the latent disagreements among his supporters. While all his major foreign policy and security advisers shared the general view that a "tougher" posture toward the Soviet Union should be adopted and that U.S. military capabilities should be "strengthened," this so-called consensus was a shallow one that only thinly covered major disagreements concerning specific strategies and policies that should be adopted. Inevitably, therefore, intense competition set in among different factions within Reagan's administration to shape and control specific policies, a struggle that was to prove time-consuming and costly. Indeed the administration soon became vulnerable to criticism that it was slow in formulating policy on key defense and diplomatic issues and lacked a coherent, consistent foreign policy.

While Haig was anointed by Reagan as his leading foreign policy adviser—his "vicar of foreign policy," as Haig referred to himself—the secretary of state found it difficult to take firm hold of the fragmented foreign policy apparatus. . . . Operating from the State Department, Haig lacked the advantages that a position in the White House would have provided, and he could not count on its firm, consistent support. Haig's own more moderate foreign policy views and some of his early appointments to positions of influence in the department marked him in the eyes of those who were to the right of him in the Reagan entourage, in Congress, and among attentive opinion leaders. This included the secretary of defense, Caspar Weinberger, one of Reagan's longstanding political friends, and a number of Weinberger's associates in the Defense Department.

Even if Allen had been neutral in the policy competition that increasingly developed between Weinberger and Haig, he was ill-equipped to play the role of a strong custodian-manager of the top-level foreign-policy-making system. Allen's office had been so downgraded in importance that he did not have direct access to the president as had his predecessors in previous administrations. Rather, Allen reported to Meese, a man who lacked any experience in foreign policy and security affairs and who, besides, was concerned with formulation of all policy—domestic and economic as well as foreign. With the passage of time it became increasingly evident that the task of coordinating the policy-making process at the White House level could not be managed effectively through the existing organizational pattern. Visible evidence of feuding among leading foreign policy advisers damaged Reagan at home and abroad.

A final component of the explanation for the disappointing performance of Reagan's foreign-policymaking system during his first year in office had to do with the president himself. Not only did Reagan bring to the White House the same preference for a formalistic chief of staff system and a management style of broad delegation of responsibility to subordinates that he had displayed as governor of California; in addition, he was relatively disinterested in foreign policy and gave higher priority in the first year and a half of his presidency to his economic policies. Reagan counted upon collegiality among his top-level advisers to smooth the workings of his administration. But while collegiality was preserved and indeed played an important role in the workings of the inner circle composed of Meese, Deaver, and Baker, it did not spread outward to lubricate the interactions of the principal advisers in the security and foreign-policymaking system—Haig, Weinberger, and Allen.

What emerged, therefore, was not a well-designed, smoothly working system which, while centered in a strong secretary of state, was complemented, as indeed it should have been, by additional high-level coordination and linkage to the president himself through the assistant for national security affairs. Rather, what emerged was a fragmented, competitive, inadequately managed system in which distrust was ever present and which gave rise repeatedly to damaging intra-administration conflicts over policy. Unlike Roosevelt's competitive *system*, which was designed to bring important issues up to the presidential level and to improve the quality of information and advice available to a president who was interested and actively involved in making the important decisions, the competitive-conflictful features of Reagan's foreign policy machinery were the consequences of a poorly structured and inadequately managed system, one that did not engage the president's attention except sporadically when international developments required him to act or intra-administration conflicts got completely out of hand and required his personal attention.

To his credit and that of his leading advisers, Reagan, well before the end of his first year in office, recognized that his foreign-policymaking system was not working and that it required reorganization and change of personnel. Early in 1982 Allen was replaced by William Clark, a close friend and a former supreme court justice in California who had been serving as undersecretary of state under Haig. In addition, Reagan now strengthened the position of assistant for national security affairs; Clark would henceforth deal directly with the president on a daily basis and no longer report to Meese. A determined effort was made to enable Clark to discharge more effectively the traditional role of custodian-manager of the system.

During the first half of 1982 relations between Haig and Clark developed with a minimum of friction. Behind the scenes, however, lay still unresolved questions between the White House and State as to the direction and control of foreign policy, questions that were severely exacerbated by the clash of styles and personalities. With Secretary of State Haig's resignation in June 1982, it became evident that the new policy machinery created by the strengthening of the role of the assistant for national security affairs had not stabilized itself sufficiently to cope with new stresses that developed in connection with the president's trip to Europe and the Israeli invasion of Lebanon, both of which occurred in June.

Thus, within less than a year and a half after his inauguration, President Reagan was forced to replace both his national security assistant and his secretary of state, an unprecedented admission of failure to develop an effective foreign-policymaking system. Insofar as personality clashes and differences of style had contributed to Haig's departure, there was every reason to expect that these impediments would disappear with the choice of George Schultz as his replacement. What was also clear by mid-1982 was that President Reagan had significantly modified his initial preference for a State-centered foreign-policy-making system. Such a model had worked effectively in past administrations and appealed to Reagan for reasons already noted. The viability of a State-centered system always depended not merely upon selecting a self-confident, competent, and experienced person as secretary of state but, even more, on developing a complementary role relationship between the president and his secretary and a working relationship based upon sufficient mutual respect, confidence, and trust to withstand the efforts of other policy advisers to undermine it.[9] Acheson had such a relationship with Truman; Dulles had such a relationship with Eisenhower; Kissinger (as secretary of state) had much the same type of relationship with Ford. Haig, in contrast, never developed such a relationship with Reagan. The role of the assistant for national security affairs, in turn, can be defined in a stable, viable manner only in conjunction with the way in which the president chooses to define his own role, the role of the secretary of state, and the working relationship between them.

Well before October 1983, when he was replaced by his deputy, Robert McFarlane, Clark had grown tired of the travails of the job of national security adviser, and he seized the opportunity that arose to move into a cabinet position as the secretary of the interior. During the two years McFarlane served as national security adviser, he gradually consolidated his position and performed the difficult task of mediating major policy conflicts between State and Defense with increasing effectiveness. McFarlane also made important progress in gaining the president's trust and his ear, and moved in a slow but purposeful way to enhance his own power and prestige.[10] However, McFarlane found himself increasingly frustrated during the first year of Reagan's second term by the changes in running the White House introduced by Donald Regan, who replaced James Baker as chief of staff after the election. Just when he was needed most, to follow up on the opportunities created by the Reagan-Gorbachev summit meeting in November, 1985, McFarlane could put up with the frustrations of his position no longer, and he resigned. He was replaced by his deputy, Admiral John Poindexter, a person who clearly lacked the broad experience, political sophistication, and reputation needed to cope with the difficult tasks that had faced all his predecessors in the position of national security adviser to President Reagan.

Before proceeding to note Poindexter's fate, it will be useful to make some additional observations regarding the weakness and vulnerability of Reagan's management style. The formalistic chief of staff model adopted by President Reagan to structure the White House policy-making system differed in important respects from that of Eisenhower. While Eisenhower gave considerable prominence to the formal NSC system and to the role of his secretary of state in foreign policy, in practice Eisenhower exercised quiet but firm leadership to ensure that the formal machinery and his cabinet officers were responsive to his own policy views and judgments on major issues. In striking contrast, Reagan distanced himself to a surprising and dangerous degree from both the substance and procedures of foreign policymaking. Unlike Reagan, Eisenhower defined the role of his national security adviser in such a way as to complement his own leadership role and style, and this enabled the special assistant to serve as an effective "custodian-manager" of the system. The result was that Eisenhower's White House achieved reasonably effective interagency coordination of policy with State, Defense, and other agencies. In contrast, in his first six years in office Reagan failed to develop a model of how the national security adviser, the secretary of state, and the secretary of defense should work together to complement and compensate for, rather than to exacerbate the risks inherent in, his own modest involvement in foreign policymaking. Moreover, Reagan's penchant for delegating responsibility to trusted advisers, a practice that had served him reasonably well in his first term, created substantial new problems when he replaced James Baker, a skillful and sophisticated political operator, with Donald Regan as chief of staff.

Nonetheless, in his first five years in office, despite the forced resignation of one secretary of state and a succession of four national security advisers, Reagan's extraordinary personal popularity and his presidency remained unscathed, and he retained the possibility of finishing his second term with a defensible record in foreign policy. All this was placed in jeopardy with the revelation in the winter of 1986–1987 that the White House had been utilizing elements of the NSC staff to sell arms covertly to Iran in order to facilitate release to American hostages in Lebanon, and that some of the proceeds from these sales were being diverted to the *contras* in Central America. National Security Adviser Admiral John Poindexter and his subordinate Colonel Oliver North, who together had orchestrated the covert activities, were quickly relieved of their duties. As details of the Iran-*contra* affair emerged, attention quickly focused on the glaring weakness of Reagan's management style and the gross inadequacies of his foreign-policymaking system. These criticisms were sharply stated and documented in the report of the Tower Commission, which the president had appointed and charged with bringing out all the facts of the Iran-*contra* scandal and with making recommendations for improving the NSC system. Even before the Tower Commission issued its report, the president appointed Frank Carlucci, a person of stature and high-level government experience, to replace Admiral Poindexter. The new national security adviser moved quickly to reorganize the staff and to replace many of its personnel.

Another casualty was Reagan's White House chief of staff, Donald Regan, who had assumed that position after the president's reelection. Regan's style and performance had been the subject of considerable criticism even before the Iran-*contra* scandal. While not centrally implicated, Regan was damaged by the affair, and the president reluctantly removed him shortly after the Tower Commission issued its report. CIA director William Casey might well have had to resign also were it not for the fact that a severe illness removed him from the scene before all the facts regarding his involvement emerged.

Regan's replacement, former Senator Howard Baker, was widely regarded as an excellent choice for the position. Together with Frank Carlucci, Baker contributed to restoring confidence in the operations of the White House staff. The president himself emerged from a period of semi-seclusion and struggled to reassert his leadership. In the early spring of 1987, however, the prospects for Reagan and his presidency remained uncertain. The country awaited the result of the investigations being conducted by the special prosecutor, Lawrence Walsh, and several congressional committees, and the possibility remained that their findings would inflict additional damage on the president's credibility and reputation.

NOTES

1. These three management styles are described and evaluated in Richard T. Johnson, *Managing the White House* (New York: Harper & Row, 1974). See particularly chapters 1 and 8. A useful discussion of the evolution of the modern presidency and of the styles of different presidents is provided by Stephen Hess, *Organizing the Presidency* (Washington, D.C.: The Brookings Institution, 1976).

2. Richard Fenno, *The President's Cabinet* (New York: Vintage Books, Knopf, 1959), pp. 44–46. See also Arthur Schlesinger, Jr., *The Age of Roosevelt*, vol. 2, *The Coming of the New Deal* (Boston: Houghton Mifflin, 1959), chapters 32–34; and Richard E. Neustadt, *Presidential Power* (New York: Wiley, 1960), chapter 7.

3. The figures in this selection (with the exception of the one describing Nixon's variant of the formalistic model) are taken directly, with minor adaptations, from John Q. Johnson, "Communication Structures Among Presidential Advisors" (seminar paper, Stanford University, September 1975). The seminal work on communication networks is that of Alex Bavelas, "Communication Patterns in Task-oriented Groups," *Journal of Acoustic Society of America* 22 (1950): 725–730. A summary of early work of this kind appears in Murray Glanzer and Robert Glaser, "Techniques for the Study of Group Structure and Behavior," *Psychological Bulletin* 58 (1961): 2–27.

4. Recently available archival materials at the Eisenhower Library evidently require a substantial revision of the conventional image of Eisenhower as an apolitical military man, one who was generally uninformed about and not very attentive to his executive responsibilities, one who was prone to overdelegate his responsibilities, and one who was naive about the art of governing. What emerges, rather, is a different executive style that Fred Greenstein refers to as Eisenhower's "invisible hand" mode of leadership in which he sought actively to secure his goals by indirection (Fred I. Greenstein, "Presidential Activism Eisenhower Style: A Reassessment Based on Archival Evidence," [paper delivered to the 1979 Meeting of the Midwest Political Science Association, January 1979]).

5. Johnson, *Managing the White House*, pp. 210–211.

6. Don Bonafede, "Brzezinski—Stepping Out of His Backstage Role," *National Journal* (15 October 1977): 1598. See also Elizabeth Drew, "A Reporter at Large: Brzezinski," *The New Yorker*, May 1978; and Marilyn Berger, "Vance and Brzezinski: Peaceful Coexistence or Guerrilla War?" *New York Times Magazine*, 13 February 1977.

7. For a remarkably incisive set of observations regarding aspects of Carter's personality and outlook that adversely affected the organization of his advisory system and his performance generally, see the series of articles published by his former speech writer, James Fallows, "The Passionless Presidency," *The Atlantic Monthly*, May and June 1979. . . .

8. Johnson, *Managing the White House*, chapter 8; reproduced with minor changes and additions in *The Stanford Business School Alumni Bulletin*, Fall 1973.

9. For an insightful critical examination of the feasibility of a State-centered foreign policy–making system, see Leslie H. Gelb, "Why Not the State Department?" *The Washington Quarterly*, Autumn 1980.

10. See the major article in the *New York Times Magazine* by Leslie H. Gelb, "Taking Charge: The Rising Power of National Security Adviser Robert McFarlane," *New York Times*, May 26, 1985.

9. THE PRESIDENCY AND THE IMPERIAL TEMPTATION

Arthur M. Schlesinger, Jr.

The imperial presidency in the United States has staged a comeback some 13 years after the fall of Richard Nixon. Both the recent renewal of presidential aggrandizement and the reaction against it recall the latter days, hectic and ominous, of the Nixon presidency, when I wrote *The Imperial Presidency*. My argument then, as now, was that the American Constitution intends a strong presidency within an equally strong system of accountability. My title referred to what happens when the constitutional balance between presidential power and presidential accountability is upset in favor of presidential power.

The perennial threat to the constitutional balance springs from foreign policy. Confronted by presidential initiatives at home, Congress and the courts—the countervailing branches of government under the separation of powers—have robust confidence in their own information and judgment. But confronted by presidential initiatives abroad, Congress and the courts, along with the press and the citizenry, generally lack confidence in their information and judgment. Consequently, in foreign policy the disposition has been to hand over power and responsibility to the president.

The presidency had always flourished in times of war. "We elect a king every four years," Secretary of State William H. Seward told a *London Times* correspondent during the Civil War, "and give him absolute power within certain limits, which after all he can interpret for himself." But in the past, peace has brought reaction against executive excess. Within a dozen years Seward's elective-kingship theory faded away, and the post-Civil War era was famously characterized by Professor Woodrow Wilson as one of "congressional government."

Then, after 1898, the Spanish-American War stimulated a flow of power back to the presidency. In the 15th edition of *Congressional Government*, Wilson called attention to "the greatly increased power . . . given the President by the plunge into international politics." When foreign policy becomes the nation's dominant concern, Wilson said the executive "must of necessity be its guide: must utter every initial judgment, take every first step of action, supply the information upon which it is to act, suggest and in large measure control its conduct." In another 15 years the First World War gave Wilson, now president himself, the opportunity to exercise those almost royal prerogatives. Then postwar disillusion again revived congressional assertiveness. In the 1930s

127

Franklin Roosevelt, a mighty domestic president, could not stop Congress from enacting the rigid neutrality legislation that put American foreign policy in a straitjacket while Hitler ran amok in Europe.

Since Pearl Harbor, however, Americans have lived under a conviction of international crisis, sustained, chronic, and often intense. The imperial presidency, once a transient wartime phenomenon, has become to a degree institutionalized.

The most palpable index of executive aggrandizement is the transfer of the power to go to war from Congress, where the Constitution expressly lodged it, to the presidency. In the bitter month of June 1940, when the French prime minister pleaded for American aid against Hitler's blitzkrieg, Franklin Roosevelt, after saying that the United States would continue supplies so long as France continued resistance, took care to add: "These statements carry with them no implication of military commitments. Only the Congress can make such commitments." How old-fashioned this sentiment sounds today!

Presidents Truman, Johnson, Nixon, and Reagan thereafter assumed that the power to send troops into combat is an inherent right of the presidency and does not require congressional authorization. Nixon carried presidential prerogative even further when he took the powers flowing to the presidency from international crisis and turned them against his political opponents at home. In Nixon's hands the claim to inherent presidential power swelled into the delusion that the presidency was above the law and the Constitution.

Congress, seized by a temporary passion to prevent future Vietnams and Watergates, enacted laws designed to reclaim lost powers, to dismantle the executive secrecy system, and to ensure future presidential accountability. The War Powers Resolution of 1973 was meant to restrain the presidential inclination to go to war. Congress set up select committees to monitor the Central Intelligence Agency. It gave the Freedom of Information Act new vitality. It imposed its own priorities—human rights and nuclear nonproliferation, for example—on the executive foreign policy.

For a season the presidency appeared in rout. Nixon's successors—the hapless Gerald Ford and the hapless Jimmy Carter—proved incapable of mastering the discordant frustrations of the day. In 1973 the concern had been the excessive power claimed by a president as his inherent right. By the end of the 1970s the republic was consumed by an opposite concern—that the presidency had become too weak to do the job. In 1980 ex-President Ford said to general applause, "We have not an imperial presidency but an imperiled presidency."

Half a dozen years later concern has shifted back from presidential weakness to presidential power. President Reagan demonstrated that the presidency was far from an insolvent office. The congressional reclamation of power after Watergate turned out to be largely make-believe. The War Powers Resolution had no effect in restraining presidents from sending troops into combat, whether in Lebanon or Grenada or Libya. Reagan reestablished the executive secrecy system. He brought the CIA back from its season of disgrace, made it once again the president's private army, and sent it off, without congressional approval, to overthrow the government of Nicaragua.

In order to escape the CIA's nominal obligation to report its dark deeds to congressional oversight committees and to evade the laws of the land, Reagan converted the National Security Council, heretofore a policy-coordination body, into an operating agency, and permitted it to indulge in the Iran-

Nicaragua flimflam. Having placed the integrity and credibility of the United States in the hands of Iranian confidence men, the administration made exposure inevitable. And, when the inevitable exposure began, the administration took refuge in a bluster of incomplete, misleading, and, on occasion, false accounts of what its members had wrought.

The reaction against executive usurpation is already provoking a counter-reaction, as it did after Watergate. We are beginning to hear again that the presidency itself is in danger. We are told that too zealous an inquiry into executive abuses will cripple the office. The prospect of a fifth consecutive failed presidency is leading some to conclude again that the fatal flaw lies not in the individuals occupying the office, but in the office itself. These apprehensions are unduly gloomy.

In the short run, if a president is inclined to do foolish things, surely a crippled presidency is better for the nation and the world than an unrepentant and unchastened one. And the crippling of a president who does foolish things does not mean a crippling of the presidential office. The reaction against Watergate did not prevent Reagan from having a successful first term, and it would not have handicapped Ford and Carter if they had been more competent.

Nor can one conclude from another failed presidency that there is something basically wrong with the system. The Constitution has never pretended to guarantee against presidential incompetence, folly, stupidity, or criminality. But through the separation of powers, it can guarantee that, when a president abuses power, corrective forces exist to redress the constitutional balance. As Senator Sam Ervin put it in Watergate days, "One of the great advantages of the three separate branches of government is that it's difficult to corrupt all three at the same time." The press, as a de facto fourth branch, serves as a powerful reinforcement of the corrective process.

No one need fear that the recurrent uproar against the imperial presidency will inflict permanent damage on the office. For the American presidency is indestructible. This is partly for functional reasons. The separation of powers among three supposedly equal and coordinate branches of government creates an inherent tendency toward inertia and stalemate. The executive branch must take the initiative if the system is to move. The men who framed the Constitution intended that it should do so. "Energy in the Executive," as Alexander Hamilton put it in the Federalist Papers, "is a leading character in the definition of good government."

Moreover, the growth of presidential initiative has resulted less from presidential rapacity for power than from the necessities of governing an ever more complex society. As the United States grew into a continental, industrial, and finally world power, the problems assailing the national polity increased vastly in number, size, and urgency. Most of these problems could not be tackled without vigorous executive leadership.

A third reason for the indestructibility of the presidency lies in the psychology of mass democracy. Americans have always had considerable ambivalence about the presidency. One year they denounce presidential despotism. The next they demand presidential leadership. Although they are proficient at cursing out presidents—a proficiency that helps keep the system in balance—they also have a profound longing to believe in and admire them. Reagan's success in his first term expressed a widespread national desire for presidents to succeed, even when he proposed policies that made little sense and to which in many cases, if public opinion polls can be believed, a majority of Americans were opposed.

The presidency will survive. The real question is what leads American presidents into the imperial temptation. When the American presidency conceives itself as the appointed savior of a world in which mortal danger requires rapid and incessant deployment of men, weapons, and decisions behind a wall of secrecy, power rushes from Capitol Hill to the White House. The imperial temptation is the consequence of a global and messianic foreign policy. Twenty years ago an apprehensive Senate Judiciary Committee established a Subcommittee on Separation of Powers under the redoubtable chairmanship of Senator Ervin. In 1973 the Ervin subcommittee declared that "the movement of the United States into the forefront of balance-of-power realpolitik in international matters has been accomplished at the cost of the internal balance-of-power painstakingly established by the Constitution."

Whether this was a necessary cost the subcommittee did not say. But a prudent balance-of-power foreign policy confined to vital interests of the United States is surely not irreconcilable with the separation of powers. A messianic foreign policy, however, aiming at the salvation of the world and involving the United States in useless wars and grandiose dreams, is another matter. Vietnam and Iran/Nicaragua were the direct consequences of global messianism, Watergate an indirect consequence.

If America's mission is to redeem a fallen world, then the United States must have a new constitution. And if a messianic foreign policy bursts the limits of our present Constitution, then the wisdom of the Framers is even greater than one could have imagined, for such a policy is hopeless on its merits and can only bring disaster to the American republic. The best insurance against a revival of the imperial presidency would be the revival of realism, sobriety, and responsibility in the conduct of foreign affairs.

10. REAGAN'S JUNTA: THE INSTITUTIONAL SOURCES OF THE IRAN-CONTRA AFFAIR

Theodore Draper

1.

This is supposed to have been the era of the imperial presidency. It has turned out to be the era of presidencies that have tried to make themselves imperial—and failed. The attempt and the failure of the Reagan presidency are only the latest of this kind. The basic elements that have gone into the Reagan effort are also not new. Other presidents have used and misused the National Security Council and its "adviser"; other presidents have deliberately kept their secretaries of state in ignorance of presidential policy; other presidents have found ways to keep Congress in the dark about what they were doing.

Yet there is something new about the Reaganite phenomenon. The elements of the present intrigue may be familiar, but they have taken a different and more ominous form. A would-be imperial president has prepared the way for a would-be presidential junta.

The transition has been a very long one. In his study of the imperial presidency, Arthur M. Schlesinger, Jr. began the story with the disputes over presidential power in George Washington's administration. But the present crisis of presidential power has a different dimension; it is a crisis not only about what a president has the power to do; it is also about the power of those around or behind him to act in his name.

The roots of the present predicament go back to the efforts of at least the last seven presidents to extricate themselves from the constitutional limitations of their office. Schlesinger places the "presidential breakaway" after the Second World War. "The postwar Presidents," he asserts, "though Eisenhower and Kennedy markedly less than Truman, Johnson, and Nixon, almost came to see the sharing of power with Congress in foreign policy as a derogation of the Presidency."[1] This version lets Franklin D. Roosevelt off on the ground that though his "destroyer deal" with Great Britain in 1940 was arranged without congressional authorization, it was done for good and sufficient reasons. Schlesinger exonerates Roosevelt because the prospect of a British collapse represented a genuine national emergency, and because Roosevelt privately con-

Note: Some footnotes have been deleted, and others have been renumbered to appear in consecutive order. The subtitle has been added.

sulted with the Republican and Democratic leadership. But Roosevelt knew that his action was constitutionally dubious and at first did not want to send the destroyers to Great Britain without legislative approval. As Schlesinger notes, the leading authority on the presidency, Professor Edward S. Corwin, regarded the deal as an "endorsement of unrestrained autocracy in the field of our foreign relations." The road to Reagan was paved with good intentions.

The imperial presidency, then, is one that acts autocratically. It does so far more in foreign than in domestic affairs. Yet it was not always so. As long as the isolationist tradition was still strong, presidents had less incentive or opportunity to act alone. Once the so-called Truman Doctrine of 1947 seemed to provide a license to intervene everywhere in the world, presidents were far less inclined to restrain themselves, especially in periods of congressional complaisance.

Before the end of the Second World War, presidents did not have the bureaucratic means to carry out policy by themselves. They might insist on making decisions unilaterally, but they could not bypass the existing bureaucracy in order to carry them out. Roosevelt did not have a Central Intelligence Agency or a national security adviser with his own staff; the "destroyer deal" was no secret from the department, Congress, or anyone else. The CIA and the National Security Council were set up in 1947, the latter with a staff headed by an assistant for national security affairs, better known as national security adviser. From a handful, the NSC professional staff has grown to about fifty, enough to divide up the entire world among its own specialists. With these two new agencies, presidents were able to do things that had not been feasible for them to do before.

Again, the change came by stages. The CIA was originally charged with coordinating, correlating, evaluating, and disseminating foreign intelligence information; the national security adviser was given the task of coordinating the policy options open to the president and the recommendations to him. A decision was made at an early stage that foreshadowed the end of the State Department's traditionally predominant role in the making and execution of American foreign policy. Truman's secretary of state, James F. Byrnes, wanted the new intelligence organization to be responsible to the State Department.[2] When he was turned down, the CIA went on to live a life of its own, increasingly at the expense of the State Department. In 1948, another new agency, loosely linked with the CIA, was set up, disarmingly called the Office of Policy Coordination, to engage in covert activities; in 1951, it was fully integrated into the CIA, which henceforth carried out both covert intelligence and covert operations.

The Truman administration was basically reponsible for these innovations; yet Truman himself did not realize where they were going to lead. Eleven years after he had left office, Truman confessed: "I never had any thought that when I set up the CIA that it would be injected into peacetime cloak-and-dagger operations." He no longer liked what he had wrought: "For some time I have been disturbed by the way CIA has been diverted from its original assignment. It has become an operational and at times a policy-making arm of the government." After watching what had resulted, he wanted no more of it: "I, therefore, would like to see the CIA be restored to its original assignment as the intelligence arm of the President, and whatever else it can properly perform in that special field—and that its operational duties be terminated or properly used elsewhere."

Finally, he reflected: "We have grown up as a nation, respected for our ability to maintain a free and open society. There is something about the way the CIA has been functioning that is casting a shadow over our historic position and I feel that we need to correct it."[3] To a correspondent, he wrote: "The CIA was set up by me for the sole purpose of getting all the available information to the President. It was not intended to operate as an international agency engaged in strange activities."[4]

These activities have grown stranger and stranger, until under Reagan the president himself claims that he does not know how they have happened. Yet there is one thing that he could not fail to know—that he used his national security adviser instead of the secretary of state as his chosen instrument in the conduct of American foreign policy. If this displacement had happened for the first time, it would be serious enough. But it has happened frequently before, though not in the extreme Reaganite form.

Too much attention has been paid to the minutiae of the Iran-*contra* affair and not enough to the implications it has for the institutions and structure of our government. Long after the exact details of the diversion of funds to the *contras* have been forgotten, the institutional cost will still have to be paid. For a full appreciation of how deep and acute the problem is, it is necessary to look back and see how it has developed over the past quarter of a century. This institutional crisis mainly concerns the president, secretary of state, and national security adviser, the first two offices as old as the Republic, the third a comparative newcomer in the American scheme of governance.

2.

The post of national security adviser did not take off until early in the Kennedy administration in 1961. The post was held by McGeorge Bundy, who with his deputy, Walt W. Rostow, according to Arthur M. Schlesinger, gave the White House "an infusion of energy on foreign affairs with which the State Department would never in the next three years . . . quite catch up." At first, it is said, Kennedy wanted the State Department to be the "central point" in all aspects of foreign affairs. But he was soon "disappointed" in its makeup and performance, with the result that he came to depend on Bundy and his staff or on Theodore Sorensen, his special counsel. The secretary of state, Dean Rusk, and Kennedy's entourage were so different from each other in outlook and manner that they hardly spoke the same language. To Kennedy himself, Rusk's views "remained a mystery."[5] Sorensen says that Rusk "deferred almost too amiably to White House initiatives and interference." If Kennedy had lived to have a second term, Bundy would have been a "logical candidate for Secretary of State."[6]

Kennedy was not the first president to make foreign policy in the White House rather than in the State Department. The pattern had been set by Franklin D. Roosevelt, who made his secretary of state, Cordell Hull, almost a figurehead. But Roosevelt had not built up a substitute or shadow foreign-policy agency; he had preferred to work through other cabinet officers, at first Under Secretary of State Sumner Welles, and then through other members of the cabinet or his personal emissary Harry Hopkins. Yet Roosevelt and the proliferation of quasi–foreign-affairs agencies during World War II were responsible for starting the State Department on its downward path. Presidents who wanted to be their own foreign ministers followed his example by choosing weak secretaries of state and depending on others to carry out their wishes.

The president who gave this system a pathological twist was Richard Nixon. We know just how pathological it was because his national security adviser, Henry Kissinger, has told us all about it. Nixon hardly knew Kissinger when he took him on; his choice as secretary of state, William Rogers, was one of Nixon's closest friends and a former law partner. When Nixon chose Rogers, Nixon knew him to be unfamiliar with foreign affairs. According to Kissinger, Nixon immediately told him to build up a "national security apparatus" in the White House. The only region that Nixon entrusted to Rogers was the Middle East—for one reason because Nixon believed at the time that any active policy there was doomed to failure. The "back channel" that Nixon and Kissinger set up with Soviet ambassador Anatoly Dobrynin cut the State Department out of the most important field of Soviet-American affairs. According to Kissinger, Nixon repeatedly lied to Rogers, especially about Kissinger's trip to China in 1971 and to Moscow in 1972.

Why did Nixon humiliate his old friend? Kissinger's explanation clearly suggests a pathological motive. In the past, it seems, Rogers had been the "psychologically dominant partner" in the relationship. Now Nixon "wanted to reverse roles and establish a relationship in which both hierarchically and substantially he, Nixon, called the tune for once." Kissinger was only too willing to collaborate in the diseased machination, of which he was the chief beneficiary. "I do not mean to suggest that I resisted Nixon's conduct toward his senior Cabinet officer," Kissinger confessed bashfully. "From the first my presence made it technically possible and after a time I undoubtedly encouraged it."

One precedent set by Kissinger has come back to haunt the present secretary of state, George Shultz. Kissinger used the US ambassador in Pakistan to prepare for his China trip without either of them informing Secretary of State Rogers. The US ambassador in Lebanon was used in the same way to help in the arms deal with Iran, without the knowledge of Secretary Shultz, who professed to be "shocked" when he learned about it and then took steps to prevent it from happening again. Shultz found it necessary to protest against the use of Kissinger's precedent as a justification for treating him as Rogers had been treated, with the argument that Kissinger was unique—"They broke the mold when they made him." Unfortunately, they did not break the mold of what he did, which was far more important in the long run than what he was. If Kissinger had been national security adviser vis-à-vis Shultz, it would seem, Shultz would have made no complaint.

In restrospect, Kissinger knew that there was something wrong with his theatrical China coup. In his memoirs, he admitted:

> The State Department should be the visible focus of our foreign policy; if the President has no confidence in his Secretary of State he should replace him, not substitute the security adviser for him. If he does not trust the State Department, the President should enforce compliance with his directives, not circumvent it with the NSC machinery. Yet, while these postulates are beyond argument as a matter of theory, they are not easy to carry out. To achieve the essential coherence of

policy there is need for a strong Secretary of State who is at the same time quite prepared to carry out Presidential wishes not only formally but in all nuances.[7]

So it was Secretary of State Rogers's fault for having been too weak to carry out the presidential wishes. But Nixon had deliberately chosen a weak secretary of state and then had made him all the weaker by treating him with open contempt and cutting him out of his own constitutional responsibilities. As for the conspiratorial secrecy which enveloped Kissinger's first trip to China in 1971, it was not anything the Chinese had wanted or demanded. They were, in fact, "extremely suspicious of our desire for secrecy." It was wholly contrived for American consumption, to confront the American public with an accomplished fact.

Nixon fancied himself a great expert in foreign affairs; Carter had no such illusions. But Carter also wanted to be seen as his own master in foreign policy and, therefore, chose a secretary of state, Cyrus Vance, who would not be too obtrusive. His national security adviser, Zbigniew Brzezinski, was from the first determined to be the President's prime agent in foreign policy. Brzezinski quickly contrived to freeze out the CIA in the daily intelligence of the President, which he insisted on giving every morning without anyone else present. He saw himself as Carter's mentor and in the first months gave him lessons in "conceptual or strategic issues." Brzezinski's National Security Council staff controlled "the policy-making output of both State and the Defense Department," as well as the activities of the CIA. Brzezinski and Secretary Vance increasingly disagreed on major issues, with Vance unable or unwilling to assert himself. Vance's "reluctance to speak up publicly, to provide a broad conceptual explanation for what our Administration was trying to do, and Carter's lack of preparation for doing it himself, pushed me to the forefront," Brzezinski later explained, adding in parenthesis, "I will not claim I resisted strongly." Finally Vance could stand no more and resigned as a result of his disagreement over the ill-fated mission to rescue the hostages from the Tehran embassy. Another secretary of state had spent almost four miserable, humiliating years in office, at least as the national security adviser later described them.[8]

Reagan's first secretary of state, Alexander M. Haig, Jr., was another casualty. Having been Kissinger's deputy on the staff of the National Security Council, Haig well knew about the rivalry and threat from that quarter to the secretary of state. When he took the office, he says, the President told him that he would be "*the* spokesman" in foreign affairs and "I won't have a repeat of the Kissinger-Rogers situation." Reagan also assured him that the new national security adviser, Richard Allen, "would act exclusively as a staff coordinator." Haig does not seem to have had much trouble with Allen. They were both deprived of direct, regular access to the President, the factor that Haig later thought had brought both of them down. For most of his tenure, Haig attributed his woes to the White House staff, especially James A. Baker and Michael K. Deaver, or as Haig put it—"Baker, Deaver, and their apparat." Without access to the President and subject to their control of what went to the President, Haig was mortally handicapped by "not knowing his methods, not understanding his system of thought, not having the opportunity of discussing policy in detail with him." The same might be said of some of his predecessors and their knowledge and understanding of the presidents who had chosen them.

After Allen's inglorious departure as national security adviser in January 1982, a real rival and threat confronted Haig in his successor, William Clark, whose deputy was Robert C. ["Bud"] McFarlane. As Haig tells the story, he began to be bypassed by Clark during the Lebanon crisis of that year. Soon Haig was worried by a situation "in which a presidential assistant [Clark], especially one of limited experience and limited understanding of the volatile nature of an international conflict [at that time the Falklands crisis], should assume powers of the Presidency." Clark would draft a message to Israel for the President to sign without showing it to Haig. Yet in the end, Haig himself came to denigrate the constitutional position of the secretary of state to such an extent that he offered the view that "it does not really matter whether the Secretary of State or the National Security Adviser, or some other official carries out the President's foreign policy and speaks for the Administration on these questions." The would-be imperial president, it seems, was permitted to use anyone to make the secretary of state a figurehead instead of a "vicar."[9]

The imperial presidency has not materialized. Kennedy's presidency was cut short. Johnson came to grief over Vietnam. Nixon was disgraced and dethroned. Carter was not successful enough to win a second term. Now Reagan has beeen exposed as a hollow idol—the great delegator who gave away his power to those to whom it had been delegated.

But though the imperial presidency has failed to come about, presidents have distorted the institution they have inherited by seeking to get rid of checks and balances in the conduct of foreign affairs. The expansion of presidential ambitions in foreign policy has been concurrent with the expansion of the country's global power. This expansion, on a scale never envisioned by pre–World War II presidents, has made foreign affairs the main test of presidential greatness. Presidents have deliberately appointed weak secretaries of state or rid themselves of those who did not bend to their will in order to free themselves from traditional or constitutional constraints. The last strong secretaries of state were Truman's George C. Marshall and Dean Acheson and Eisenhower's John Foster Dulles a quarter of a century ago. It is unthinkable that any president would have treated them the way Rusk, Rogers, Vance, and Haig have been treated, or that Marshall and Dulles would have submitted to such treatment.

The fate that has overtaken Secretary Shultz both resembles that of the other recent secretaries of state and also differs from anything experienced before. It is the extra dimension that deserves the most attention in making sense of the Iran-*contra* imbroglio.

3.

While much is murky about the entire affair, the main thing is indisputable. The essentials can now be reconstructed without the aid of a congressional inquiry or pleading with Rear Admiral John M. Poindexter and Lieutenant Colonel Oliver L. North to come clean.

On January 17, 1986, President Reagan signed a secret intelligence "finding" authorizing the sale of weapons and spare parts to Iran. This directive also enjoined that it should not be made known to Congress, and, even more remarkably, to four of the eight members of the National Security Council. The four left out were: Secretary of State Shultz, Secretary of Defense Caspar

Weinberger, the Chairman of the Joint Chiefs of Staff, Admiral William J. Crowe, Jr., and Secretary of the Treasury James A. Baker III. The four in the know were: Vice President George Bush, CIA director William J. Casey, Attorney General Edwin Meese, and presidential chief of staff Donald T. Regan. The "finding" attributed the need to exclude Congress to "extreme sensitivity" and "security risks." So secretive was the order that only one copy was made of it and it was deposited in the safe of National Security Adviser Poindexter.

This "finding" was not made by President Reagan in a fit of absent-mindedness. It can be understood only by going back to two previous meetings of the National Security Council. On December 6, 1985, a "full-scale" discussion had been held on the subject of arms sales to Iran. It was not a new subject for Secretary Shultz; he said that he and the then national security adviser Robert C. McFarlane had been considering it ever since June of that year. Whatever Shultz knew or did not know, one shipment of American arms was sent from Israel in August 1985 with the approval of the President, according to McFarlane, and a second in September. At the meeting of December 6, both Shultz and McFarlane came out against the proposal—Shultz evidently on principle, McFarlane because he had been disappointed in his previous dealings with the Iranians. The decision at that time went in favor of engaging "in a dialogue [with the Iranians] if they release our hostages but that we would not sell them arms," as Shultz put it in his testimony of December 8, 1986.

But the President was somehow prevailed on to reopen the subject. Another "full-scale discussion" was held on January 7, 1986. This time both Shultz and Weinberger openly opposed changing the policy of not selling arms to Iran. Nevertheless, as Shultz disclosed, he could see that he was now on the losing side. Thus the January 7 meeting led to the secret decision of January 17. Shultz, Weinberger, and the two others were "cut out" of the subsequent dealings, because they were opposed to the arms sales or were not sufficiently enthusiastic. In any case, the critical decision of January 17 had been made after about six weeks of intensive discussion and conflicting views.

Whatever the vagaries of President Reagan's decision-making process may be, he made this decision fully aware of what it entailed. No one else can be held responsible for it.

Of the four trusted with the decision, there is reason to believe that the most influential and zealous was Casey. For the task of drafting the January 17 finding was given to Stanley Sporkin, then the CIA's general counsel and now a federal judge. The evident objective in drafting the order was to shield the CIA, among others, from breaking the law prohibiting the United States from selling weapons directly to Iran without notification to Congress.

Ordinarily, the CIA would have been given the task of carrying out the January 17 directive; it had all the means to do so and in any case the plan could not be implemented without it. But past misbehavior had made the CIA suspect and dictated that a less exposed agency should be put out in front. The national security adviser and his staff served the purpose because they were considered to be responsible to the President alone and not even to the National Security Council as such, let alone to Congress. Yet Poindexter and his main aide in the operation, Lieutenant Colonel North, had no physical means to carry out an arms deal with Iran. They were helpless without the cooperation of the CIA and the arms which could be obtained only from the Defense Department.

Thus, as Casey explained, the CIA put itself in a "support mode" to Poindexter.[10] The CIA requested the arms from the secretary of defense, who ordered the army to release them from its stocks and transfer them to the CIA. Secretary Weinberger, who did not approve of the deal but was aware that it was the President's wish, did nothing to hinder it. A stickler for form, he knew that he was bound by the Economy Act, which regulated the transfer of property between government agencies. Weinberger insisted that the Defense Department should be paid $12 million for the arms, a price obviously far less than they were worth but with the inestimable advantage that it was $2 million less than arms sales that had to be reported to Congress. The arms were then transported to Israel and elsewhere in chartered planes of companies controlled by the CIA. The money obtained from the Iranian intermediaries was put into secret bank accounts in Switzerland. Almost every step in the transaction was actually carried out through the CIA, while at the same time director Casey was able to shift the responsibility to the NSC, which, he later claimed, "was operating this thing."

Thus was set up what amounted to a presidential junta. It was not led by a single, outstanding personality of the Kissinger type. Its main figures were relatively obscure military characters—a rear admiral and a lieutenant colonel on active service. They could get things done only by acting in the President's name, generally through the CIA. Even Secretary Weinberger, who must have suspected that something untoward was afoot when he was told to "sell" arms to the CIA, apparently entrusted the transaction to only two of his closest aides. How many besides Poindexter and North were directly involved in the deal with Iran is not known, but they could not have been many, because extraordinary measures were taken to keep the affair a secret—and it was kept a secret for months.

The diversion of funds to the *contras*, whatever it amounted to, was only a minor byproduct of the deal with Iran. It was made possible by the junta-like operation, which was so self-contained and so far removed from the rest of the government, even from the CIA, if we can believe its director, that it could be managed by a single insider. The worst that North can be charged with is having done something illegally—providing the *contras* with funds that Congress had refused to approve—that Reagan and Casey wanted done unobtrusively, in a way that would not technically violate the Boland Amendment prohibiting the government from supplying such funds. North's transgression has been a godsend to Reagan and Casey, because it has diverted attention from the government-by-junta that they set up and that made possible the diversion of funds.

Far more important than the diversion of funds to the *contras* was the damage done to the conduct of a credible, responsible American foreign policy. For years official American spokesmen had fulminated against making deals with terrorists or terrorist nations, and especially against selling arms to Iran. On October 1, 1986, however, Secretary of State Shultz met in New York with the six Persian Gulf foreign ministers, organized in the Gulf Cooperation Council. He assured them that the United States was intensifying its efforts to discourage the sale of arms to Iran, feared by all of them. By that time, the United States had been secretly, for months, intensifying its efforts to sell arms to Iran, directly and indirectly.

No doubt Secretary Shultz did not mean to deceive. But he was not a member of President Reagans' junta, which was pursuing an altogether different foreign policy. Thus arose the curious phenomenon of two conflicting American foreign policies—the junta's and the secretary of state's. Both in a sense emanated from the President, but only one was credible and genuine on October 1, 1986, when Shultz conferred with the gulf ministers.

Yet government-by-junta cannot operate without the voluntary ignorance and complaisance of those who are in a position to resist it. Shultz, Weinberger, and probably others were aware of "bit and pieces of evidence," as Shultz put it, that arms were going to Iran. They knew as much as they wanted to know, which was just enough to permit them to protest that they did not know enough. So long as it was the President's policy, they looked the other way, despite a conviction that it was indefensible. Secretary Weinberger permitted himself to say that the President had received "very bad" advice and that "there aren't any moderate elements in Iran with whom we can deal." But he had authorized the transfer of arms to the CIA for Iran and, like Shultz, had put loyalty to the President ahead of faithfulness to the best interests of the country.

4.

. . . [R]eactions to President Reagan's predicament tell us something about its implications. The Iran-*contra* affair has evoked demands for absolute loyalty to the President, outcries against traditional Republicans or conservatives in general, charges against Congress as the main enemy, and justifications of an admittedly illegal diversion of funds.

Another response has been put forward by Charles Krauthammer of *The New Republic,* which touches a deeper level of the problem. "This affair," he holds, "is not a Reagan crisis nor a presidential crisis, but a recurring American crisis, rooted ultimately in the tension between America's need to act like a great power and its unwillingness to do so." He further explains: "The problem is not democracy. Democracy is instrumental. Its role is faithfully to transmit the popular will. The problem is American popular will, which is deeply divided on whether to accept the responsibilities of a great power."

Krauthammer finally presents his case in the form of a dilemma. The presidency

> finds itself in a permanent bind: to fulfill its obligations as leader of a superpower or to fulfill its obligations as leader of a democracy. Confronted with the choice, a president must choose the latter. But it is the choice itself—not the identity of the president or his management style—that is the source of our recurring crisis.[11]

This view conveniently exculpates every president and every "management style" by putting the onus on the "choice." Even as Krauthammer puts it, however, the choice should not be so difficult or culpable. We are told that confronted with the choice, the president "must choose" to fulfill his obligations as leader of a democracy. If that is how he *must* choose, why should the choice itself be responsible for creating the crisis instead of the president who does not make the right and necessary choice?

Yet Krauthammer is clearly of two minds about the primacy of democracy. If democracy is merely "instrumental," then it is not fundamental, as it has long been assumed to be in the American political tradition. Krauthammer himself implies that democracy is something more than "instrumental" if presidents must choose to be faithful to it and must subordinate superpower status to it. Krauthammer would have much less trouble with presidents making the choice if he himself had less trouble making it.

Still, there is something revealing in Krauthammer's dilemma that bears closely on Reagan's "management style" in the Iran-*contra* affair. Reagan's choice of a presidential junta to carry out his policy was more characteristic of a leader of a runaway superpower than a leader of a healthy democracy. The deliberate decision to exclude Congress for many months from all knowledge, the degrading ex-communication of the secretary of state, the implied edict that disagreement cannot be tolerated and is punishable by exclusion from decision making, the morbid secrecy of the entire enterprise—these are political monstrosities in a democracy such as ours. They are of a piece with those other monstrosities that have recently been advanced—absolute loyalty to the President, repudiation of tradtional conservatism in favor of adventurist neoconservatism, the conception of Congress as enemy, and the absolution given to lawlessness on the part of presidential agents, even military officers.

Despite my reservations about the way Krauthammer has dealt with the problem that he poses, it is not a problem that can be easily disposed of. If, as he says, America is unwilling to act like a great power, or the "American popular will" is deeply divided on whether to accept the responsibilities of a great power, what are the further implications of such a "permanent bind"?

The most far-reaching implication of this line of reasoning is that the President and those around him must substitute their will for the "popular will." If a president must choose between being the leader of a superpower or the leader of a democracy, the former must take precedence over the latter or he will be no leader of a superpower. President Reagan made precisely such a choice when he decided to act through a presidential junta instead of the existing structure of government. The argument that he was forced to rely on his junta because he could not trust Congress, the secretary of state, the secretary of defense, and any others who might disagree with him merely reinforces the ultimate nature of this choice. But there was another way open to him. If he could not trust them it should have meant that he could not carry through a policy without or against them. At that point, the leader of a democracy would call a halt.

In fact, then, the Krauthammer dilemma is unreal. The reason so many presidents have failed to make their rule imperial is that they have always, ultimately, come up against the basic institutions of this country, backed by the "popular will." In order for these institutions and will to be overcome, a radical change would have to take place in this country. We are still far from that, but the threat exists so long as the President and his apologists think that he must act like the leader of a superpower instead of the leader of a democracy.

In the end, setting up a presidential junta as a solution to the problem of being both a superpower and a democracy is self-defeating. Without the support of our democratic structure backed up by popular approval, a president will end up the leader neither of a superpower nor of a democracy. Whenever we act as a superpower at the expense of our democracy, the price is too high. It would be safer and sounder to seek openly to establish a balance between the responsibilities of a superpower and those of a democracy. Whenever the two

responsibilities conflict and democracy loses, our system of government becomes unbalanced and finally takes revenge on those who would, in fact,
impose an imperial presidency.

The founders still have something to teach us. "The history of human conduct does not warrant that exalted opinion of human virtue which would make
it wise in a nation to commit interests of so delicate and momentous a kind as
those which concern its intercourse with the rest of the world to the sole
disposal of a magistrate, created and circumstanced, as would be a president of
the United States," wrote Alexander Hamilton in No. 75 of *The Federalist*.
"The constitution supposes, what the History of all Gov[ernmen]ts demonstrates, that the Ex[ecutive] is the branch of power most interested in war, &
most prone to it," wrote James Madison to Jefferson in 1798. "It has accordingly with studied care vested the question of war in the Legisl[ature]."[12]

Notes

1. Arthur M. Schlesinger, Jr., *The Imperial Presidency* (Houghton Mifflin, 1973), p. 206.

2. Harry S. Truman, *Years of Trial and Hope* (Doubleday, 1956), p. 57.

3. *The Washington Post* (December 22, 1963).

4. *Off the Record: The Private Papers of Harry S. Truman*, edited by Robert H. Ferrell
(Harper and Row, 1980), p. 408.

5. Arthur M. Schlesinger, Jr., *A Thousand Days* (Houghton Mifflin, 1965), pp. 150, 407,
420–421, 435.

6. Theodore C. Sorensen, *Kennedy* (Harper and Row, 1965), pp. 263, 270.

7. Henry Kissinger, *White House Years* (Little, Brown, 1979), p. 728. All the evidence of the
dealings by Nixon and Kissinger comes from this book.

8. Zbigniew Brzezinski, *Power and Principle* (Farrar, Straus and Giroux, 1983), pp. 37, 65–
66, 72.

9. Alexander M. Haig, Jr., *Caveat: Realism, Reagan, and Foreign Policy* (Macmillan, 1984),
pp. 12, 53, 84, 306–307, 339, 341, 356.

10. Interview with Casey, *Time* (December 22, 1986), p. 31.

11. *The New Republic* (December 22, 1986).

12. Both of these citations appear in Schlesinger's *The Imperial Presidency*, p. 5.

11. WHY STATE CAN'T LEAD

Duncan L. Clarke

Questions again have arisen about the management of U.S. foreign policy. In light of the real and feared roles of the National Security Council (NSC) in the arms-for-hostages arrangement with Iran, predictable calls for the State Department to assume overall direction of U.S. foreign policy are being made. The calls should go unheeded. The idea will not work.

Since 1947, with a few exceptions, the secretary of state has been a significant foreign-policy adviser to the president. Often he has been the leading adviser. Moreover, after the president, he usually has been the country's chief foreign-policy advocate and diplomat. These roles for the secretary receive broad endorsement.

But it also is often asserted that the secretary's own department should have the central, or at least leading, role in making and coordinating foreign policy. This view is wrong. In fact, there is a growing perception among informed observers that the State Department is ill-equipped to assume such a position of prominence. Contributors to a 1975 study by the Commission on the Organization of the Government for the Conduct of Foreign Policy (Murphy commission), for example, concluded that establishing the State Department as the centerpiece of foreign policymaking by constructing coordinating mechanisms around it simply would not work. Neither formal delegations of presidential authority nor powerful secretaries have enabled the department in the past to coordinate important activities of other departments and agencies.

There is a powerful bureaucratic reason for this persistent failure. The department encounters vehement resistance from other departments when the policy issues it tries to control affect their areas of jurisdictional responsibility and interest. Neither the Defense Department nor the Treasury Department will accept State's lead in their respective areas. Indeed, relatively few secretaries of state and defense have enjoyed close working partnerships. More often their relationships have been described as ranging from "peaceful coexistence" to "open warfare." Tensions in a State-centered system would burden the president with a disproportionate number of interagency disputes to resolve.

It is true that the NSC has not been notably successful in integrating defense and international economic policy into overall national security policy. But

Note: Some footnotes have been deleted.

there is no indication that State can perform these functions more effectively. And the NSC has one key advantage over State: Only the NSC has the potential to integrate the various policy strands as a neutral broker. If the problem is ever to be mitigated, therefore, it is to the NSC and the White House, not to State, that an administration must look. If, by some miracle, State were offered the role of neutral broker, it probably should reject it. For State, like any other department, must be an advocate and representative within interagency councils to fulfill its essential missions. A stance of neutrality would ensure inadequate representation of State positions within interagency councils.

The two times that State has been assigned central coordinative responsibility it performed poorly. Presidents Dwight Eisenhower and Lyndon Johnson gave State central coordinative responsibility through the Operations Coordinating Board and the National Security Action Memorandum 341, respectively. Both systems failed partly because of the opposition of other departments and State's unwillingness or inability to play the role assigned. The historical record does not end there, however. Most modern presidents, either before or shortly after their inauguration, have indicated a desire for the secretary and the Department of State to play a leading role in formulating and directing foreign policy. Although some secretaries proceed to assume such a role, the department rarely does. A major reason for this is the gap between what presidents want and expect and what they come to believe State can or will give them. Among other things, they expect loyalty, responsiveness to their needs and directives, an opportunity to exercise foreign-policy leadership, and sensitivity to their domestic political requirements. No recent president has found the department able or willing to perform as expected.

Upon assuming office, President Richard Nixon reportedly told his staff that foreign policy was to be handled by the White House, "not by the striped-pants faggots in Foggy Bottom." The offensive language apart, such uneasiness about the State Department appears to be the rule rather than the exception. Recent presidents seem quickly to have concluded that, except for the secretary and a handful of others, people in State are not to be trusted. Many New Deal, Kennedy, and Carter Democrats believed State to be hidebound and resistant to progressive policies; many Eisenhower, Nixon, and Reagan Republicans were convinced it was infested with suspect left-wingers and liberals. Regardless of party, presidents often are disposed to blame State for unauthorized leaks of sensitive information.

Some of the more telling reasons for presidential suspicions relate to various traits and attitudes of the Foreign Service "subculture." I. M. Destler, an articulate advocate in favor of a strong role for State, has acknowledged that the department is "strikingly 'un-Presidential,' " and that the Foreign Service subculture constitutes "a formidable problem for those who would make State *the* central foreign affairs agency."[1]

In any administration, the president's confidence is gained through demonstrated loyalty and competence, which normally come only through daily interaction with the president. Usually only the president's White House advisers, including the national security assistant (NSA), and cabinet officials like the secretary of state can meet this condition. A sprawling bureaucracy cannot. Consequently, no postwar president has sought to build lines of confidence down through the State Department bureaucracy.

Every recent administration, therefore, has an inclination to center foreign policymaking in the White House, an inclination that is further strengthened by a sense that State is insufficiently responsive to presidential requirements and directives. Secretaries themselves must be responsive to presidents if they are to retain the chief executive's confidence, but they confront a dilemma: They can either distance themselves from their own department, thereby setting it adrift, or become State's advocate at the risk of being suspect themselves. Either way, State suffers. Former Secretary of State Cyrus Vance was reasonably successful for a while in balancing these two roles, but as the struggle with former national security adviser Zbigniew Brzezinski for the president's ear intensified, he found the task more and more difficult. And former President Jimmy Carter finally was to conclude that "Cy Vance mirrored the character of the organization he led. He was . . . extremely loyal to his subordinates, and protective of the State Department and its status."

The notion of responsiveness does not imply that State's advice is invariably wrong. But one element often mentioned by presidents and NSAs is State's reluctance to implement faithfully and promptly White House directives. Carter was disturbed by the apparent unwillingness in the State Department to carry out his directives fully and with enthusiasm; Brzezinski wrote in his book *Power and Principle* (1983) that he was "amazed at how skillful the State Department was in delaying the execution of decisions which it had not in the first place favored"; and former Secretary of State Henry Kissinger remarked in *White House Years* (1979) that Foreign Service officers (FSOs) "will carry out clear-cut instructions with great loyalty, but the typical Foreign Service officer is not easily persuaded that an instruction with which he disagrees is really clear-cut."

This perception that the secretary and, more often, the Department of State are insensitive to domestic politics also encourages presidents to favor the advice of NSAs. With some exceptions, State devotes little attention to framing its proposals in terms that will draw domestic political support. Presidents soon come to know that they and their staffs can frame decisions in a more politically acceptable manner. When the White House becomes convinced that State is irremediably out of touch with politics, the White House staff is well on its way to commanding policy.

Another factor inexorably pulls policymaking into the White House. Presidents searching for areas in which to demonstrate international leadership have always found foreign policy much easier to dominate than defense policy. When the White House decides to move boldly into a foreign-policy area, the State Department, and sometimes even the secretary, is often shunted aside. Reinforcing this tendency is the need to respond effectively to the growing global interdependence in international economic and security affairs during an era of instant worldwide communication. The requirements for policy integration and responsiveness to public opinion can best be met by the White House, not by State Department foreign-policy professionals.

Another shortcoming of the department is its lack of expertise. The Murphy commission and a 1970 State Department study informally known as the Macomber Report both agreed that State lacked the expertise to "manage and contain" officials from other departments in the international economic, defense, and intelligence areas. Nor has reform taken place. William Bacchus, special assistant to the undersecretary for management, wrote in 1983 that "State does not have the functional competence . . . to play anything resembling an integrative, policy development role. . . . And there is little current indication that significant improvement is likely."[2]

Since the mid-1970s, some effort has been made to address this issue, particularly in the international economic and political-military fields. Yet the Foreign Service continues to be predominantly generalist in background and orientation and resists recruitment of specialists. . . .

A problem distinct from, but related to, inadequate expertise is the quality of State Department analysis and reporting. The analytic caliber of State's papers and reports has been criticized roundly by many inside and outside the building. Critics complain that State Department studies are long and too descriptive and often unsatisfactory. Based heavily on intuition, and almost never conceptual, many of the analyses are unaccompanied by reliable sources and information, or reflect the FSO's lack of adequate training and expertise; papers are so cautious and vague as to be of little use to policymakers who long ago concluded that such "waffling" constitutes the quintessential character of the "Fudge Factory at Foggy Bottom."

Another perception widely held outside the State Department is that the need to maintain "good relations" with a country or region predisposes FSOs to identify excessively with that country's interests at the expense of American interests. Many FSOs will confide privately that such clientism is a risk to be guarded against, though one that is starkly overdrawn by those whose norms, policy preferences, or bureaucratic interests put them in frequent conflict with the State Department. Others react heatedly—often in private, sometimes in public—to allegations of clientism, which they see as impugning their patriotism.

But whether there is truth to the charge matters much less than the fact that it is widely believed by officials in other departments, in Congress, and in the White House. FSOs may, with sound reason, argue that long-term U.S. interests are at times best advanced by accommodating legitimate concerns of other countries. Most foreign-policy decisions, and not a few domestic ones, are unlikely to be well informed if taken without an understanding of the thinking and concerns of foreign governments and peoples. Few officials have better insight into such matters than career diplomats who immerse themselves in the culture, politics, society, and language of another country. But presidents often view such "accommodationist" advice as soft and out of touch with more pressing American interests. Their inclination, once again, is to discount State's advice.

The notion that "the striped-pants" types are selling out to foreigners probably is held even more firmly in Congress. The department's usual relationship with Congress is at best uncomfortable, and State alone among executive departments lacks a significant public constituency. This is no help to the able FSO country specialist who, like the responsible intelligence analyst, often bears bad news that decision makers must hear. But there are few rewards for the messenger.

Other aspects and attitudes of the Foreign Service collectively diminish the prospect that the State Department will assume a central place in the direction and formulation of foreign policy.

Elitism. Except for many junior officers, FSOs see themselves as members of an elite corps of talented, nonpartisan, close-knit, and unjustly beleaguered professionals. Many Americans and their elected representatives also view the Foreign Service as an elite—one that is an ingrown, exclusive club enjoying undeserved perquisites. Although the public, or sectors of it, might admire or acknowledge certain elites—the Boston Celtics or the United States Marine Corps—most Americans seem to distrust self-perceived elites. And although the image of the Foreign Service probably has improved somewhat as terrorist incidents have taken their toll among the dedicated diplomats who serve the United States overseas, perceived FSO elitism remains a political liability for the department.

Elitism has other costs. It increases pressures for conformity within a system that already stifles individual initiative and creativity. It contributes to a certain "laager mentality," an "us-against-them" attitude frequently exhibited by FSOs toward many outside of State and even toward some political appointees and those with specialized expertise within the department. This can only distance the Foreign Service from the political leadership and larger governmental foreign affairs community with which it must interact.

Essence of the Foreign Service. The essence of Foreign Service work is another factor limiting the department's ability and disposition to play a leading policy role. FSOs are thought of (and think of themselves) as diplomats whose principal duty is to execute, not make, policy. The FSOs' "essence" is to represent their country overseas, send reports back to Washington, and negotiate with foreign governments. Successful performance of these functions requires a certain compromising, accommodating, and unabrasive style that does not easily lend itself to the combative, aggressive quality of Washington decision making.

In short, the very qualities that serve FSOs well in their diplomatic capacity impede their performance in the Washington policymaking environment. Indeed, decision makers are often informed by analyses that are best prepared by a group that is only grudgingly tolerated by FSOs—experts with specialized knowledge and skills in, for instance, military, economic, or scientific affairs.

Lack of Innovation and Risk Avoidance. The historian Arthur Schlesinger, Jr., once observed that the Foreign Service officer has come to be known as a person for whom the risks always outweigh the opportunities. This may relate partly to the nature of the diplomatic profession. Diplomats are expected to reflect not their own, but their government's views. Great care must be taken not to exceed one's instructions. Every word must be carefully measured.

The Macomber Report found that the mores of the Foreign Service are not conducive to creative thinking and that conformity is prized above all other qualities. But there is more to it than this. Prevalent norms within the State Department inhibit direct confrontation of particularly sensitive issues and penalize risk takers. It can be hazardous to be creative, to go out on a limb. Initiative or premature insight may set back or destroy careers even when FSOs correctly read or predict evolving international events. An example is the fate of the department's old China hands, who were purged for submitting what are now regarded as perceptive reports on communist China. But there are others. Officers working on arms control issues or U.S.-Soviet relations have been especially vulnerable during the transition from one administration to another. The prudent course is the cautious course. "Fitting in" has a higher value than "standing out."

Management Is Merely Housekeeping. Internal State Department feuding and the department's lack of effective management practices also make a State-centered foreign policy seem implausible. Even casual observers have at least a general awareness of fights for turf between and among various regional and functional bureaus and other departmental units, and informed observers describe State as deeply divided and analogize its intradepartmental bickering to tribalism and clannishness.[3]

Of course, internal spats are common to other agencies as well. But what is less frequently encountered elsewhere in the executive branch are resistance to the very notion of management and a tradition that de-emphasizes the standing and importance of managers. Among FSOs, management is equated with housekeeping or administration. Most FSOs, like most university professors, neither admire nor aspire to be administrators. Such attitudes mean that, despite several efforts, career development programs designed to augment State's managerial competencies have met with only limited success. Moreover, only senior officials are positioned to be senior managers. If they take no personal interest in the subject and delegate this function entirely to subordinates, it will not have sufficient priority. This is true at the highest level: Few secretaries of state since George Marshall have paid adequate attention to managing their own department.

In summary, the State Department is so beset with problems and weaknesses that it cannot now or in the foreseeable future assume a central foreign-policy role. Therefore, it is time to put the illusion of a State-centered system to rest.

This does not mean that extreme centralization in the White House is an appealing alternative. . . .

The president and the NSA alone lack the time to handle all vital issues themselves, let alone secondary or tertiary ones. This inclines an administration toward a crisis or "front-burner" orientation, since critical matters will claim much, if not all, of its time. Long-term problems—nuclear proliferation, Middle East peace, NATO cohesion, for example—invariably receive scant attention. Fortunately, there is virtually no support for a highly centralized system. . . .

No system is acceptable . . . unless it meets the president's needs and style. Personal considerations will largely determine the NSC's role as well as the quality of advice the president receives. But whatever process a president decides upon, some structure is essential. Those who neglect the mechanisms and procedures for formulating and implementing policy—as the Reagan administration did in 1981 and to a considerable degree thereafter—will encounter difficulties. Although there is no universally correct way to structure an NSC system, experience suggests certain guidelines:

- Although a president's subsequent behavior will speak much louder than formal directives, a written directive should be issued in the first week of the administration setting forth the NSC system and delineating the functions of the NSA, the secretary of state, and other key officials.
- There should be a formal method for preparing national security policy studies and issuing presidential decisions to facilitate White House policy direction.
- Senior interagency coordinating committees chaired by the NSC should have clear areas of responsibility and be supported by interagency working groups that develop option papers and oversee the policy analysis effort.

Most senior-level interagency management of the national security system must be delegated to the NSA and the NSC staff. As argued above, neither the

State Department nor any other line department can perform this function effectively, and the president has neither the time nor the ability to manage the executive branch. However, presidents must take some interest in their policy processes and at times intervene personally. . . .

The secretary of state can still be important. However, recent history—certainly since 1961, and probably earlier—cautions against holding out great expectations for the secretary's own department.

Three categories of significant activities can reasonably be expected of State. Foremost among them are the implementation of foreign-policy decisions and the continued fulfillment of the traditional missions of the Foreign Service: representation, negotiation, and reporting. In this diplomatic arena the department and the Foreign Service possess unique experience and talent. Second, though less likely, an influential secretary who has the president's confidence might be able to draw some immediate staff and perhaps two or three senior departmental officers into a closer, more comfortable relationship with the White House. This is a far cry from a State-centered system, but it expands the scope of contact. Finally, State can and must continue to contribute to the whole range of substantive foreign-policy issues—in senior and lower inter-agency committees, in less formal contexts, and through the secretary and the seventh-floor staff. But in most instances the department will remain a contributor, not a leader, in the policy-formulation process. For it to aspire higher is only to court yet another blow to its prestige and reputation.

NOTES

1. I. M. Destler, "A Job that Doesn't Work," FOREIGN POLICY 38(Spring 1980): 80–88; Destler, "State: A Department or 'Something More'?" in Public Policy and Political Institutions: United States Defense and Foreign Policy—Policy Coordination and Integration, ed. Duncan L. Clarke (Greenwich, Conn.: JAI Press, 1985), 104.

2. William I. Bacchus, Staffing for Foreign Affairs: Personnel Systems for the 1980's and 1990's (Princeton: Princeton University Press, 1983), 52. See also Robert L. Rothstein, Planning, Prediction, and Policymaking in Foreign Affairs: Theory and Practice (Boston: Little, Brown, 1972), 39–41.

3. Destler, "State: A Department or 'Something More'?" 99; Destler, Presidents, Bureaucrats and Foreign Policy: The Politics of Organizational Reform (Princeton: Princeton University Press, 1972), 159; Bacchus, Staffing for Foreign Affairs, 69; Henry Kissinger, White House Years (Boston: Little, Brown, 1979), 27; Donald P. Warwick, A Theory of Public Bureaucracy: Politics, Personality, and Organization in the State Department (Cambridge: Harvard University Press, 1975), 33; Barry Rubin, Secrets of State: The State Department and the Struggle over U.S. Foreign Policy (New York: Oxford University Press, 1985), 245.

12. PRESIDENT, CONGRESS, AND AMERICAN FOREIGN POLICY

Thomas E. Cronin

Who makes foreign policy? Who should make foreign policy in America? The United States is unique among major world powers because it is neither a parliamentary democracy nor a wholly executive-dominated government. Our Constitution invites both Congress and the president to set policy and govern the nation.[1]

Article I of the Constitution grants to Congress "all legislative powers," but limits them to those "herein granted." It then sets forth in detail the powers vested in Congress. Article II, in contrast, grants to the president "the executive power," but describes these powers only in vague terms. Is this difference significant? Some scholars and most presidents have argued that a president has additional undefined power to act to promote the well-being of the United States, especially in the area of national security. Thus, they contend, a president is not limited to the powers spelled out in the Constitution as is Congress.

Such a position leads to the view that the presidency ought to have the primary responsibility for foreign policy-making. Because a president, it is added, is the only elected official in the nation answerable to the entire nation, so presidents should be uniquely qualified to pursue foreign policy on behalf of the entire nation. It is merely the next logical step to assert then that Congress should not seek to tie the president's hands when the security of the nation is at stake.

Many scholars and most members of Congress, however, contend that the president has no such inherent power, that the Framers intended Congress to play at least a coequal role in foreign policy-making and that recent presidents such as Lyndon Johnson, Richard Nixon, and Ronald Reagan have too often violated the principles of constitutionalism and the shared responsibilities for setting foreign policy.

Whatever the language of the Constitution, our presidents have often exercised powers not expressly defined in it. These powers have a variety of names: implied or inherent powers, or moral, residual, and emergency powers.

The Framers expected presidents to be a major influence in conducting treaty negotiations and directing military strategy in wartime. Presidents would also send and receive envoys and ambassadors. Yet the authors of our 1787 Constitution most assuredly did not want the president to be the only agent in the making of foreign policy. Indeed, several of the powers specified in the Constitution as being vested in Congress (making laws, declaring war, appropriating funds, approving treaties, confirming top personnel, and so on) were designed to bring Congress directly into the making and setting of foreign policy.

As times have changed and as the roles of Congress and the presidency have changed, tensions between the branches have been inevitable. These were not only anticipated but planned: The branches were designed with different constituencies, different-length terms, and different responsibilities. The branches are also organized differently, and they are jealous of their prerogatives and powers.

Still, even though the Constitution disperses power and invites a continuing struggle between the two branches, it also requires the two branches to integrate the fragmented parts of the system into workable policies. The media tend to emphasize conflict between the two branches, but in practice the Congress and the president cooperate far more often than the stalemates, deadlocks, and antagonism so emphasized in the media would suggest. For example, most presidential nominations win confirmation. The vast bulk of presidential budgetary requests win approval. Few presidential vetoes are overridden. And a considerable amount of constructive compromising characterizes the month-to-month policy-setting relations between the two branches.

Conflicts, however, do regularly occur. Why? In part, because the whole process was designed to maximize checks and balances and deliberation— rather than cooperation and speedy action. The Framers created a system that deliberately involved overlapping, ambiguous, and conflicting powers and responsibilities. They built in not one but several arrangements of checks and balances. And most Americans, by and large, want it this way. However much they may like a president, they do not want that president dictating policies and laws. They want a reasonably strong Congress. And they want presidents to abide by the general principles of constitutionalism.

Much of the time, then, a president must deal with a Congress that moves according to its own pace and that responds to a variety of interests above and beyond those coming from the White House. Members of Congress are influenced—most of the time—more by their own philosophical and ideological convictions, their colleagues in Congress, and the interests of their districts back home than they are by instructions or pleas from the White House. These realities remain central features in presidential-congressional relations.

The abuses of foreign policy-making powers in the Johnson, Nixon, and Reagan administrations aroused many critics to condemn the development of what they called "the imperial presidency."

THE IMPERIAL PRESIDENCY ARGUMENT

Many critics held that, because of abuse of power by presidents, especially abuse of the war powers and secrecy during the 1960s, the early 1970s, and again in the mid-1980s, the presidency became an imperial institution. In his book *The Imperial Presidency*, historian and former Kennedy adviser Arthur M. Schlesinger, Jr., argued that presidential power was so expanded and misused by 1972 that it threatened our constitutional system.[2] Schlesinger claimed that an imperial presidency was created as a result of America's wartime experiences, particularly Vietnam.

Proponents of the "imperial presidency" view contend that the difficulty stems in part from ambiguity concerning the president's power as commander in chief: It is an undefined *office*, not a *function*. Schlesinger and others acknowledge that Nixon and Johnson did not create the imperial presidency; they merely built on some of the more questionable practices of their predecessors. But observers contend there is a distinction between the *abuse* and the *usurpation* of power. Abraham Lincoln, FDR, and Harry Truman temporarily usurped power in wartime. Johnson and Nixon abused power, even in peacetime, by claiming absolute powers to be a part of their office. Reagan's Iran-*contra* abuses are equally condemned as a major abuse of power.[3]

Secrecy has often been used to protect and preserve a president's national security power. It is argued that Nixon pushed the doctrine beyond acceptable limits. Before Eisenhower, Congress expected to get the information it sought from the executive branch. Instances of secrecy and the claim of executive privilege were the rare exceptions. By the early 1970s they had become the rule. And a Congress that knows only what the president wants it to know is not an independent body.

Those who are critical of Nixon contend that he made the presidency not only fully imperial but also revolutionary. For example, in authorizing members of his own White House staff to retaliate against his political opponents, Nixon became the first president in our history to establish an extralegal investigative force, paid for by the taxpayers but unknown to Congress and accountable to no one but himself. Because Nixon also misused intelligence agencies and authorized breaking and entering, he became the only American president known to have supervised lawless actions in peacetime.

Political scientist Theodore Lowi contends that presidents have little choice but to be imperial, given the development of the American national state and the significant practical role of the executive in that development. He suggests that Schlesinger's interpretation exaggerates the case of personal abuse of power by Nixon and others and underestimates the fact that the modern presidency is largely the construction of the Congress with the cooperation of the federal courts. He suggests that the vast growth of presidential power began with the coming of New Deal domestic programs and cannot be linked solely or even primarily with the expansion of the president's foreign policy powers. Although "there may be many specific cases of usurpation by modern presidents, these are extreme actions in pursuit of powers and responsibilities by and large willingly and voluntarily delegated to the president by Congress."[4]

Still, Schlesinger's book is a useful point of departure for discussing the allegedly too powerful presidency. The chief complaints involve such presidential activities as war making, emergency power, diplomacy by executive agreement, covert CIA activities, and undeclared, secretive, and privatized foreign policy operations.

Presidential War Making

The Constitution delegates to Congress the authority to *declare* the legal state of war (with the consent of the president), but in practice the commander in chief often starts or initiates war (or actions that lead to war). This power has been used by the chief executive time and time again. In 1846 President James

K. Polk ordered American forces to advance into disputed territory; when Mexico resisted, Polk informed Congress that war existed by act of Mexico, and a formal declaration of war was soon forthcoming. William McKinley's dispatch of a battleship to Havana, where it was blown up, helped precipitate war with Spain in 1898. Again, the United States was not formally at war with Germany until late 1941, but before Pearl Harbor Franklin Roosevelt ordered the Navy to guard convoys to Great Britain and to open fire on submarines threatening the convoys. Since World War II every president, from Truman through Reagan, has sent forces into combat without specific congressional authorization—to Korea, Berlin, Vietnam, Lebanon, Grenada, Cuba, Libya— in fact, around the world.[5]

Thus, from Washington's time on, by ordering troops into battle, the president has often decided when Americans will fight and when they will not. When the cause has had political support, the president's use of this authority has been approved. Abraham Lincoln called up troops, spent money, set up a blockade, and fought the first few months of the Civil War without even calling Congress into session. More recently it has become obvious that the president needs the power to respond to sudden attacks and to protect the rights and property of American citizens. The State Department has described this enlarged mandate as follows:

> In the twentieth century the world has grown much smaller. An attack on a country far from its shores can impinge directly on the nation's security... The Constitution leaves to the President the judgment to determine whether the circumstances of a particular armed attack are so urgent and the potential consequences so threatening to the security of the U.S. that he should act without formally consulting the Congress.[6]

But Congress became upset when it learned (several years after the fact) that in 1964 President Johnson had won approval of his Vietnam initiatives on the basis of misleading information. In 1969 and 1970 a secret air war was waged in Cambodia with no formal congressional knowledge or authorization. The military also operated in Laos without formally notifying Congress. It was to prevent just such acts as these that the Framers of the Constitution had given Congress the power to declare war, and many members of Congress believe that what happened in Indochina was the result of the White House's bypassing the constitutional requirements. But they also agree that presidential excesses came about because Congress either agreed with presidents or did nothing to stop them.

What the Johnson and Nixon war experiences also show is that at the beginning of hostilities, the country and Congress rally behind a president. As casualties mount and fighting continues, support usually falls off. In both Korea and Vietnam presidential failure to end the use of American ground forces led to increased political trouble. Dwight Eisenhower swept into power in 1952 saying "I shall go to Korea" and thus arousing hope among voters that he would bring about an end to the Korean War. Nixon won in 1968 when Johnson was forced out over Vietnam. But even though Congress may have been misled during the Vietnam War, it enthusiastically supported the president and went along with his actions. Not until the war turned sour did senators and representatives begin to charge misrepresentation. Why, then, were they so easily talked into approving funds for the war? They continued to pass appropriations for it right up to April 1975. The more general lesson appears to be that the country and Congress (and the courts) tend to go along with a president's judgments about military action overseas.

There are additional reasons why no formal congressional declarations of war have been issued in recent times. During a state of war the president assumes certain legal prerogatives that Congress might not always be willing to grant. There are also international legal consequences of a formal declaration of war—regarding foreign assets, the rights of neutrals, and so on—which our allies would not always be willing to recognize and which would be difficult to insist upon. Moreover, there is the psychological consequence of declaring war, compounded by the fact that—according to Article 2, Section 2, of the United Nations Charter—war is illegal except in self-defense.

Diplomacy by Executive Agreement

Before a president can ratify a treaty, two-thirds of the Senate must consent. But a president can enter into formal agreements with a foreign nation, by executive agreements, without senatorial approval. These agreements have been recognized as distinct from treaties since George Washington's day, and their use by the executive has been upheld by the courts. What irked Congress in the 1960s and 1970s was that the Senate was being asked to ratify international accords only on trivial matters. Critically important mutual-aid and military agreements were being arranged by the White House without its even informing Congress.

For example, while the Senate was ratifying treaties to preserve archaeological artifacts in Mexico and to maintain certain rights in the Red Sea, the president was using executive agreements to make vital decisions about U.S. presence in Vietnam, Laos, Korea, and Thailand. Several senators and others argued that these practices violated the Constitution's intent that Congress share in making foreign policy. And so the members of Congress began to look for ways to limit a president's executive-agreement authority.

Ironically, during the 1940s and 1950s conservative members of Congress had tried to check the president's power to make executive agreements. In 1953 Senator John Bricker (R-Ohio) introduced a constitutional amendment that would have required Congress to approve all executive agreements. He was opposed by liberals, especially liberal political scientists and historians, who feared the Bricker Amendment would reintroduce mindless isolationism. Bricker was opposed too by Eisenhower's secretary of state, who called the amendment dangerous to our peace and security. In the wake of Vietnam, and especially during the Nixon administration, the shoe was on the other foot: The liberals, fearing an interventionist foreign policy, now wanted to limit executive agreements.[7]

Government by the CIA and Undeclared Foreign Policy

Presidents have also been charged with abusing the intelligence and spying agencies. The Central Intelligence Agency (CIA) was established in 1947, when the threat of "World Communism" led to a vast number of national security efforts. When the CIA was established, Congress recognized the dangers to a free society inherent in such a secret organization. Hence, it stipulated that the

CIA was not to engage in any police work or to perform operations within the United States.

From 1947 through the 1980s, however, with only rare exceptions, no area of national policy-making was more removed from Congress than CIA operations, especially covert, secret operations. There is considerable evidence that both Congress and the White House have been lax in supervising CIA operations.[8]

By 1973, the CIA was accused of plotting assassinations, experimenting with mind-altering drugs, carrying out extensive foreign paramilitary operations, and, most important, spying on American citizens during the Watergate era.

In the Reagan years, the CIA was again charged with the abuse of its responsibilities and with failure to inform congressional intelligence committees of many of its activities—most notably its widespread coordinating role in providing American assistance to the Nicaraguan *contras* and its mining of Nicaraguan harbors. In late 1984, it became known that the CIA had aided the publication and distribution of a training manual for the *contras*. It instructed the rebels about sabotoge, blackmail, and "neutralization" of public officials through the use of selective violence. Reagan's critics, including former CIA officials, contended that such language urged political assassinations as a means of undermining the Nicaraguan government. Reagan denied these charges, but several lower-echelon CIA employees were dismissed for their role in this affair. The CIA role in helping to arrange arms sales to Iran and in diverting funds from these sales and other fundraising efforts to the Nicaraguan rebels also came under attack in 1987.

CIA Director William Casey personally directed White House aide Oliver L. North's effort to assist the Nicaraguan *contras* during the 1984 to 1986 period, when Congress prohibited U.S. military assistance to them. These and similar activities bent the rules, misled Congress, and violated various laws. Casey, for example, supervised North's secret program to place American military trainers in the *contras'* camps in Honduras, loaned CIA staff and equipment to these training schemes, and gave Lt. Colonel North advice on how to evade congressional restrictions on such aid.

President Reagan and CIA Director Casey also approved arms sales to Iran and ignored various statutory requirements for congressional notification of such arms transfers. The Tower Commission Report speaks to these questions:

> Throughout the Iran initiative, significant questions of law do not appear to have been adequately addressed. In the face of a sweeping statutory prohibition and explicit requirements relating to Presidential consent to arms transfers by third countries, there appears to have been at the outset in 1985 little attention, let alone systematic analysis, devoted to how presidential actions would comply with U.S. law. The Board [Tower Board] has found no evidence that an evaluation was ever done during the life of the operation to determine whether it continued to comply with the terms of the January 17 Presidential Finding. Similarly, when a new prohibition was added to the Arms Export Control Act in August of 1986 to prohibit exports to countries on the terrorism list (a list which contained Iran), no evaluation was made to determine whether this law affected authority to transfer arms to Iran in connection with intelligence operations under the National Security Act. This lack of legal vigilance markedly increased the chances that the initiative would proceed contrary to law.[9]

The Iran-*contra* affair is merely the latest, if one of the worst, illustrations of the imperial presidency. White House aides and advisors with access to millions of dollars (some of it taxpayers' dollars and some of it privately recruited from either wealthy U.S. citizens or friendly allies) and an intimate understanding of Ronald Reagan's foreign policy priorities took foreign policy into their own hands. These aides and advisors deliberately deceived Congress, most of the cabinet, much of the CIA regular staff, and sometimes even the president.

Why did the Reagan people go to such lengths to bypass the Congress? In part, they had run into extensive congressional opposition. Congress was increasingly skeptical of the Reagan administration's policies in Central America. Moreover, several White House advisors became frustrated with what they viewed as the fragmentation or parochialism in Congress.

This is how Reagan's staff and the CIA director apparently viewed the situation: Congress was poorly suited to micromanage U.S. foreign policy. Its 535 members were too tied to parochial interests to pursue the steady realization of coherent policy goals. Congress bent like a reed in the wind, one month bending this way, a few months later bending another way.

Further, Congress had enacted a number of restrictions, such as against providing aid to the *contras* and against transferring arms to a terrorist nation. Yet to the White House, new and special circumstances existed that they believed justified White House covert operations and undeclared foreign policy activities. Secrecy was of the essence, and Congress could not, in their view, be informed.

President Reagan later acknowledged that he and his staff had erred. Speaking to the American people on March 4, 1987, Reagan said he would change his ways:

> As a start, yesterday I met with the entire professional staff of the National Security Council. I defined for them the values I want to guide the national security policies of this country. I told them that I wanted a policy that was as justifiable and understandable in public as it was in secret. I wanted a policy that reflected the will of the Congress, as well as the White House. And I told them that there will be no more freelancing by individuals when it comes to our national security.[10]

Reagan also said, in the wake of the Iran-*contra* scandal, that proper procedures in consultation with the Congress will be followed not only in letter, but in spirit.

Why do White House aides sometimes violate the law? One noteworthy response was offered by one of Richard Nixon's White House staffers, as he stood before a U.S. district judge awaiting sentencing for his role in one of the several Watergate episodes. This episode involved breaking into the office of the psychiatrist of a Nixon foreign policy critic, in an effort to discredit him and lessen pressure on Nixon's policies. This is how the repentant aide suggested the word "national security" affected him:

> While I early concluded that the operation had been a mistake, it is only recently that I have come to regard it as unlawful. I see now that the key is the effect that the term "national security" had on my judgment. The very words served to block critical analysis. . . . Freedom of the President to pursue his planned course was the ultimate national security objective. . . . The invocation of national security stopped me from asking the question "is this the right thing to do. . . ."

I see now that sincerity of my motivation was not a justification but indeed a contributing cause of the incident. I hope that the young men and women who are fortunate enough to have an opportunity to serve in government can benefit from this experience and learn that sincerity can often be as blinding as it is worthy. I hope they will recognize that the banner of national security can turn perceived patriotism into actual disservice. . . .[11]

CONGRESS'S EFFORTS TO REASSERT ITSELF AS A CO-EQUAL PARTNER IN FOREIGN POLICY-MAKING

From 1970 through the Reagan administration Congress has sought, often in a fitful and incoherent fashion, to define for itself a more assertive role in shaping foreign and national security policy. As can be seen from the short list below, its efforts have placed constraints on the executive as much if not more than they have defined a larger role for Congress. A few of these will be discussed at length in the pages that follow:

- *Cooper-Church Amendment* (1971)—Stipulated that no funds could be used to introduce U.S. troops into Laos or Thailand.
- *War Powers Resolution* (1973)—Requires the president to notify Congress within forty-eight hours of sending U.S. troops into combat and states that the troops must be withdrawn after sixty days unless Congress has voted to declare war.
- *Jackson-Vanik Amendment* (1974)—A provision of the 1974 Trade Act that linked granting the Soviet Union most-favored-nation trade status to Soviet policy toward emigration.
- *Amendment to the Arms Export Control Act* (1974)—Gave Congress thirty calendar days to review major proposed arms sales and to vote on whether to block the sales by concurrent resolution approved by both the House and the Senate.
- *The Hughes-Ryan Amendment to the Foreign Assistance Act* (1974)—Required that Congress be regularly informed about covert operations and called for the President to certify the necessity of all such operations. The key language of the amendment stated that "no funds . . . may be expended by or on behalf of the Central Intelligence Agency . . . unless and until the President finds that such operation is important to the national security of the United States."
- *Clark Amendment to the International Security Assistance and Arms Export Control Act* (1976)—Prohibited covert assistance to Angolan rebels.
- *Embargo on Sale of U.S. Arms to Turkey* (1975)—Prohibited sales of arms to Turkey until 1978.
- *Intelligence Oversight Act* (1980)—Requires the CIA director to report all significant intelligence activities to the House and Senate Intelligence Committees "in a timely fashion."
- *The Boland Amendment to the Defense Appropriations Bill* (1982)—Prohibited funds provided by this appropriations measure to be used by the CIA or Defense Department to furnish military equipment, military

training, or advice or any other support for the overthrowing of the government of Nicaragua.

The War Powers Resolution of 1973

In 1973 Congress overrode a presidential veto and enacted the War Powers Resolution. Congress declared that henceforth the president can commit the armed forces of the United States only (1) after a declaration of war by Congress; (2) by specific statutory authorization; or (3) in a national emergency created by an attack on the United States or on its armed forces. After committing the armed forces under the third circumstance, the president is required to report to Congress within forty-eight hours. Unless Congress has declared war, the troop commitment will be ended within sixty days. The president is allowed another thirty days if he claims the safety of U.S. forces requires their continued use. A president is also obligated by this resolution to consult Congress "in every possible instance" before committing troops to battle. Moreover, at any time, by concurrent resolution *not subject to presidential veto,* Congress may direct the president to disengage such troops. Because of a 1983 court ruling, whether Congress can remove the troops by concurrent resolution or legislative veto is now in doubt.

Not everyone was pleased by the passage of the War Powers Resolution. But many experts believed the legislation to be of symbolic and institutional significance, because it reflected a new determination in Congress. Presidents now know that commitment of American troops is subject to congressional approval. They will have to persuade the nation that their actions are justified by the gravest of national emergencies.

All our recent presidents, including Reagan, have opposed the War Powers Resolution as unwise and overly restrictive. They claim it gives to Congress the right to force them to do what the Constitution says they do not have to do—to withdraw American forces at some arbitrary moment. The War Powers Resolution has not been tested in the courts, and probably will not be, because it raises political questions, with which judges are unwilling to be involved.

How has the resolution worked? Since its adoption in 1973 the process it spells out has been used several times. It was used, for example, when Marines were sent in 1975 to free the merchant cargo ship *Mayagüez,* which had been captured by the Cambodians. In 1982 President Reagan reported to Congress, along the lines of the resolution, after he sent troops into Lebanon. Yet he made clear in a written statement that his compliance did not "cede any of the authority vested in me under the Constitution as President and as commander in chief. . . . Nor should my signing be viewed as any acknowledgment that the President's constitutional authority can be impermissibly infringed by statute."[12] Then, in the 1983 U.S. invasion, or rescue mission, in Grenada, Reagan acted completely on his own until after the troops had already landed. Furthermore, he acted as though he did not need any sort of authorization. What did Congress do? Virtually nothing. A few members grumbled.

Nor did President Reagan invoke the War Powers Resolution provisions for military operations in Honduras. He also employed military power against Libya twice in 1986, and in neither case did he seek prior advice from Congress. Although he sent reports about these actions to Congress after the incidents, he went out of his way to make it clear that he was not acting in accordance with the

War Powers Resolution. Both military actions against Libya won widespread support in Congress and in the country, although Congressman Dante Fascell (D-Fla.), chair of the House Foreign Affairs Committee, complained that the president was waltzing around the War Powers Resolution and was developing "a new way of going to war which totally bypasses the Constitution" and its requirement that only Congress can declare war.[13] Reagan responded that he was acting in self-defense against terrorism. His State Department spokesperson said "the deployment of anti-terrorist units . . . would seem to fall completely outside the scope of the [War Powers] Resolution."[14]

For the most part, then, the War Powers Resolution has not hindered presidential military and war-making action. Nor has it, as Nixon had argued, weakened the presidency in any visible way. Even its chief sponsor in the Senate recognized its inadequacies.[15]

What is the future of the War Powers Resolution? It will remain, as will the considerable disputes over its effectiveness and constitutionality. Someday Congress is likely to improve it by defining a group of congressional leaders with whom the president should consult prior to commitment of American forces abroad.

Congress's Efforts to Oversee the CIA

Congress has tried to reassert control over the CIA. It now requires the agency to report to two committees—the House and the Senate oversight committees—any plans for clandestine operations. In 1976, in an unprecedented exercise of power, Congress amended the Defense Appropriations Bill to terminate American covert intervention in Angola. But skeptics doubt whether Congress will be able to maintain control over the CIA.

The Intelligence Oversight Act of 1980 is yet another effort by the Congress to reassert its claim on the authority it shares with the White House to set foreign policy. This 1980 act reaffirmed earlier legislation requiring presidential approval of covert activities, but it required of the director of central intelligence and the heads of other agencies involved in intelligence activities that they report such activities in a timely fashion to the congressional intelligence committees.

According to most experts, the Reagan administration violated the letter and the spirit of this act when it chose not to inform the Congress of its arms sales to Iran in 1985 and 1986. Two students of the act suggest Reagan was wrong to do so, yet the ambiguities of the law may have led the president and his aides to believe they were merely circumventing the law:

> Prior notice was not given, notice in a timely fashion apparently was not intended, and the CIA director may have failed to report unauthorized intelligence activity. The major ambiguity is the status of a delay in reporting under the "due regard" clause. In any case, a central purpose of the act [the Intelligence Oversight Act of 1980], to provide a mechanism for consultation with Congress, was deliberately undermined. The only defense for such a sweeping avoidance of notification requirements can be a constitutional one. That is, the administration must argue that the President's right to keep national security secrets from Congress is inherent in his commander-in-chief authority. If this is a valid defense, it undermines both the prior notice and timely fashion requirements of the Act, contrary to Congress' hope.[16]

Presidents have criticized Congress for weakening the CIA—for going too far in making covert operations too difficult. President Carter especially pressed this case during the Iranian and Afghan crises of 1980. The Reagan administration gave the CIA a new era of prominence, enhanced powers, and generous budgets.

Former CIA Director Stansfield Turner argues that congressional oversight has been useful. It forces intelligence officers to exercise greater judiciousness and to maintain a healthy sense of the national temper, he contends. He also believes that congressional oversight strengthens the hand of the CIA director in controlling what has always been a notoriously independent agency.[17] On balance we have to conclude that for all the talk of greater congressional control, the CIA and the president have not been seriously hampered in carrying out what they deem necessary. To be sure the Iran-*contra* revelations were a setback for Reagan and the CIA. On the other hand, however, they revealed how independent and evasive of Congress were many of its activities.

Confirmation Politics

The Framers of the Constitution regarded the confirmation process and its advice and consent by the Senate as a check on executive power. Alexander Hamilton viewed it as a way for Congress to prevent the appointment of "unfit characters." Even today, the Senate and the president often struggle over control of top personnel in the executive and judicial branches. The Constitution leaves the question somewhat ambiguous: "The President . . . shall nominate, and by and with the advice and consent of the Senate, shall appoint Ambassadors, other public Ministers and Consuls, Judges of the Supreme Court, and all other officers of the United States . . ." Presidents, however, have never enjoyed exclusive control over hiring and firing in the executive branch. The Senate jealously guards its right to confirm or reject major appointments; during the period of congressional government after the Civil War, presidents had to struggle to keep their power to appoint and dismiss. But for most of the twentieth century, presidents have gained a reasonable amount of control over top appointments. This has happened in part because public-administration experts warned that a chief executive cannot otherwise be held accountable.

In recent years, however, the Senate has taken a somewhat tougher stand on presidential appointments. Senators are especially concerned about potential conflicts of interest. Time spent evaluating and screening presidential nominations has increased. "Our tolerance for mediocrity and lack of independence from economic interests is rapidly coming to an end," said one senator. Another summed it up this way: "Surely, we have learned that one item the government is short on is credibility." Screening became somewhat tighter; Presidents Ford and Carter had several high-level appointees turned down. Reagan lost several potential nominees because of conflict-of-interest problems, and others were denied confirmation because of their policy views. In the course of one session of Congress today, presidents regularly submit as many as 8,000 civilian and over 100,000 military nominations that require Senate confirmation.

The confirmation provisions in the Constitution have fulfilled most of the intentions of the Founders. The Senate has been able to use its power to reject unqualified nominees. It has sometimes also been able to prevent those with conflicts of interest from taking office. In addition, senators have been able to use the confirmation process to make their views known to prospective executive officials. Indeed, the very existence of the confirmation process deters presidents from appointing weak, questionable, or "unfit characters." Yet, by and large, presidents have still been able to appoint the people they want to important positions.

The Senate's role in the confirmation process was never intended to eliminate politics, but rather to use politics as a safeguard. Some conservatives in the Reagan years objected that the Senate rejected occasional nominees because of their political beliefs and thus interfered with the executive power of presidents. In such instances, so this complaint goes, the Senate's decision is not a reflection of the fitness of a nominee but rather of the political strength of the president.

Despite the importance of this constitutional power, the Senate has never established clear guidelines or a systematic process for screening presidential nominees. The Senate's participation during the past twenty-five years has become more thorough, more independent, and even somewhat more consistent. "Unfortunately, the process has also become more tedious, time-consuming, and intrusive for the nominees," according to one recent study. "For some, this price is too high, particularly in conjunction with the requirements of the Ethics in Government Act. For others, the process is annoying and distasteful but not enough of a roadblock to prevent them from going forward."[18]

Other Actions

Congress has also become more involved in general foreign policy. Shaking off years of inertia, Congress imposed a cutoff of aid to Vietnam and a bombing halt in Cambodia. As of 1972 it required the secretary of state to submit to Congress the final texts of executive agreements. It also restrained the Ford administration from getting involved in Portugal and Angola. This was clearly a case of Congress's imposing its goals on the executive. Congress has also demanded, and won, a greater role in arms sales abroad and in determining U.S. involvement in Lebanon, Central America, and the Caribbean. In late 1982, for example, Congress attempted to curb covert training activities by amending the Defense Appropriations Bill to prohibit funding in support of any forces aiming to overthrow the Nicaraguan government. This became known as the Boland Amendment.

In addition, individual members of Congress are likely to travel around the world to international trouble spots, to conduct their own investigations and sometimes even their own negotiations. Presidents Ford, Carter, and Reagan became increasingly bothered by such second-guessing and attempts by Congress to interfere with presidential foreign policy-making. These and myriad other actions were all parts of an effort by Congress to reclaim its lost authority and to respond to a public that seemed to want power shared in a way that placed Congress on a more equal footing than had been the case.

Not every effort by Congress succeeded, nor did every effort guarantee that Congress was playing a better or more creative role. Indeed, many well-intentioned reforms that sought to reclaim authority for the national legislature were merely congressional victories that stopped or inhibited presidents from carrying out their policy plans. Rarely did such reforms ensure that Congress would formulate better policy alternatives; more typically it meant that Congress could delay or modify what a president sought to achieve. And sometimes, it merely brought about a deadlock.

THE REAGAN REASSERTION AND ITS SETBACK

Most informed observers now believe that Congress did not really gain back many of its alleged lost powers, and are skeptical of Congress's ability to match the advantages of the presidency for setting the long-term policy direction of the nation. Clearly, Ronald Reagan demonstrated that a popular president who knew what he wanted to do could not only influence the national policy agenda but also win considerable cooperation from the Congress.

Even before Reagan won the 1980 presidential election, support for a restrengthened presidency was gaining public support. Some people believed Congress (and the press) had overreacted to both Vietnam and Nixon's antics and abuses of power. Others believed Congress was correct to try to win back some of its powers, but felt it had gone a bit too far. Others could understand what Congress was doing, but soon realized that our system functions best when a strong, positive president is willing to play a key role in initiating legislative and budgetary proposals.

The American public may have lost confidence in its leaders, but it had not lost hope in the efficacy of strong, purposive leadership. Whether or not people believed in Ronald Reagan's policy priorities, many supported his view that the country needed a strong president who would strengthen the presidency and make the office a more vital center of national policy than it had been in the years immediately following the Watergate scandals.

A central question during the late 1970s and early 1980s was whether, in the wake of a somewhat diminished presidency, the Congress could furnish the necessary leadership to govern the country. Most people, including many members of Congress, did not think Congress could play that role. The routine answer as we approach the 1990s is that the United States will need a presidency of substantial power if we are to solve the trade and budget deficits, productivity, and other economic and national security problems we currently face. We live in a continuous state of emergency, where terrorist acts and especially nuclear warfare threaten to destroy our country. In addition, global competition of almost every sort highlights the need for swift and sure leadership, and a certain amount of efficiency and unity, in our government. Many people realize too that weakening the presidency may, as often as not, strengthen the vast federal bureaucracy more than strengthen Congress.

It is clear today that the congressional reassertion efforts of the 1970s were more a groping and often unsystematic, if well-intentioned, attempt by Congress to be taken seriously than an effort to weaken the presidency. It did not take long for close observers to appreciate that when a president is unable to exercise authority and leadership, no one else is able to supply comparable purpose and initiative. Not only was the pre-Watergate view that history has usually shown the presidency to be the most effective instrument for innovation, experimentation, and progress reaffirmed, but a majority of Americans concurred that to the extent the country is governable on a national basis, it is governed from the White House by a president and his top advisers, in cooperation with the Congress.

How did Reagan infuse the presidency with more energy and effectiveness? First, he came to office with enormous self-confidence and optimism and a personal style that celebrated the promise of American success and achievements. He much more fully appreciated the symbolic and morale-building functions of the modern presidency than had his predecessors. Second, he knew the power of ideas and themes, and he cleverly focused both his own energies and the attention of the nation on four or five fresh policy initiatives (such as tax cuts and tax reform, increased military spending, and reductions in what he claimed were unnecessary federal regulations).

Perhaps his most important successes came in clarifying and redefining for the average American some basic values about the role of government. Time and again he stressed that we should turn to the federal government mainly for national defense needs, but that we should return more of the domestic activities of the national government to state and local governments and, if possible, even back to the private sector and individual responsibility. His consistent trumpeting of these views and his effective use of the media soon enabled him to score victories in Congress. Reagan was also almost always ready to accept less than all of his proposed legislative programs; in so doing, he often appeared to be a conciliatory legislative leader.

Reagan was not always successful in winning cooperation from Congress, but in his first six years he pushed vigorously to expand presidential authority. He often succeeded in minimizing, or even ignoring, congressional interference and in deflecting some of the reassertions of the 1970s.

But in his second term Reagan's style of management, his overreliance on chief of staff Donald Regan, and his failure to use the National Security Council for full debates and review of his policies undid many of the institutional achievements of his first term. The Congress and the American public reacted very negatively to the findings that Reagan, his CIA director, and several other of his aides and advisers deliberately withheld information from Congress and engaged in additional cover-up activities about their mistaken actions in Iran and Nicaragua.

The Tower Commission Report and subsequent congressional investigations about the Reagan administration's abuses of foreign policy-making powers dealt a major political blow to Reagan's presidency and weakened its credibility in the eyes of the public.

These investigations pointed out anew the need for a strong National Security Council that meets regularly and provides frank and regular advice to the president. Reagan was hurt, in many respects, not from too strong an NSC but one that was too weak, too dominated by military aides (40 percent of its membership at one point), and from too much turnover in the key position of national security assistant to the president.

Plainly the main fault was Reagan's own lack of curiosity and interest in having the NSC system operate as the serious multiple-advocacy system it was intended to be. In hindsight, too, it is clear the NSC system failed because it was too often preoccupied with covert operations and various managerial activities it was unwilling or unable to delegate to the CIA or State and Defense Departments. There may be rare occasions when the NSC is justified in executive implementation of a president's policies, yet these very activities can undermine the NSC's ability to serve the president as a staff assigned to gather and evaluate impartial policy options and advice.

The senior NSC assistant to the president, as the Tower Commission Report correctly recommended, should serve just one master—the president—and hence should not be subject to confirmation by the U.S. Senate.

Congress, for its part, may also have been too lax in the performance of its responsibilities. Perhaps the time has come for a joint national security committee in Congress, composed of the ranking leaders of both chambers plus the chair and ranking minority member of the foreign affairs, armed services and intelligence committees in both chambers. Such a committee could meet monthly with the president and secretary of state, and tough questions could be posed by each side to the other. Properly designed and staffed, such a committee might become the congressional group a president consults with on vital questions of military intervention and covert operations. Doubtless there are many objections to the formation of such a committee, but I think these objections—such as that certain relevant committees might be left out and that partisan gamesmanship might follow divided (partisan) government—would be overcome by Congress's need for some structure within its own sprawling branch to meet the presidency on these vital matters of state—and to meet the president on its terms rather than on his.

Our system of checks and balances, of deliberation and consultation, must be strong enough for effective leadership, while dispersing power enough to ensure liberty. It is precisely when the "national security" is at stake that uncertainties and confusion arise. Justice Robert Jackson long ago warned us that "security is like liberty in that many crimes are committed in its name."[19] This was true in the 1960s and 1970s, and in the mid- and late 1980s we discover it once again.

THE PRESIDENT AND CONGRESS: THE CONTINUING STRUGGLE

However much the public may want Congress to be a major partner with the president and a major check on the president, the public's support for Congress is always subject to deterioration. Power is dispersed in Congress. Its deliberations and quarrels are public. After a while, the public begins to view Congress as "the bickering branch," especially if a persuasive activist is in the White House.

Polls show that people think Congress pays more attention to public views than does the president. Assuredly, Congress is a splendid forum that represents and registers the diversity of America. But that very virtue makes it difficult for Congress to provide leadership, and difficult for it to challenge and bargain effectively with presidents. Not surprisingly, a wary public—dissatisfied with programs that do not work and policies that do not measure up to the urgencies of the moment—will look elsewhere, often to the president or to an aspiring presidential candidate.

A theory of cyclical relations between the president and Congress has long been fashionable. It holds that there will be periods of presidential ascendancy followed by periods of congressional ascendancy. Usually these periods last a decade or more, and sometimes they are a generation in length. Analysis suggests that a moderate but real congressional resurgence did take place in the immediate post-Watergate years. But the responsibilities of the presidency these days, coupled with the complexities of foreign and economic policy, do not really permit any serious weakening of the office. Congress has regained some of its own lost power, and it has tried to curb the misuse and abuse of power—but it has not really weakened the presidency.

Many will continue to worry about future imperial presidents and about the possible alienation of the people from their leaders as complex issues continue to centralize responsibilities in the hands of the national government and the executive. Those who are concerned about these matters will not content themselves, nor should they, with the existing safeguards against the misuse of presidential powers. It is not easy, however, to contrive devices that will check the president who would misuse powers, without hamstringing the president who would use those same powers for purposive and democratically acceptable ends.

Both the president and Congress have to recognize they are not supposed to be two sides out to "win" but two parts of the same government, elected to pursue together the interests of the American people. Too much has been made, by too many presidents and by too many scholars, of that ancient but partial truth that only the president is the representative of all the people. Members of Congress do not represent the people exactly as a president does, but the two houses collectively represent them in ways a president cannot and does not.

In the end, the issue is not so much whether the presidency should be stronger than Congress, or vice versa. The real issue is that Congress and the presidency must both be strengthened to do the pressing work required for the well-being of the nation.

NOTES

1. I have borrowed here and at several points in this essay from some of my earlier writings: *The State of The Presidency* (Boston: Little, Brown and Co., 1980); "A Resurgent Congress and The Imperial Presidency," *Political Science Quarterly*, 95 (Summer, 1980), pp. 209–237, and from a text I co-author, *Government By The People* (Englewood Cliffs, N.J.: Prentice-Hall, 1987).

2. Arthur M. Schlesinger, Jr., *The Imperial Presidency*, (Boston: Houghton Mifflin, 1973).

3. R. W. Apple, Jr., ed., *The Tower Commission Report* (N.Y.: Times Books 1987).

4. Theodore Lowi, *The Personal President* (Ithaca, N.Y.: Cornell University Press, 1985), p. 179.

5. See Thomas A. Bailey, *The Pugnacious Presidents: War Presidents on Parade* (New York: Free Press, 1980).

6. Leonard C. Meeker, "The Legality of U.S. Participation in the Defense of Vietnam," *Department of State Bulletin* (March 28, 1966), pp. 484–485.

7. On executive agreements and treaties see Lawrence Margolis, *Executive Agreements and Presidential Power in Foreign Policy* (New York: Praeger, 1986), and William L. Furlong and Margaret E. Scranton, *The Dynamics of Foreign Policymaking: The President, The Congress and the Panama Canal Treaties* (Boulder, Colo.: Westview Press, 1984).

8. See Stansfield Turner, *Secrecy and Democracy: The CIA in Transition* (Boston: Houghton Mifflin, 1985).

9. *The Tower Commission Report*, p. 79. See also James M. McCormick and Steven S. Smith, "The Iran Arms Sales and the Intelligence Oversight Act of 1980" *P.S.* (Winter, 1987), pp. 29–37.

10. President Ronald Reagan, address to the nation in response to the Tower Commission Report, March 4, 1987.

11. Egil Krogh, Jr., statement released in U.S. District Court, Los Angeles, January 24, 1974, published in *The New York Times* (January 25, 1974), p. 16.

12. Quoted in Christopher Madison, "Despite His Complaints Reagan Going Along with Spirit of War Powers Law," *National Journal* (May 19, 1984), p. 990.

13. Quoted in "In Wake of Libya, Skirmishing over War Powers," *Congressional Quarterly* (May 10, 1986), p. 1021.

14. Abraham D. Sofaer, "The War Powers Resolution and Antiterrorist Operations." Statement before the Subcommittee on Arms Control, International Security and Science, House Foreign Affairs Committee, April 29, 1986.

15. Jacob K. Javits, "War Powers Reconsidered," *Foreign Affairs* (Fall 1985), pp. 130–140.

16. James M. McCormick and Steven S. Smith, "The Iran Arms Sale and the Intelligence Oversight Act of 1980" *P.S.* (Winter, 1987) p. 32.

17. Stansfield Turner, *Secrecy and Democracy: The CIA in Transition* (Boston: Houghton Mifflin, 1985).

18. Christopher J. Deering, "Damned If You Do and Damned If You Don't: The Senate Role in the Appointment Process," in G. Calvin Mackensie, ed., *The In-and-Outers: Presidential Appointees and the Problems of Transient Government in Washington* (Baltimore, Md.: Johns Hopkins Press, 1987), chap. 5.

19. Justice Robert Jackson, *United States ex. rel. Knauff v. Shaughnessy*, 338 U.S. 537, 551 (1950).

13. POLITICS OVER PROMISE: DOMESTIC IMPEDIMENTS TO ARMS CONTROL

Steven E. Miller

Disappointment with negotiated arms control as it has been practiced over the past two decades is widespread and is found as much among proponents as among critics. This disappointment, caused largely by the decade-long failure to achieve telling limitations on strategic offensive nuclear forces, has spawned a veritable cottage industry of writings on the future of arms control, writings which seek new, more fruitful approaches to arms control or new recipes for success in given negotiations. Lavish attention has been given to the problem of rethinking, restructuring, restarting, fixing, or otherwise improving the prospects for and the effectiveness of negotiated arms control. . . .

A common premise of this outpouring of effort and ideas is that further attention to the substantive issues of arms control will yield answers that will somehow make possible significant progress. But the arms control process has never wanted for ideas and proposals, only for success and impact. New ideas and new proposals are unlikely to change that fact.

Largely unconfronted in any systematic way in the current disarray with respect to arms control is one overriding, fundamentally important reality: that the promise of arms control as an instrument of national security policy has been stunted as much by domestic political factors as by any other. Indeed, the lesson that emerges most strongly from the record of the past twenty-five years is that domestic political impediments to negotiated arms control regularly triumph over its substantive possibilities.[1] There are, of course, other serious obstacles: the Soviet Union is a notoriously difficult negotiating partner, obstinate, opaque, and inflexible; the asymmetric forces possessed by the two sides complicate negotiations; the march of technology raises hard, sometimes seemingly intractable negotiating problems; and, on the American side, at least, the sensibilities of allies must be taken into account. But these have not proven insurmountable. . . .

THE MODERN THEORY OF ARMS CONTROL

The intellectual foundations of arms control in the nuclear age were laid more than twenty years ago and have scarcely been modified since.[2] Except insofar

Note: Some footnotes have been deleted, and others have been renumbered to appear in consecutive order.

as . . . there are unilateral measures that advance the purposes of arms control, very little attention was given to domestic politics. . . .

Much of this early work on arms control was devoted to demonstrating its potential benefits by showing that there existed plausible arms control solutions to pressing security concerns. Arms control, it was said, could reduce, if not eliminate, the incentives to strike first and so rid the strategic relationship of dangerous fears of surprise attack. It could diminish the chances of accidental or inadvertent war. It would inhibit the spread of nuclear weapons. In general, arms control was offered as a potential means of enhancing the stability, and thereby increasing the safety, of the nuclear balance, and the early theorists of nuclear arms control were keen to explain how it was that it could be so. It is a measure of how far we have come that these notions now seem commonplace. . . .

But to be persuasive, arms control proponents had to do more than just prove that arms control could be useful; they also had to show that it was feasible. This, in the late 1950s and early 1960s, was a harder task. It entailed addressing the two major obstacles to arms control: the difficulty in achieving an effective means of monitoring compliance and the daunting prospect of dealing with the Soviet Union as a negotiating partner. . . .

In sum, three questions troubled those who struggled with these issues during the formative period of 1958 to 1961 when arms control was beginning to emerge as a truly substantive component of national policy: (1) Could arms control be accepted as an instrument of security policy with a role to play in helping to address important security problems? (2) Would it be possible to monitor compliance with arms control treaties? and (3) Would the Soviet Union be willing to play a constructive role in arms control negotiations?

In subsequent years, each of these questions has been answered in the affirmative. It is widely accepted, even by those who have doubts about the particulars of a given treaty, that arms control is, in theory and often in practice, a legitimate and useful activity that can contribute to national security. The rapid improvement of satellite reconnaissance technologies has made verification a far more tractable problem than anyone could have expected twenty-five years ago; the development of national technical means (NTM) of verification has obviated the need for on-site inspection that was once assumed a prerequisite of negotiated agreements. Finally, in the course of a number of negotiations, the Soviets have shown themselves to be tough but serious negotiators with whom it is possible to reach agreement. These points should not be overstated: some still doubt the value of arms control; verification is still a major stumbling block; and some still doubt Soviet seriousness and trustworthiness. But, nevertheless, the main conditions identified by the early theorists as necessary for progress in arms control have been met.

Given this development, it might be expected that arms control had entered its heyday. Certainly the early arms control theorists were quite optimistic about its prospects. But has there been great progress?

GAINS AND DISAPPOINTMENTS FOR ARMS CONTROL

Although negotiated arms control has some significant accomplishments to its credit, the net record is sufficiently disappointing to indicate that simply meeting the conditions of the early theorists was not enough to usher in a new age of negotiated restraint. While the achievements of arms control should not be belittled, it seems fair to say that it has not lived up to the hopes invested in it; the plus side of the arms control ledger is accompanied by a substantial slate of minuses.

On the plus side, there has been, first, a tremendous amount of arms control activity. A fairly steady stream of treaties has been negotiated, beginning with the Antarctic Treaty of 1959 and including the Hot Line Agreement (1963), the Limited Test Ban Treaty (1963), the Outer Space Treaty (1967), the Non-Proliferation Treaty (1968), the Seabed Arms Control Treaty (1971), the Biological Weapons Convention (1972), the SALT I Agreements (1972), the Threshold Test Ban Treaty (1974), as well as the SALT II Treaty (signed in 1979 but never ratified)—and there are others. These treaties are the product of a huge investment in the preparation for and the participation in arms control negotiations. Formal discussion of a ban on nuclear testing began in 1958 and has continued, with occasional interruptions, into the 1980s. The question of non-proliferation occupied statesmen throughout much of the 1960s, and recurred on the arms control agenda of the 1970s in such guises as the Nuclear Suppliers Club discussions of the mid-1970s and the International Nuclear Fuel Cycle Evaluation of the late 1970s. The confrontation of conventional military forces in Central Europe has been the subject of more than a decade of continuous (albeit fruitless) negotiations. And setting aside an occasional hiatus, strategic nuclear arms negotiations have been underway more or less continuously since 1969.

Even during the Reagan Administration, at a time of great acrimony in U.S.–Soviet relations and with an American administration . . . unenthusiastic about arms control, three separate negotiations were conducted—the Strategic Arms Reduction Talks (START); the negotiations on intermediate-range nuclear forces (INF) in Europe; and the Mutual and Balanced Force Reduction talks (MBFR). . . . Moreover, arms control is well established as high-level policy, which attracts the attention of presidents, secretaries of state, national security advisers, and of the general public as well.

Second, and much more important than the mere fact of activity, several of the agreements impose restraints on central aspects of the arms competition. The Limited Test Ban Treaty prohibits atmospheric testing of nuclear weapons. The Non-Proliferation Treaty has established a regime which inhibits the spread of nuclear weapons to additional states. And in strategic arms control, the ABM Treaty succeeded in bringing the testing and deployment of defensive systems under stringent control, thereby restraining one large area of weapons technology and closing off, for the time being, the possibility of an interaction between offensive and defensive systems that has the potential to lead to huge increases in the cost and size of the strategic forces of the superpowers. With respect to offensive forces, SALT I did place a ceiling on numbers of delivery systems, and SALT II added to this constraints on numbers of warheads and some modest restrictions on modernization. These were constructive developments and represent considerable improvement over a completely unconstrained environment whose possible costs and dangers make it undesirable compared to the moderately limited environment of today.

Set against these achievements, however, are the disappointing aspects of arms control diplomacy. Surveying the record of the past twenty-five years, one cannot avoid three negative conclusions. First, the recent history of arms control is littered with as many failures as successes. In this, the two conferences of

1958 which initiated the era of serious arms negotiations (the Surprise Attack Conference and the Geneva Conference on the Discontinuance of Nuclear Weapons Tests) were unfortunately symptomatic: both ended unsuccessfully. But beyond those first false starts have been many other failed efforts. There is still no comprehensive test ban treaty. MBFR has to date produced no agreement, despite years of endless discussion. The conventional arms transfer talks were unsuccessful. Discussion of anti-satellite arms control proved abortive. Negotiations on naval limitations in the Indian Ocean led nowhere. The Threshold Test Ban Treaty and the SALT II agreement remain unratified. Even in cases where agreement was eventually reached, progress was often painfully slow.

Second, and more importantly, the impact of arms control has been modest, especially relative to the level of effort invested in it. As one exceptionally cynical commentator put it, "Arms control negotiations have served as a long-term source of employment for diplomats and of copy for journalists and academics but they have had little military impact."[3] Many of the agreements that have been reached have prohibited weapons from being put in places where there were none anyway—such as Antarctica, the sea-bed, or outer space—or have constrained weapons that nobody had much incentive to use—such as biological weapons. Such agreements are not without value, but they do not address the central problems and dangers that confront us.

In the cases where arms control agreements have confronted major aspects of the arms race, their effect has generally been limited. The Limited Test Ban Treaty has safeguarded the environment but has not proven especially constraining to the nuclear weapons programs of the superpowers (and several of the smaller nuclear powers are not signatories of the treaty). The Non-Proliferation Treaty has contributed to a regime of restraints that has probably slowed the spread of nuclear weapons, but the most worrisome cases remain outside the treaty or seek to elude its constraints.

And strategic arms control, the centerpiece of arms control in the past fifteen years and the primary interest of most defense and arms control analysts, has produced results that have disappointed supporters and critics alike. For in the 1970s, the decade of SALT, there occurred an enormous buildup of strategic nuclear forces *on both sides*. Both the United States and the Soviet Union added thousands of nuclear weapons to their arsenals during this period; between 1971 and 1980 the American stockpile of deployed nuclear warheads doubled while the Soviet Union's tripled. In addition, modernization proceeded apace. The United States deployed the Minuteman III MIRVed ICBM during the first half of the decade, and spent the latter part of the decade upgrading it with a new warhead and guidance system. Poseidon and later Trident I submarine-launched missiles (SLBMs) were added to the strategic submarine force. The B-52 force was steadily modernized and provided with new armament—the short range attack missile (SRAM)—designed to improve its ability to penetrate Soviet air defenses. And throughout the decade, a whole new generation of strategic weapons—the MX, the Trident submarine, the B-1 bomber, and the air-launched cruise missile—was developed, most of which will likely be deployed during the next few years. On the Soviet side, the modernization effort was even more energetic, resulting in the tiresomely familiar litany of "the Soviet buildup": several new, modern, accurate, multiple-warhead ICBMs (including the SS-18 "heavy" missile), several new strategic submarines and SLBMs, deployment of the Backfire bomber and hints of the development of a new strategic bomber, and indications of more systems on the way. In the face of all this, many liberals concluded in despair that strategic arms control simply legitimized the continuing arms race while many conservatives concluded with alarm that it served merely to camouflage an unrelenting Soviet buildup.

And what about the risk of war? Did SALT help to reduce it? Has it contributed to the stability of the strategic balance? As the Oppenheimer Panel on disarmament thirty years ago commented in one of the first serious efforts to analyze arms control, "the basic objective of any scheme of arms regulation should be to eliminate" the capacity for what the Panel then called a "surprise knockout blow."[4] But strategic arms control has not prevented the emergence of disturbing vulnerabilities, in particular the problem of ICBM vulnerability and the less widely appreciated vulnerability of command and control facilities—both borne of the great accuracy of contemporary ballistic missiles combined with the advent of multiple warheads. Of course, a significant fraction of both superpower strategic arsenals remain survivable and would be available for retaliation, so the fundamental deterrence relationship is not presently jeopardized by this development. But if there is some degree of safety against the possibility of a disarming first strike, it is because of a multiplication of weapons and delivery systems rather than the result of negotiated arms control. Measured by this standard, then, strategic arms control must be judged insignificant if not deficient.

The third negative conclusion that emerges—along with the failures of arms control and its modest impact—is that these twenty-five years of efforts to bring the arms competition under some form of limitation have had the effect of tarnishing the arms control process. The failures, the inadequacies, the sluggishness, the occasional irrelevance of arms control have understandably harmed its image. If the writings on and the successes of arms control in the early 1960s resulted in the legitimizing of arms control, the experiences of more recent years have gone far toward discrediting it. . . .

In short, arms control has not lived up to its promise. Those who took up the cause of arms control in the early 1960s felt that it offered the prospect of substantial benefits in the form of a more stable nuclear balance and a more restrained arms competition. But, as former Secretary of Defense Harold Brown has written, "Measured against these glittering possibilities, the achievements of arms negotiations to date have been modest indeed, as are their immediate prospects. . . . In all, not much to show for thirty-five years of negotiations and twenty years of treaties."[5] But why has this been the case? It is certainly possible for arms control to provide more benefit than it has. There are fairly straightforward arms control solutions to many of the strategic problems that most trouble us. The main obstacles—verification and negotiability—seem more manageable than anyone expected them to be. And yet great exertions have not yielded great results. What has gone wrong?

THE DOMESTIC POLITICAL IMPEDIMENTS TO ARMS CONTROL

A major part of the answer lies in the ability of internal politics to shape and limit the results of arms negotiations. Each of the two main phases of arms control policymaking—the politics of policy formulation and the politics of ratification—is fraught with possibilities for preventing ambitious proposals or resisting agreements. These two phases in turn intersect in a complicated way with the larger domestic political process of which they are a part. In this way, electoral and Congressional politics, as well as public opinion, come to play a role in determining the possibilities of arms control.

The origin of U.S. arms control policy lies, obviously, in the policy formulation phase—in the negotiation primarily within the executive branch of the U.S. government. Here lurk several potential impediments to arms control. It is necessary to get all the many relevant parties within the government to agree on what should or should not be proposed and to get them to support whatever agreement is achieved. This may be the most difficult part of arms control. President Carter has observed, for example, that SALT II required as much negotiation in the United States as it did with the Soviet Union.[6] These internal negotiations can be fully as difficult as the international ones.

The players in the internal game are many: the White House, which often has its own agenda of political, budgetary, and foreign policy concerns; the State Department, with its concern for the international political relationships involved; the Arms Control and Disarmament Agency, a weak player in its own game; the various divisions and subdivisions of the Defense Department, which often have the most directly at stake; and occasionally key individuals from Congress. . . . The goal of the game is to produce an arms control proposal or position that is essentially acceptable to all. The structure of the game is simple: each of the organizations involved will seek, within the limits of its influence and effectiveness in the bureaucratic politics of the situation, to preserve its own interests or, at the least, to avoid having them badly violated.

Here lies the crux of the problem. For while it is commonly said that arms control and military policy are compatible and indeed ought to be integrated, the fact is that the *practice* of arms control, whether as a process or in the particulars of a given agreement, can and usually does affront the interests of some of the players in the game. In particular, few offices in the Pentagon have their interests furthered by arms control, and the wariness of the military toward arms control is evident to participants in the process and is sometimes remarked upon by the military itself. And because military support for agreements is thought to be, and probably is, crucial to the *ratification* process, as well as because military programs are directly affected, the military voice is a powerful one in the *policy formulation process.* . . . The strength of the military hand in shaping arms control policy and in safeguarding its interests against the intrusions of negotiated restraints explains why the JCS [Joint Chiefs of Staff] has, in general, consistently supported ratification of agreements that are reached, for having been satisfied in the policy formulation phase, it is free to take the high ground in the ratification process—as it did with SALT II. In short, although arms control and military policy share many of the same goals, they seek to achieve those goals through different, often incompatible means.

After all, arms control is an effort to interfere with the defense policy process, to constrain certain kinds of weapons, options, and practices for the larger good of national security. But this engages the interests of a large, powerful, complex, and not well understood process of defense decision-making and weapons acquisition, a process that generally seeks security not be constraining or eliminating weapons and military options but by providing them; this, it should not be forgotten, is the job that the Pentagon is hired to do, and it should come as no surprise that it seeks to fulfill that responsibility. But, as William Hyland (himself a long-time participant in the process) has written, "Arms control lends itself well to infringements on defense policy," and further, it creates "an environment for bureaucratic guerilla warfare against military programs. . . ."[7] As the modest impact of arms control agreements to date attests, proponents of defense programs and weapons systems are far from helpless in this particular form of warfare. And given the size and complexity of the defense policy process and the potential for antagonism between military policy and arms control, it is very difficult to coordinate the two and to manage the bureaucratic and organizational politics effectively.

Several important points flow from this analysis. First, arms control proposals are usually the result of internal bargaining. Consequently, deliberations are slow and changing proposals can be difficult. Considerable time and effort must be spent overcoming bureaucratic standoffs and adjudicating internal disputes. Second, in these internal negotiations, some participants often have to be bought off—their positions accommodated or their sacrifices in one area made up in another. Third, losers in the process need not give up. They can oppose or circumvent restrictions, take their case to the public, or air their disagreements before Congress—in short, broaden the fight to the ratification phase, having lost it internally. Such tactics will inevitably obstruct the smooth passage to a signed and ratified agreement. Fourth, internal critics will usually have to be paid for their public support of the treaty, as was the case, for example, with SALT I, where Secretary of Defense Laird and the Joint Chiefs of Staff made Administration support of a broad program of strategic modernization the fairly explicit condition of their support of the treaty. Finally, policy formulation is the President's game if he and his advisers in the White House have the will and the skill to seize control of the process. This John Kennedy did in 1963; Nixon and Kissinger did likewise during SALT I—with some important decisions being made by the two of them in the Kremlin during the Moscow summit; and Carter attempted the same in formulating his bold March 1977 comprehensive proposal. Unlike the ratification process, which can elude presidential control, policy formulation can be marked by decisive presidential interventions. Even if this happens, problems remain, for the Soviets still must agree and the Senate must still ratify. But the President does at least possess substantial power to shape the policy formulation process, and when that power has been exercised, progress has often ensued.

With respect to the politics of ratification, the second dimension of the domestic process of arms control, it is the Senate, rather than the President, that can be the decisive player in the game. In the Senate is vested the authority to ratify treaties, and so the Senate can determine the fate of an agreement even if it is only a marginal influence on the formulation of arms control policy. And the key fact, as *The New Republic*'s Richard Strout has . . . commented, is that, "In a Congress of 535 members, 33 Senators plus one can block a treaty." This may be, as Strout remarks, "a queer system."[8] But it is the system nevertheless, and it requires that the politics of ratification be tended to rather carefully so that a minority is not able to gather sufficient strength to defeat an agreement. This can involve a significant amount of cajolery and appeasement of key Senators, the involvement of Senators in policy formulation, permitting Senators to observe the negotiations first-hand, and political logrolling on military programs (or on other unrelated issues) to secure or assure the support of important votes, as well as an effort to mobilize public opinion. This may sound like the routine business of politics but it is not necessarily easy to do, . . . particularly . . . when there is skillful and determined public opposition to arms control, as there often seems to be, by what has been called "the vigilance lobby."[9] SALT I showed that ratification can be easy . . . ; the Threshold Test Ban Treaty showed that ratification cannot be taken for granted; and SALT II showed that ratification can be a major hurdle, not easily overcome even with great effort.

Both the formulation of arms control policy and the ratification of treaties take place in the larger domestic arena, and are affected by the general political process normally at work. One substantial domestic political impediment is the electoral process, especially at the presidential level. The quadrennial electoral cycle has several possible disruptive consequences for the arms control process. For one thing, arms control policy tends to get caught up in partisan politics, with one party attacking the approach of the other, and often unsubstantiated charges and countercharges flung about in public debate. This clearly occurred in the 1980 election, and President Carter strove to paint Reagan as a warmonger while Reagan accused Carter of following policies of weakness, with distinct tendencies toward unilateral disarmament. . . .

A second way that electoral politics can disrupt the arms control process is that administrations that are taking heat on this issue and perceive themselves to be on the political defensive may backpedal from arms control. Thus President Ford, in the midst of his struggle with Ronald Reagan for the 1976 Republican nomination, banished the word "detente" from his political vocabulary and placed SALT II, then nearly completed, on hold. This was a decision that Ford came to regret, but in the event it contributed to a several year delay in the signing of the SALT II agreement. Of course, this phenomenon can cut the other direction as well: when Richard Nixon sought in 1972 to bolster his image as peacemaker against the attacks of critics of the Vietnam War, the SALT I agreement became politically useful to him. But the potential for disruption remains.

Third, elections often result, as they are intended to do, in changes of government. It seems to be a rule of thumb, if past experience is any guide, that roughly a year is lost in the transition from one administration to the next. Those new to power generally need time to overcome the instinct to substantially repudiate the policies of their predecessors, to study the issues anew from their own perspectives, to organize the policy machinery, and to formulate their own policies. Thus when the Nixon Administration inherited the incipient SALT process from the Johnson Administration in 1969, its first impulse was to slow the momentum toward negotiations so that it could review the situation. The Carter Administration sought to avoid delay but nevertheless derailed the SALT II negotiations for a time with its impulsive March 1977 comprehensive proposal, which was a substantial departure from the negotiating record with which the Soviets were familiar and comfortable. And more recently, of course, the Reagan Administration held arms control in abeyance for nearly a year before embarking first on the INF and then the START negotiations. This recurrent pattern is not necessarily negative. Indeed, it is probably preferable that new administrations be cautious and careful as they begin to formulate arms control policy. But, when combined with the risk that election years may also be disruptive, this means that as many as two years out of every four may be bad ones from the perspective of furthering arms control. This represents a substantial constraint on the process, one that helps to account for the slowness of many negotiations.

The accountability of members of Congress to the public is yet another way that the electoral process can influence the fate of arms control. Congressmen especially tend to be quite sensitive to public opinion, and so will reflect the favorable . . . or unfavorable political mood of the country about arms control. But the politician's finely honed instinct for self-preservation causes many to be ever-ready to duck a hot issue or to avoid taking a clear stand on a controversial one. This rule does not apply equally to all Congressmen and Senators at all times on all issues—obviously much depends on the specific circumstances in each case. But it is clear, for example, that when the strength of public opposition to SALT II became evident in 1979, even Senators sympathetic to the treaty were glad to avoid a vote. And the behavior of key figures—for example, Senator Frank Church—seems to be explained by concern over electoral considerations.

In politics, of course, public opinion counts, although not in any easily traceable way. Because it has often been supportive of arms control, it may seem curious or even incorrect to label it an impediment. But, as we have seen in the recent, rapid reversal of public opinion from supporting to doubting the Reagan defense buildup, it is volatile. And, moreover, it is at the same time manipulable—up to a point—and yet to a considerable extent uncontrollable. This means that it is vulnerable to the blandishments of sellers and opposers of strategic arms control (with success going to the side that most effectively mounts its public relations campaign) but that the efforts of both can be overwhelmed by events—usually to the benefit of one side or the other, depending on whether the event is the Soviet invasion of a neighboring country or slips of the tongue by high-level American officials about fighting limited nuclear war.

In addition, public attitudes towards defense and arms control are schizophrenic. Put most simply, the public fears both nuclear war and the Soviet Union, and the political climate of the moment is determined by which of these fears is predominant. The contradictions in public opinion are manifest in a number of ways. It supports arms control in the abstract but is often lukewarm or negative about specific agreements. It often favors both arms control and American military superiority, both negotiated restraint and military buildup. The public seems to believe in negotiating with the Russians but is mistrustful of Soviet power. Moreover, as the Committee on the Present Danger found in its polls (and demonstrated by its success), there is a sizable anti-arms control constituency that can be mobilized to oppose arms agreements.[10] What all this suggests is that, while public opinion can occasionally be a supporting, or even . . . a driving force in the arms control process, it does not provide consistent backing for arms negotiations and agreements. For politicians, this means that support of an arms agreement can be a political liability as well as (and perhaps as often as) a strength.

Public opinion, moreover, is the medium through which international politics reverberates in the American body politic. Indeed, the linkage of arms control with international politics or, more specifically, with Soviet behavior, is the most frequently remarked upon political impediment to successful negotiation. At least twice, the strategic arms control process has been disrupted by provocative Soviet behavior, once in 1968 when it invaded Czechoslovakia and again in the fall of 1979 when first the Cuban brigade episode and then the invasion of Afghanistan proved to be the death of SALT II. Allegations about Soviet use of chemical weapons in Cambodia and Afghanistan, which though not proven have not been conclusively disproven, have caused doubts about Soviet willingness to comply with treaties. And more generally, the absence of restraint in Soviet activity in the Third World—in Indochina, the Horn of Africa, Angola, and Afghanistan—has eaten away at what little trust and good will existed toward the Soviet Union in the United States. It has also destroyed the tentative cooperation in the political relationship between the two powers that was partially created by, but which also sustained, the strategic arms control process.

There are some who welcome this linkage, and indeed urge that it be American policy. The reasoning is that the conduct of arms control with the U.S.S.R. can be a reward for Soviet restraint (thereby providing an incentive for restraint if the Soviets are genuinely interested in arms control) and the abandonment of arms negotiations can be, if not punishment, then at least an appropriate gesture of disapproval of Soviet misbehavior. For others, however, the aim should be to isolate strategic arms control as much as possible from international relations so that it is not constantly buffeted by the vicissitudes of what will continue to be a stormy superpower relationship. . . .

The problem is, however, that, whether or not linkage is policy, it is an unavoidable political fact. This is so because of the way that global politics are refracted by the American polity. The Soviet Union is not likely to modify its interests and the general lines of its foreign policy simply to avoid violating American sensibilities. This means there will be crises and problems in the future just as there have been in the past. And international developments that grab headlines and attract coverage on the evening news will inevitably have an impact on public opinion and therefore on the political fortunes of those in the public arena. Consequently, they will as well help to define the realm of the possible in American politics with respect to foreign policy. So it is not simply the linkage of strategic arms control to Soviet international behavior that must be addressed, but also the linkage between international developments and American politics.

CONCLUSION: RUNNING THE GAUNTLET OF POLITICAL IMPEDIMENTS

In summary, then, the disappointing results of arms control seem to be a consequence of the effects of an imposing set of political impediments: policy formulation, the ratification process, electoral politics, congressional politics, bureaucratic politics, public opinion, even international politics have to be aligned properly or managed effectively if arms control is to be pursued successfully. And it is not enough to have only some pieces of the puzzle in place. In 1979, for example, the White House was eager for SALT II ratification, but public and congressional enthusiasm was lacking and Soviet foreign policy behavior was uncooperative. Today [1984], there is passionate public support for arms control, but the White House is more interested in deployments than limitations. Hence, arms control progress requires that all the internal political factors be brought into positive alignment; any agreement will have to run the gauntlet of these potential impediments. Several implications follow from this fact.

First, because the whole of this political process is so slow, it raises another problem: a technological impediment. The pace of technological improvement is sufficiently rapid and the rate of modernization sufficiently fast that force postures change dramatically during the course of negotiations, raising new issues and problems before old ones are completely resolved. During the course of SALT II (1972–1979), for example, both U.S. and Soviet forces changed markedly and some of the more difficult issues—cruise missiles, Backfire bombers, MIRVed heavy missiles—were not in view when the negotiations began.

Second, any agreement that successfully runs the gauntlet of impediments will necessarily be modest in impact—otherwise it would not have survived. Consequently, the failure of arms control to fully live up to its promise is perfectly understandable. But it has led to disillusionment with arms control at both ends of the spectrum: hawks because it has not solved U.S. strategic problems (for example, ICBM vulnerability), doves because it has not ended the arms race.

Third, the strong and direct commitment of the President and his close associates in the White House seems to be a decisive element in determining whether and how much arms control can succeed. John Kennedy, for example, played an important role in pushing the Limited Test Ban Treaty to completion. Nixon and Kissinger played pivotal roles in the achievement of SALT I. And Jimmy Carter's personal determination helped to make the SALT II agreement possible. The President is the one player in the game who is powerful enough to override many of the political impediments to agreement. But, as the experience of the Carter Administration demonstrates, it is possible for the impediments to defeat even the President.

Fourth, it must be recognized that the effective pursuit of arms control is incompatible with a number of strategic worlds. For arms control to be a significant constraint on the arms competition and for it to contribute to strategic stability, it must preclude many many counterforce systems and render impossible many if not all nuclear war-fighting options; in short, it must close off the paths toward a more heavily armed and heavily counterforce world. But that world appears to be preferable to the Soviet military and desirable to a significant portion of the American strategic community, military and civilian. Others disagree with this direction and attempt to use arms control to stop it. But because we cannot agree among ourselves on the strategic environment toward which we should be moving, it is virtually impossible for arms control to play a constructive role in shaping that environment. Those whose strategic visions are foreclosed by arms control (whether war-fighters or disarmers) will always find its part to be unsatisfactory. . . .

Finally, it is worth noting that some of these domestic impediments can be avoided by pursuing the aims of arms control in a different fashion. An arms control strategy that placed less emphasis on formal treaties and negotiations and more on routinized, less public consultations, such as those of the SALT Standing Consultative Commission, would bring these domestic factors much less into play. Moreover, as the early arms control theorists emphatically pointed out, there are many unilateral steps that can be taken in defense policy that further the objectives of arms control, and much more effort could be invested in these. It is often said that the goals of arms control are no different from those of sound military policy. But the latter is not easy to achieve either, and is necessary whether or not there is great success in arms control.

NOTES

1. This may well be as true for the Soviet Union as for the United States. Because little is known about the politics of arms control within the Soviet Union, however, this essay will focus on the American political scene. For some evidence on the Soviet side of the equation, see David Holloway, *War, Militarism, and the Soviet State,* World Order Models Project, Working Paper Number 17 (1981), which examines obstacles to disarmament in the Soviet system; and Rose Gottemoeller, "Decisionmaking for Arms Limitation in the Soviet Union," in Hans Guenter Brauch and Duncan L. Clarke, eds., *Decisionmaking for Arms Limitation: Assessment and Prospects* (Cambridge, Mass: Ballinger, 1983), pp. 53–80. Suggestive on this point is the Soviet claim, made privately to the Carter Administration, that Brezhnev has "spilled political blood" in order to achieve the Vladivostok Accord and consequently could not easily depart from it, as the Carter Administration had proposed in March 1977. See Strobe Talbott, *Endgame: The Inside Story of SALT II* (New York: Harper and Row, 1980), p. 73.

2. In one extraordinary year, 1961, there were published four books which still constitute the basic core of thought on arms control. The discussion which follows is based primarily on a reading of them. The books are: Thomas C. Schelling and Morton H. Halperin, *Strategy and Arms Control* (New York: Twentieth Century Fund, 1969); Hedley Bull, *The Control of the Arms Race: Disarmament and Arms Control in the Missile Age* (New York: Praeger Publishers, for the International Institute for Strategic Studies, 1961); Donald G. Brennan, *Arms Control, Disarmament, and National Security* (New York: George Braziller, 1961); and Arthur T. Hadley, *The Nation's Safety and Arms Control* (New York: Viking Press, 1961). . . .

3. Trevor Taylor, "Arms Control: The Bankruptcy of the Strategist's Approach," in David Carlton and Carlo Schaerf, eds., *The Arms Race in the 1980s* (New York: St. Martin's Press, 1982), p. 59. . . .

4. McGeorge Bundy, "Early Thoughts on Controlling the Nuclear Arms Race: A Report to the Secretary of State, January 1953," *International Security,* Vol. 7, No. 2 (Fall 1982), p. 25.

5. Harold Brown, *Thinking About National Security: Defense and Foreign Policy in a Dangerous World* (Boulder, Col.: Westview Press, 1983), p. 185.

6. Jimmy Carter, *Keeping Faith* (New York: Bantam Books, 1982), p. 218.

7. Hyland, "Institutional Impediments," [in Richard Burt, ed., *Arms Control and Defense Postures in the 1980s* (Boulder, Colo.: Westview Press, 1983)] pp. 100–101.

8. "Views from Backstage," *The New Republic,* April 18, 1983, p. 39.

9. The phrase is from Talbott, *Endgame,* p. 104. A revealing glimpse at the skill, wealth, and organization of groups that tend to be skeptical of arms control may be found in Sidney Blumenthal, "The Ideology Makers," *The Boston Globe Magazine,* August 8, 1982. . . .

10. See, for example, the Committee's pamphlet, *Public Attitudes on SALT II,* March 1979, which reported the results of a poll in which 71 percent of the respondents who had an opinion about SALT II either opposed it or felt it required further protection of American interests before they could support it. In contrast, only 20 percent of those polled supported the treaty.

14. THE PRESIDENT, "INTERMESTIC" ISSUES, AND THE RISKS OF POLICY LEADERSHIP

Ryan J. Barilleaux

For many years it has been a commonplace of presidential studies to note the existence of "two presidencies": one in foreign affairs and one in domestic matters. Ever since Wildavsky's classic analysis in 1966,[1] scholars have accepted the unevenness of presidential influence over policy and the fact that presidential initiatives are expected to provide leadership more in the foreign realm than at home. Yet, for all its worth in clarifying the nature of the presidency, the idea of "two presidencies" is being overshadowed by the growing importance of a third force that presents new problems and opportunities for presidential policy making: that realm of problems known as "intermestic issues."[2]

"Intermestic issues" refers to those matters of international relations which, by their very nature, closely involve the domestic economy of a nation. In the United States, such issues as international trade, oil imports, immigration, and transnational pollution (acid rain, etc.) are "intermestic," for they all combine American foreign relations with the state of the economic health of the nation. . . .

. . . In many ways, trade is the classic intermestic issue: it is about the American economy as it interacts with the rest of the world.

Two important cases of presidential initiatives in this area, the Trade Expansion Act of 1962 and the Trade Act of 1970, can illuminate the risks and opportunities involved in presidential policy making for intermestic affairs. By contrasting these cases, one a presidential success and the other a failure, it will be possible to draw some conclusions about the prospects for presidential policy leadership in this area. . . .

THE TRADE EXPANSION ACT OF 1962

The case of the Trade Expansion Act of 1962 represents a success in presidential policy leadership, for in this case President Kennedy was able to achieve his goal of passage of a new international trade bill which included broad presiden-

Note: Some footnotes have been deleted, and others have been renumbered to appear in consecutive order.

tial authority to negotiate tariff reductions. Not only did he achieve enactment of this bill, but he did so with what one observer called "resounding margins"[3] in both Houses of Congress.

The issue of international trade was high on the new President's list of economic priorities for his Administration. Moreover, it was an issue of national concern. For the Kennedy Administration faced an important juncture in American trade relations: the Reciprocal Trade Agreements Act of 1934 was due to expire in June 1962, and the sagging American economy was confronted by the Common External Tariff and growing power of the European Common Market. Furthermore, in July 1961, Britain announced its intention of seeking membership in the Common Market, which if accepted would both broaden the reach of the Common External Tariff and increase the power of the Common Market. This changing international environment presented a challenge to American trade policy, for the advance of European integration presented both a threat and an opportunity to the United States: the Common Market, particularly with British membership, meant an extremely broad area of preferential treatment for member nations, from which the United States was excluded; at the same time, however, if the United States could negotiate lower tariffs with the E.E.C., it could offset the additional trade preferences the Common Market would gain from British membership, avoid a trade war with Europe and strengthen Western unity, and help boost the American economy through freer trade with Europe.

Even before the British announcement in July 1961, Kennedy was aware of the issue of trade, due to the upcoming expiration of the 1934 law. During his pre-inaugural transition, he commissioned George Ball, a Washington lawyer active in the antiprotectionist Committee for a National Trade Policy (CNTP), to head a Task Force on Trade Policy, which examined the issue and provided the President-elect with recommendations for new trade legislation to strengthen presidential tariff-negotiating authority.

This attention to the trade issue continued in the first year of the Kennedy Administration, as the demise of the 1934 law drew nearer. In essence, the complex question of trade policy revolved around two fundamental issues: the scope and timing of trade legislation. In the first matter, the question was whether to request merely an extension with minor modifications of the old act, as had been done in the past, or to proceed with a new initiative involving more presidential authority for a longer period to accomplish more ambitious goals. On this question, Kennedy's advisors generally favored a new law, but there was concern about opposition from certain industries and their friends in Congress. The textile industry, for example, would be particularly concerned about the adverse effects of freer trade.

Because of this concern, Kennedy's advisors were divided over the second issue, that of timing. Here, the question was whether to pursue the new legislation in 1962, or to wait for the new Congress in 1963. Ball, who was a firm advocate of a new bill, counseled delay until 1963, in order to avoid clashing with protectionists during an election year. In this advice he was opposed by Howard Petersen, the President's Special Assistant for Trade Policy and a member of the Ball Task Force, and Lawrence O'Brien, the President's chief lobbyist on Capitol Hill. O'Brien and Petersen argued that a new trade bill would receive a warm welcome from some highly influential members of Congress, including Hale Boggs and House Ways and Means Committee chairman

Wilbur Mills. For his own part, the President was inclined toward an act in 1962, so that, as Sorensen noted, "the fierce fight which even a simple extension would entail might better be fought, and fought only once, for [a] wholly new trade instrument."[4]

Nevertheless, because of the possible strength of opposition in such an act, the President proceeded to test the political climate with a few trial balloons. On November 1, 1961, George Ball, now Undersecretary of State for Economic Affairs, addressed the National Foreign Trade Council on the changes in the international economy wrought by the establishment of the Common Market, and argued that existing trade legislation was inadequate for meeting this challenge. He avoided specific policy recommendations, but read a message from the President which concluded "It is essential that we have new tools to deal with the problems of international trade in a new and challenging world."[5] One week later, the President spoke at a news conference of the need for new tools to deal with the challenge of the Common Market. In early December, Hale Boggs began hearings in the Subcommittee on Foreign Economic Policy of the Joint Economic Committee. At these hearings, former Secretary of State Christian Herter and former Undersecretary of State William Clayton testified on the inadequacy of the old Reciprocal Trade Act. Finally, on November 29 the President announced that a tentative decision had been made to seek wider authority to cut tariffs, and on December 6 and 7 made a pair of speeches to the National Association of Manufacturers and the AFL-CIO advocating changes in American trade law. After all these efforts were favorably received, a final decision was made to proceed with a new trade initiative in 1962.

The Trade Expansion Act of 1962 was sent to Congress on January 25, 1962, where it was introduced into the House by Representative Wilbur Mills. It contained tariff-cutting authority for the President, with particular provisions for dealing with [the] Common Market. Second, it included safeguards for domestic industries and labor adversely affected by tariff reductions, with provision for "adjustment assistance" to injured parties. By expanding presidential authority to cut tariffs and simplifying the procedures for [doing] so, the bill authorized a major change in United States trade policy.

The new trade proposal now received highest priority, and the Administration immediately mobilized for the campaign to sell the bill to Congress. All lobbying efforts on the bill's behalf were directed from the White House, where Petersen's Trade Policy staff was increased in size to handle the responsibility of orchestrating the congressional and public campaigns. Petersen and congressional liaison O'Brien were equipped, inter alia, with promotional literature for the campaign, including separate brochures for each state. Moreover, the White House assisted free-trade groups in their efforts on behalf of the bill, using the Committee for a National Trade Policy as coordinator for and liaison with other free-trade groups.

The Administration's chief spokesman for the bill was Commerce Secretary Luther Hodges, who was chosen over Ball because the Undersecretary was unpopular with many members of Congress. Hodges, former governor of North Carolina with friends in the textile industry, led the assault on Capitol Hill. Exhaustive hearings were held before the House Ways and Means and Senate Finance committees, and Hodges led the lengthy parade of Administration and friendly private spokesmen who testified in favor of the bill.

The President himself was also involved in this campaign. The Trade Expansion Act had received special attention in the 1962 State of the Union message, and after submitting the bill Kennedy predicted in a news conference that it would receive bipartisan support. In May, he and four members of his Cabinet participated in a day-long conference of twelve hundred people representing one hundred organizations supporting the bill. He also hammered on the need for the bill in his speeches.

Beyond these efforts at lobbying, the Kennedy Administration also acted to undercut opposition to the bill. It focused special attention on the textile and timber industries, but also worked on other groups as well. Textiles and timber were particularly threatened by adverse effects of reduced tariffs, so Kennedy announced a six-point plan to help the lumber industry and raised tariffs on carpets and glass. Soon, support from the textile industry and legislators from affected states was forthcoming.

At the same time, undercutting opposition meant acceding to congressional demands to modify the structure of executive authority for conducting trade negotiations. First, to alleviate congressional concerns that the State Department, which had previously been the agency with primary responsibility for trade negotiations, gave insufficient attention to the domestic impact of trade liberalization, Kennedy accepted Wilbur Mills' proposal for a Special Trade Representative, to be located in the Executive Office of the President. This official would lead the American delegation in all international trade negotiations, and was called upon to consult with Congress on such matters. Second, to minimize congressional concerns about misuse of the broader negotiating authority given to the President under this act, the President accepted a provision whereby two members (not of the same party) of each House would be accredited as members of the U.S. trade delegation. Finally, the President accepted an amendment to make it easier for Congress to override a presidential decision on the use of the "escape clause" in the bill.

With these concessions by the President, to both Congress and industry opponents, the bill was able to pass into law. Wilbur Mills' handling of the bill in the House prevented attachment of a series of protectionist amendments, and in the Senate the bill avoided any serious changes. The only amendment to the Administration bill forced by Congress over presidential objections forbade the granting of most-favored-nation status to Communist nations, a provision Kennedy had sought but could live without.

The House passed the Trade Expansion Act on June 28, 1962, by a vote of 298–125. Three months later, on September 19, the Senate passed the bill by a vote of 78–8. On October 11, the President signed the Trade Expansion Act in a ceremony at the White House, calling it ". . . the most important international piece of legislation, I think, affecting economics since the Marshall Plan. It marks a decisive point for the future of our economy, for our relations with our friends and allies, and for the prospects of free institutions and free societies everywhere."

THE TRADE ACT OF 1970

The case of the Trade Act of 1970 represents a clear failure in presidential policy making for intermestic affairs, for in this case President Nixon's attempt to achieve passage of his international trade proposals was frustrated in Congress. He was thus defeated in his first major initiative in the area of international trade policy.

Richard Nixon had long been an advocate of freer international trade, but at the same time was sensitive to political pressures which moderated that view. In his 1968 campaign for the presidency, he had reaffirmed his commitment to free trade as a matter of principle, but cited textiles as a "special case" to be given special treatment. The textile industry, concentrated in the South, had been hardest hit by Japanese competition, and Nixon sought to win Southern votes by promising that aforementioned special treatment. Consequently, he stated in the campaign that he would take steps toward an expansion of free international trade, while at the same time clearly promising to do something about textile imports.

The result of this combined pledge of free trade and help for textiles was the Trade Act of 1970,[6] sent to Congress on November 18 of that year. The bill had three broad purposes: 1) to reestablish presidential authority to reduce tariffs, which had lapsed in 1967, and to grant the President the power to eliminate the American Selling Price (ASP) system of evaluating imports for calculation of duties; 2) liberalization of the current criteria for providing relief and assistance to industries, firms, and workers adversely affected by imports; and, 3) greater presidential authority to retaliate against unfair trade practices by other nations. In general, it sought to enhance free trade by renewing the lapsed tariff-cutting authority of the 1962 Trade Expansion Act, modify and expand presidential control over trade barriers and retaliation to barriers, and protect domestic industry. In his accompanying message, the President said of the bill: "It is modest in scope, but significant in its impact."

The bill was soon caught up in a whirl of protectionist trade proposals submitted to the 91st Congress. Responding to a poor balance-of-trade and pressure from domestic interests, over three hundred members of the House had introduced some sort of import quota legislation. The Ways and Means Committee had before it fifty-nine bills related to steel imports, forty-seven to textiles, forty to dairy imports, twenty-four to footwear, and fifty-five which authorized the President to set ceilings on imports threatening American industries.[7] Of great importance was the fact that among this crowd was Wilbur Mills, chairman of the committee and long an advocate of free trade. At the Administration's request, he introduced a textile-import quota bill, although he preferred adjustment assistance as a means for coping with the adverse effects of trade on domestic industry.[8]

The Mills bill was part of an overall strategy for dealing with the complex problem of trade, by dealing with an issue closely related to the Nixon trade proposal. That issue was an Administration effort to negotiate a voluntary agreement with Japan to reduce textile exports by that country, which the Mills bill was intended to facilitate. Honoring his campaign pledge, and interested in the 1970 congressional elections, Nixon sought an agreement with the Japanese in order to aid the domestic textile industry through Japanese restraint. In pursuit of this goal, the Administration conducted extensive negotiations with Japanese officials. These efforts were both public, in talks conducted by either Commerce Secretary Maurice Stans or presidential assistant Peter Flanigan, and private, in "backchannel" discussions between presidential assistant Henry Kissinger and an emissary of the Japanese prime minister. In this strategy, a quota bill from the Ways and Means chairman was intended to put pressure on Japan to agree to self-restraint or face statutory quotas. Nevertheless, despite extensive secret and public discussions, meetings between President Nixon and Japanese prime minister Eisaku Sato, and Mills' proposal, no agreement was ever reached.

Yet the Mills bill was not dead, for it was endorsed by the Administration following the collapse of yet another effort to reach an agreement with Japan. After a June 1970 meeting between Commerce Secretary Stans and his counterpart in the Japanese government once again failed to produce an agreement, the President "reluctantly" endorsed textile quota legislation as a further prod to Japanese concurrence. He did not, however, endorse the bill's provision for footwear quotas, and explicitly stated his opposition to quotas on any items other than textiles. Consequently, the Administration supported both the original bill and the Mills bill.

After these actions, and exhaustive hearings conducted in May and June 1970, the Ways and Means Committee drafted a "clean bill" incorporating most of the Nixon proposals and the Mills quota on textiles, but also including provisions which the Administration opposed. Specifically, it retained oil import quotas, and implemented mandatory quotas for footwear and restrictions on imports of other products. Furthermore, it failed to include two provisions which Nixon had proposed: tax advantages to American exporting firms and continuation of American participation in the International Coffee Agreement.

Nevertheless, the Nixon Administration still hoped for ultimate success. It was counting on changes in the bill in the Senate, to be negotiated in a conference committee. To that end, the President declared on July 20 that he would veto any law containing mandatory quotas on products other than textiles: "I would not be able to sign the bill because that would set off a trade war." He feared that these other quotas would stimulate even more quotas, and so pressed his "special case" argument for textiles. This veto threat, along with congressional lobbying and pressure on the Japanese to reach an export agreement, were all part of Nixon's effort to achieve passage of his trade proposals and avoid protectionist legislation.

On the floor of the House, Mills defended the "clean" bill, quotas and all. He argued that these quotas were only temporary, and pointed to the failure of the Japanese to submit to a voluntary agreement as evidence of the need for new barriers. On November 19, 1970, Nixon suffered the first half of his defeat as the House passed the Committee bill by a vote of 205–165.

Meanwhile, in the Senate, trouble was mounting for the President. Aware that time was running out for the 91st Congress, the Finance Committee began working on the trade bill in October. It held two days of hearings, and then the committee began its markup of the bill. Unfortunately for the President, the committee was chaired by Senator Russell Long, who favored protection of American industry because he felt that the United States was not being treated fairly by its trading partners. Under Long's influence, the committee voted on October 13 to attach the trade bill to the Social Security Amendments Act of 1970, which had been passed by the House and was scheduled to go to the Senate floor before the end of the session. This action not only moved the bill closer to floor action, but nullified the threat of a presidential veto: The Finance Committee's version of the trade bill was not to the Administration's liking, but that bill was now protected by the Social Security Act, to which the Administration was already committed.

The Administration now made its last efforts to prevail. The White House stepped up efforts to reach an agreement with Japan, and drew attention to its consideration of a November 15 proposal by the Japanese government. William Timmons, Chief of Congressional Liaison in the White House, tried unsuccessfully to delay a vote on the bill in the House, and was equally unsuccessful in trying to persuade Long to separate the trade bill from the Social Security bill.

On November 20, the Finance Committee reported the combined trade and Social Security bill to the Senate. Not only was it caught up in the controversy over free trade and protection, but over welfare and provisions in the Social Security bill as well. By the time the Senate convened on December 28 to consider the combined bill, the chance of agreement with Japan appeared dim once again, and the bill was wrapped in a tangle of parliamentary maneuvers. At the urging of Senator Long, the Senate deleted the trade provisions of the combined bill and thus killed what remained of the Trade Act of 1970.

EXPLAINING THE OUTCOMES OF THE CASES

As the two case summaries above imply, Presidents Kennedy and Nixon each mounted strong efforts at policy development, management of policy-making processes, and consensus-building to win passage of their respective proposals. Yet the outcomes of these two cases were quite different: one an important success, the other an embarrassing failure. What factors influenced these outcomes? The answer to that question lies in two areas: 1) the political environment of intermestic issues; and, 2) the risks of presidential policy leadership.

All policy issues exist in an environment that affects policy-makers' perceptions and attitudes toward those issues. In security affairs, the balance of power between the United States and the Soviet Union, the behavior of allies and adversaries, the course of recent history, and other factors all combine to create an environment that helps to shape the world as policy makers see it. In this area, the President is given great leeway in choosing how to respond to that environment, and Congress traditionally relies on presidential initiatives as guides to action.

With intermestic affairs, however, the political environment is different, for it involves domestic politics to a much greater degree than do security affairs. Moreover, Congress feels much less reluctant to act on its own, as the spate of trade bills introduced in 1969 and 1970 demonstrate, or as can be seen in recent congressional initiatives on immigration policy. In the cases of the Trade Expansion Act and the Trade Act of 1970, the political environment significantly affected the outcomes of each case.

In the 1962 case, that environment had two aspects: international and domestic. The international environment aided the President by giving a particular relevance to his call for new trade legislation. No matter what the success of the Common Market had been in the previous years, it was the 1961 British application for membership in that community which gave urgency to his request for broader powers in negotiating tariff reductions. For the British application was a precipitous event: not only did it provide focus and support for all the existing reasons why a new law for freer trade was necessary, but it also demanded an American response before too long. It presented both a threat and an opportunity: at that time, British membership in the E.E.C. was expected to be quickly followed by that of several other European nations, so the British announcement heralded a wide expansion of the Common Market. On the one hand, such an expansion, because it excluded the United States from this European trade preference area, threatened to spark a trans-Atlantic trade war. At the same time, however, if the United States could negotiate tariff reductions with the Common Market, conflict could be avoided and Western unity enhanced. Without the British decision, whatever the other reasons for a new law, Kennedy's case for broader power would have been much less compelling.

The domestic political environment of this case had two facets, friendly congressional leadership and the attitude of the American business and labor communities. First, Kennedy's bill was likely to receive a favorable welcome from two important members of Congress, Wilbur Mills and Hale Boggs, no matter the effectiveness of the President's efforts at consensus-building. Boggs had independently called for new legislation in 1961, and Mills indicated to O'Brien that same year his receptiveness to a new bill. With this support, particularly that of the powerful Ways and Means Committee chairman, passage of the President's initiative was greatly facilitated.

Beyond this support, the attitude of the business community was likewise important. In this regard, the activities of the Committee for a National Trade Policy were particularly important. This committee, composed of executives from several large corporations and such other figures as George Ball and Charles Taft (brother of the late Senator), had worked for years to promote the idea of freer trade with the American business community. Throughout the 1950s, it waged a public relations war for freer trade, disseminating information and evidence in support of its cause and helping to coordinate the efforts of other likeminded groups. It participated in the battle over the extension of the Reciprocal Trade Act of 1954–55, and maintained its publicity campaign after that. While it was not a powerful organization in the sense of being able to sway a large number of votes in Congress, it was effective in bringing many business leaders around to the cause of free trade. Indeed, in their exhaustive study of *American Business and Public Policy*, Bauer, Pool, and Dexter traced the activities of the Committee and concluded "But for the basic changes in business attitudes generated in the 1950s [at the impetus of the Committee], the Trade Expansion Act would not have passed in 1962, no matter what deals were made in its favor."[9] In sum, then, the Committee helped to make Kennedy's domestic audience more receptive to his initiative.

Business and labor, then, largely supported the Kennedy bill, with the notable and temporary exceptions of the textile and timber industries. The U.S. Chamber of Commerce, the National Association of Manufacturers, AFL-CIO, and even the American Cotton Manufacturers Institute all supported the bill. Had the domestic political environment been hostile to the very idea of free trade, the President would probably not have been able to sell the bill to Congress. The domestic attitude in favor of such an act could not be obtained overnight: it existed before President Kennedy took office.

In both its domestic and international aspects, then, the political environment certainly contributed to the President's success in this case. Indeed, the two facets complemented one another: the domestic attitude was receptive to a move toward freer trade, which the British application to the Common Market made more urgent. The political environment thus facilitated Kennedy's effort at consensus-building, by providing an impetus for a new law and a domestic audience acceptant of such a proposal.

In the 1970 case, the force of domestic politics worked in the opposite direction. Congress was keenly sensitive to the force of domestic opposition to free trade in 1970, because that force generally pushed in one direction and because of the congressional elections that year. As the *National Journal* noted in describing the domestic political scene that year,[10]

> Pressure on Congress for protective legislation has been building for several years as increased imports, foreign barriers of U.S. exports and now rising unemployment have gradually won converts from the free trade camp.
>
> Almost 300 members of the House have introduced quota legislation of one sort or another in the 91st Congress—among them 20 or 25 members of the key Ways and Means Committee, which generally initiates all trade legislation.

In the late 1950s and early 1960s, domestic political pressure for protection was much weaker. In 1970, however, strong pressure for protection now dominated the political scene. It was this same sort of domestic political pressure which had moved candidate Richard Nixon to promise help for the Southern textile industry, and was now pressing for protection of other industries as well.

Throughout the 1960s, there was growing sentiment in the United States that, as Senator Long had expressed it, the United States was not being treated fairly by its trading partners. Increases in industrial and agricultural imports led to a declining balance of trade surplus, down from $7.1 billion in 1964 to $300 million in 1968 and $1.3 billion in 1969. In this environment, with concern that unfair trade practices by the Japanese were injuring American enterprise, even traditionally pro-free trade labor unions shifted to a protectionist stance. The AFL-CIO called for import quotas to protect American jobs, and the resulting labor-management coalition favoring protection created a powerful force, keenly felt in Congress. This general labor-management coalition was especially pronounced in certain areas and industries, such as the textile industry in the South and the shoe industry in Massachusetts, Pennsylvania, and New York. The result was strong pressure on Congress to do something about imports.

THE RISKS OF POLICY LEADERSHIP

While of considerable importance to these cases, the political environment was not the only factor affecting their outcome. Other factors lie in the risks of policy leadership.

Presidential policy leadership always entails risks: that the President may fail, that he may anger or alienate groups who formerly supported him, that the political costs of winning support for his initiatives may be higher than anticipated, or that even in winning support for his initiatives the President may be committing the nation to the wrong policy. Yet the risks of leadership in intermestic affairs are greater than for other foreign-policy issues.

Richard Nixon discovered this fact in the case of his trade bill. His support for the "special case" of Southern textiles angered other groups who felt adversely affected by imports, while his general free-trade approach bucked the tide of protectionist sentiment in Congress and the nation. For a President whose reputation was being built on mastery in foreign affairs, this trade policy initiative was politically costly and embarrassingly unsuccessful. Nixon was never able to win support for his trade proposals, either in 1970 or afterward, and he discovered the risks of policy leadership.

Intermestic issues naturally invite presidential initiatives, because they lie partially in the traditionally presidential realm of foreign affairs. At the same time, however, they also involve interests not affected by other foreign issues, or which are not affected to the same degree: jobs and labor, specific regions of the country or sectors of the economy, ethnic group interests, etc. Consequently, while in one sense lying in the realm of foreign affairs, intermestic issues also incorporate all the risks attending domestic policy leadership, e.g., interest-group politics and congressional particularism (each Congressman seeking to write legislation to protect his district), with the additional problem of running afoul of nationalist feelings (the idea that the President is more concerned about other nations than about the United States). Moreover, as is probably clear by this point, in intermestic issues the President receives almost none of the "benefit of the doubt" that members of Congress and others are willing to give him on even highly controversial security issues (Vietnam, Grenada). This means that intermestic policy initiatives often involve uphill battles for the President unless, like Kennedy, the political environment works to his advantage.

As far as Congress is concerned, intermestic issues are domestic issues, because the immediate concerns of members and their constituents are how such questions as imports, immigration, and energy resources affect the local economy and national life. Presidents who seek to provide policy leadership on intermestic issues will have to sell their initiatives on the domestic-policy merits of those proposals. Kennedy's Trade Expansion Act was promoted in that way, while Nixon's Trade Act encountered trouble because it was perceived to exacerbate American trade disadvantages for the majority (expanding free trade) while providing protection for a minority (Southern textiles).

Policy initiatives on intermestic issues offer Presidents a chance to assume a position of leadership in matters that will profoundly affect the future of the nation. Moreover, presidential leadership in this area may forestall congressional attempts to gain near-absolute control over these issues. In other words, if a President seizes the initiative, he may be able to make Congress work with him, and this ultimately exercises influence over intermestic policy. But, for all these opportunities that intermestic issues offer, Presidents must never forget the risks these subjects entail. . . .

Intermestic issues obscure the conventional distinctions between the "two presidencies," and in doing so mix the hazards of domestic policy leadership with the demands of foreign policy leadership. The two cases examined here illuminate these hazards, and obliquely suggest how the President might deal with an area of growing importance.

NOTES

1. Aaron Wildavsky, "The Two Presidencies," *Trans-Action* (December 1966): 7–14.
2. Bayless Manning, "The Congress, the Executive, and Intermestic Affairs: Three Proposals," *Foreign Affairs* 55 (January 1977): 306–324.

3. Lawrence F. O'Brien, *No Final Victories* (Garden City, NY: Doubleday and Co., 1974), p. 131.

4. Theodore Sorensen, *Kennedy* (New York: Harper and Row, 1965), p. 411.

5. [Robert A. Pastor, *Congress and the Politics of U.S. Foreign Economic Policy 1929–1976* (Berkeley, Calif.: University of California Press, 1980)], p. 106.

6. Nixon's proposal was originally entitled the Trade Act of 1969, but it was not taken up in Congress until the following year, when the designation was changed.

7. Pastor, pp. 124–125. See also *CQ Weekly Report*, March 27, 1970, p. 861.

8. *CQ Weekly Report*, July 18, 1969, pp. 1292 and 1296. Mills would later change his view and support quotas. . . .

9. [Raymond Bauer, Ithiel deSola Pool, and Lewis Anthony Dexter, *American Business and Public Policy*, 2nd ed. (Chicago: Aldine-Atherton, Inc., 1972)], p. 387.

10. Frank V. Fowlkes, "Pressure Mounting on Congress to Enact Import Quota Legislation," *National Journal*, May 16, 1970, p. 1034.

Part III: Decision Makers and Their Policy-Making Positions

To the question "What factors most influence the direction of American foreign policy?" the answer that comes immediately to mind is "the people who are responsible for its formulation." The president figures prominently in such thinking, followed by those immediately surrounding him.

The popularity of explanations that emphasize the impact political leaders have on foreign policy is easy to understand. Most people operate instinctively from a "great leader" image of politicians—one which equates actions on policy with the preferences of the most highly placed officials—because it is comforting to believe that elected and appointed officials are "leaders" empowered to chart the nation's destiny. In fact, the conviction that the individual who holds office makes a difference is one of the major premises underlying the electoral process in a democratic society.

The view that individuals matter is reinforced by the tendency to attach to policies the names of presidents (for example, the Truman Doctrine, the Kennedy Round, Reaganomics), a propensity that suggests that policies are synonymous with the people who first promulgated them and that national policies are determined exclusively by those presumed to be most responsible for their formulation. The widespread belief that in a democratic society leaders will make public policy in accordance with public preferences also strengthens the image of the importance of leaders, for they alone interpret what public preferences are. From these perspectives, it would seem that all history is biography.

Clearly, the characteristics unique to the individuals who make American foreign policy exert a potentially powerful influence on the nation's external behavior, and no account of the sources of American foreign policy would be complete without a discussion of them. But despite their importance, apparently confirmed in theory as well as fact, it would be misleading and simplistic to ascribe too much influence to the individuals responsible for the conduct of American foreign policy or to assume that influence is the same for all leaders in all circumstances. The thesis that the individuals make a difference is unassailable, but more meaningful questions to ask are "Under what circumstances do the idiosyncratic qualities of leaders exert their greatest impact?" and, secondarily, "What kinds of policy outcomes are likely to result from different types of officials?" Addressing these questions forces an examination of how individual characteristics find expression in foreign policy outcomes and of the subtle ways the impact of leaders' influence may be circumscribed by the policy-making *roles* they occupy.

When the mediating impact of policymakers' roles on their behavior is taken into account, attention is drawn to the fact that many different people, widely dispersed throughout the government, contribute to the making of foreign policy. Some of the departments and other agencies of government involved with foreign policy were examined in the preceding part of this book. In Part III, we are concerned with decision makers and with how the roles established by the way the government is organized for the conduct of foreign policy influence the behavior of the policymakers occupying those roles, and, ultimately, American foreign policy itself. As a rival hypothesis to the "great man" image of political leadership, "role theory" assumes that the positions and the processes, rather than the characteristics of the people making the decisions, influence most potently the course of action the United States pursues abroad. Furthermore, changes in policy are assumed to result from changes in role conceptions rather than from changes in the individuals who occupy these roles.

As a source of American foreign policy-making, policy-maker roles highlight how the nature of the office shapes the behavior of its occupants: decision makers' actions are molded by the socially prescribed behaviors and legally sanctioned norms that are attached to a given position. Bureaucratic roles in the decision-making machinery carry with them certain expectations, obligations, rights, and images of appropriate behavior, and they produce pressures that influence policy performance and policy outcomes.

If the positions policymakers hold substantially shape their behaviors, merely changing the person sitting behind the desk in the Oval Office will not bring about fundamental alterations in the nation's policies. Nor, for that matter, would massive changes of personnel within the foreign affairs government bring about policy innovations. To proponents of role theory, roles determine behavior more than do the qualities and characteristics of individuals.

Because large-scale organizations manage the nation's international activities, it is also important to examine the related effects of collective decision making by and within the many large bureaucratic organizations that bear responsibility for the implementation of American foreign policy.

Here the evidence points to pressures that lead to inertial respect for the orthodox views of such agencies. Such tendencies are clearly more conducive to policy continuity than to policy change. In addition, role factors help account for the capacity of entrenched bureaucratic personnel to prevent presidents from getting their decisions implemented. "The outsider believes," Secretary of State Henry A. Kissinger once noted, that "a presidential order is consistently followed. Nonsense. I have to spend considerable time seeing that it is carried out in the spirit the president intended." Role theory anticipates the reasons for this kind of bureaucratic intransigence.

To develop these ideas, the essays assembled in Part III explore various ways in which decision makers and the policy positions or roles they occupy influence the foreign policy of the United States. In this context the selections address such questions as, What consequences result from the president's dependence on the bureaucratic organizations created to serve him? and, Are bureaucracies "ruling servants" in control of policy by virtue of their power to impede? If so, is a "rational" foreign policy, dictated by the national interest of the country as determined by the president and his advisers, rather than by the parochial interests of the foreign affairs establishment, possible?

DECISION MAKERS AND POLICY-MAKER ROLES AS INFLUENCES ON AMERICAN FOREIGN POLICY

What is the most meaningful way to conceptualize the process by which foreign policy decisions are reached? The conventional view maintains that policymakers—notably the president and his principal advisers—devise strategies and implement plans to realize objectives "rationally," that is, in terms of calculations regarding national interests defined by the relative costs and benefits associated with alternative goals and means. Many scholars have questioned the accuracy of this popular model, however. Much of the evidence drawn from case studies points in another direction: to the likelihood that foreign policy-making is shaped more by bargaining among competing actors within the foreign affairs establishment than by the rational calculations of a unitary actor. Correspondingly, what has come to be known as the "bureaucratic-politics model" of decision making stresses the roles within large-scale organizations and the struggles that occur among their constituent units. The result is often policy-making by negotiated compromise between and among the many rival actors. Proponents of the bureaucratic-politics model claim it captures the essence of the highly politicized foreign policy–decision-making process more completely and accurately than does the model of rational behavior.

Of the many features of American foreign policy that may be explained by reference to the kind of policy-making roles that exist within the U.S. government, defense policy stands out. This is because the Pentagon—with the most personnel and the biggest budget of any governmental agency—exerts a powerful sway over the kinds of national security policies undertaken and over the ways in which they are implemented. But size and clout do not necessarily make for efficiency. On the contrary, a fragmented decision-making structure may make for inefficiency and waste. This thesis is explored in David C. Jones's essay, "What's Wrong with Our Defense Establishment." General Jones served as Chairman of the Joint Chiefs of Staff longer than any previous occupant of that important position, and thus brings authority, experience, and expertise to his analysis of policy-making and policy coordination—and lack thereof—in U.S. defense policy. Indeed, his critique, against the backdrop of the historical evolution of the defense establishment, was instrumental in provoking a movement to reform defense policy-making. That culminated in passage in late 1986 of the Goldwater-Nunn Bill, which strengthened the influence of field commanders and the chairman of the Joint Chiefs of Staff, in the hope of correcting the proclivity of the Defense Department to rely more on symbols of strength than on actual preparedness for the conduct of war. But Jones's evaluation shows that developing a link between defense strategies and defense resources poses a serious challenge. The reason lies in the fact that, as Jones put it, "The bureaucratic resistance to change is enormous and is reinforced by many allies of the services—in Congress and elsewhere—who are bent on keeping the past enthroned." General Jones's assessment suggests that the organizational apparatus from which defense policy emanates, and in particular interservice rivalries, impedes a more effective and efficient approach to the formulation and execution of national security policy.

Some of the tenets of this thesis are illuminated in the way in which the United States became involved in and attempted to conduct its prolonged war in Vietnam. For a variety of often incompatible reasons, most observers regard America's involvement in the Vietnam War as an unfortunate, even tragic, event. The protracted series of decisions that took the United States into Indochina and, after years of fighting and the loss of thousands of lives, eventually out of it on unsatisfactory terms, raises serious questions about the manner in which American foreign policy is conducted. "How Could Vietnam Happen?" asks James C. Thomson, Jr., almost rhetorically. His answer—that the tragedy was rooted in the roles and bureaucratic processes embedded in the way the U.S. government organizes itself for the making of foreign policy— illustrates the dysfunctional consequences that may emanate from a system characterized by bureaucratic policy-making. Thomson's case study thus documents the thesis underlying role theory and the bureaucratic-politics model, namely, that some of the most catastrophic of America's foreign policy initiatives are the result, not of evil or stupid people, but of misdirected behaviors that are encouraged by the nature of the policy-making system. The failure of Vietnam, Thomson contends, was the failure of America's policy-making process, not of its leadership. His argument, however disturbing, gives insight into the milieu of decision making and introduces a number of concepts crucial to understanding how the roles created by the organizational setting of decision making influences the kinds of decisions that leaders make and that bureaucracies implement.

Extending this interpretation and the perspective that informs it, a thoughtful critique of the bureaucratic-politics perspective is provided that focuses on the 1962 Cuban missile crisis, and in particular on perhaps the most famous bureaucratic treatment of that critical juncture in Soviet-American relations, Graham Allison's *Essence of Decision*. Stephen D. Krasner's "Are Bureaucracies Important?: A Re-examination of Accounts of the Cuban Missile Crisis" finds Allison's interpretation wanting. Krasner argues that the picture Allison and others provide of foreign policy-making, emphasizing bureaucratic roles as all-powerful determinants of policy outcomes, is greatly exaggerated. Indeed, Krasner's reexamination of the facts surrounding the Cuban missile crisis reveals evidence that, while bureaucracies do exert an impact on foreign policy, decision makers nonetheless have a capacity for rational choice, and that the choices they make—rather than those made by bureaucratic organizations— ultimately matter most. Hence, the individuals elected by and responsible to the people they represent do matter, and how those leaders define their decision-making roles can prove decisive.

Some of the principles underlying the thesis Krasner advances are exemplified in the comparative case studies Fen Osler Hampson provides in "The Divided Decision-Maker: American Domestic Politics and the Cuban Crises." Through an analysis of a series of *crisis* decisions made by American policymakers with respect to Cuba, Hampson sheds light on the ways in which countervailing pressures are exerted on American decision makers, pressures that can divide the policymaker's attention and force him or her to satisfy competing constituencies by pursuing incompatible goals. Undesired policy responses to crises can result, and those pressures can inhibit the nation's capacity to choose among policy alternatives rationally. By extension, Hampson's examples expose a wider syndrome, explaining some of the puzzling directions American foreign policy has occasionally taken under conditions of stress. Discontinuities in the overall pattern of American foreign policy can be explicated by reference to the impact of domestic politics on external behavior, as can the disarray that episodically surfaces in the processes through which crisis decisions are reached.

Krasner's essay and Hampson's historical evidence pose a challenge to those whose explanations of American foreign policy ignore either the preferences of presidents or the influence of domestic political pressures on crisis decision making. In so doing, they set the stage for a critical theoretical and empirical evaluation of the impact of large-scale bureaucratic organizations on American foreign policy. In an essay derived from comparative studies of bureaucratic performance and their consequences, Charles F. Hermann's "New Foreign Policy Problems and Old Bureaucratic Organizations" probes the ways the operating procedures of bureaucratic organizations affect the conduct of American foreign policy. His broad-ranging treatment shows how disarray and incoherence in foreign policy can be traced to how presidents have dealt with the bureaucratic organizations on which successful foreign policy necessarily depends. "What is there," Hermann asks, "about the large, complex bureaucratic organizations upon which all modern governments depend that often leads to ineffectiveness?" His analysis of past bureaucratic practice suggests that "often the heart of the difficulty lies with certain structural characteristics of organizations, not with willful bureaucrats who deliberately seek to frustrate presidents." These characteristics are identified and submitted to theoretical interpretation, a treatment that leads to the conclusion that "significantly more resources and energy [should be devoted] to the design of, and experimentation with, bureaucratic approaches to new forms of collective problem recognition."

Ultimate responsibility for the management of American foreign policy rests with the nation's leaders. Thus we conclude *The Domestic Sources of American Foreign Policy* with an evaluation of the capacity of leaders to control American foreign policy and, through the exercise of that control, to frame coherent responses to the multiple challenges confronting the United States from abroad. Margaret G. Hermann's essay, "The Role of Leaders and Leadership in the Making of American Foreign Policy," examines the complex analytical problems that surround interpretation of the impact of leaders on foreign policy-making. While clarifying several key concepts that relate to that topic, she explores the properties of leadership that are likely to most influence the way American foreign policy is made and the kinds of policies that are produced by the impact of these influences. Her essay introduces "the leadership dilemma" that emerges from popular but incompatible images Americans maintain of their leaders—images that are often not grounded in realistic awareness of the prevailing constraints on the capacity of American leaders to lead. Arguing that multiple factors are involved in assessing the impact of leaders on foreign policy, these are analyzed in terms of leaders' characteristics (worldview, political style, motivation, interest and training in foreign affairs, and political socialization), their multiple constituencies (the American people, Congress, executive-branch departments and agencies, their own staff aides and political appointees, and foreign leaders), and the functions they perform in relation to their constituencies (as motivators, policy advocates, consensus builders, recruiters, and managers). These characteristics, Hermann argues, are the ones that most shape how American leaders will respond to the situations they encounter. Her comprehensive overview adds to our awareness of the manner in which the human dimension of American diplomacy makes itself felt. The illustrative material provided in the essay also contributes to an understanding of how individuals' definitions of the roles they occupy can influence their subsequent behavior (and, correspondingly, the degree to which leaders can reduce the influence of role factors by redefining their requirements). Hence, the essay serves as an antidote to the belief that individuals do not make a difference, for it demonstrates convincingly that "American foreign policy is made by people and what those people are like shapes what happens."

15. WHAT'S WRONG WITH OUR DEFENSE ESTABLISHMENT

David C. Jones

At a late-afternoon meeting at the White House . . . , President Reagan, who had just returned from horseback riding at Quantico, turned to me in jest, but with a touch of nostalgia, and asked, "Isn't there some way we can bring back the horse cavalry?" My reply was: "Just wait, Mr. President. We are starting by resurrecting battleships."

Below the surface of this lighthearted exchange lie two pervasive problems within defense:

- We are too comfortable with the past.
- We do not make a sufficiently rigorous examination of defense requirements and alternatives.

By their very nature, large organizations have a built-in resistance to change. As the largest organization in the free world, our defense establishment—the Department of Defense—has most of the problems of a large corporation but lacks an easily calculated "bottom line" to force needed change. At the core are the Army, Navy, Air Force and Marine Corps: institutions that find it difficult to adapt to changing conditions because of understandable attachments to the past. The very foundation of each service rests on imbuing its members with pride in its mission, its doctrine and its customs and discipline—all of which are steeped in traditions. While these deep-seated service distinctions are important in fostering a fighting spirit, cultivating them engenders tendencies to look inward and to insulate the institutions against outside challenges.

The history of our services includes striking examples of ideas and inventions whose time had come, but which were resisted because they did not fit into existing service concepts. The Navy kept building sailing ships long after the advent of steam power. Machine guns and tanks were developed in the United States, but our Army rejected them until long after they were accepted in Europe. The horse cavalry survived essentially unchanged right up until World War II despite evidence that its utility was greatly diminished decades earlier. Even Army Air Corps officers were required to wear spurs until the late 1930's.

But the armed services are only part of the problem: The Defense Department has evolved into a grouping of large, rigid bureaucracies—services, agencies, staffs, boards and committees—which embrace the past and adapt new technology to fit traditional missions and methods. There is no doubt that the

195

cavalry leaders would have quickly adopted a horse which went farther and faster—a high-technology stallion. The result of this rigidity has been an ever-widening gap between the need to adapt to changing conditions and our ability to do so. Over the last two to three years the American public has become increasingly concerned over our deteriorating position in military power and convinced that we must devote more to our defenses than we did in the 1960's and 1970's. But after serving on the Joint Chiefs of Staff longer than anyone else in history and under more Presidents and Secretaries of Defense (four of each), and being a student of military history and organizations, I am convinced that fundamental defense deficiencies cannot be solved with dollars alone—no matter how much they are needed.

We do not think through our defense problems adequately, and we are getting less capability than we should from our increased defense budgets. There is reason to believe that, faced with a contingency requiring a major joint operation, our performance would be below the level we should expect or need.

No one element of our defense establishment is singularly responsible for our defense problems. The problems I will identify, and for which I will propose solutions, have existed too long to be the fault of any particular administration or of particular personalities in or out of uniform.

History books for the most part glorify our military accomplishments, but a closer examination reveals a disconcerting pattern:

- Unpreparedness at the onset of each new crisis or war.
- Initial failures.
- Reorganizing while fighting.
- Building our defenses as we cranked up our industrial base.
- Prevailing by wearing down the enemy—by being bigger, not smarter.

We could do things poorly at the start of past wars and still recover because time was on our side.

The North was a striking example of a bureaucratized military-establishment during the Civil War. Initially, the South had better leadership, was far more flexible and was able to do a great deal more with its limited resources and forces. The North suffered early defeats and encountered many leadership problems, but finally won by virtue of overwhelming industrial output and military manpower.

We also had serious organizational problems during the Cuban campaign of the Spanish-American War. The interservice wrangling had been so great that the Army commander refused to let the Navy be represented at the formal surrender. Unfortunately, this was not the last case of split responsibilities and interservice conflicts obstructing our conduct of a war.

In the aftermath of the 1898 war, the services, particularly the Army, instituted some organizational reforms. Despite a great deal of opposition, a Chief of Staff of the Army was created in 1903 and a Chief of Naval Operations was established in 1916. But the War Department (the precursor of the Department of the Army and the Department of the Air Force) and the Navy Department continued to be riddled with semi-autonomous, often intractable fiefdoms, branches, corps, departments, bureaus, and so forth.

World War I was the most tragic example of trying to win a war through mass and attrition. Thousands of young men gave their lives to advance a few yards over the enemy trenches, only to be thrown back the next day at an equal cost to the enemy.

The emergence of the airplane as a major military asset during World War I should have alerted us to the need to adjust our doctrines and our organizations to changing realities. The continued development of air power could not help but blur the traditional distinction between land and naval warfare, but the nation reacted to this phenomenon in a traditionally bureaucratic manner: Each service developed its own air power (today there are *four* air-power entities), and protected it with artificial barriers to obscure the costly duplications. One barrier, established in 1938 (later rescinded), prohibited any Army Air Corps airplane from flying more than 100 miles out to sea.

The Army and Navy began World War II with authority and responsibility diffused. Each still had many semiautonomous agencies with little coordination below the chief-of-service level. Soon after Pearl Harbor, Gen. George C. Marshall, the Army Chief of Staff, streamlined the Army by reducing the number of officers with direct access to him from 61 to 6. The Navy also made some adjustments. (The services have since slipped back into the old patterns. The number of officers having direct access to most service chiefs—especially when the joint system is considered—is again very high.)

The Joint Chiefs of Staff were established early in 1942 as a counterpart to the British Chiefs of Staff Committee. Although the wartime Chiefs addressed certain priority issues, to a great extent World War II was fought along service lines. . . . [M]any of the fundamental problems of the World War II joint system still exist below the surface.

We won World War II despite our organizational handicaps, not because we were smarter, but once again because we and our allies were bigger. We had the time and geographic isolation to mobilize American industry and a superb code-breaking effort to aid our intelligence gathering.

As the war drew to a close, an exhaustive debate ensued on how to organize the postwar military. The Army favored a highly integrated system, but the Navy and others were strongly opposed, some fearing that the Army would dominate any integrated system. The Air Force, then still a part of the Army, supported integration, but was primarily interested in becoming a separate service.

Those opposed to integration were backed by stronger constituencies, including powerful forces in Congress, than were the advocates of unification. Arguments that unification threatened civilian control over the military soon dominated the debate. . . .[It] became quite clear to the advocates that major change was unlikely. . . .

. . . So after nearly two years of studies, debate and political maneuverings, the National Security Act of 1947 emerged with a compromise military establishment: a loose confederation of large, rigid service bureaucracies—now four rather than three—with a Secretary of Defense powerless against them. . . .

One of [James V.] Forrestal's last acts as [the country's first] Secretary of Defense was to recommend a much more integrated Department of Defense, but changes came slowly. Amendments to the National Security Act in 1949, 1953 and 1958 strengthened the Secretary's authority and expanded the size and purview of his staff, but did little to alter the relative influence of the joint military system and the services.

President Eisenhower had recommended a much stronger joint system in 1953 and 1958, and his wisdom was borne out by our conduct of the Vietnam War—perhaps our worst example of confused objectives and unclear responsibilities, both in Washington and in the field. Each service, instead of integrating efforts with the others, considered Vietnam its own war and sought to carve out a large mission for itself. For example, each fought its own air war, agreeing only to limited measures for a coordinated effort. "Body count" and "tons dropped" became the measures of merit. Lack of integration persisted right through the 1975 evacuation of Saigon—when responsibility was split between two separate commands, one on land and one at sea; each of these set a different "H-hour," which caused confusion and delays.

Our soldiers, sailors, airmen and marines have acted bravely throughout our history. With few exceptions, our forces have performed well at the unit level. And there have been bright moments at the higher levels also. The landing at Normandy, Patton's charge across France, the battle of Midway and the landing at Inchon were brilliant strategic conceptions, valiantly executed. But these peaks in martial performance followed valleys in which the nation found itself poorly prepared, poorly organized and imperiled by inadequacies in Washington. In the past, we had time to overcome our mistakes. Our allies often bore the initial brunt, and we had the industrial capacity for a quick buildup in the military capacity needed to turn the tide. Today we can expect no such respite. Our allies could not delay the Soviet Union while we prepared, and our industrial base has fallen into a state of disrepair. Nuclear weapons have added new dimensions which make constant readiness even more critical. If we are to deter another conflict, or to succeed if one be thrust upon us, we must be prepared to do things right on the battlefield the first time.

A sound defense posture should begin with sound long-term planning, a means to measure progress, and authoritative direction and control to insure that all elements contribute to a well-defined objective. On the surface, our system *appears* to provide such an orderly approach. The process starts with a defense guidance document prepared by the office of the Under Secretary of Defense for Policy, based on Administration policy and fiscal guidance and on inputs from field commanders, the services, the Joint Chiefs, the Secretary of Defense's staff and other relevant sources. The services build their annual programs on the basis of the defense guidance's objectives and budget targets and then submit them to the Secretary of Defense. The Secretary convenes a committee to review the documents and recommend changes to bring the service programs into conformance with the nation's priorities. After being submitted to the President and Congress for approval, the budgets are administered by the services and agencies assigned to the Department of Defense.

But this process begins to break down at the very beginning because the military strategy contained in the defense guidance always demands greater force capabilities than the budget constraints will allow. Some administrations have attempted to limit the requirements by calling for the capability to fight "one and a half" or "two and a half" wars, while others have proposed preparing for global war almost without limits. In any case, the guidance almost invariably leads to what the Joint Chiefs have long called the "strategy-force mismatch" as requirements outpace capabilities. . . .

Since requirements exceed resources, the military services invariably allocate resources among their traditional missions, and seek ways to justify a greater share of the budget. But additional funds are likely to come only from another service's share, so each attempts to outgame the others without sufficient regard for cross-service programs.

The vast array of service programs is then submitted to the defense committee. The name and composition of the committee may vary from administration to administration, but its function remains the same. Currently it is called the Defense Resources Board, and its chairman is the Secretary or the Deputy Secretary of Defense, and includes the service Secretaries, Assistant Secretaries of Defense and the Chairman of the Joint Chiefs of Staff. The service chiefs attend as observers.

Week after week, the board meets in an attempt to examine major issues, but the focus is primarily on the service programs, which include many hundreds of items deemed essential by their advocates. The board fusses over marginal changes in the service programs, but it is literally impossible for it to address them in sufficient depth or to focus on the most critical cross-service issues.

The Joint Chiefs of Staff and the Joint Staff are assigned a role in this process, but each service usually wants the Joint Staff merely to echo its views. Since four of the five members of the Joint Chiefs of Staff are also service chiefs, a negotiated amalgam of service views almost invariably prevails when inputs are finally proposed by the Joint Staff. The Chairman of the Joint Chiefs of Staff is the only military member of the Defense Resources Board and can offer independent opinions, but the chairman has only five people working directly for him to sift through the various issues. (The Joint Staff belongs to the Joint Chiefs' corporate body, not to the chairman.) Consequently, chairmen traditionally focus on a few critical items. In my case, they were readiness, command and control, and mobility.

The result of this tedious process is a defense budget that is derived primarily from the disparate desires of the individual services rather than from a well-integrated plan based on a serious examination of alternatives by the civilian and military leadership working together. Inevitably, a Secretary of Defense either supports a total program that is roughly the sum of the service inputs (limited by fiscal guidance) or resorts to forcing changes, knowing that advocates of disapproved programs will continue the opposition into the Congressional hearings.

But resource allocation by the board is only the beginning of the problem. The optimism expressed in program proposals seldom comes true. The chairman of the Defense Science Board, Norman Augustine, has written that [since the 1940s] our major weapons systems have met performance goals 70 percent of the time (not bad), but have met schedules only 15 percent of the time, and cost estimates only 10 percent of the time, even after accounting for inflation.

As costs increase, programs are stretched out. Weapons are usually ordered in numbers well below efficient production rates, to the detriment of the "industrial base." This only leads to further cost increases, the cycle repeats itself, and we find ourselves trapped in a Catch-22 situation. Tough decisions are not made, so the financial "bow wave" that always spills ahead is magnified. Attempts to improve efficiency, such as the [Reagan] Administration's multiyear procurement contracts, are very helpful, but do not get to the fundamental problems of planning and resources.

The lack of discipline in the budget system prevents making the very tough choices of deciding what to do and what not to do. Instead, strong constituencies in the Pentagon, Congress and industry support individual programs, while the need for overall defense effectiveness and efficiency is not adequately addressed.

Pentagon leadership finds it virtually impossible to spend the time necessary to impose discipline on the budget process. Cycles overlap and . . . we usually find Congress considering a last-minute multibillion-dollar supplemental appropriation at the end of one fiscal year and unable to agree on the budget before the start of the next fiscal year. At the same time, the Pentagon is struggling with the next five-year defense plan and the subsequent budget submission. This immerses the leadership constantly in confusing external struggles for public and Congressional support and bewildering internal disputes over resources and turf.

The same pressures burden the service leaders as they attempt to cope with managing procurement programs, recruiting and training the forces, and maintaining discipline and esprit. Chiefs are judged by their peers and services on their success in obtaining funding for their own major systems and on protecting service interests in the three afternoons a week they spend in meetings of the Joint Chiefs of Staff. Furthermore, a service chief, who is a service advocate in one hat and supposedly an impartial judge of competing requirements in his other hat as a member of the Joint Chiefs of Staff, has a fundamental conflict of interest.

To sum up, our defense establishment suffers serious deficiencies, including the following:

- Strategy is so all-encompassing as to mean all things to all men.
- Leaders are inevitably captives of the urgent, and long-range planning is too often neglected.
- Authority and responsibility are badly diffused.
- Rigorous examination of requirements and alternatives is not made.
- Discipline is lacking in the budget process.
- Tough decisions are avoided.
- Accountability for decisions or performance is woefully inadequate.
- Leadership, often inexperienced, is forced to spend too much time on refereeing an intramural scramble for resources.
- A serious conflict of interest faces our senior military leaders.
- The combat effectiveness of the fighting force—the end product—does not receive enough attention.

. . . [T]hese problems have been with us for decades and there are no easy solutions.

What all this adds up to is that it is an uphill struggle for anyone—including a Secretary of Defense—to gain real control of our defense establishment. An earlier study on defense organization stated that everyone was responsible for everything and no one was specifically responsible for anything. The top leadership is too often at the mercy of long-entrenched bureaucracies. It is ironic that the services have, with considerable help from outside constituencies, been able to defeat attempts to bring order out of chaos by arguing that a source of alternative military advice for the President and Secretary of Defense runs the risk of undermining civilian control.

There has for some time been an imbalance in the degree of control that our civilian leadership exercises over operational and other defense matters. In operational matters, it is pervasive. An order cannot go out of Washington to move a ship or any combat unit or to take any other specific operational action without the specific approval and initialing of the directive by the Secretary of Defense. At times, Defense Secretaries and their staffs have been involved in the most minute details of operations.

In other areas, civilian influence is more often apparent than real. Defense Secretaries are given very little comprehensive advice on alternative strategies or systems. In an attempt to fill the void, Defense Secretaries have often turned to civilian analysts for such advice. Such consultants can provide a useful service, but they cannot make up for the absence of alternative advice from experienced, serving military officers. That the Joint Chiefs of Staff, a committee beholden to the interests of the services, has not been able to provide such advice during its existence is amply documented in scores of studies over many years.

Civilian accountability within the Defense Department is undermined further by the rapid turnover or by inexperience in the senior leadership. In the [40] years since the department was founded [in 1947], there have been 15 Secretaries of Defense, and there have been 19 Deputy Secretaries of Defense in the 33 years since the establishment of that position. A recent study revealed that the civilian policy makers in the Defense Department stay on the job an average of only 28 months.

Little of what I have said is new. Reams of paper have been used since World War II to describe these same deficiencies. President Eisenhower, who knew well both sides of the civilian-military equation, tried to resolve the basic problem, but the effects of his efforts were limited. Others have also tried, but with even less success. The bureaucratic resistance to change is enormous and is reinforced by many allies of the services—in Congress and elsewhere—who are bent on keeping the past enthroned. Civilian defense leaders have been reluctant to push hard for changes, either because they thought they could not succeed or because they did not want to expend the necessary political capital which they believed was better spent on gaining support for the defense budget. Many have feared that raising basic organizational issues might distract attention from the budget and give ammunition to opponents, who would use admissions of organizational inefficiency to argue for further budget cuts. Yet, since the public already believes that all is not right with the Department of Defense, bold reforms would not only increase our defense effectiveness, but would strengthen public support as well.

That the balance of influence within the defense establishment is oriented too much toward the individual services has been a constant theme of many past studies of defense organization. A special study group of retired senior officers [in 1982] found it necessary to report that "a certain amount of service independence is healthy and desirable, but the balance now favors the parochial interests of the services too much and the larger needs of the nation's defenses too little."

It is commonly accepted that one result of this imbalance is a constant bickering among the services. This is not the case. On the contrary, interactions among the services usually result in "negotiated treaties" which minimize controversy by avoiding challenges to service interests. Such a "truce" has its good points, for it is counterproductive for the services to attack each other. But the lack of adequate questioning by military professionals results in gaps and unwarranted duplications in our defense capabilities. What is lacking is a counterbalancing system, involving officers not so beholden to their services, who can objectively examine strategy, roles, missions, weapons systems, war planning and other contentious issues to offset the influence of the individual services.

President Eisenhower tried to resolve this problem in 1958 by removing the services from the operational chain of command. In essence, two separate lines of authority were created under the Secretary of Defense: an operational line and an administrative line. The operational line runs from the President, through the Secretary of Defense, to the combat commands—those theater or functional commands headed by the Eisenhowers, the Nimitzes, the Mac-Arthurs of the future. The Joint Chiefs of Staff are not directly in this line of command but do, through the Joint Staff, provide the Secretary oversight of the combat commands, and pass his orders to them. The administrative line runs to the service departments responsible for recruiting, training, procurement and a myriad of other tasks necessary to develop the forces assigned to the combat commands.

President Eisenhower intended that the operational side would assist the Secretary of Defense in developing strategy, operational plans and weapons and force-level requirements based on the needs of "truly unified commands." The Joint Chiefs of Staff and the Joint Staff were to be the *Secretary's* military staff in this effort. The services would remain the *providers* of the forces needed by the combatant commands but would not determine *what* to provide or how those forces would be employed. But President Eisenhower did not achieve what he wanted. The scales of influence are still tipped too far in favor of the services and against the combat commanders.

Although the combat commanders now brief the Defense Resources Board and have every opportunity to communicate with the Secretary of Defense and the Chiefs, virtually their only power is that of persuasion. The services control most of the money and the personnel assignments and promotions of their people wherever assigned, including in the Office of the Secretary of Defense, the Joint Staff and the Unified Command Staffs. Officers who perform duty outside their own services generally do less well than those assigned to duty in their service, especially when it comes to promotion to general or admiral. The Chiefs of Staff of the services almost always have had duty on service staffs in Washington but almost never on the Joint Staff. Few incentives exist for an officer assigned to joint duty to do more than punch his or her ticket, and then get back into a service assignment. I cannot stress this point too strongly: He who controls dollars, promotions and assignments controls the organization— and the services so control, especially with regard to personnel actions. . . .

Yet it is very difficult to break out of the Department of Defense's organizational maze. Many have struggled vainly within the system to make improvements in the balance between the operational and administrative lines. Solutions to some of the basic interservice problems are heralded every few years but to this date have not addressed the fundamental causes. To provide a balance, the services must share some of their authority, but they have proved to be consistently unwilling to do so. A service chief has a constituency which, if convinced that he is not fighting hard enough for what the service sees as its fair share of defense missions and resources, can destroy the chief's effectiveness.

Only the Chairman of the Joint Chiefs of Staff is unconstrained by a service constituency, but he is in a particularly difficult position. His influence stems from his ability to persuade all his colleagues on the Joint Chiefs of Staff to agree on a course of action and any disagreement requires by law a report to the Secretary of Defense. A Chairman jeopardizes his effectiveness if, early in his tour, he creates dissension within the corporate body by trying to force the services to share some of their authority.

By the summer of 1980, after serving as Chairman of the Joint Chiefs of Staff for two years, I had become convinced that we could not begin to overcome our defense problems without a basic restructuring of military responsibility. . . .

It is no secret that the greatest opposition to any change came from the Department of the Navy, just as it did in 1947 and has ever since. I believe I understand, even though I cannot agree with the reasons. The Department of the Navy is the most strategically independent of the services—it has its own army, navy and air force. It is least dependent on others. It would prefer to be given a mission, retain complete control over all the assets, and be left alone.

The Army is and always has been the most supportive of the services in cross-service activities and the strongest advocate of organizational changes which would improve unity of effort. Its reasons, too, are understandable— and I agree with them. The Army is the least strategically independent service. It depends on the Air Force for much firepower and on the Air Force and Navy for mobility; the Army can, in fact, do very little in isolation and hence is particularly short-changed by a lack of integration and cooperation among the services.

The Air Force has some missions requiring the cooperation of the other services, and some which it can pursue independently. Not surprisingly, Air Force officers generally have been more ambivalent about change.

Given these circumstances, we cannot expect the services to agree on profound changes no matter how badly needed, for the changes inevitably would result in the services' giving up some of their sovereignty. . . .

. . . There is always great reluctance in Washington to take on entrenched bureaucracies in the absence of some consensus for change.

. . . [My] proposals are designed to provide the Secretary of Defense more balanced military advice and staff support in order to *strengthen* civilian control. I believe we must provide a proper balance between the services and the joint system—the administrative and operational lines of authority and responsibility. So long as the leadership of the operational side remains within the control of the four services, individual service interests—which are oriented to independent capabilities—will continue to dominate the military advice offered to the Secretary of Defense.

In broad outline, this is what I believe must be done:

To eliminate service domination of the channels of military advice to the Secretary and the President, the Chairman of the Joint Chiefs of Staff—rather than the five-man committee of the Chiefs—should represent the operational side, while the service chiefs should continue to represent the administrative side of our military organization. The Chairman would receive advice from both the service chiefs and the combat commanders in preparing his recommendation to the Secretary of Defense. . . .

To insure that he can meet his responsibility to the Secretary and the President, the Chairman should be authorized a deputy chairman and the Joint Staff should be assigned to the Chairman rather than the corporate body of the Joint Chiefs. The service chiefs and their staffs (most of which dwarf the Joint Staff) would still have access to the Joint Staff but would not have a de facto veto of all proposals which subordinated service interests to greater cross-service effectiveness.

Systems analysts should be transferred from the office of the Secretary of Defense to the Chairman's office to insure a good balance of civilian and military perspectives on alternatives offered to the Secretary. As a related action, many of the more than 500 military officers assigned to the Office of the Secretary of Defense should be reassigned back to their services as the Joint Staff becomes defensewide oriented rather than service dominated.

Discipline should be imposed on the guidance-program-budget cycle. Not only should there be a requirement for an independent cost analysis on every major program, but greater reliance should be placed on the results. . . .

Administrative matters should be decentralized to the services, with their leadership, military and civilian, being held more accountable for performance. Fixing responsibility for defensewide advice more clearly on a joint system not dominated by the services would allow the service chiefs and their staffs to spend much more time on running their services.

Substantial changes should be made in military personnel policies so that officers could develop a broader vision than that of their own service and could be prepared better for both service and interservice assignments. . . .

The professional education system should be changed to stress the joint needs in defense by providing the National Defense University limited oversight of part of the curriculum of the Service War Colleges.

We should re-examine the retirement system which provides great incentives for officers to serve for 20 years, but very few incentives for the best to stay longer. We still lose too many of our best officers at the peak of their capabilities. . . .

Finally, the Congressional restrictions on tenure of assignment on the Joint Staff should be removed so that we do not continue to experience a 100 percent turnover in a little over two years. Collectively, the above should provide opportunities for greater stability and experience in officer assignments and, thus, the opportunity for better accountability of performance.

I do not claim that my proposals will solve all of our defense problems, but these or similar major changes can set us on the right course. . . .

16. HOW COULD VIETNAM HAPPEN? AN AUTOPSY

James C. Thomson, Jr.

As a case study in the making of foreign policy, the Vietnam War will fascinate historians and social scientists for many decades to come. One question that will certainly be asked: How did men of superior ability, sound training, and high ideals—American policy-makers of the 1960s—create such a costly and divisive policy?

As one who watched the decision-making process in Washington from 1961 to 1966 under Presidents Kennedy and Johnson, I can suggest a preliminary answer. I can do so by briefly listing some of the factors that seemed to me to shape our Vietnam policy during my years as an East Asia specialist at the State Department and the White House. I shall deal largely with Washington as I saw or sensed it, and not with Saigon, where I . . . spent but a scant three days, in the entourage of the Vice President, or with other decision centers, the capitals of interested parties. Nor will I deal with other important parts of the record: Vietnam's history prior to 1961, for instance, or the overall course of America's relations with Vietnam.

Yet a first and central ingredient in these years of Vietnam decisions does involve history. The ingredient was *the legacy of the 1950s*—by which I mean the so-called "loss of China," the Korean War, and the Far East policy of Secretary of State Dulles.

This legacy had an institutional by-product for the Kennedy Administration: in 1961 the U.S. government's East Asian establishment was undoubtedly the most rigid and doctrinaire of Washington's regional divisions in foreign affairs. This was especially true at the Department of State, where the incoming Administration found the Bureau of Far Eastern Affairs the hardest nut to crack. It was a bureau that had been purged of its best China expertise, and of far-sighted, dispassionate men, as a result of McCarthyism. Its members were generally committed to one policy line: the close containment and isolation of mainland China, the harassment of "neutralist" nations which sought to avoid alignment with either Washington or Peking, and the maintenance of a network of alliances with anti-Communist client states on China's periphery.

Another aspect of the legacy was the special vulnerability and sensitivity of the new Democratic Administration on Far East policy issues. The memory of the McCarthy era was still very sharp, and Kennedy's margin of victory was too thin. The 1960 Offshore Islands TV debate between Kennedy and Nixon

206 James C. Thomson, Jr.

had shown the President-elect the perils of "fresh thinking." The Administration was inherently leery of moving too fast on Asia. As a result, the Far East Bureau (now the Bureau of East Asian and Pacific Affairs) was the last one to be overhauled. Not until Averell Harriman was brought in as Assistant Secretary in December, 1961, were significant personnel changes attempted, and it took Harriman several months to make a deep imprint on the bureau because of his necessary preoccupation with the Laos settlement. Once he did so, there was virtually no effort to bring back the purged or exiled East Asia experts.

There were other important by-products of this "legacy of the fifties":

The new Administration inherited and somewhat shared a *general perception of China-on-the-march*—a sense of China's vastness, its numbers, its belligerence; a revived sense, perhaps, of the Golden Horde. This was a perception fed by Chinese intervention in the Korean War (an intervention actually based on appallingly bad communications and mutual miscalculation on the part of Washington and Peking; but the careful unraveling of the tragedy, which scholars have accomplished, had not yet become part of the conventional wisdom).

The new Administration inherited and briefly accepted *a monolithic conception of the Communist bloc.* Despite much earlier predictions and reports by outside analysts, policy-makers did not begin to accept the reality and possible finality of the Sino-Soviet split until the first weeks of 1962. The inevitably corrosive impact of competing nationalisms on Communism was largely ignored.

The new Administration inherited and to some extent shared *the "domino theory" about Asia.* This theory resulted from profound ignorance of Asian history and hence ignorance of the radical differences among Asian nations and societies. It resulted from a blindness to the power and resilience of Asian nationalisms. (It may also have resulted from a subconscious sense that, since "all Asians look alike," all Asian nations will act alike.) As a theory, the domino fallacy was not merely inaccurate but also insulting to Asian nations; yet it has continued to this day to beguile men who should know better.

Finally, the legacy of the fifties was apparently compounded by an uneasy sense of a worldwide Communist challenge to the new Administration after the Bay of Pigs fiasco. A first manifestation was the President's traumatic Vienna meeting with Khrushchev in June, 1961; then came the Berlin crisis of the summer. All this created an atmosphere in which President Kennedy undoubtedly felt under special pressure to show his nation's mettle in Vietnam—if the Vietnamese, unlike the people of Laos, were willing to fight.

In general, the legacy of the fifties shaped such early moves of the new Administration as the decisions to maintain a high-visibility SEATO (by sending the Secretary of State himself instead of some underling to its first meeting in 1961), to back away from diplomatic recognition of Mongolia in the summer of 1961, and most important, to expand U.S. military assistance to South Vietnam that winter on the basis of the much more tentative Eisenhower commitment. It should be added that the increased commitment to Vietnam was also fueled by a new breed of military strategists and academic social scientists (some of whom had entered the new Administration) who had developed theories of counterguerrilla warfare and were eager to see them put to the test. To some, "counterinsurgency" seemed a new panacea for coping with the world's instability.

So much for the legacy and the history. Any new Administration inherits both complicated problems and simplistic views of the world. But surely among the policy-makers of the Kennedy and Johnson Administrations there were men who would warn of the dangers of an open-ended commitment to the Vietnam quagmire?

This raises a central question, at the heart of the policy process: Where were the experts, the doubters, and the dissenters? Were they there at all, and if so, what happened to them?

The answer is complex but instructive.

In the first place, the American government was sorely *lacking in real Vietnam or Indochina expertise*. Originally treated as an adjunct of Embassy Paris, our Saigon embassy and the Vietnam Desk at State were largely staffed from 1954 onward by French-speaking Foreign Service personnel of narrowly European experience. Such diplomats were even more closely restricted than the normal embassy officer—by cast of mind as well as language—to contacts with Vietnam's French-speaking urban elites. For instance, Foreign Service linguists in Portugal are able to speak with the peasantry if they get out of Lisbon and choose to do so; not so the French speakers of Embassy Saigon.

In addition, the *shadow of the "loss of China"* distorted Vietnam reporting. Career officers in the Department, and especially those in the field, had not forgotten the fate of their World War II colleagues who wrote in frankness from China and were later pilloried by Senate committees for critical comments on the Chinese Nationalists. Candid reporting on the strengths of the Viet Cong and the weaknesses of the Diem government was inhibited by the memory. It was also inhibited by some higher officials, notably Ambassador Nolting in Saigon, who refused to sign off on such cables.

In due course, to be sure, some Vietnam talent was discovered or developed. But a recurrent and increasingly important factor in the decision-making process was *the banishment of real expertise*. Here the underlying cause was the "closed politics" of policy-making as issues become hot: the more sensitive the issue, and the higher it rises in the bureaucracy, the more completely the experts are excluded while the harassed senior generalists take over (that is, the Secretaries, Undersecretaries, and Presidential Assistants). The frantic skimming of briefing papers in the back seats of limousines is no substitute for the presence of specialists; furthermore, in times of crisis such papers are deemed "too sensitive" even for review by the specialists. Another underlying cause of this banishment, as Vietnam became more critical, was the replacement of the experts, who were generally and increasingly pessimistic, by men described as "can-do guys," loyal and energetic fixers unsoured by expertise. In early 1965, when I confided my growing policy doubts to an older colleague on the NSC staff, he assured me that the smartest thing both of us could do was to "steer clear of the whole Vietnam mess"; the gentleman in question had the misfortune to be a "can-do guy," however, and [was subsequently] highly placed in Vietnam, under orders to solve the mess.

Despite the banishment of the experts, internal doubters and dissenters did indeed appear and persist. Yet as I watched the process, such men were effectively neutralized by a subtle dynamic: *the domestication of dissenters*. Such "domestication" arose out of a twofold clubbish need: on the one hand, the dissenter's desire to stay aboard; and on the other hand, the nondissenter's conscience. Simply stated, dissent, when recognized, was made to feel at home. On the lowest possible scale of importance, I must confess my own considerable sense of dignity and acceptance (both vital) when my senior White House employer would refer to me as his "favorite dove." Far more significant was the case of the former Undersecretary of State, George Ball. Once Mr. Ball began to express doubts, he was warmly institutionalized: he was encouraged to become the inhouse devil's advocate on Vietnam. The upshot was inevitable: the process of escalation allowed for periodic requests to Mr. Ball to speak his piece; Ball felt good, I assume (he had fought for righteousness); the others felt good (they had given a full hearing to the dovish option); and there was minimal unpleasantness. The club remained intact; and it is of course possible that matters would have gotten worse faster if Mr. Ball had kept silent, or left before his final departure in the fall of 1966. There was also, of course, the case of the last institutionalized doubter, Bill Moyers. The President is said to have greeted his arrival at meetings with an affectionate, "Well, here comes Mr. Stop-the-Bombing . . . " Here again the dynamics of domesticated dissent sustained the relationship for a while.

A related point—and crucial, I suppose, to government at all times—was *the "effectiveness" trap*, the trap that keeps men from speaking out, as clearly or as often as they might, within the government. And it is the trap that keeps men from resigning in protest and airing their dissent outside the government. The most important asset that a man brings to bureaucratic life is his "effectiveness," a mysterious combination of training, style, and connections. The most ominous complaint that can be whispered of a bureaucrat is: "I'm afraid Charlie's beginning to lose his effectiveness." To preserve your effectiveness, you must decide where and when to fight the mainstream of policy; the opportunities range from pillow talk with your wife, to private drinks with your friends, to meetings with the Secretary of State or the President. The inclination to remain silent or to acquiesce in the presence of the great men—to live to fight another day, to give on this issue so that you can be "effective" on later issues—is overwhelming. Nor is it the tendency of youth alone; some of our most senior officials, men of wealth and fame, whose place in history is secure, have remained silent lest their connection with power be terminated. As for the disinclination to resign in protest: while not necessarily a Washington or even American specialty, it seems more true of a government in which ministers have no parliamentary back-bench to which to retreat. In the absence of such a refuge, it is easy to rationalize the decision to stay aboard. By doing so, one may be able to prevent a few bad things from happening and perhaps even make a few good things happen. To exit is to lose even those marginal chances for "effectiveness."

Another factor must be noted: as the Vietnam controversy escalated at home, there developed *a preoccupation with Vietnam public relations as opposed to Vietnam policy-making*. And here, ironically, internal doubters and dissenters were heavily employed. For such men, by virtue of their own doubts, were often deemed best able to "massage" the doubting intelligentsia. My senior East Asia colleague at the White House, a brilliant and humane doubter who had dealt with Indochina since 1954, spent three quarters of his working days on Vietnam public relations: drafting presidential responses to letters from important critics, writing conciliatory language for presidential speeches, and meeting quite interminably with delegations of outraged Quakers, clergymen, academics, and housewives. His regular callers were the late A. J. Muste and Norman Thomas; mine were members of the Women's Strike for Peace.

Our orders from above: keep them off the backs of busy policy-makers (who usually happened to be nondoubters). Incidentally, my most discouraging assignment in the realm of public relations was the preparation of a White House pamphlet entitled *Why Vietnam*, in September, 1965; in a gesture toward my conscience, I fought—and lost—a battle to have the title followed by a question mark.

Through a variety of procedures, both institutional and personal, doubt, dissent, and expertise were effectively neutralized in the making of policy. But what can be said of the men "in charge"? It is patently absurd to suggest that they produced such tragedy by intention and calculation. But it is neither absurd nor difficult to discern certain forces at work that caused decent and honorable men to do great harm.

Here I would stress the paramount role of *executive fatigue*. No factor seems to me more crucial and underrated in the making of foreign policy. The physical and emotional toll of executive responsibility in State, the Pentagon, the White House, and other executive agencies is enormous; that toll is of course compounded by extended service. Many ... Vietnam policy-makers [had] been on the job for from four to seven years. Complaints may be few, and physical health may remain unimpaired, though emotional health is far harder to gauge. But what is most seriously eroded in the deadening process of fatigue is freshness of thought, imagination, a sense of possibility, a sense of priorities and perspective—those rare assets of a new Administration in its first year or two of office. The tired policy-maker becomes a prisoner of his own narrowed view of the world and his own clichéd rhetoric. He becomes irritable and defensive—short on sleep, short on family ties, short on patience. Such men make bad policy and then compound it. They have neither the time nor the temperament for new ideas or preventive diplomacy.

Below the level of the fatigued executives in the making of Vietnam policy was a widespread phenomenon: *the curator mentality* in the Department of State. By this I mean the collective inertia produced by the bureaucrat's view of his job. At State, the average "desk officer" inherits from his predecessor our policy toward Country X; he regards it as his function to keep that policy intact—under glass, untampered with, and dusted—so that he may pass it on in two to four years to his successor. And such curatorial service generally merits promotion within the system. (Maintain the status quo, and you will stay out of trouble.) In some circumstances, the inertia bred by such an outlook can act as a brake against rash innovation. But on many issues, this inertia sustains the momentum of bad policy and unwise commitments—momentum that might otherwise have been resisted within the ranks. Clearly, Vietnam [was] such an issue.

To fatigue and inertia must be added the factor of internal confusion. Even among the "architects" of our Vietnam commitment, there [was] persistent *confusion as to what type of war we were fighting* and, as a direct consequence, *confusion as to how to end that war.* (The "credibility gap" [was], in part, a reflection of such internal confusion.) Was it, for instance, a civil war, in which case counterinsurgency might suffice? Or was it a war of international aggression? (This might invoke SEATO or UN commitment.) Who was the aggressor—and the "real enemy"? The Viet Cong? Hanoi? Peking? Moscow? International Communism? Or maybe "Asian Communism"? Differing enemies dictated differing strategies and tactics. And confused throughout, in like fashion, was the question of American objectives; your objectives depended on whom you were fighting and why. I shall not forget my assignment from an Assistant Secretary of State in March, 1964: to draft a speech for Secretary McNamara which would, *inter alia*, once and for all dispose of the canard that the Vietnam conflict was a civil war. "But in some ways, of course," I mused, "It *is* a civil war." "Don't play word games with me!" snapped the Assistant Secretary.

Similar confusion beset the concept of "negotiations"—anathema to much of official Washington from 1961 to 1965. Not until April, 1965, did "unconditional discussions" become respectable, via a presidential speech; even then the Secretary of State stressed privately to newsmen that nothing had changed, since "discussions" were by no means the same as "negotiations." Months later that issue was resolved. But it took even longer to obtain a fragile internal agreement that negotiations might include the Viet Cong as something other than an appendage to Hanoi's delegation. Given such confusion as to the whos and whys of our Vietnam commitment, it is not surprising, as Theodore Draper has written, that policy-makers [found] it so difficult to agree on how to end the war.

Of course, one force—a constant in the vortex of commitment—was that of *wishful thinking*. I partook of it myself at many times. I did so especially during Washington's struggle with Diem in the autumn of 1963 when some of us at State believed that for once, in dealing with a difficult client state, the U.S. government could use the leverage of our economic and military assistance to make good things happen, instead of being led around by the nose by [foreign dictators]. If we could prove that point, I thought, and move into a new day, with or without Diem, then Vietnam was well worth the effort. Later came the wishful thinking of the air-strike planners in the late autumn of 1964; there were those who actually thought that after six weeks of air strikes, the North Vietnamese would come crawling to us to ask for peace talks. And what, someone asked in one of the meetings of the time, if they don't? The answer was that we would bomb for another four weeks, and that would do the trick. And a few weeks later came one instance of wishful thinking that was symptomatic of good men misled: in January, 1965, I encountered one of the very highest figures in the Administration at a dinner, drew him aside, and told him of my worries about the air-strike option. He told me that I really shouldn't worry; it was his conviction that before any such plans could be put into effect, a neutralist government would come to power in Saigon that would politely invite us out. And finally, there was the recurrent wishful thinking that sustained many of us through the trying months of 1965–1966 after the air strikes had begun: that surely, somehow, one way or another, we would "be in a conference in six months," and the escalatory spiral would be suspended. The basis of our hope: "It simply can't go on."

As a further influence on policy-makers I would cite the factor of *bureaucratic detachment*. By this I mean what at best might be termed the professional callousness of the surgeon (and indeed, medical lingo—the "surgical strike" for instance—seemed to crop up in the euphemisms of the times). In Washington the semantics of the military muted the reality of war for the civilian policy-makers. In quiet, air-conditioned, thick-carpeted rooms, such terms as "systematic pressure," "armed reconnaissance," "targets of opportunity," and even "body count" seemed to breed a sort of games-theory detachment. Most memorable to me was a moment in the late 1964 target planning when the question under discussion was how heavy our bombing should be, and how extensive our strafing, at some midpoint in the projected pattern of systematic pressure. An Assistant Secretary of State resolved the point in the following words: "It seems to me that our orchestration should be mainly violins, but with periodic touches of brass." Perhaps the biggest shock of my return to Cambridge, Massachusetts, was the realization that the young men, the flesh and blood I taught and saw on these university streets, were potentially some of the numbers on the charts of those faraway planners. In a curious sense, Cambridge [was] closer to this war than Washington.

There is an unprovable factor that relates to bureaucratic detachment: the ingredient of *cryptoracism*. I do not mean to imply any conscious contempt for Asian loss of life on the part of Washington officials. But I do mean to imply that bureaucratic detachment may well be compounded by a traditional Western sense that there are so many Asians, after all; that Asians have a fatalism about life and a disregard for its loss; that they are cruel and barbaric to their own people; and that they are very different from us (and all look alike?). And I *do* mean to imply that the upshot of such subliminal views is a subliminal question whether Asians, and particularly Asian peasants, and most particularly Asian Communists, are really people—like you and me. To put the matter another way: would we have pursued quite such policies—and quite such military tactics—if the Vietnamese were white?

It is impossible to write of Vietnam decision-making without writing about language. Throughout the conflict, words [were] of paramount importance. I refer here to the impact of *rhetorical escalation* and to the *problem of oversell*. In an important sense, Vietnam [became] of crucial significance to us *because we . . . said that it [was] of crucial significance*. (The issue obviously relates to the public relations preoccupation described earlier.)

The key here is domestic politics: the need to sell the American people, press, and Congress on support for an unpopular and costly war in which the objectives themselves [were] in flux. To sell means to persuade, and to persuade means rhetoric. As the difficulties and costs . . . mounted, so [did] the definition of the stakes. This is not to say that rhetorical escalation is an orderly process; executive prose is the product of many writers, and some concepts— North Vietnamese infiltration, America's "national honor," Red China as the chief enemy— . . . entered the rhetoric only gradually and even sporadically. But there [was] an upward spiral nonetheless. And once you have *said* that the American Experiment itself stands or falls on the Vietnam outcome, you have thereby created a national stake far beyond any earlier stakes.

Crucial throughout the process of Vietnam decision-making was a conviction among many policy-makers: that Vietnam posed a *fundamental test of America's national will*. Time and again I was told by men reared in the tradition of Henry L. Stimson that all we needed was the will, and we would then prevail. Implicit in such a view, it seemed to me, was a curious assumption that Asians lacked will, or at least that in a contest between Asian and Anglo-Saxon wills, the non-Asians must prevail. A corollary to the persistent belief in will was a *fascination with power* and an awe in the face of the power America possessed as no nation or civilization ever before. Those who doubted our role in Vietnam were said to shrink from the burdens of power, the obligations of power, the uses of power, the responsibility of power. By implication, such men were soft-headed and effete.

Finally, no discussion of the factors and forces at work on Vietnam policy-makers can ignore the central fact of *human ego investment*. Men who have participated in a decision develop a stake in that decision. As they participate in further, related decisions, their stake increases. It might have been possible to dissuade a man of strong self-confidence at an early stage of the ladder of decision; but it is infinitely harder at later stages since a change of mind there usually involves implicit or explicit repudiation of a chain of previous decisions.

To put it bluntly: at the heart of the Vietnam calamity [was] a group of able, dedicated men who [were] regularly and repeatedly wrong—and whose standing with their contemporaries, and more important, with history, depended, as they [saw] it, on being proven right. These [were] not men who [could] be asked to extricate themselves from error.

The various ingredients I have cited in the making of Vietnam policy . . . created a variety of results, most of them fairly obvious. Here are some that seem to me most central:

Throughout the conflict, there [was] *persistent and repeated miscalculation* by virtually all the actors, in high echelons and low, whether dove, hawk, or something else. To cite one simple example among many: in late 1964 and early 1965, some peace-seeking planners at State who strongly opposed the projected bombing of the North urged that, instead, American ground forces be sent to South Vietnam; this would, they said, increase our bargaining leverage against the North—our "chips"—and would give us something to negotiate about (the withdrawal of our forces) at an early peace conference. Simultaneously, the air-strike option was urged by many in the military who were dead set against American participation in "another land war in Asia"; they were joined by other civilian peace-seekers who wanted to bomb Hanoi into early negotiations. By late 1965, we had ended up with the worst of all worlds: ineffective and costly air strikes against the North, spiraling ground forces in the South, and no negotiations in sight.

Throughout the conflict as well, there [was] *a steady give-in to pressures for a military solution* and only minimal and sporadic efforts at a diplomatic and political solution. In part this resulted from the confusion (earlier cited) among the civilians—confusion regarding objectives and strategy. And in part this resulted from the self-enlarging nature of military investment. Once air strikes and particularly ground forces were introduced, our investment itself had transformed the original stakes. More air power was needed to protect the ground forces; and then more ground forces to protect the ground forces. And needless to say, the military mind develops its own momentum in the absence of clear guidelines from the civilians. Once asked to save South Vietnam, rather than to "advise" it, the American military could not but press for escalation. In addition, sad to report, assorted military constituencies, once involved in Vietnam, . . . had a series of cases to prove: for instance, the utility not only of air power (the Air Force) but of supercarrier-based air power (the Navy). Also, Vietnam policy . . . suffered from one ironic by-product of Secretary McNamara's establishment of civilian control at the Pentagon: in the face of such control, interservice rivalry [gave] way to a united front among the military—reflected in the new but recurrent phenomenon of JCS unanimity. In conjunction with traditional congressional allies (mostly Southern senators and representatives) such a united front would pose a formidable problem for any President.

Throughout the conflict, there [were] *missed opportunities, large and small,*

to disengage ourselves from Vietnam on increasingly unpleasant but still accept-
able terms. Of the many moments from 1961 onward, I shall cite only one, the
last and most important opportunity that was lost: in the summer of 1964 the
President instructed his chief advisers to prepare for him as wide a range of
Vietnam options as possible for postelection consideration and decision. He
explicitly asked that all options be laid out. What happened next was, in effect,
Lyndon Johnson's slow-motion Bay of Pigs. For the advisers so effectively
converged on one single option—juxtaposed against two other, phony options
(in effect, blowing up the world, or scuttle-and-run)—that the President was
confronted with unanimity for bombing the North from all his trusted counsel-
ors. Had he been more confident in foreign affairs, had he been deeply informed on Vietnam and Southeast Asia, and had he raised some hard questions
that unanimity had submerged, this President could have used the largest electoral mandate in history to de-escalate in Vietnam, in the clear expectation that
at the worst a neutralist government would come to power in Saigon and
politely invite us out. . . .

In the course of these years, another result of Vietnam decision-making [was]
the abuse and distortion of history. Vietnamese, Southeast Asian, and Far
Eastern history [was] rewritten by our policy-makers, and their spokesmen, to
conform with the alleged necessity of our presence in Vietnam. Highly dubious
analogies from our experience elsewhere—the "Munich" sellout and "containment" from Europe, the Malayan insurgency and the Korean War from Asia—
[were] imported in order to justify our actions. And [later] events [were] fitted
to the Procrustean bed of Vietnam. Most notably, the change of power in
Indonesia in 1965–1966 has been ascribed to our Vietnam presence; and
virtually all progress in the Pacific region—the rise of regionalism, new forms
of cooperation, and mounting growth rates—has been similarly explained. The
Indonesian allegation is undoubtedly false (I tried to prove it, during six
months of careful investigation at the White House, and had to confess failure); the regional allegation is patently unprovable in either direction (except,
of course, for the clear fact that the economies of both Japan and Korea . . .
profited enormously from our Vietnam-related procurement in these countries;
but that is a costly and highly dubious form of foreign aid).

There is a final result of Vietnam policy I would cite that holds potential
danger for the future of American foreign policy: *the rise of a new breed of*
American ideologues who saw Vietnam as the ultimate test of their doctrine. I
have in mind those men in Washington who have given a new life to the
missionary impulse in American foreign relations: who believe that this nation,
in this era, has received a threefold endowment that can transform the world.
As they see it, that endowment is composed of, first, our unsurpassed military
might; second, our clear technological supremacy; and third, our allegedly
invincible benevolence (our "altruism," our affluence, our lack of territorial
aspirations). Together, it is argued, this threefold endowment provides us with
the opportunity and the obligation to ease the nations of the earth toward
modernization and stability: toward a full-fledged *Pax Americana Technocra-*
tica. In reaching toward this goal, Vietnam [was] viewed as the last and crucial
test. Once we . . . succeeded there, the road ahead [was seen to be] clear. In a
sense, these men [were] our counterpart to the visionaries of Communism's
radical left: they are technocracy's own Maoists. . . .

Long before I went into government, I was told a story about Henry L.

Stimson that seemed to me pertinent during the years that I watched the Vietnam tragedy unfold—and participated in that tragedy. It seems to me more pertinent than ever . . .

In his waning years Stimson was asked by an anxious questioner, "Mr. Secretary, how on earth can we ever bring peace to the world?" Stimson is said to have answered: "You begin by bringing to Washington a small handful of able men who believe that the achievement of peace is possible.

"You work them to the bone until they no longer believe that it is possible.

"And then you throw them out—and bring in a new bunch who believe that it is possible."

17. ARE BUREAUCRACIES IMPORTANT? A RE-EXAMINATION OF ACCOUNTS OF THE CUBAN MISSILE CRISIS

Stephen D. Krasner

Who and what shapes foreign policy? In recent years, analyses have increasingly emphasized not rational calculations of the national interest or the political goals of national leaders but rather bureaucratic procedures and bureaucratic politics. Starting with Richard Neustadt's *Presidential Power*, a judicious study of leadership published in 1960, this approach has come to portray the American President as trapped by a permanent government more enemy than ally. Bureaucratic theorists imply that it is exceedingly difficult if not impossible for political leaders to control the organizational web which surrounds them. Important decisions result from numerous smaller actions taken by individuals at different levels in the bureaucracy who have partially incompatible national, bureaucratic, political, and personal objectives. They are not necessarily a reflection of the aims and values of high officials. . . .

. . . Analyses of bureaucratic politics have been used to explain alliance behaviour during the 1956 Suez crisis and the [1962] Skybolt incident, Truman's relations with MacArthur, American policy in Vietnam, and now most thoroughly the Cuban missile crisis in Graham Allison's *Essence of Decision: Explaining the Cuban Missile Crisis*, published in 1971 (Little Brown & Company). Allison's volume is the elaboration of an earlier and influential article on this subject. With the publication of his book this approach to foreign policy now receives its definitive statement. The bureaucratic interpretation of foreign policy has become the conventional wisdom.

My argument here is that this vision is misleading, dangerous, and compelling: misleading because it obscures the power of the President; dangerous because it undermines the assumptions of democratic politics by relieving high officials of responsibility; and compelling because it offers leaders an excuse for their failures and scholars an opportunity for innumerable reinterpretations and publications.

The contention that the Chief Executive is trammelled by the permanent government has disturbing implications for any effort to impute responsibility to public officials. A democratic political philosophy assumes that responsibility for the acts of governments can be attributed to elected officials. The charges of these men are embodied in legal statutes. The electorate punishes an erring official by rejecting him at the polls. Punishment is senseless unless high officials are responsible for the acts of government. Elections have some impact only if government, that most complex of modern organizations, can be controlled. If the bureaucratic machine escapes manipulation and direction even by the highest officials, then punishment is illogical. Elections are a farce not because the people suffer from false consciousness, but because public officials are impotent, enmeshed in a bureaucracy so large that the actions of government are not responsive to their will. What sense to vote a man out of office when his successor, regardless of his values, will be trapped in the same web of only incrementally mutable standard operating procedures?

THE RATIONAL ACTOR MODEL

Conventional analyses that focus on the values and objectives of foreign policy, what Allison calls the Rational Actor Model, are perfectly coincident with the ethical assumptions of democratic politics. The state is viewed as a rational unified actor. The behaviour of states is the outcome of a rational decision-making process. This process has three steps. The options for a given situation are spelled out. The consequences of each option are projected. A choice is made which maximizes the values held by decision-makers. The analyst knows what the state did. His objective is to explain why by imputing to decision-makers a set of values which are maximized by observed behaviour. These values are his explanation of foreign policy.

The citizen, like the analyst, attributes error to either inappropriate values or lack of foresight. Ideally the electorate judges the officeholder by governmental performance which is assumed to reflect the objectives and perspicacity of political leaders. Poor policy is made by leaders who fail to foresee accurately the consequences of their decisions or attempt to maximize values not held by the electorate. Political appeals, couched in terms of aims and values, are an appropriate guide for voters. For both the analyst who adheres to the Rational Actor Model, and the citizen who decides elections, values are assumed to be the primary determinant of government behaviour.

The bureaucratic politics paradigm points to quite different determinants of policy. Political leaders can only with great difficulty overcome the inertia and self-serving interests of the permanent government. What counts is managerial skill. In *Essence of Decision*, Graham Allison maintains that "the central questions of policy analysis are quite different from the kinds of questions analysts have traditionally asked. Indeed, the crucial questions seem to be matters of planning for management." Administrative feasibility not substance becomes the central concern.

The paradoxical conclusion—that bureaucratic analysis with its emphasis on policy guidance implies political non-responsibility—has most clearly been brought out by discussions of American policy in Vietnam. Richard Neustadt on the concluding page of *Alliance Politics* . . . muses about a conversation he would have had with President Kennedy in the fall of 1963 had tragedy not intervened. "I considered asking whether, in the light of our machine's performance on a British problem, he conceived that it could cope with South Vietnam's. . . . [I]t was a good question, better than I knew. It haunts me still." For adherents of the bureaucratic politics paradigm, Vietnam was a failure of the "machine," a war in Arthur Schlesinger's words "which no President . . .

desired or intended."[1] The machine dictated a policy which it could not success-fully terminate. The machine not the cold war ideology and hubris of Kennedy and Johnson determined American behaviour in Vietnam. Vietnam could hardly be a tragedy for tragedies are made by choice and character, not fate. A knowing electorate would express sympathy not levy blame. Machines cannot be held responsible for what they do, nor can the men caught in their workings.

The strength of the bureaucratic web has been attributed to two sources: organizational necessity and bureaucratic interest. The costs of coordination and search procedures are so high that complex organizations *must* settle for satisfactory rather than optimal solutions. Bureaucracies have interests defined in terms of budget allocation, autonomy, morale, and scope which they defend in a game of political bargaining and compromise within the executive branch.

The imperatives of organizational behaviour limit flexibility. Without a divi-sion of labor and the establishment of standard operating procedures, it would be impossible for large organizations to begin to fulfill their statutory objec-tives, that is to perform tasks designed to meet societal needs rather than merely to perpetuate the organization. A division of labor among and within organizations reduces the job of each particular division to manageable propor-tions. Once this division is made, the complexity confronting an organization or one of its parts is further reduced through the establishment of standard operating procedures. To deal with each problem as if it were *sui generis* would be impossible given limited resources and information processing capacity, and would make intra-organizational coordination extremely difficult. Bureaucra-cies are then unavoidably rigid; but without the rigidity imposed by division of labor and standard operating procedures, they could hardly begin to function at all.

However, this rigidity inevitably introduces distortions. All of the options to a given problem will not be presented with equal lucidity and conviction unless by some happenstance the organization has worked out its scenarios for that particular problem in advance. It is more likely that the organization will have addressed itself to something *like* the problem with which it is confronted. It has a set of options for such a hypothetical problem and these options will be presented to deal with the actual issue at hand. Similarly, organizations cannot execute all policy suggestions with equal facility. The development of new standard operating procedures takes time. The procedures which would most faithfully execute a new policy are not likely to have been worked out. The clash between the rigidity of standard operating procedures which are abso-lutely necessary to achieve coordination among and within large organizations, and the flexibility needed to spell out the options and their consequences for a new problem and to execute new policies is inevitable. It cannot be avoided even with the best of intentions of bureaucratic chiefs anxious to faithfully execute the desires of their leaders.

THE COSTS OF COORDINATION

The limitations imposed by the need to simplify and coordinate indicate that the great increase in governmental power accompanying industrialization has not been achieved without some costs in terms of control. Bureaucratic organizations and the material and symbolic resources which they direct have enormously increased the ability of the American President to influence the international environment. He operates, however, within limits set by organizational procedures.

A recognition of the limits imposed by bureaucratic necessities is a useful qualification of the assumption that states always maximize their interest. This does not, however, imply that the analyst should abandon a focus on values or assumptions of rationality. Standard operating procedures are rational given the costs of search procedures and need for coordination. The behaviour of states is still determined by values although foreign policy may reflect satisfactory rather than optimal outcomes.

An emphasis on the procedural limits of large organizations cannot explain nonincremental change. If government policy is an outcome of standard operating procedures, then behaviour at time t is only incrementally different from behaviour at time t-1. The exceptions to this prediction leap out of [such] events . . . [as Nixon's] visit to China and [his] new economic policy. Focusing on the needs dictated by organizational complexity is adequate only during periods when policy is altered very little or not at all. To reduce policymakers to nothing more than the caretakers and minor adjustors of standard operating procedures rings hollow in an era rife with debates and changes of the most fundamental kind in America's conception of its objectives and capabilities.

Bureaucratic analysts do not, however, place the burden of their argument on standard operating procedures, but on bureaucratic politics. The objectives of officials are dictated by their bureaucratic position. Each bureau has its own interests. The interests which bureaucratic analysts emphasize are not clientalistic ties between government departments and societal groups, or special relations with congressional committees. They are, rather, needs dictated by organizational survival and growth—budget allocations, internal morale, and autonomy. Conflicting objectives advocated by different bureau chiefs are reconciled by a political process. Policy results from compromises and bargaining. It does not necessarily reflect the values of the President, let alone of lesser actors.

The clearest expression of the motivational aspects of the bureaucratic politics approach is the by now well-known aphorism—where you stand depends upon where you sit. Decision-makers, however, often do not stand where they sit. Sometimes they are not sitting anywhere. This is clearly illustrated by the positions taken by members of the ExCom during the Cuban missile crisis, which Allison elucidates at some length. While the military, in Pavlovian fashion, urged the use of arms, the Secretary of Defense took a much more pacific position. The wise old men, such as Acheson, imported for the occasion, had no bureaucratic position to defend. Two of the most important members of the ExCom, Robert Kennedy and Theodore Sorensen, were loyal to the President, not to some bureaucratic barony. Similarly, in discussions of Vietnam in 1966 and 1967, it was the Secretary of Defense who advocated diplomacy and the Secretary of State who defended the prerogatives of the military. During Skybolt, McNamara was attuned to the President's budgetary concerns, not those of the Air Force.

Allison, the most recent expositor of the bureaucratic politics approach, realizes the problems which these facts present. In describing motivation, he backs off from an exclusive focus on bureaucratic position, arguing instead that decision-makers are motivated by national, organizational, group, and personal interests. While maintaining that the "propensities and priorities stemming from position are sufficient to allow analysts to make reliable predictions about a player's stand" (a proposition violated by his own presentation), he also notes that "these propensities are filtered through the baggage that players bring to positions." For both the missile crisis and Vietnam, it was the "baggage" of culture and values, not bureaucratic position, which determined the aims of high officials.

Bureaucratic analysis is also inadequate in its description of how policy is made. Its axiomatic assumption is that politics is a game with the preferences of players given and independent. This is not true. The President chooses most of the important players and sets the rules. He selects the men who head the large bureaucracies. These individuals must share his values. Certainly they identify with his beliefs to a greater extent than would a randomly chosen group of candidates. They also feel some personal fealty to the President who has elevated them from positions of corporate or legal to ones of historic significance. While bureau chiefs are undoubtedly torn by conflicting pressures arising either from their need to protect their own bureaucracies or from personal conviction, they must remain the President's men. At some point disagreement results in dismissal. The values which bureau chiefs assign to policy outcomes are not independent. They are related through a perspective shared with the President.

The President also structures the governmental environment in which he acts through his impact on what Allison calls "action-channels." These are decision-making processes which describe the participation of actors and their influence. The most important "action-channel" in the government is the President's ear. The President has a major role in determining who whispers into it. John Kennedy's reliance on his brother, whose bureaucratic position did not afford him any claim to a decision-making role in the missile crisis, is merely an extreme example. By allocating tasks, selecting the White House bureaucracy, and demonstrating special affections, the President also influences "action-channels" at lower levels of the government.

The President has an important impact on bureaucratic interests. Internal morale is partially determined by Presidential behaviour. The obscurity in which Secretary of State Rogers languished during the China trip affected both State Department morale and recruitment prospects. Through the budget the President has a direct impact on that most vital of bureaucratic interests. While a bureau may use its societal clients and congressional allies to secure desired allocations, it is surely easier with the President's support than without it. The President can delimit or redefine the scope of an organization's activities by transferring tasks or establishing new agencies. Through public statements he can affect attitudes towards members of a particular bureaucracy and their functions.

THE PRESIDENT AS "KING"

The success a bureau enjoys in furthering its interests depends on maintaining the support and affection of the President. The implicit assumption of the bureaucratic politics approach that departmental and Presidential behaviour are independent and comparably important is false. Allison, for instance, vacillates between describing the President as one "chief" among several and as a "king" standing above all other men. He describes in great detail the deliberations of the ExCom implying that Kennedy's decision was in large part determined by its recommendations and yet notes that during the crisis Kennedy vetoed an ExCom decision to bomb a SAM base after an American U-2 was shot down on October 27. In general, bureaucratic analysts ignore the critical effect which the President has in choosing his advisors, establishing their access to decision-making, and influencing bureaucratic interests.

All of this is not to deny that bureaucratic interests may sometimes be decisive in the formulation of foreign policy. Some policy options are never presented to the President. Others he deals with only cursorily, not going beyond options presented by the bureaucracy. This will only be the case if Presidential interest and attention are absent. The failure of a Chief Executive to specify policy does not mean that the government takes no action. Individual bureaucracies may initiate policies which suit their own needs and objectives. The actions of different organizations may work at cross purposes. The behaviour of the state, that is of some of its official organizations, in the international system appears confused or even contradictory. This is a situation which develops, however, not because of the independent power of government organizations but because of failures by decision-makers to assert control.

The ability of bureaucracies to independently establish policies is a function of Presidential attention. Presidential attention is a function of Presidential values. The Chief Executive involves himself in those areas which he determines to be important. When the President does devote time and attention to an issue, he can compel the bureaucracy to present him with alternatives. He may do this, as Nixon apparently [did] by establishing an organization under his Special Assistant for National Security Affairs, whose only bureaucratic interest [was] maintaining the President's confidence. The President may also rely upon several bureaucracies to secure proposals. The President may even resort to his own knowledge and sense of history to find options which his bureaucracy fails to present. Even when Presidential attention is totally absent, bureaus are sensitive to his values. Policies which violate Presidential objectives may bring Presidential wrath.

While the President is undoubtedly constrained in the implementation of policy by existing bureaucratic procedures, he even has options in this area. As Allison points out, he can choose which agencies will perform what tasks. Programs are fungible and can be broken down into their individual standard operating procedures and recombined. Such exercises take time and effort but the expenditure of such energies by the President is ultimately a reflection of his own values and not those of the bureaucracy. Within the structure which he has partially created himself he can, if he chooses, further manipulate both the options presented to him and the organizational tools for implementing them.

Neither organizational necessity nor bureaucratic interests are the fundamental determinants of policy. The limits imposed by standard operating procedures as well as the direction of policy are a function of the values of decision-makers. The President creates much of the bureaucratic environment which surrounds him through his selection of bureau chiefs, determination of "action-channels," and statutory powers.

THE MISSILE CRISIS

Adherents of the bureaucratic politics framework have not relied exclusively on general argument. They have attempted to substantiate their contentions with detailed investigations of particular historical events. The most painstaking is Graham Allison's analysis of the Cuban missile crisis in his *Essence of Decision*. In a superlative heuristic exercise Allison attempts to show that critical facts and relationships are ignored by conventional analysis that assumes states are unified rational actors. Only by examining the missile crisis in terms of organizational necessity, and bureaucratic interests and politics, can the formulation and implementation of policy be understood.

The missile crisis, as Allison notes, is a situation in which conventional analysis would appear most appropriate. The President devoted large amounts of time to policy formulation and implementation. Regular bureaucratic channels were short-circuited by the creation of an Executive Committee which included representatives of the bipartisan foreign policy establishment, bureau chiefs, and the President's special aides. The President dealt with details which would normally be left to bureaucratic subordinates. If, under such circumstances, the President could not effectively control policy formulation and implementation, then the Rational Actor Model is gravely suspect.

In his analysis of the missile crisis, Allison deals with three issues: the American choice of a blockade, the Soviet decision to place MRBM's and IRBM's on Cuba, and the Soviet decision to withdraw the missiles from Cuba. The American decision is given the most detailed attention. Allison notes three ways in which bureaucratic procedures and interests influenced the formulation of American policy: first, in the elimination of the nonforcible alternatives; second, through the collection of information; third, through the standard operating procedures of the Air Force.

In formulating the U.S. response, the ExCom considered six alternatives. These were:

1. Do nothing
2. Diplomatic pressure
3. A secret approach to Castro
4. Invasion
5. A surgical air strike
6. A naval blockade

The approach to Castro was abandoned because he did not have direct control of the missiles. An invasion was eliminated as a first step because it would not have been precluded by any of the other options. Bureaucratic factors were not involved.

The two non-military options of doing nothing and lodging diplomatic protests were also abandoned from the outset because the President was not interested in them. In terms of both domestic and international politics this was the most important decision of the crisis. It was a decision which only the President had authority to make. Allison's case rests on proving that this decision was foreordained by bureaucratic roles. He lists several reasons for Kennedy's elimination of the nonforcible alternatives. Failure to act decisively would undermine the confidence of members of his Administration, convince the permanent government that his Administration lacked leadership, hurt the Democrats in the forthcoming election, destroy his reputation among members of Congress, create public distrust, encourage American allies and enemies to question American courage, invite a second Bay of Pigs, and feed his own doubts about himself. Allison quotes a statement by Kennedy that he feared impeachment and concludes that the "non-forcible paths—avoiding military measures, resorting instead to diplomacy—could not have been more irrelevant to *his* problems." Thus Allison argues that Kennedy had no choice.

Bureaucratic analysis, what Allison calls in his book the Governmental Politics Model, implies that any man in the same position would have had no choice. The elimination of passivity and diplomacy was ordained by the office and not by the man.

Such a judgment is essential to the Governmental Politics Model, for the resort to the "baggage" of values, culture, and psychology which the President carries with him undermines the explanatory and predictive power of the approach. To adopt, however, the view that the office determined Kennedy's action is both to underrate his power and to relieve him of responsibility. The President defines his own role. A different man could have chosen differently. Kennedy's *Profiles in Courage* had precisely dealt with men who had risked losing their political roles because of their "baggage" of values and culture.

Allison's use of the term "intra-governmental balance of power" to describe John Kennedy's elimination of diplomacy and passivity is misleading. The American government is not a balance of power system; at the very least it is a loose hierarchical one. Kennedy's judgments of the domestic, international, bureaucratic, and personal ramifications of his choice were determined by *who* he was, as well as *what* he was. The central mystery of the crisis remains why Kennedy chose to risk nuclear war over missile placements which he knew did not dramatically alter the strategic balance. The answer to this puzzle can only be found through an examination of values, the central concern of conventional analysis.

The impact of bureaucratic interests and standard operating procedures is reduced then to the choice of the blockade instead of the surgical air strike. Allison places considerable emphasis on intelligence-gathering in the determination of this choice. U-2 flights were the most important source of data about Cuba; their information was supplemented by refugee reports, analyses of shipping and other kinds of intelligence. The timing of the U-2 flights, which Allison argues was determined primarily by bureaucratic struggles, was instrumental in determining Kennedy's decision:

> Had a U-2 flown over the western end of Cuba three weeks earlier, it could have discovered the missiles, giving the administration more time to consider alternatives and to act before the danger of operational missiles in Cuba became a major factor in the equation. Had the missiles not been discovered until two weeks later, the blockade would have been irrelevant, since the Soviet missile shipments would have been completed ... An explanation of the politics of the discovery is consequently a considerable piece of the explanation of the U.S. blockade.

The delay, however, from September 15 to October 14 when the missiles were discovered reflected Presidential values more than bureaucratic politics. The October 14 flight took place 10 days after COMOR, the interdepartmental committee which directed the activity of the U-2's, had decided the flights should be made. "This 10 day delay constitutes some form of 'failure,' " Allison contends. It was the result, he argues, of a struggle between the Central Intelligence Agency and the Air Force over who would control the flights. The Air Force maintained that the flights over Cuba were sufficiently dangerous to warrant military supervision; the Central Intelligence Agency, anxious to guard its own prerogatives, maintained that its U-2's were technically superior.

However, the 10-day delay after the decision to make a flight over western Cuba was not entirely attributable to bureaucratic bickering. Allison reports an attempt to make a flight on October 9 which failed because the U-2 flamed out. Further delays resulted from bad weather. Thus the inactivity caused by bureaucratic in-fighting amounted to only five days (October 4 to October 9) once the general decision to make the flight was taken. The other five days' delay caused by engine failure and the weather must be attributed to some higher source than the machinations of the American bureaucracy.

However, there was also a long period of hesitation before October 4. John McCone, Director of the Central Intelligence Agency, had indicated to the President on August 22 that he thought there was a strong possibility that the Soviets were preparing to put offensive missiles on Cuba. He did not have firm evidence, and his contentions were met with skepticism in the Administration.

INCREASED RISKS

On September 10, COMOR had decided to restrict further U-2 flights over western Cuba. This decision was based upon factors which closely fit the Rational Actor Model of foreign policy formulation. COMOR decided to halt the flights because of the recent installation of SAM's in western Cuba coupled with the loss of a Nationalist Chinese U-2 increased the probability and costs of a U-2 loss over Cuba. International opinion might force the cancellation of the flights altogether. The absence of information from U-2's would be a national, not simply a bureaucratic, cost. The President had been forcefully attacking the critics of his Cuba policy arguing that patience and restraint were the best course of action. The loss of a U-2 over Cuba would tend to undermine the President's position. Thus, COMOR's decision on September 10 reflected a sensitivity to the needs and policies of the President rather than the parochial concerns of the permanent government.

The decision on October 4 to allow further flights was taken only after consultation with the President. The timing was determined largely by the wishes of the President. His actions were not circumscribed by decisions made at lower levels of the bureaucracy of which he was not aware. The flights were delayed because of conflicting pressures and risks confronting Kennedy. He was forced to weigh the potential benefits of additional knowledge against the possible losses if a U-2 were shot down.

What if the missiles had not been discovered until after October 14? Allison argues that had the missiles been discovered two weeks later the blockade would have been irrelevant since the missile shipments would have been completed. This is true but only to a limited extent. The blockade was irrelevant even when it was put in place for there were missiles already on the island. As Allsion points out in his Rational Actor cut at explaining the crisis, the blockade was both an act preventing the shipment of additional missiles and a signal of American firmness. The missiles already on Cuba were removed because of what the blockade meant and not because of what it did.

An inescapable dilemma confronted the United States. It could not retaliate until the missiles were on the island. Military threats or action required definitive proof. The United States could only justify actions with photographic evidence. It could only take photos after the missiles were on Cuba. The blockade could only be a demonstration of American firmness. Even if the missiles had not been discovered until they were operational, the United States might still have begun its response with a blockade.

Aside from the timing of the discovery of the missiles, Allison argues that the standard operating procedures of the Air Force affected the decision to blockade rather than to launch a surgical air strike. When the missiles were first discovered, the Air Force had no specific contingency plans for dealing with such a situation. They did, however, have a plan for a large-scale air strike carried out in conjunction with an invasion of Cuba. The plan called for the air bombardment of many targets. This led to some confusion during the first week of the ExCom's considerations because the Air Force was talking in terms of an air strike of some 500 sorties while there were only some 40 known missile sites on Cuba. Before this confusion was clarified, a strong coalition of advisors was backing the blockade.

As a further example of the impact of standard operating procedures, Allison notes that the Air Force had classified the missiles as mobile. Because this classification assumed that the missiles might be moved immediately before an air strike, the commander of the Air Force would not guarantee that a surgical air strike would be completely effective. By the end of the first week of the ExCom's deliberations when Kennedy made his decision for a blockade, the surgical air strike was presented as a "null option." The examination of the strike was not reopened until the following week when civilian experts found that the missiles were not in fact mobile.

This incident suggests one caveat to Allison's assertion that the missile crisis is a case which discriminates against bureaucratic analysis. In crises when time is short the President may have to accept bureaucratic options which could be amended under more leisurely conditions.

NOT ANOTHER PEARL HARBOR

The impact of the Air Force's standard operating procedures on Kennedy's decision must, however, to some extent remain obscure. It is not likely that either McNamara who initially called for a diplomatic response, or Robert Kennedy who was partially concerned with the ethical implications of a surprise air strike, would have changed their recommendations even if the Air Force had estimated its capacities more optimistically. There were other reasons for choosing the blockade aside from the apparent infeasibility of the air strike. John Kennedy was not anxious to have the Pearl Harbor analogy applied to the United States. At one of the early meetings of the ExCom, his brother had passed a note saying, "I now know how Tojo felt when he was planning Pearl Harbor." The air strike could still be considered even if the blockade failed. A chief executive anxious to keep his options open would find a blockade a more prudent initial course of action.

Even if the Air Force had stated that a surgical air strike was feasible, this might have been discounted by the President. Kennedy had already experienced unrealistic military estimates. The Bay of Pigs was the most notable example. The United States did not use low flying photographic reconnaissance until after the President had made his public announcement of the blockade. Prior to the President's speech on October 22, 20 high altitude U-2 flights were made. After the speech there were 85 low level missions, indicating that the intelligence community was not entirely confident that U-2 flights alone would reveal all of the missile sites. The Soviets might have been camouflaging some missiles on Cuba. Thus, even if the immobility of the missiles had been correctly estimated, it would have been rash to assume that an air strike would have extirpated all of the missiles. There were several reasons, aside from the Air Force's estimate, for rejecting the surgical strike.

Thus, in terms of policy formulation, it is not clear that the examples offered by Allison concerning the timing of discovery of the missiles and the standard operating procedures of the Air Force had a decisive impact on the choice of a blockade over a surgical air strike. The ultimate decisions did rest with the President. The elimination of the nonforcible options was a reflection of Kennedy's values. An explanation of the Cuban missile crisis which fails to explain policy in terms of the values of the chief decision-maker must inevitably lose sight of the forest for the trees.

The most chilling passages in *Essence of Decision* are concerned not with the formulation of policy but with its implementation. In carrying out the blockade the limitations on the President's ability to control events became painfully clear. Kennedy did keep extraordinarily close tabs on the workings of the blockade. The first Russian ship to reach the blockade was allowed to pass through without being intercepted on direct orders from the President. Kennedy felt it would be wise to allow Khrushchev more time. The President overrode the ExCom's decision to fire on a Cuban SAM base after a U-2 was shot down on October 27. A spy ship similar to the Pueblo was patrolling perilously close to Cuba and was ordered to move further out to sea.

Despite concerted Presidential attention coupled with an awareness of the necessity of watching minute details which would normally be left to lower levels of the bureaucracy, the President still had exceptional difficulty in controlling events. Kennedy personally ordered the Navy to pull in the blockade from 800 miles to 500 miles to give Khrushchev additional time in which to make his decision. Allison suggests that the ships were not drawn in. The Navy being both anxious to guard its prerogatives and confronted with the difficulty of moving large numbers of ships over millions of square miles of ocean failed to promptly execute a Presidential directive.

There were several random events which might have changed the outcome of the crisis. The Navy used the blockade to test its antisubmarine operations. It was forcing Soviet submarines to surface at a time when the President and his advisors were unaware that contact with Russian ships had been made. A U-2 accidentally strayed over Siberia on October 22. Any one of these events, and perhaps others still unknown, could have triggered escalatory actions by the Russians.

Taken together, they strongly indicate how much caution is necessary when a random event may have costly consequences. A nation like a drunk staggering on a cliff should stay far from the edge. The only conclusion which can be drawn from the inability of the Chief Executive to fully control the implementation of a policy in which he was intensely interested and to which he devoted virtually all of his time for an extended period is that the risks were even greater than the President knew. Allison is more convincing on the problems concerned with policy implementation than on questions relating to policy formulation. Neither bureaucratic interests nor organizational procedures explain the positions taken by members of the ExCom, the elimination of passivity and diplomacy, or the choice of a blockade instead of an air strike.

CONCLUSION

. . . Before the niceties of bureaucratic implementation are investigated, it is necessary to know what objectives are being sought. Objectives are ultimately a reflection of values, of beliefs concerning what man and society ought to be. The failure of the American government to take decisive action in a number of critical areas reflects not so much the inertia of a large bureaucratic machine as a confusion over values which afflicts the society in general and its leaders in particular. It is, in such circumstances, too comforting to attribute failure to organizational inertia, although nothing could be more convenient for political leaders who having either not formulated any policy or advocated bad policies can blame their failures on the governmental structure. Both psychologically and politically, leaders may find it advantageous to have others think of them as ineffectual rather than evil. But the facts are otherwise—particularly in foreign policy. There the choices—and the responsibility—rest squarely with the President.

NOTE

1. Quoted in Daniel Ellsberg, "The Quagmire Myth and the Stalemate Machine," *Public Policy*, Spring 1971, p. 218. [For an exemplary treatment of this thesis, see James C. Thomson's essay in this volume—*eds.*]

18. THE DIVIDED DECISION-MAKER: AMERICAN DOMESTIC POLITICS AND THE CUBAN CRISES

Fen Osler Hampson

How does domestic politics affect the way decision-makers define a foreign policy crisis? How does it affect crisis decision-making and methods of crisis management? In a confrontation between the superpowers that raised the risks of nuclear war, how might domestic political pressures influence efforts to defuse the crisis and reduce the likelihood of military—and maybe nuclear—conflict? The existing literature on crisis decision-making suggests that there is a single appropriate answer to all of these questions: "Not much." Despite compelling evidence that the causes of war have sometimes had their origins in the internal politics of the state, analysts of crisis behavior and decision-making have underplayed the role of domestic politics on the grounds that there is little time for Congress to act, or interest groups and the public to mobilize, to have influence in a crisis.

On the basis of three case studies of foreign policy crises involving Cuba, however, this essay will argue that domestic politics influences crisis decision-making not in the usual "pluralistic" sense we understand of domestic political processes, but rather through the political expectations and concerns of the decision-maker and the values he assigns to the consequences of his actions for his domestic political standing. . . . Not only may [such concerns] fundamentally influence the way decision-makers define a "crisis," but they may also influence the manner in which they develop and choose options. The structure of this value system and the way such expectations through the internalization of domestic political constraints shape policy choices in a crisis are the subjects of this essay.

THE CONVENTIONAL VIEW OF CRISIS

The accepted wisdom about foreign policy crises is that they are threatening situations, happen suddenly, and pose a direct challenge to the vital interests of the state. They usually occur when one state (or group of states) tries to change the international status quo, threatening the security of other states. . . .

Note: Some footnotes have been deleted, and others have been renumbered to appear in consecutive order.

The conventional view is that the impact of domestic political pressures on the decision-making process during a crisis is attenuated because the contraction of authority in the executive branch limits the number of individuals and groups who are involved in the decision-making process. "In crises, responsibility for action moves upward precisely because important values are threatened, standard operating procedures are inadequate, and necessary decisions exceed the authority and competence of junior, often less experienced officials. At the top, there is apt to be greater reliance on *ad hoc,* rather than formal decision-making groups. . . . *During crises, initially at least, there is also likely to be a reduction in the salience of domestic politics, in part because of the desirability of maintaining secrecy.*"[1]

The concentration of authority, the premium on secrecy, and the need to act decisively and quickly have an important secondary effect: they limit the impact of bureaucratic and organization factors in decisions. As Lloyd Jensen points out, "decisions made . . . in the context of a crisis are less likely to be watered down through bureaucratic compromise, and the decision-makers themselves may be less concerned with the sometimes uninformed and selfish demands of the mass public and special interests."[2]

Once a crisis becomes public, a third factor may contribute to the freedom and latitude enjoyed by the President: the tendency for the American public to rally around the flag. Regardless of the apparent success or failure of a policy, Presidential popularity peaks with crises: "Kennedy's popularity rose from 61 to 74 percent after the Cuban missile crisis, but it stood at an even higher 85 percent following the Bay of Pigs fiasco in 1961; Truman had an impressive 81 percent of the public supporting his commitment to South Korea in 1950, despite his low popularity at the time, and Nixon's escalation of the Vietnam War in 1972 also enhanced his public support despite the increasing opposition to that war."[3]

The high degree of Presidential involvement in a crisis, combined with limited institutional and domestic political constraints, has led many observers to emphasize the importance of psychological and personal idiosyncratic factors in crisis decision-making. During a crisis, especially when there is little time to explore options thoroughly, and information is highly ambiguous, decision-makers—and the President in particular—are likely to rely upon preexisting beliefs and images and draw upon historical analogies to assess the problem at hand. Predetermined preferences will guide the decision, rather than the unique contingencies of the situation itself. Instead of being captured by organizational and public interests, decision-makers will be the captives of their own psychological make-up, the psychological dynamics of the decision-making unit, and their perceptions.

Three foreign policy crises that have involved the United States, the Soviet Union, and Cuba provide a good set of cases to test the hypothesis that domestic political pressures play a negligible role in crisis decision-making and that psychological and personal idiosyncratic factors are the chief explanatory variables. The three cases are the Cuban missile crisis (1962), the Cienfuegos crisis (1970), and the Cuban brigade crisis (1979). All had the general characteristics of crisis . . . ; they involved a major confrontation between the United States and the Soviet Union; and in all three, the situation was characterized by threat, surprise, and relatively short decision times.

For the purposes of comparison, however, what makes these cases interesting is that the magnitude of the crisis varied enormously among them, despite the fact that the military threat—at least in two of them—was quite similar. The Cuban missile crisis saw a direct political clash between the superpowers, where military force was threatened, and the risks of nuclear war loomed large. In contrast, the Cienfuegos crisis, which erupted when the Soviets began construction of a naval base at Cienfuegos Bay in Cuba, was remarkably bereft of confrontation, the high drama of crisis, or the sense that both parties were peering into the nuclear abyss. Even though the strategic threat was prominent in the Cienfuegos crisis, the risks of direct military conflict were much lower than in the Cuban missile crisis. In every respect, it was a mini-crisis overshadowed by other events.[4]

The Cuban brigade crisis, sparked by the "discovery" of a Soviet troop brigade in Cuba in 1979 that appeared to be deployed for "offensive" purposes, was principally a crisis of domestic proportions. Nevertheless, as such, it had long-term foreign policy implications for U.S.-Soviet relations. . . . The differing degree of crisis between the 1962 and 1970 cases is explained by the varying impact of domestic politics on decision-making. The 1979 case, by contrast, illustrates how a relatively trivial military threat was inflated into a major domestic political crisis which had repercussions in the foreign policy realm. . . .

THE CUBAN MISSILE CRISIS

The events that took place over the critical thirteen days of the Cuban missile crisis are familiar and have been described in detail elsewhere.[5] The crisis began to brew in the late summer and early fall of 1962. With Cuba firmly rooted in the socialist bloc, the Soviets began a massive military buildup on the island as a show of support for Castro and to prevent his overthrow by the United States, which had found his turn to communism particularly difficult to accept. The buildup was viewed with a great deal of apprehension in the United States, especially since mixed with the steady stream of refugee and intelligence reports were rumors that missiles were included. President Kennedy's critics were quick to seize on these reports to challenge his administration for its lackadaisical approach to the Cuban problem.

The administration's response was that its intelligence only detected anti-aircraft missiles for "defensive" purposes, lacking the capability to attack American cities. On September 4, President Kennedy went on the record that there was "no proof of offensive ground-to-ground missiles or other significant offensive capability," but he also warned that, "were it otherwise, the gravest issues would arise." On September 13, he further clarified his administration's policy: "If at any time the communist buildup in Cuba were to endanger or interfere with our security . . . ," he stated, "or if Cuba should ever . . . become an offensive military base of significant capacity for the Soviet Union, then this country will do whatever must be done to protect its own security and that of its allies."

The ultimate test of the administration's resolve came barely a month later. On October 14, a U-2 reconnaissance flight over Cuba revealed that the Soviets were constructing 9 new missile sites, with launching positions for 24 Soviet medium-range (1020 mile) and 12 intermediate-range (2200 mile) ballistic missiles. In addition, 42 IL-28 bombers, having an operating radius of 600 miles, were also discovered. On the morning of October 16, McGeorge Bundy, Special Assistant for National Security Affairs, informed the President about the missiles.

From October 16 to October 22, the President and his closest advisers thrashed out, in secret, the problem of how to deal with the missiles. During those deliberations, six basic operations were developed: (1) do nothing; (2) diplomatic pressure; (3) a secret approach to Castro; (4) invasion; (5) a surgical air strike; (6) a naval blockade. Eventually, the blockade option was chosen and, in the early evening of Monday, October 22, President Kennedy went on national television to break the news and to announce the immediate imposition of what was described as a naval "quarantine," intended to prevent the shipment of more missiles and to pressure the Soviets to remove the ones they had already installed.

In the Cuban missile crisis, the President and his advisers had to deal with a problem that had important domestic and international repercussions: the administration was politically vulnerable over its policies with respect to Cuba and the Soviet deception had far-reaching geostrategic implications. But why did Kennedy choose the *means* he did to deal with the problem and were they appropriate, especially in view of the enormous risks they entailed? There are several competing explanations for why Kennedy acted the way he did— springing the discovery on Khrushchev by announcing publicly, to the world, their existence and simultaneously imposing a naval blockade to prevent additional deployments and force Khrushchev's hand.

Challenge to U.S. Credibility and Commitments

It was acknowledged by the participants at the time, and has been generally accepted by most observers since then, that the missiles in Cuba did not substantially alter the strategic balance, at least in the short term; this was not the principal reason why their immediate removal was considered necessary. . . .

A major concern with the Cuban deployments was the international political consequences. As Sorensen states, the President

> was concerned less about the missiles' military implications than with their effect on the global political balance. The Soviet move had been undertaken so swiftly, so secretly and with so much deliberate deception—it was so sudden a departure from Soviet practice—that it represented a provocative change in the delicate status quo. Missiles on Soviet territory or submarines were very different from missiles in the western hemisphere, particularly in their political and psychological effect on Latin America. The history of Soviet intentions toward smaller nations was very different from our own. Such a step, if accepted, would be followed by more; and the President's September pledges of action called this step unacceptable. While he desired to combine diplomatic moves with military action, he was not willing to let the UN debate and Khrushchev equivocate while the missiles became operational.[6]

Kennedy feared that the missiles would substantially alter political appearances. If the Soviet probe succeeded, more would follow. As Kennedy stated in the Ex Comm, "Then they start getting ready to squeeze us in Berlin. . . ." In view of those concerns, were the methods that were chosen—public confrontation of the Soviets and a naval blockade—appropriate? The arguments are not compelling.

First, the naval blockade did *not* prevent the missiles from becoming operational. . . . Only a U.S. air strike or a military invasion of Cuba, or both, would have achieved this objective.

Second, instead of withdrawing the missiles, Khrushchev could have stalled for time, by initiating proposals for a summit dialogue under the auspices of the U.N. or even outside it. A blockade did not prevent the Soviets from trying to finesse the American initiative with a diplomatic offensive.

Third, if Kennedy's concern was that the missiles were merely a prelude to another Berlin crisis, a blockade was probably not only ineffectual but also ran the risk of sending the wrong signal to the Soviets, which could have led to horizontal escalation of the conflict. A naval blockade around Cuba did not prevent the Soviets from doing likewise with their land forces in Berlin. It almost invited it, and their previous behavior provided strong reasons for believing that this would be exactly how the Soviets would respond. Such an outcome would have been disastrous for the alliance. If alliance relations and security were what worried Kennedy, a blockade was surely a risky course, because of the precedent it set for a Soviet countermove.

Fourth, a blockade was a difficult action to control, and *force majeure* might have driven the United States and the Soviet Union into military confrontation. Recall during the height of the crisis, Saturday, October 27, an American U-2 was shot down over Cuba, almost precipitating an attack on Soviet surface-to-air missiles. Suppose this incident had occurred simultaneously with one or more of the following: a Soviet submarine refusing to surface was depth-charged by an American destroyer and sunk; a U-2 on a reconnaissance flight over the Aleutian Islands inadvertently strayed into Soviet air space and was attacked; or the captain of a Soviet cargo ship "didn't get the message" and ran the blockade. The simultaneous combination of events could have very easily precipitated a catastrophic confrontation. . . .

If the issue was one of standing up to the Soviet challenge, it is not self-evident why the blockade was preferable to the diplomatic route. As is discussed at greater length below, Kennedy could have asked the Soviets to remove the missiles first through a diplomatic ultimatum; then, if that failed, he could have imposed a blockade. Certainly, an ultimatum did not foreclose this option. If it worked, then the United States would have successfully proven its "resolve" and its ability to "stand up" to the Soviets. If it failed, then a further test of wills could have taken place.

That a naval blockade did not serve these general foreign policy objectives well, and was also an extremely risky course of action, was not lost on the participants. As Sorensen vividly recounts:

> It seemed almost irrelevant to the problem of the missiles, neither getting them out nor seeming justifiable to our many maritime allies, who were sensitive to freedom of the seas. Blockade was a word so closely associated with Berlin that it almost guaranteed a new Berlin blockade in response. Both our allies and world opinion would then blame the U.S. and impose as a "solution" the lifting of both blockades simultaneously, items accomplishing nothing.

Moreover, blockade had many of the drawbacks of the air-strike plan. If Soviet ships ignored it, U.S. forces would have to fire the first shot, provoking Soviet action elsewhere. . . .

We could not even be certain that the blockade route was open to us. Without obtaining a two-thirds vote in the OAS—which appeared dubious at best—allies and neutrals as well as adversaries might well regard it as an illegal blockade in violation of the UN Charter and international law.

But the greatest single drawback to the blockade . . . was time. Instead of presenting Khrushchev and the world with a *fait accompli,* it offered a prolonged and agonizing approach, uncertain in its effect, indefinite in its duration, enabling the missiles to become operational, subjecting us to counterthreats from Khrushchev, giving him a propaganda advantage, stirring fears and protests and pickets all over the world, causing Latin American governments to fall, permitting Castro to announce that he would execute two Bay of Pigs prisoners for each day it continued, encouraging the UN or the OAS or our allies to bring pressure for talks, and in all these ways making more difficult a subsequent air strike if the missiles remained.[7]

Of course, none of these things happened, but one can only say that with hindsight. At the time, blockade seemed very risky, especially given the high degree of uncertainty about how Khrushchev would react. Sorensen's explanation that, compared to an air strike, a blockade was preferable because it "offered Khrushchev the choice of avoiding a direct military clash—which is why it gained strength—begs the question why the less risky diplomatic option was not chosen.

Process, Group Dynamics, and Perceptions

Can one explain the decision by the bargaining and consensus-building methods of the Ex Comm? Did group dynamics affect decision-making? To what extent were images and perceptions the determinants of behavior?

According to Graham Allison, what finally persuaded the President was the consensus reached by his key advisers—Robert Kennedy, Robert McNamara, and Ted Sorensen—that the blockade was the preferred alternative.[8] He rejected the advice of the Joint Chiefs of Staff, McCone, Rusk, Nitze, and Acheson, who urged an air strike, on personal grounds: "*Who* supported the air strike . . . counted as much as *how* they supported it. This *entente cordiale* was not composed of the President's natural allies."[9] But as Allison himself recognizes, the President had framed the original parameters of the problem by rejecting the diplomatic option quite early in the crisis. The Ex Comm was acting within the scope of Presidential preferences and priorities. The bargaining and consensus-building model, while important, fails to explain why the President narrowed the wide array of options to military ones (blockade, air strike, or invasion) in the first place.

Irving Janis argues that small decision-making groups have a tendency towards "group-think." Although Janis's model is quite complex, it suggests that small groups will develop stereotyped images that "dehumanize out-groups against whom they are engaged in competitive struggles" and shift "toward riskier courses of action than the individual members would otherwise be prepared to take."[10] Was this the case in the Ex Comm? Janis thinks not. According to Janis, the group "met all the major criteria of sound decision-

making." They considered a wide variety of options, weighed the costs, benefits, and risks of each, were on the constant watch for new information, and
carefully assessed the consequences of each alternative. This conclusion ignores
the very real risks to which the President and his advisers exposed themselves in
choosing the blockade, in which case the "group-think" phenomenon may be
more pervasive and insidious than Janis thinks.

A more fundamental objection to the "group-think" argument is that it
ignores the *multiple risks* that decision-makers face in their environment and
the difficult trade-offs they often have to make. . . . Kennedy's decision to
blockade Cuba was risky from a foreign policy and military standpoint, but it
was an action that partially reduced his exposure to vocal domestic critics, who
charged that the administration was soft on communism. From a domestic
political standpoint, the blockade was a less risky course of action.

While cognitive theorists have tended to focus upon information failures in
the Cuban missile crisis and the inability of U.S. intelligence to detect the
missiles early on, the importance of perceptions and preexisting beliefs in the
Ex Comm's deliberations are stressed as well. Was Kennedy acting on historical analogy, reading the present in the light of the past? In the early discussions,
when the majority opinion seemed to be for an air strike, Robert Kennedy
passed a note to his brother: "I now know how Tojo felt when he was planning
Pearl Harbor." The analogy struck home, as did the moral implication, that it
was unwise for a superpower to use such force against a comparably defense-
less small power, although Acheson did his best to debunk the comparison.
This may help to explain further why Kennedy rejected the air strike option,
but it does not explain why he rejected other options. At best, the actors'
perceptions of history was only a partial guide to their actions.

Domestic Politics and Political Risk Aversion

There are a number of studies of the missile crisis which have argued, quite
convincingly, that domestic politics was indeed "the essence of decision." Kennedy was politically vulnerable on the Cuban issue. He was on the public
record that the missiles in Cuba were only for defensive purposes, and the
discovery of "offensive" systems raised serious doubts about his credibility
before an important congressional election, only three weeks off when the
presence of the missiles was confirmed on October 15. A "do-nothing" or
diplomatic approach to the missiles was simply not acceptable to him. The
President *had* to act forcibly.

These arguments have a rather conspiratorial tone to them. They suggest
that the President was only worried about the election, and was willing to risk
war with the Soviets in the process. This characterization flies in the face of
virtually every account of decision-making in the crisis. Moreover, to assert
categorically that domestic politics was the cause of the crisis is merely to
substitute one partial explanation for another. . . .

More important, the argument overlooks the very important political risks
to which the President exposed himself in adopting the course of action he did.
Suppose all those things Sorensen, Kennedy, and others feared might happen at
the time had: Khrushchev seized the propaganda advantage, stalled for time by
going to the U.N. to plead for a negotiated settlement, did not challenge the
blockade, but did not remove the missiles either. The crisis could have very

easily continued *into* the November elections, or have ended up in a mangled military operation (like the Bay of Pigs) or in war with the Soviets. Kennedy would have then been accused of bungling the crisis and the Democrats would have been beaten at the polls. The blockade was not an easy way out of the President's political dilemma by any means.

Is there a way to explain how the President reconciled these enormously difficult costs, risks, and tremendous uncertainties? One possible route is suggested by the theory of political risk aversion I have developed elsewhere.[11] The theory accepts the premise that elites will often face the difficult choice of reconciling multiple values in the process of making decisions. Faced with a difficult decision where a variety of key values are threatened and cannot be maximized simultaneously, they will seek to foster those values they cherish most. The hypothesis is that these values form a hierarchy and can be rank-ordered accordingly. At the top of this scale is the leadership's concern with his (or her) continued political health, legitimacy, and survival. Further down the scale of values, in decreasing order of importance, are political institutions, the polity, the economy, social stability, external political relations, and external economic relations. Short-term threats to each will be treated more seriously than those which have longer-term consequences. . . .

Thus, if a conflict arises among these values, the temptation will be to maximize the higher value on the scale to the greatest extent possible, even if it means sacrificing, to at least some extent, the fulfillment of other values. This is not to say that these decisions will be easy; but, to take the extreme case, when a leader has to decide between two possible courses of action where the alternatives are mutually exclusive, and one involves doing something that will enhance his domestic political standing but has high foreign policy costs and risks, whereas the other weakens his domestic standing but has beneficial foreign policy consequences (or fewer costs and risks), he will lean towards the former. Though choices are rarely this stark, domestic political considerations will be an important factor in decision-making when elites feel vulnerable.

Although there are cases of statesmanly behavior when leaders have taken actions which fly in the face of public opinion at great cost to themselves (such as President Truman's decision not to support Chiang Kai-Shek's Nationalist forces in China and to "decouple" in 1949, or President Carter's handling of the Iranian hostage crisis), these are by-and-large the exception in politics rather than the norm. Rare is the President who is prepared to sacrifice his own political interests, when they are threatened, for the sake of some broader national purpose, particularly when the two cannot be reconciled.

The model emphasizes that most political decisions involve enormously difficult trade-offs in which policy makers cannot maximize all of their values at once, but when presented with a strong challenge to his leadership or political survival, it hypothesizes that a leader will attach greater importance to his own, immediate, short-term, political interest than to other goals or values. . . . It is important to note that this model of decison-making stresses the internalization of domestic political constraints. It is precisely this internalization that makes political risk analysis possible. This view of the political process is very different from the sorts of domestic pressures and the sorts of political risks evident in, for example, the politics of the regulation of farm product prices or of tax policy. In these latter cases, there are ample external constraints on the policymaker, but what is dramatic in the following cases is the internal constraints and how individual perceptions of political risk shape policy choices.

Reconciling Difficult Trade-offs

Given the long-term military, political, and strategic threats posed by the Cuban missiles, especially if the buildup had been allowed to continue, letting the Soviets get away with it was simply not in the cards. It was clear the missiles had to go, but was the blockade the right way to go about it?

At the diplomatic level the options were essentially two:

1. NEGOTIATED REMOVAL. The President could have tried to negotiate the removal of the missiles with the Soviets in a summit meeting with Khrushchev or through a third party like the U.N.

2. NON-NEGOTIABLE ULTIMATUM. The President could have notified Khrushchev, quietly or publicly, that the missiles had to be removed or the United States would remove them forcibly. . . .

Both of these options were considered but then rejected in the Ex Comm. The first would have required some sort of *quid pro quo* with the Soviets (such as the removal of the American Jupiter missiles from Turkey, concessions on Berlin, etc.), and it was feared that either one would have handed the propaganda advantage to Khrushchev, given the Soviets warning (thereby making further military action, like an air strike against the missiles, much more difficult), and not prevented the missiles from becoming operational.

While a negotiated removal of the missiles had clear disadvantages, since Kennedy would have been forced to give up something in exchange for their removal (although it must not be forgotten that in the end Kennedy agreed not to invade Cuba and to remove the Jupiters from Turkey once the crisis was resolved), an ultimatum did not have this problem. It is true that an ultimatum had other problems, but it is not clear they were any worse than a blockade. It did not prevent the missiles from becoming operational, but then neither did the blockade. It would have given the Soviets warning, but then so did the blockade. It could have handed the propaganda advantage to Khrushchev, but that could have happened with the blockade too (Khrushchev could have heeded the blockade and then gone to the U.N. or some other forum to plead for a negotiated removal of the missiles). Unlike the blockade, an ultimatum did not risk military confrontation on the high seas, either through advertent or inadvertent escalation. If it worked, the crisis would have obviously ended there; if it didn't, it did not foreclose military action.

This is not to say diplomacy *would* have worked, but it perhaps should have been tried first since certainly an ultimatum ran fewer risks of escalation than public confrontation of the Soviets combined with a blockade. For domestic political reasons, however, the President and his advisers felt this option was not acceptable and that some sort of military action was necessary. It was not simply the danger of defeat in the upcoming congressional elections Kennedy feared, however; it was the consequence of failure to act decisively *now* for his whole Presidency. His authority, status, and prestige were on the line. As Richard Neustadt wrote, in a book Kennedy himself read, "The greatest danger to a President's potential influence . . . is not the show of incapacity he makes today, but its apparent kinship to what happened yesterday, last month, last year. For if his failures seem to form a pattern, the consequence is bound to be a loss of faith in his effectiveness 'next time.' The boy who cried 'wolf' came to a sad end because nobody paid attention to his final cry."[12]

Kennedy placed an enormous value on his Presidency. He perceived that his failure to act decisively and quickly would have very high costs: a complete erosion of his authority and prestige and maybe even loss of the Presidency itself. In addition to the military and foreign policy implications of the missiles, what made the situation a "crisis" was the President's belief that the situation posed a direct threat to himself and his Presidency. The members of the Ex Comm recognized the President's political dangers right away. . . . [V]ery early in the crisis, October 16, McNamara was already trying to devise a package of military options which would address the domestic political aspects of the problem.

McNamara:	Now, the second alternative I'd like to discuss just a second, because we haven't discussed it fully today, and I alluded it to, to it a moment ago. I, I, I'll be quite frank. I don't think there is a military problem here. This is my answer to Mac's question . . .
Bundy:	That's my honest [judgment?]
McNamara:	. . .and therefore, and I've gone through this today, and I asked myself, well, what is it then if it isn't a military problem? Well it's just exactly *this* problem, that, that, uh, if Cuba should possess a capacity to carry out offensive activities against the U.S., the U.S. would act.
Speaker:	That's right.
Speaker:	That's right.
McNamara:	Now, it's that problem this . . .
Speaker:	You can't get around that one.
McNamara:	. . . *This, this is a domestic, political problem.* [My emphasis] The announcement [apparently Kennedy's September 13 speech]—we didn't say we'd go in and not, and kill them, we said we'd *act*. Well, how will we act? Well, we want to act to prevent their use, and it's really the . . .
Bundy:	Yeah.
McNamara:	. . .the act. Now, how do we pre-, act to prevent their use? Well, first place, we carry out open surveillance, so we know what they're doing. All times. Twenty-four hours a day from now and forever, in a sense indefinitely. What else do we do? We prevent any further offensive weapons coming in. In other words we blockade offensive weapons.
McNamara:	And what I really tried to do was develop a little package that meets the action requirement of that paragraph I read.
Speaker:	Yeah.
McNamara:	Because, as I suggested, I don't believe it's primarily a military problem. It's primarily a, a domestic political problem.
Ball:	*Yeah, well, as far as the American people are concerned, action means military action, period.* [My emphasis]
McNamara:	Well, we have a blockade. Search and, uh, removal of, of

	offensive weapons entering Cuba. Uh, [word unintelligible] again, I don't want to argue for this . . .
Ball:	No, No, I . . .
McNamara:	because I, I don't think it's . . .
Ball:	I think it's an alternative.
McNamara:	. . . a perfect solution by any means . . .

It is important to note that the way the problem was defined had enormous consequences for the decision itself. For largely domestic reasons, some sort of military action was deemed essential as a way of handling the crisis. In the context of the President's political difficulties, the blockade *was* the most sensible option since it did not involve direct military conflict and left most other military options open. While the risks of escalation pushed the decision down the ladder to the blockade, the President's domestic political interests favored military action over diplomacy. . . .

It does seem that the President and his advisers were quite uncomfortable with the consequences of the decision they took. Although the President was willing to take enormous foreign policy and military risks to preserve his Presidency (both for himself and the nation), he never did quite reconcile himself to that fact, at least until the crisis had passed and his gamble seemed to have worked. . . . [A]t one point, in the middle of the confrontation, [Kennedy] wondered out loud to his brother how the whole mess had started. There was little comfort in Robert Kennedy's reply, "If you hadn't acted, you would have been impeached."

The value structure of the President explains not only why he made the kinds of trade-offs that he did, but also why he was prepared to embark on a course which itself had great political risks if things turned out badly. Although Kennedy worried about the implications of the crisis for his Presidency, he focused on the short-term aspects of the problem. The President felt that he had to take decisive military action if his Presidency was not to be severely challenged and his political credibility undermined. Diplomacy of any kind simply did not meet this requirement. . . .

THE CIENFUEGOS CRISIS

On September 9, 1970, U.S. intelligence revealed an unusual degree of activity in the Bay of Cienfuegos, Cuba.[13] A large Soviet flotilla, which included a submarine tender, was spotted and seemed to be on more than just a routine training exercise. A U-2 reconnaissance flight on September 16, which investigated the situation more closely, found more than ships: undergoing rapid construction at Cayo Alcatriz was a full-scale naval facility, and there was compelling evidence the Soviets were behind it.

National Security Adviser Henry Kissinger hastily convened an interagency group known as the WSAG (Washington Special Action Group) to discuss the implications of the Soviet action and to decide what ought to be done. The Group divided: the Pentagon favored strong diplomatic action, whereas the State Department urged a more moderate approach that would have sought a clarification from the Soviets before any action was taken. Kissinger sided with the Pentagon.

Informed of his options, President Nixon favored a tough response, but wanted to postpone a decision until he returned from his upcoming trip to Europe (September 27–October 5). He told Kissinger that he wanted a full report on the following set of actions: (1) what the CIA could do to "irritate" Castro; (2) what the U.S. could do, in addition to what it had already done, to boycott nations that had diplomatic and trade relations with Castro; and (3) how the U.S. could go about either covertly or overtly putting missiles in Turkey or submarines in the Black Sea that would give it some "trading stock" with the Russians.

Matters would have probably stood that way had not a Pentagon briefing officer inadvertently revealed the details of the base under construction in a press conference. The "leak" forced the President's hand, and Kissinger was authorized to do what he could to get the Soviets to cease construction immediately.

Kissinger quietly summoned Soviet Ambassador Anatoly Dobrynin to his office and informed him that "Moscow should be under no illusion; we would view continued construction with the 'utmost gravity'; the base could not remain."[14] Dobrynin sought and received assurances that the United States would not launch a press campaign that would magnify the issue and cause a loss of face if the Soviets retreated.

On October 5, following Kissinger's return from the President's European tour, Dobrynin met with him again, affirming that the Soviets would not do anything that would violate the 1962 understandings between Kennedy and Khrushchev prohibiting the deployment of any sort of strategic offensive systems in Cuba. Dobrynin subsequently indicated that, while the Soviets could not agree that their submarines would never call on Cuban ports, they were prepared to avow that no ballistic missile-carrying submarines would call there in an operational capacity and that they would not establish a submarine base in Cuba. Although the Soviets tested the agreement almost as soon as it was made, they never actually sent a nuclear-powered, ballistic missile-launching submarine to Cuba.

The Cienfuegos crisis had many of the same ingredients as the Cuban missile crisis: it involved a major effort by the Soviet Union to gain a strategic advantage using Cuba as a base; the Soviets took action secretly and without warning; they sought a major change in the political status quo; and the crisis erupted on the brink of a congressional election. This time, however, there was no major confrontation with the Soviet Union, no risk of nuclear war. The crisis, to the extent that it was a crisis at all, was resolved peacefully through diplomatic channels. Why?

Challenge to U.S. Credibility and Commitments

A possible explanation for the difference between the Cuban missile crisis and the Cienfuegos "mini-crisis" is that the Soviet action in the latter was *not* perceived as a challenge to U.S. credibility and commitments, at least to the same extent it was in 1962. . . .

Nevertheless, . . . the . . . information available about the decision-making processes . . . suggests the strategic threat at Cienfuegos was taken very seriously. No one sums up the views of the principal actor in the crisis better than Kissinger himself:

Even if no further facilities were added, it would increase the Soviet capacity to keep ballistic missile submarines at combat stations. If expanded, it might effectively double the Soviets' sea-based missile force against us. If the Soviets proceeded in their usual fashion, the first deployments, if not resisted, would be followed by a further rapid increase. The experience of the missile buildup along the Suez Canal would be repeated, this time against us. If we acquiesced in the original installation, we would have difficulty in resisting its expansion.[15]

Like in the missile crisis, the strategic threat was long-term rather than short. In 1970, the Soviets only had 22 SSBNs, out of which only 14 were of the Yankee class, the only submarine with a long-range cruising capability. Although each submarine was equipped to carry 16 SS-N-6s, the total number of warheads threatening targets in the United States would have been well below 224 because not all Soviet submarines would be out of port at any one time and some would be dedicated to missions elsewhere on the globe. In the context of the rapid expansion of the Soviet SSBN force that took place in the seventies (by 1980, for example, the total force numbered 71), the base *would*, however, have had important long-term strategic implications. . . .

The political consequences of the Soviet action were just as important if not more so to Kissinger. He felt the base was simply part of a larger Soviet design aimed at "testing" the United States "in different parts of the world." He therefore "favored facing the challenge immediately lest the Soviets misunderstand our permissiveness. . . . "[16] His view certainly resonates with Kennedy's in the Cuban missile crisis. Whether it was correct or not cannot be proven definitely, but Kissinger was right about two things: first, the Soviet action did constitute a violation of the 1962 Kennedy-Khrushchev "understandings"—or at least, in the most favorable light, a fundamental and unilateral revision of them; and second, if the United States did not act quickly, the Soviets would believe that it was acquiescing, because they knew Cuba was being watched closely by U.S. intelligence. Any sort of future confrontation would have put their prestige on the line and reinforced "their belief that they had been set up for humiliation."[17]

Kissinger surmised that the problem was best handled by a private communication to the Soviets before the base was completed and became operational. This would leave them an easy way out and not challenge their prestige. . . . Informed of his options, Nixon favored a much tougher response to the Soviets that would have included some sort of military action. To explain the response that was eventually adopted, one must look beyond the immediate strategic and political issues raised in the mind of the President's National Security Adviser to other factors.

Process, Group Dynamics, and Perceptions

Bureaucratic politics and group-dynamic models of decision-making are not terribly applicable to an analysis of the Cienfuegos crisis. Kissinger and Nixon were the key players and pretty much left their subordinates in the dark, withholding important information from them and not revealing their own policy preferences or objectives. For example, on August 4 and 7, 1970, when Kissinger discussed with Soviet Chargé d'Affaires Yuli Vorontsov U.S. views on the 1962 Kennedy-Khrushchev understandings about deployment of offensive systems in Cuba, he failed to inform members of the WSAG or key government officials what the substance of the exchanges was. Thus, there was no way for the group to properly review what the essence of the Soviet violation was or the degree to which it breached the 1962 understandings. Nor did Kissinger issue the WSAG group with a directive, as Kennedy did with the Ex Comm, to reach a consensus about what ought to be done. Instead, he simply used the WSAG as a sounding board to explore, in rather general and loosely defined terms, the strategic and political implications of Soviet action. The decision about what to do and the methods about how to go about doing it were left up to Kissinger and the President.

Process was important insofar as poor coordination and improper instructions led a Pentagon briefing officer to break the news to the press before the President wanted to deal with it. The leak forced a decision upon the President and his National Security Adviser, but such timing factors do not explain the substance of the decision.

Perceptions did play an important role in determining how the key players viewed the crisis. Kissinger saw the Soviet action as having far-reaching strategic and political consequences which were linked to their actions and objectives in other parts of the world. Kissinger's belief that Soviet behavior in Cuba was part of a global design was based on a much profounder set of values and attitudes about world history. There is nothing to suggest that the President disagreed with Kissinger's assessment of Soviet intentions or the implications of the crisis for American foreign policy. Where he was in disagreement with his National Security Adviser was over methods: both how to deal with the crisis and when. He wanted to hit the Soviets hard, but only after he had returned from his trip abroad.

To explain *why* the President felt the way he did and why he eventually succumbed to Kissinger's view on how to manage the crisis, we need to look beyond the perceptions of the players to their values and to the domestic politics of the decision.

Domestic Politics and Political Risk Aversion

Nixon initially wanted to play hard ball with the Soviets over their actions in Cuba, but then changed his mind. Why? No better explanation is available than the one given by his National Security Adviser:

> Cuba was a neuralgic problem for Nixon. When he ran for the Presidency in 1960, it featured in the famous television debates with Kennedy. A few days before the debate of October 21, 1960, Kennedy had advocated intervention by American forces to topple Fidel Castro. . . . Nixon, who was aware of the planning for what turned out to be the abortive Bay of Pigs invasion, felt constrained to disavow the proposal. . . . In his memoirs, Nixon related with some bitterness: 'In that debate, Kennedy conveyed the image—to 60 million people—that he was tougher on Castro and communism than I was.' Nixon was determined that no one would ever be able to make this charge again.
>
>   . . . In 1962, when he was running for the governorship of California, the Cuban missile crisis dominated the last three weeks of the campaign—the period Nixon always considered crucial to the outcome. Though he had already fallen behind by then, he was convinced that the crisis had deprived him of the opportunity to

recover. He never ceased believing that Kennedy had timed the showdown to enhance Democratic prospects in the midterm elections. For Nixon the coincidence of Cuba with an electoral campaign set off waves of foreboding and resentment. In his view, nothing was more to be avoided than a Cuban crisis in a Congressional election year.[18]

On the one hand, Nixon felt personally vulnerable over the Cuba issue and instinctively wanted to play it tough: "For anyone who knew him it was out of the question that he would tolerate the establishment of a Soviet naval base in Cuba. . . . Too much of his political life had been tied up with taking a tough stance on this issue. . . . " On the other hand, Nixon feared "that while Vietnam unleashed media and Congressional assaults on Presidential credibility, a new Cuban missile crisis in an election year would generate a massive *public* cynicism." For these reasons, "Nixon's preferred strategy was to confront the Soviets right after the election."[19]

There are extraordinary parallels between Nixon's sense of political vulnerability over Cuba and Kennedy's, but there is a crucial difference in the challenge the Soviet action in each crisis posed to the President. This difference lies in the domestic political context of the two crises. When President Kennedy received word that the Soviets were putting offensive ballistic missiles in Cuba, Cuba was the spotlight of national attention: there were members of Congress who were screaming about the Administration's "do nothing policy"; there were daily press reports about the Soviet military buildup; Republicans had made Cuba the central foreign policy issue in the upcoming congressional election campaign. Nothing could have been further from reality in 1970. Cuba was not even an issue. Vietnam and the events that were unravelling in the Middle East were the topics of national concern. Although both Kennedy and Nixon had a natural aversion to just about *anything* having to do with Cuba for rather obvious political reasons, the key difference in the two crises was that Kennedy's job was on the line over Cuba—at least he felt it was—whereas Nixon's was not. . . .

For these reasons, it is easy to see why Nixon behaved the way he did when news of the submarine base leaked, his hand was forced, and Kissinger proposed the diplomatic route to "confront" the Soviets. Kissinger's "quiet" approach provided not only a face-saving way out of the problem for the Soviets but also one for Nixon. It avoided a showdown with the Soviet Union which would have been costly for the Republicans in the upcoming congressional elections, but it left options open for a tough response and confrontation with the Soviets if it did not work. Unlike Kennedy, who felt that his options were greatly limited because domestic political pressures threatened his Presidency and therefore "action," given these pressures, "meant military action," Nixon felt under no such constraints. If there were pressures, they ran the other way: to keep the crisis under wraps until the elections were over.

In the Cuban missile crisis, the President's central political values—his concern for his own political survival and that of his Presidency—were threatened; in the Cienfuegos crisis they were not. The either/or predicament that Kennedy faced was not Nixon's. There was not the tug of conflicting values—the dilemma of whether to take foreign policy risks to save the Presidency or to risk the Presidency in the interests of policy moderation. The distinguishing characteristic of these two crises is that the degree to which domestic politics mattered, in the way I have defined it here, was much greater in the Cuban missile crisis. Supreme political values were perceived to be at risk in the missile crisis; they were not at Cienfuegos.

THE CUBAN BRIGADE CRISIS

The Cuban brigade crisis illustrates that congressional actors are also prone to politically risk-averse behavior, and that the foreign policy costs of such behavior can be enormous. The ways in which political elites evaluate threats in the congressional branch of government are quite similar to those in the executive. Indeed, the proclivity to sacrifice long-term interests for short-term gain is probably stronger, expecially when an important change in national politics threatens the political tenure of "established" members of the House or Senate. . . .

The origins of the Cuban brigade crisis date back to the days of the Cuban missile crisis.[20] Recall that the deployment of the missiles in Cuba was preceded by a massive Soviet troop buildup. When the missiles were removed, most of the troops left with them, but some stayed to help train Castro's army and to instruct Cuban troops in how to use Soviet military hardware and technology. The dispersal, followed by a regrouping and reorganization of Soviet troops in Cuba after the removal of the missiles, confounded U.S. intelligence: in the absence of extensive ground intelligence-gathering capabilities, it was impossible to discover with any degree of precision where Soviet troops were located and what their various missions were. The absence of hard intelligence was to have very important implications for subsequent events.

In 1978, President Carter's National Security Adviser Zbigniew Brzezinski instructed the CIA to do a complete assessment of the location, size, and activities of Soviet and Cuban troops throughout the world. Brzezinski was worried about what seemed to be a growing trend of military involvement by the Soviets and their surrogate, the Cubans, in Third World conflicts. . . .

Brzezinski's directive resulted in stepped-up monitoring of Soviet activities in Cuba by satellite reconnaissance. Photographs revealed the existence of what seemed to be a new Soviet unit. It was deployed in a way which suggested it was not an advisory force to the Cubans but had some sort of independent mission. A June 1979 National Security Agency Report concluded that the newly discovered brigade did have a separate purpose and speculated that its role might be either a combat one or to guard nuclear weapons. The NSA study was hotly disputed in the intelligence community, with the CIA, the Defense Intelligence Agency, Air Force and Navy Intelligence, and the Department of State disagreeing strongly with NSA's conclusions.

The Report's findings surfaced in the Senate Foreign Relations Committee's mid-July hearings on SALT II. From the outset, SALT II was in trouble: congressional and public critics charged that the Soviet Union could not be trusted to live up to its side of the agreement; the Soviet threat was much greater than the administration believed; and U.S. intelligence would not be able to detect whether or not the Soviets were living up to their commitments. When certain members of the Foreign Relations Committee got wind of the Soviet brigade in Cuba through intelligence channels, they were quick to dredge up further details in their efforts to build a case for Soviet duplicity and the ineptitude of the Carter Administration.

Immediately recognizing the threat to SALT, if rumors persisted, the administration sent some of its most senior officials to Capitol Hill to assure the members of the Foreign Relations Committee that there was no brigade in Cuba. In response, Senator Frank Church, Committee Chairman, who was guiding SALT through the Senate, issued a public statement denying the existence of a brigade or a buildup of Soviet troops in Cuba.

Continued surveillance of Cuba, however, during the month of August confirmed the presence of a Soviet force equipped with tanks, artillery, armored personnel carriers, etc., which appeared to have no relation to training of Cuban troops. Although the administration decided that the best strategy was to downplay the news while at the same time issuing the Soviets with a sharp note of protest, the story leaked with imminent threat of publication. The approach chosen was for the State Department to issue a short announcement downplaying the significance of the Soviet troops, but only after key congressional leaders had been informed.

When Senator Frank Church, the first on this list, was notified about the brigade's existence from the State Department, he was back in Idaho on the campaign trail. The news caught him at a bad moment. The National Conservative Political Action Committee had launched a stiff compaign to unseat him in the next election, and he was already in serious political trouble. Church requested and received permission from Secretary of State Cyrus Vance to break the brigade story to the public himself. Having been chief congressional defender of the administration's assertion that there were no new Soviet forces in Cuba, he felt it would be less damaging to his own credibility if he were to reveal the truth about their existence himself. In the full glare of the television lights of the major networks, Church told the nation about the brigade.

As the administration feared, the brigade became the focal point of the Senate Foreign Relations Committee hearings on SALT II in September, acting as a lightning rod to critics of SALT. The administration found itself on the defensive. To allay public concerns, Vance announced that he would "not be satisfied with the status quo in Cuba," adding, with characteristic understatement but a not-so-thinly-disguised threat, that the administration would not object if Congress delayed ratification of SALT II until the Soviets removed their troops.

Bewildered and outraged, the Soviets replied that no new troops had been sent to Cuba. Whatever troops were there had been in Cuba since 1962. The American "sightings" were simply of Soviet troops on a regular training exercise with the Cubans.

The continuing intelligence assessment corroborated Soviet denials. It was plausible, indeed likely, that there had only been a regrouping of Soviet forces in Cuba which only the intensive surveillance beginning in 1978 was capable of detecting. Although it seemed the Soviet force was not on a training mission, it was self-evident that it was not an offensive force either since it lacked necessary airlift and sealift capabilities. By the time this revised intelligence assessment surfaced, however, the damage had been done. SALT II had stalled sufficiently long in the Senate that whatever hope there was that it might be ratified was lost when the Soviets invaded Afghanistan on December 25, 1979. The Treaty was quietly withdrawn by the Carter Administration, not only with enormous political cost to itself but also to the détente process and U.S.-Soviet relations.

Challenge to U.S. Credibility and Commitments

Was the Cuban brigade crisis provoked by a direct Soviet military or political threat (or both) to vital U.S. security interests? The evidence is unambiguously negative. . . . Even if the brigade had had an offensive mission, it is difficult to see what the Soviets could have achieved with a force numbering a mere 5,000 men. Compared to the strategic threat proposed by missiles or a submarine base, this "threat" was inconsequential. . . .

Process

As a study in crisis management, the Cuban brigade incident provides a valuable contrast to the Cuban missile and Cienfuegos crises. Congress played a much more significant role both in defining the nature of the crisis itself—it was not just based on the perceptions and values of the executive—and delimiting the options available to the executive.

Press leaks and clumsy management of congressional-executive relations by the Carter Administration certainly contributed to the crisis. . . . It is also true that had Cyrus Vance been more forceful, he might have persuaded Church to downplay the importance of the news or forgo the announcement altogether, leaving it to be made by some minor official in the State Department in a background briefing to the press. . . . Indeed, had there been no SALT Treaty requiring congressional approval, there would have probably been no crisis at all. . . . These counterfactuals, however, explain neither Senator Church's behavior nor the administration's. After all, both Church and the administration contributed greatly to the sense of crisis by dramatizing the newsworthiness of the brigade; by refusing to challenge openly their critics . . . ; and by confronting the Soviets, linking ratification of SALT II to removal of the troops. None of these things had to have happened. Why did they? . . .

Domestic Politics and Political Risk Aversion

One of the great ironies of the Cuban brigade crisis is that one of the principal advocates of arms control in the Senate and a staunch supporter of SALT II turned out to be its executioner. A long-standing and well-known "dove," Church was the Carter Administration's point man for ensuring that SALT II made it through the Senate. If there was anyone who should have recognized the enormous risks posed by the brigade affair to the ratification process, it was Church. Yet he was the first to sound the alarm bells about the brigade instead of being the first to signal the "all clear." The explanation for Church's rather extraordinary behavior is found in the extreme political vulnerability of his position when the crisis erupted. Gloria Duffy describes Church's problem well: ". . . Frank Church had put his name on the Senate Foreign Relations Committee statement a month earlier, affirming that no change had occurred in Soviet forces in Cuba. Fighting a National Conservative Political Action Committee campaign in Idaho which branded him 'soft' on defense and the Soviet Union, Church was worried that the news leak would make his earlier denial of Soviet forces look either gullible or irresponsible. An anti-Church commercial on Idaho television just the night before had shown Church and Fidel Castro smoking cigars together on Church's recent trip to Havana."[21]

Although not until after some agonizing over the matter with his aides and Cyrus Vance, Church decided the news had to come from him. He was fighting for his political life in the face of a growing wave of conservatism. He was one of the chief targets on the NCPAC "hit list," an organization which sought the removal of ultra-liberal senators nationwide. In less tumultuous times, Church would have probably taken a different stance on the brigade; this time, however, with his political life in jeopardy, he could not afford to appear "soft" on the Soviets or communism. The value Church placed on his political survival led him to embark on a course of action which he knew would have high foreign policy costs, but he obviously felt he had no choice.

Church's perception of his political vulnerability was undoubtedly magnified by his earlier political experience with Cuba as well. As a young Senator at the time of the Cuban missile crisis, he had been one of the first to support the Kennedy Administration's early denials that the Soviets were putting offensive missiles in Cuba. When Kennedy's October 22 television announcement proved the contrary to be true, Church was "hamstrung." It was only Kennedy's invitation to Church to accompany Senator Adlai Stevenson to the U.N. to press formal charges against the Soviet Union that saved him from being discredited. The past undoubtedly weighed heavily on Church's mind as he pressed Vance for "permission" to be the first to break the news of the brigade. This time, however, Church could not be saved. His face-saving effort was lost in the tide of Reaganism which swept Republicans into office throughout the country in 1980. . . .

. . .[O]ne simple reality underlies [the] many mistakes in the brigade fiasco. At every step of the way, the Carter Administration and Senator Church were pushed beyond the bounds of prudence by their perception of political vulnerability. Behind Senator Church's overly hasty announcement was fear of criticism from groups such as the National Conservative Political Action Committee. Secretary Vance felt he had to use the ambiguous yet fateful phrase 'status quo unacceptable' to deal with popular pressure. The Administration felt pressured to begin negotiations with the Soviets before they were even certain what the situation was in Cuba, and to elicit concessions in order to protect the SALT II agreement from further criticism. . . .

. . .The affair was a diplomatic defeat for the U.S., and a sure sign that politics can have an ill effect on American foreign policy.

FURTHER IMPLICATIONS OF THE ARGUMENT

On the basis of this analysis, we can reject the simple proposition that domestic political pressures have little impact on crisis decision-making, even when key decisions are made *in camera* out of the immediate political spotlight. Political decision-makers are Janus-like creatures: while one head is turned towards the international arena, the other is firmly fixed on the arena of domestic politics. . . . In the Cuban missile crisis, the President's perception of the domestic political consequences of his actions played a decisive role in affecting the *means* chosen to deal with a foreign policy crisis. In the Cienfuegos crisis, such perceptions affected means as well, but in a way that led the actors to downplay the crisis and avoid confrontation with the Soviets. The brigade crisis, by contrast, shows how politically risk-averse behavior on the part of key Congressional actors created enough ripples to rock the boat in foreign policy.

The reason why domestic pressures can have such a decisive impact on crisis decisions is that decision-makers do not approach a crisis with a mind that is a *tabula rasa*. Their view of events will always be structured by their beliefs, perceptions, and values and their own *internal* political calculation of the costs, benefits, and risks of any given course of action. If the domestic political atmosphere in which the crisis erupts is already menacing and key values held by the decision-maker are threatened, the definition, evaluation of, and solution to the problem will be structured largely by those values which are at risk. In such situations, the decision-maker will feel enormous constraints.

The conventional definition of crises as situations characterized by high threat, surprise, and short decision times is therefore incomplete. Threats are not just external, they frequently have an internal, domestic political dimension too. . . .

Is the impact of domestic politics on crisis behavior likely to be negative? Some, like Richard Neustadt, argue that a President's personal power stake in an issue will be the best guide to a wise policy.[22] Others argue that one neither wants foreign policy to be decided through democratic public opinion nor entirely insulated public officials.[23] It could even be argued that domestic political pressures are usually likely to dampen swings in foreign policy, causing hawks to be less hawkish and doves to be less dovish. While this may be generally true of foreign policy management, during a crisis when supreme political values are at stake, the prevailing political climate at the time the crisis breaks (which may suffer from either extreme) can exert a decisive influence on the policy choices of the decision-maker to the detriment of the national interest.

NOTES

1. John R. Oneal, "The Appropriateness of the Rational Actor Model in the Study of Crisis Decision Making," Paper prepared for delivery at the 1983 Annual Meeting of the American Political Science Association, The Palmer House, September 1–4, 1983, p. 5. This essay provides an excellent review of the assertions and propositions of the crisis decision-making literature and is the basis for this and subsequent observations, along with Lloyd Jensen, *Explaining Foreign Policy* (Englewood Cliffs, N.J.: Prentice-Hall, 1982).

2. The process of arriving at a decision in a crisis is to be contrasted with the process of implementing a decision in a crisis. As Graham Allison points out in his study of the Cuban missile crisis, bureaucratic and organizational interests played a key role in determining how the naval blockade was implemented during the crisis and also affected intelligence gathering operations. See *Essence of Decision: Explaining the Cuban Missile Crisis* (Boston: Little, Brown, 1971).

3. Jensen, *Explaining Foreign Policy*, p. 151. . . .

4. The Cienfuegos crisis erupted in the middle of the Jordanian crisis. Syria had invaded Jordan in support of a PLO revolt against King Hussein.

5. The major studies of the crisis are Elie Abel, *The Missile Crisis* (Philadelphia: J.B. Lippincott, 1966); Allison, *Essence of Decision;* Herbert S. Dinerstein, *The Making of a Missile Crisis: October 1962* (Baltimore: Johns Hopkins University Press, 1976); Alexander L. George and Richard Smoke, *Deterrence in American Foreign Policy: Theory and Practice* (New York: Columbia University Press, 1974), pp. 447–499; Roger Hilsman, *To Move A Nation: The Politics of Foreign Policy in the Administration of John F. Kennedy* (New York: Doubleday, 1967), pp. 160–229; Robert F. Kennedy, *Thirteen Days: A Memoir of the Cuban Missile Crisis* (New York: W.W. Norton, 1971); Henry M. Pachter, *Collision Course: The Cuban Missile Crisis and Coexistence* (New York: Praeger, 1963); Arthur M. Schlesinger, Jr., *A Thousand Days* (New York: Fawcett Premier Books, 1965), pp. 250–277; and Theodore C. Sorensen, *Kennedy* (New York: Harper and Row, 1965), pp. 667–718.

6. Sorensen, *Kennedy*, p. 684.

7. [Ibid.]

8. Allison, *Essence of Decision*, pp. 203–204.

9. Ibid., p. 204.

10. [Irving L. Janis, *Victims of Group Think: A Psychological Study of Foreign Policy Decisions and Fiascoes* (Boston: Houghton, Mifflin, 1972)], p. 6.

11. Fen Osler Hampson, "Fraught with Risk: The Political Economy of Petroleum Policies in Canada and Mexico," Ph.D. Dissertation, Department of Government, Harvard University, 1982, pp. 42–82.

12. Richard E. Neustadt, *Presidential Power: The Politics of Leadership* (New York: John Wiley, 1960), p. 129.

13. The following chronology is drawn from Gloria Duffy, "Crisis Prevention in Cuba," in Alexander George, ed., *Managing U.S.-Soviet Rivalry: Problems of Crisis Prevention* (Boulder, Colo.: Westview Press, 1983), pp. 285–318; Raymond L. Garthoff, "Handling the Cienfuegos Crisis," *International Security*, Vol. 8, No. 1 (Summer 1983), pp. 46–66; and [Henry A. Kissinger, *White House Years* (Boston: Little, Brown, 1979)], pp. 632–652.

14. Kissinger, *White House Years*, p. 647.

15. Ibid, p. 640.

16. Ibid., p. 641.

17. Ibid.

18. Ibid., pp. 633–634.

19. Ibid., pp. 641–642.

20. The following brief description of events and subsequent analysis is based on Gloria Duffy, "Crisis Mangling and the Cuban Brigade," *International Security*, Vol. 8, No. 1 (Summer 1983), pp. 67–87, and "Crisis Prevention in Cuba."

21. Duffy, "Crisis Mangling and the Cuban Brigade," p. 78.

22. Neustadt, *Presidential Power*, pp. 249–263.

23. The classic discussion of these issues is George F. Kennan's *American Diplomacy 1900–1950* (Chicago: University of Chicago Press, 1951).

19. NEW FOREIGN POLICY PROBLEMS AND OLD BUREAUCRATIC ORGANIZATIONS

Charles F. Hermann

At the White House on January 17, 1987, the national security adviser, Vice Admiral John Poindexter, briefed President Reagan on a memorandum he had prepared concerning the continuing efforts to develop productive contacts with Iran. The memorandum accompanied a document that required the president's signature to authorize the Central Intelligence Agency to engage in covert activity. (Law requires that the CIA engage in covert activity only when the president formally substantiates that such an effort is important to U.S. national security.) The national security adviser's plan "proposed that the CIA purchase 4000 TOWs [portable antitank weapons] from DoD [the U.S. Department of Defense] and, after receiving payment transfer them directly to Iran. . . . That day President Reagan wrote in his diary: 'I agreed to sell TOWs to Iran.' " (Tower, Muskie, and Scowcroft, 1987:38).

Earlier efforts to promote renewed contacts with Iran by encouraging sales to Iran from Israel had failed to produce the desired results. Now, in one of the most controversial episodes of the Reagan administration, the U.S. government decided to become the direct supplier of weapons to Iran. That decision and the much larger sequence of events of which it was a part raise profound questions: Was the American objective to seek an improved relationship with Iran as part of an effort to gain influence in an area that could become pivotal in future Soviet-American rivalry? Was the real overriding concern the release of seven American citizens captured in Beirut, Lebanon, and held hostage by groups that Iran could pressure? Was the major objective actually to generate revenue that could be transferred by third parties to the *contras* fighting in Central America? Whatever the goal, what about the declared American policy of neutrality in the prolonged Iran-Iraq war and our insistence on an arms embargo by our allies as well as ourselves? What about the stern and often repeated policy that the United States would not negotiate with terrorists and would not pay ransoms for their release? Could we continue to pressure friendly countries to follow such a strategy if we violated it ourselves? How were the funds owed to the United States for the arms supplied to Iran to be used? Were they to be diverted, contrary to law, to provide assistance to the *contras* fighting the Nicaraguan government forces?

These questions touch on issues of considerable significance for American foreign and national security policy. Most revealing is the list of advisers present and absent when the president decided to engage in a major escalation of the potentially dangerous program. In their subsequent investigation the Tower Commission (1987:38) reports that in addition to the president the session was attended by Admiral Poindexter and one of his NSC staff members, Vice President Bush, and the chief of the White House staff, Donald Regan. Absent were Secretary of State Shultz, Secretary of Defense Weinberger, and Director of the CIA Casey. In earlier discussions, Secretaries Shultz and Weinberger and the departments they represented opposed any arms shipments to Iran. The CIA, whose agents might have been expected to direct the sale, was not represented, and in fact supervision of the operation was given to the NSC staff rather than the CIA.

In important respects, the decision was an anomaly in contemporary foreign policy, in part because of the configuration of presidential advisers participating and not participating. Most American foreign policy decisions involve extensive preparation by the relevant departments and agencies. When the decisions involve extensive action, as this one did, the complex government bureaucracies routinely assume responsibility for the implementation. That there appears to have been a serious attempt to skirt the major foreign policy organizations in this instance highlights some classic dilemmas concerning bureaucracy that confront every modern president of the United States. Consider these illustrations:

- Presidents need the professional expertise of career specialists in the major foreign and security agencies of government, *but* they want faithful execution of both the spirit and the letter of their decisions (and too frequently presidents feel bureaucracies fail to provide such implementation).

- Presidents need to conduct foreign and security policy in a manner that assures accountability to the Congress, the people, and the law of the land, *but* sensitive issues often require secrecy that easily becomes violated as the number of people involved increases and written records are kept.

- Presidents need to have sufficient knowledge about the international issues with which they must deal to ensure the best possible decisions, *but* the president is responsible for the complete spectrum of executive-branch operations, and knowledge about all potential key issues can overload any individual, particularly when the person's prior knowledge and interests in some areas inevitably must be less than in others.

It is against such a backdrop that this essay seeks to sketch a framework for the operation of bureaucratic organizations in the conduct of American foreign policy. Governments of complex contemporary societies, such as the United States, find it necessary to assemble many specialized organizations for the conduct of foreign and defense policy. Among the key executive-branch bureaucracies in the United States dealing with international affairs are the Department of State, the Department of Defense (including the individual military services), the Central Intelligence Agency, the National Security Agency, the Agency for International Development, the Treasury, the United States Information Agency, the Arms Control and Disarmament Agency, and many others.

Even though the Iran-*contra* episode in the Reagan administration may have been an anomaly because key organizations were frequently sidestepped, part of its root causes can be traced to the frustrations that all presidents have in dealing with the very organizations upon which successful foreign policy depends. As President Reagan learned, attempting to conduct policy without them is filled with peril. But he and other presidents have seen their visions of effective policy dashed by systematically inadequate bureaucratic support. What is there about the large, complex bureaucratic organizations upon which all modern governments depend that often leads to ineffectiveness? Why do presidents and their White House advisers become so discouraged with the established organizations that they sometimes try risky alternatives? Often the heart of the difficulty lies with certain structural characteristics of organizations, not with willful bureaucrats who deliberately seek to frustrate presidents.

To begin with, governments—all governments—act only in response to recognized problems. Bureaucratic organizations are designed to be foreign policy problem-solving entities. Before examining certain critical organizational properties, we must examine what we mean by *problem* and by two important related concepts, *problem recognition* and *problem definition*.

BASIC DEFINITIONS

Problem

A problem exists when there is a discrepancy or imbalance between a preferred state of affairs and the present or possible future state of affairs. A number of corollaries follow from this definition. First, a problem requires that the actor be aware of one or more goals. If a government's foreign policy goals are poorly defined, then so are any problems that might arise from them. A critical problem arises when a government disagrees internally on its goals and the priorities among them.

Consider the Iran-*contra* case. Was the primary goal to get the release of the seven American hostages in the Middle East, and, if so, at what costs? Did the government also want to continue its policy of punishing governments that supported terrorists? In other words, would the United States be prepared to cancel delivery of its part of the bargain once the hostages were released? Such goals might be incompatible with another goal—improved relationships with some parts of the power structure in Teheran. Any kind of bargain would almost certainly be seen by some officials and American allies as incompatible with the stated policy of not negotiating with terrorists. Despite these seeming contradictions among preferred goals, almost all of them seem to have been held at some point by one or more high officials in the Reagan administration. Unless the goals are clearly defined and ordered—and this is often an extremely difficult task to achieve among government organizations—the problem cannot be fully recognized and the appropriate government response determined.

It should be noted that goals may be identified and refined in an interactive process. As an analogy, consider a small child who may not attach much value to a toy until another child shows interest in playing with it. Suddenly, maintaining possession of the toy becomes an important goal and the interest displayed in that object by the other child becomes the problem. After asserting ownership over the object, the first child may again lose interest in it and even forget its whereabouts. Applied to more complex matters, the analogy can reveal something about the behaviors of collective entities such as governments. Conditions or objects that are the subjects of goals need not be continuously valued at the same level of importance. The significance and the attainment of a foreign policy goal may emerge more or less suddenly in response to developing circumstances. The American commitment to the direct protection of South Korea in 1950 may be a case in point. Not until after the North Korean invasion did American policymakers fully articulate that goal; in fact, they had earlier implied that Korea's security was the United Nations' responsibility.

A second result of stipulating that the concept of problem depends on an entity's goals is that problems are relative. Whenever individuals or organizations have different goals or have assigned significantly different priorities to the same goal, then the possibility exists that what is seen as a problem for one will not necessarily be a problem for another. The same circumstances in different countries may create very different problems.

Somewhat less frequently acknowledged is the idea that different departments, agencies, or bureaus within a government may have different—even competing—goals and, hence, they may see different problems. For example, the U.S. Commerce and Defense Departments may have the goal of generating revenue and reducing unit costs of weapons by selling sophisticated arms to an ally, but the same arms sale may be viewed differently by the Arms Control and Disarmament Agency and the Department of State if each has a goal of restricting the distribution of certain armaments and maintaining an equilibrium in regional arms supplies. Thus, one of the first tasks of those who set agendas within a government may be to convince other government agencies of the importance of adopting a particular goal as having priority over others.

A third corollary of the proposed definition of a problem is that the government must have some knowledge of present conditions and possible trends. In other words, for a problem solver in government to identify a discrepancy, that person must be aware not only of the government's goals but also of the existing or emerging conditions that seem likely to affect those goals. Such intelligence about the environment, and the interpretation of what effect it may have on the government's goals, need not necessarily be accurate to generate action. The foreign policy literature as well as research on other kinds of problem solving contain numerous illustrations and evidence of misperception and erroneous estimates of cause and effect.[1] However, accuracy in the interpretation of the environment and of changes within it is essential for effective responses.

A fourth aspect of the term problem involves the concept of discrepancy. Often one thinks of discrepancies that result from negative circumstances such as punishment or threats of punishment. Potential opportunities, which are positive circumstances, can also produce a discrepancy and, hence, a problem. Suppose the presence of an American military base in a foreign country is obstructing the goal of increasing popular support for the United States within the country. If changing world conditions and improved military technology substantially reduce the importance of the base to the United States, the opportunity exists for moving toward the U.S. goal of improving its image with the foreign public. Unless a given development will transpire automatically without any government action, it remains only a potential opportunity. Recognizing a potential opportunity and the need for action to bring about its realization creates a discrepancy and a problem for a government in much the same way as a threat. Moreover, failure to realize the opportunity becomes a deprivation.

Problem Recognition

An individual with cancer may ultimately die from it if not successfully treated. Until the individual's condition is detected, however, the cancer is not a recognized problem; an undetected disease is not a matter for concern or action, and hence no discrepancy exists between the individual's preferred state of health and present health. An equivalent situation can occur for governments. The requirement that a policymaker be aware of a discrepancy between a preferred and an existing condition introduces another basic concept in need of specification—problem recognition. The human characteristic of selective attention and perception is well established (e.g., Tajfel, 1969; Tagiuri, 1969). Both individuals and organizations normally operate in environments so rich in stimuli that they cannot possibly attend to all of them, so they systematically screen out many signals—perhaps most—and select only a few to which they give conscious attention. Recognition of relevant stimuli is that first analytical step necessary for coping with a problem.

For any problem-solving entity—whether an individual, a nation, or a civilization—the failure to recognize a major problem in time could mean severe deprivation and even destruction. In the early post–World War II years some in U.S. government believed that the Soviet Union posed a deadly military threat to our European and Asian allies and ultimately to America. They feared that the American democracy, lacking a strong tradition of a large and expensive peacetime military establishment, would fail to take adequate precautions and would neglect to respond to the problem in time. Debates within the government over the Marshall Plan, the Truman Doctrine, and NSC-68 (which, during the Truman administration, outlined a strategy for implementing the containment foreign policy) reflected the profound concern on the part of these individuals and their efforts to mobilize the government and society to respond to the alleged threat.[2]

More recently others have examined with alarm the vast U.S. military establishment and its theoretical justification (particularly the doctrine of strategic nuclear deterrence) and have argued that we have generated a problem of awesome proportions that could destroy civilization. For example, Jonathan Schell (1982:217) contends:

> Now deterrence, having rationalized the construction of the [nuclear military] machine, weds us to it, and, at best, offers us, if we are lucky, a slightly extended term of residence on earth before the inevitable human or mechanical mistake occurs and we are annihilated.

Both parties—those individuals and groups who either advocate or decry a certain course of action—fear that the government will fail to recognize the problems and take corrective measures in time.

For organizations, problem recognition demands more coordination than for individuals. The individual has the capacity for both problem recognition and problem coping, although the latter may be inadequate under some circumstances. By contrast, the specialization and division of labor in large organizations or in a set of organizations (such as those that normally deal with foreign affairs) separate the functions of problem recognition from those of decision and policy implementation. It is the political officer in an embassy, the military assistance officer in the field, the intelligence analyst, or the arms-control negotiator who is often the first member of the government to become aware of a problem. In most cases, however, such an official will not have the authority to resolve the problem and must report to superiors in the organization.

Studies of foreign policy are full of problems identified at the periphery of an organization only to be lost, discounted, or simply set aside until later.[3] From the perspective of problem solving, organizational problem recognition occurs only when awareness of the problem reaches those within the organization with sufficient authority to decide whether any action is appropriate and, if so, to implement the policy selected.

Problem Definition

Analytically it is useful to distinguish problem recognition from problem definition. Problem definition means the interpretation of a problem by policymakers. Snyder, Bruck, and Sapin (1962) have referred to this as the "definition of the situation." In the practical world, it seems clear that an interpretation must be at least tentatively made at the time a problem is recognized. Thus, the question might arise as to why definition should be analytically separated from recognition. At least two reasons can be offered. First, to interpret a problem usually requires attributing cause and effect. This becomes a precondition for prescribing a means of coping with the problem. What is interpreted as the source or cause of the problem? God? Nature? An enemy nation? What is the consequence or effect? Death? Flood? Aggression? At the core of many organizations is a capability designed to deal with problems presumed to have a certain cause-and-effect combination. Just as the Red Cross may be able to deal with problems that seem to be caused by the natural disasters that effect populations in a given area, so the Agency for International Development may be able to address problems associated with certain stages of economic development.

A second difference between problem recognition and problem definition is that the former tends to be constant whereas the latter—the meaning attached to a problem (e.g., the definition)—is dynamic. It can change dramatically across a period of months, weeks, days, or even hours. Such change in the definition of a problem can result either because the actual problem is evolving or because the policymakers' perceptions of the problem are changing.

We know that the same problem may be defined differently by different individuals, organizations, and nations. The matter of a shared definition of a problem is particularly acute in foreign affairs because of cross-cultural differences, governmental motivations for keeping signals ambiguous or deceptive, and conflicting messages sent from different parts of one government to another (e.g., Jervis, 1976). For example, what meaning should the United States attach to the discovery that the Soviet Union is enlarging certain intercontinental ballistic missile (ICBM) silos? Is the move simply the expression of a long-standing cultural need to build ever-larger weapons systems? Or is it a provocative attempt to create a first-strike capability by deploying larger missiles capable of destroying American land-based missiles?

Not only must one contend with multiple interpretations by different individuals, agencies, and governments, but the same group's definition of the problem may vary through time. Paige (1968) illustrates the rapidity with which the interpretation of a problem can undergo change, in his study of the Truman administration's decision to enter the Korean War. At first, the president and his advisers believed the South Koreans could stop the invasion by themselves. Within less than a week, their interpretation of the Korean situation with regard to the expected effect had changed substantially, and American ground forces were committed. In contrast to the Korean example, however, problems are sometimes redefined out of existence. For example, the American concern in the 1970s over the need for alternative sources of energy virtually disappeared in the early 1980s after the Reagan administration concluded that the problem should be handled by the private sector. No element of the private sector found the development of new energy sources to be economically competitive with existing ones. Without government or private-sector research and development of alternative energy sources, the problem disappeared from the national agenda—at least for the time being.

Attention has been devoted to definitions and their implications. The major task of foreign policy organizations is to deal with problems—that is, discrepancies between preferred and actual, or expected, conditions. Monitoring the external environment for potential foreign policy problems also requires consideration of the many tasks associated with the concepts of problem recognition (perception by those capable of action that a discrepancy exists) and definition (assigning meaning with respect to cause and expected effect). Further insights about organizations intended to operate as problem solvers can be gained by examining some of their basic characteristics or qualities and combining them with the ideas associated with the problem concept.

ORGANIZATIONAL QUALITIES

If most foreign policy officials spend much of their careers working in governmental organizations, it is not surprising that the qualities of those organizations can influence what problems are recognized and how they are defined. That is both good news and bad. When compared to individuals working alone or in small groups, those in large organizations are potentially better able to *recognize* a problem, even though more coordination is required. Because of hierarchical structure and competing interests in an organization, however, bureaucracies may have greater difficulties than isolated individuals in *defining* a foreign policy problem. Furthermore, even though an organization should have the necessary human skills and technology for problem recognition, it can fail to do so if the problem is extremely unusual or if its effective treatment requires a radically different approach from those used previously. These strengths and weaknesses become more evident when one examines some particular qualities of governmental organizations.

Organizational Restructuring and Personnel Changes

Problems can emerge from perceived changes in the foreign environment or from internal restructuring within the foreign policy machinery of the government. Restructuring means the new interpretation of existing information through reassessments, often caused by the shift of organizational personnel or changes in organizational mission and operation. As a result of new assignments, people who hold different interpretations of the same available information may suddenly have new power to enable them to shape government action. Not only do people's positions change, but so do those of organizations. Technology, budget shifts, or revised organizational mandates can alter organizations and affect how their members view the world.

In the early years after the National Security Council was established in 1947, the assistant to the president for national security and his staff remained limited to basic functions of coordination and record keeping. Over time, the responsibilities of that presidential adviser and his staff grew, so that when Henry Kissinger held the position, it was he, not the secretary of state, who conducted secret negotiations with China to explore reestablishing relations with that country. As was noted at the outset of this essay, in the Reagan administration the NSC staff conducted critical overseas operations in Iran and elsewhere. For better or worse, such changes in the structure of organizations are inevitable. When the United States assigned the Navy responsibility for operating submarines armed with nuclear ballistic missiles capable of traveling many thousands of miles, the mission of that armed service expanded. Not only did the new mission change the Navy's view of world problems, but it led inevitably to strains between the Navy and the Air Force, and between those in the Navy committed to its traditional missions and those charged with its new responsibilities.

Of course, American foreign policy personnel changes can be most dramatic following the election of a new president who makes hundreds of new appointments. The shift can be quite significant when the movement is between administrations with substantially different political outlooks. It could be argued that the actual foreign policy environment of the United States changed only slightly between the last months of the Carter administration and the first months of the Reagan administration, but the perception of problems and the perceived best means of treating them changed substantially. Everything from human rights to the basing of the MX missile was reinterpreted by the incoming Reagan appointees.

The general conclusion is that the more a foreign policy organization reassigns personnel—particularly across hierarchical levels of authority or through the recruitment of new personnel into the organization—the more likely are new problems to be recognized or old ones to be redefined. There is, however, an important exception. While the new personnel are learning the office routines and the information retrieval system as well as the substance of an unfamiliar foreign policy area, they may miss information or be less able to piece it together than would an "old hand." The subtle shift in a trend or a small change in a foreign position might be more likely to alert the more experienced person that a problem is developing. Thus, organizational restructuring can have short-run liabilities arising from a loss of problem recognition. A president who must depend on organizations undergoing major personnel changes may suffer the consequences. Many observers have noted that the attempted invasion of Cuba at the Bay of Pigs in 1961 was approved and implemented by foreign policy advisers who all had just begun learning their new jobs when the Kennedy administration took office that year.

Selective and Differential Search

The other way policy problems emerge is through changes in the organization's external environment. Foreign policy organizations must establish search routines to discover any such possible changes. Organizations by their nature must develop specialization and role differentiation. Specialists establish routines or standard operating procedures by which they search or monitor their assigned domains. For example, in the Department of State, as in most other foreign policy agencies, specialization involves grouping personnel into a mix of geographical and functional categories for defining search capabilities. Special facilities can be developed for monitoring particular types of situations (e.g., the Crisis Communication Center, the Berlin Task Force) and procedures for transmitting information can be made systematic (e.g., under specified conditions cables of only a certain priority are to be transmitted; or instructions are given the watch officer to awaken key individuals during the night if certain occurrences transpire).

A difficulty arises because search routines, decision rules, and standard operating procedures by definition focus the search for potential foreign policy problems on some cues or particular kinds of signals, but not on others. The unavoidable question thus becomes: What about critical problems that do not have the characteristics established by the specialized search routines? Searching for the unexpected will always pose major challenges to foreign policy organizations, but they can at least avoid certain kinds of common biases. Pool and Kessler (1969:669–670) provide a convenient list of selective attention patterns applicable to bureaucratic specialists as well as isolated individuals:

1. People pay more attention to information that deals with them.
2. People pay less attention to facts that contradict their views.
3. People pay more attention to information from trusted, liked sources.
4. People pay more attention to information that they will have to act on or discuss, because of the attention by others.
5. People pay more attention to information bearing on actions they have already taken—i.e., action creates commitment.[4]

Consider the implications of item 3. Political officers in an American embassy may find it much easier to maintain contact with leaders in that country who are friendly to the United States (and perhaps even speak English). But relying primarily on such sources can seriously bias their understanding of what is taking place. Knowledge of this natural tendency that most of us have can be used to limit the effects of selective attention, but organizational officials must appreciate the possibility and be vigilant against its effects. This does not always happen.

Internal Communication

Another consequence of organizational role specialization and task differentiation is the separation of the individuals and units engaged in search and intelligence activities from those who ultimately make a decision as to whether action should be taken on a particular problem. If the internal communication system between the initial perceiver of a problem and the individual with authority fails for any reason, then the organization's behavior will not reflect the discovery. In a meaningful sense the organization can be said not to have recognized the problem at all. Therefore, a critical feature of any organization is the speed and accuracy of its internal communication system. But communication among parts of an organization can be inadequate for numerous reasons. The need for security and protection of sensitive information can obstruct the flow of information, as can struggles for bureaucratic power—in which the old adage that "knowledge is power" applies. If the foreign policy problem does not fit squarely within the domain of a single organizational unit, but instead cuts across multiple units, then communication can be slowed (particularly if the concerned units are unaccustomed to dealing with one another). Although modern communications technology can sometimes be used to ease the problem, it can occasionally give the illusion of information exchange when in fact little is occurring. These issues concern the failure to provide information when and where it is needed, but there is also the problem of too much information on too many problems, resulting in overload.

Problem Load

The failure of problem recognition can result not only from weaknesses in the internal communication system of foreign policy organizations, but also because of the heavy decision load on the middle and higher political levels of the organization. Study after study (e.g., Kissinger, 1966; Hoffmann, 1968) has noted the decision overload on foreign policy makers at this level of government. It is reasonable to speculate that the broader the base of an organization's authority structure, and the greater the delegation of authority, the more likely are external problems to be recognized, provided internal communication is well maintained. The difficulty in such a configuration arises when the collected information and analysis must be passed up through the organization, and becomes part of the load on a small number of top-level officials.

A word of caution is required about one of the consequences of overloading the problem-management process. In order to capture a position on the overcrowded agenda of senior policymakers, earnest subordinates may attempt to mobilize support from other parts of the government, the media, the public, and even from foreign nations. In the process of creating such support, the characterization of the problem may become distorted; frequently, the future consequences of failing to deal with the issue are exaggerated to promote attention. This problem deserves separate consideration, not as a matter of inadequate information or communication overload, but instead as illustrative of information distortion.

Responsiveness to Public Pressure

Why do public campaigns to mobilize support to deal with a problem lead to distortion in the perception of the problem? Two major reasons can be advanced. First, in order to motivate people to act it is necessary to persuade them that their vital interests are affected. To shape a foreign policy issue into an effective appeal for public support may require associating the immediate issue with a greater substantial danger—for example, the threat of war, severe economic loss, militant Communism, increased taxes, or the possibility of a military draft. In the process of linking the issue to a widely perceived concern, the definition of the problem may become distorted. Second, to reach millions of people requires the use of the media—especially radio and television. Because new stories in the media must be short and easily grasped, mass media can serve as another force acting to simplify and exaggerate aspects of an issue. The result is another constraint on the ability of the government to define the problem accurately. And public involvement may actually decrease the likelihood that quick agreement can be reached on any definition of a problem.

Foreign policy bureaucracies, or groups within them, search for and sustain public constituencies that support their general worldview and specific interpretation of policy problems. These supporters can include friendly media representatives, lobby and interest groups, and even foreign governments. When the Congress of the United States restricted military assistance to the *contras* fighting the government forces of Nicaragua, members of the NSC staff sought financial support from private groups and friendly foreign governments. One danger of such practices is the possibility of commitments and future obligations incurred in exchange for such support, as well as the tendency to shape the problem in a way most congenial to those from whom support is sought.

Organizational Goals

At the beginning of this essay, a problem was described as involving goals or preferred conditions. Goals are both formal and informal, and this brings us to a final organizational characteristic. The literature on bureaucratic organizations has made the point repeatedly that organizations and bureaus within organizations often have different missions and goals. If individuals see their promotions and careers as dependent on how well they succeed in their particular bureau or organization, then it will be natural for them to promote the goals of their bureaucratic units. The result is that individuals in different bureaucracies will have a built-in disposition to interpret problems in terms of their organization's goals and mission.

This process is at the heart of bureaucratic politics. It also makes the task of reaching consensus within the government on goals and on their relative priorities difficult unless other factors intervene (e.g., a strongly expressed presidential preference). To facilitate agreement, goals and objectives may be poorly specified and actual contradictions among them may be ignored. Furthermore, once consensus on goals and the related definition of a problem has been reached within an organization, inertia sets in and works against any revision of definition that may become necessary. The evolution of a problem's definition thus tends to be more gradual for bureaucratic organizations than for individuals; exceptions might arise, however, when the top of an organization changes suddenly, when a new administration comes to power, or when a coalition whose interpretation of a problem had prevailed collapses.

IMPLICATIONS OF A SHIFT IN THE ARRAY OF PROBLEMS

In this final section we will examine how the characteristics of American bureaucratic organizations could prove to be constraints in recognizing and defining the foreign policy problems of the 1990s. Basic to the discussion is the contention that the types of major foreign affairs problems in need of attention are undergoing a profound change.

Post–Cold War Problems

For much of the period since the end of World War II, most American organizations concerned with monitoring foreign affairs problems were influenced greatly by the Cold War. The protracted and intense antagonism between the United States and the Soviet Union shaped the problems that were recognized and the ways in which they were defined. Even issues that in other periods might have been interpreted very differently were defined as Cold War problems—such as the end of colonialism, the emergence of nationalistic forces and the efforts at economic development in the Third World, and national innovations in science and technology.

Of course not every problem became an adjunct of the Cold War, but the budgets of major agencies, the time allocations of presidents and other officials, and the foreign policy debates in Congress and the media point to the prominence of the Cold War framework in American foreign policy problem recognition and definition.

The political and military problems stemming from the conflict between the Communist and Western powers certainly have not disappeared. In fact some of these problems may even become more acute in the future. There could be an accelerated tendency on the part of the USSR to engage in conflicts that are far removed from its borders. The Soviets may be less prepared than in the Cuban missile crisis of 1962 to make concessions to avert a nuclear confrontation. Perhaps the most troubling aspect for the United States is its loss of clear superiority, relative to the Soviet Union, in many areas of military technology and nuclear forces. For most of the Cold War period, America enjoyed unquestioned predominance, at least with respect to nuclear weapons and military technology. However, with Soviet military advances and with changes in destructive capabilities that have robbed the concept of nuclear superiority of useful meaning, a fundamental transformation has occurred. Even if this loss of clear Western military superiority in certain areas were not to create problems, and even if the Soviets were to exercise restraint, the American coalitions that developed as a result of the Cold War might continue to interpret problems in the framework of the Cold War. Such problem definitions would conform to needs and experiences of many individuals and groups. Unfortunately the developments in much of the 1980s suggest a far more ambiguous record of Soviet behavior; the inclination to continue interpreting many problems in the Cold War framework therefore remains strong.

Having noted this continuing Cold War legacy, we must nevertheless recognize that many individuals inside and outside the American foreign policy community are identifying and debating problems that cannot be understood by reference to Cold War antagonisms. Even if problems with the Soviet Union continue to be of major importance to the United States, they may exclusively dominate our foreign policy agenda only if we ignore other pressing and urgent challenges. Consider again the problem with which this essay began. The Reagan administration's struggle to determine the future of U.S. relations with Iran and to shape a strategy for gaining the release of American hostages does not fit easily into a Cold War perspective. The government of Iran, rooted in fundamental concepts of Islam, holds both the United States and the Soviet Union in contempt. And the captors of American hostages in Lebanon are nonstate actors whose motivations arise from issues in the Middle East, not Communism.

Some observers warn of emerging problems that seem even more remote from the traditional political-military issues of the Cold War. A study done for the Commission on the Organization of the Government for the Conduct of Foreign Policy (known for short as the Murphy Commission) identified eight global problem areas that could have major adverse effects on the United States and the rest of the world after the year 2000 if not effectively handled before then. These problems, which were drawn exclusively from the area of global environmental and resource interdependence, were ocean pollution, atmospheric pollution, weather modification, resource monitoring satellites, communications-satellite jurisdiction, nuclear reactors, food, and population (Keohane and Nye, 1975). Given the environmental orientation of this list, it is perhaps understandable that the entire range of economic problems was excluded. However, economic problems—ranging from trade deficits and widespread inflation to the calls for a new international economic order—illustrate the emergence of acute foreign policy problems that seem to have little or no direct relationship to the Cold War.

From a somewhat different perspective, Mesarovic and Pestel (1974) have noted a set of unprecedented crises emerging in population, energy, raw materials, and pollution that are a result of undifferentiated growth and of rapidly increasing interdependence. From yet another perspective, the shaping of the world economy in the next quarter of a century constitutes "the greatest challenge to industrial civilization since it began to take shape two centuries ago" (Rostow, 1978).

Only time will tell whether Keohane and Nye (1975), Mesarovic and Pestel (1974), Rostow (1978), or other forecasters (e.g., Platt, 1969; Schell, 1982) have enumerated accurately the most demanding set of foreign policy problems of the future. Because we are interested in the recognition and definition of new international challenges, the particular problems identified by various individuals are less important to us than the apparent shift away from what appear to be Cold War–type problems. If there are likely to be significantly different types of problems threatening the well-being of the United States in the 1990s, how will situational characteristics and organizational properties influence their successful recognition and definition?

Interaction of Situational and Organizational Properties

How well foreign policy organizations meet future challenges depends not only on the organizational qualities discussed above but also on the nature of the situations they encounter. Do they differ in any important respects from the situations foreign policy organizations have been addressing for more than four decades? In considering such characteristics of situations as threats, opportunities, complexity, awareness, and decision time, the impression emerges that many future situations could be of a different nature from those of the past.

With respect to future threats, they may be directed not only (through war) at physical survival, but at a variety of social, political, and economic institutions, and even at ecological systems as well. Both threats and opportunities may well emerge from sources other than those with which we have grown accustomed to dealing. They may involve not only familiar antagonists, but also nonstate actors—such as terrorists, multinational corporations, nonterritorial nations—and, in general, arise from human interaction with nature.

Complexity can be interpreted as an interaction betwen the multiplicity of interacting demands created by a problem and the capabilities of the problem solvers. The problem side of this equation might be expected to become more complex in several respects. First, the growth in interdependence between international social and economic systems may complicate attempts at resolution by requiring coordination of a number of politically separate units inside and outside the United States. Those units outside the United States may not be particularly susceptible to American governmental influences. Interdependence may increase the likelihood that "solutions" to problems have more unanticipated secondary and tertiary effects that trigger new problems or confound the treatment of the original one. What may confuse detection of such problems is a breakdown of any clear idea about cause and effect. A second source of complexity may result from an increased tendency for many large, demanding problems to arise simultaneously. Platt (1969:1116) refers to this difficulty when he notes: "What finally makes all of our crises more dangerous is that they are now coming on top of each other." Our concentration on one may deflect attention from the presence of others.

Awareness of problems also affects the other side of the complexity equation—the ability of foreign policy agencies to cope with these problems. For example, as dangerous as the repeated crises over West Berlin were, the United States in time gained familiarity with some recurrent features of the problem and characteristics of the adversary. This general awareness might not have prevented a tactical surprise in any particular crisis, but it made it easier for American policymakers to recognize the problem and define it within the context of the Cold War whenever a crisis suddenly arose. One of the difficulties facing policymakers in an era of emerging new foreign policy problems could be the absence of familiarity with these problems and with their associated indicators and danger signs.

Many of the problems of the Cold War—such as in the Cuban missile crisis or the invasion of South Korea—emerged as crises in which decision time was extremely short. Although one can envision some future nuclear confrontation in which decision time is reduced to something less than the thirty minutes required for ICBMs to reach their targets, the Cold War problems of the past may have established benchmarks for acutely short decision times that are unlikely to be surpassed in the vast majority of new challenges. In fact, some of the emerging problems could be just the reverse, in that they may have long lead times before they become a major danger (an example would be the problem of ocean pollution). However, the time during which action must be initiated to avert or correct a dangerous problem may far precede the time when the full danger is actually experienced.[5]

The previous paragraphs have tried to illustrate the possible nature of situational characteristics of problems different from those that have dominated American attention during the Cold War. Assuming that such different types of problems become more important for American foreign policy, how would the organizational characteristics identified previously affect recognition and identification of these new problems?

Perhaps the most critical organizational feature concerns the selective search processes of organizations. We have suggested that governmental organizations, just as individuals, must be selective in the domains they search. The Cold War provided a framework that for more than forty years served as a structure indicating to the U.S. government's foreign policy organizations what situations to monitor and what meaning to attach to problems that arose. These highly established search routines and interpretative processes may now become increasingly dysfunctional, not directing monitoring activities to situations that could pose new kinds of dangers or opportunities, or imposing a inappropriate Cold War definition on a detected problem.

The organizational restructuring that regularly marks foreign policy agencies as new people assume key positions could aid in more rapidly eroding the Cold War framework. A darker side, however, also must be considered. If more of the foreign policy problems of the future demand attention far ahead of a crisis to avoid severe adverse effects, no leadership that expects to remain in power only a few years may find it desirable or politically feasible to attend to them. The frequent turnover of political leadership also may make it more difficult to construct coalitions with a shared definition of the problem.

Many agencies of the U.S. government participate in foreign policy decisions, but the Cold War gave certain agencies dominance—including the State and Defense Departments, the Joint Chiefs of Staff, the CIA, the Agency for International Development and its precursors, and, increasingly, the National Security Council staff. Established channels of communication, clearance processes, and interagency working groups have gradually evolved. Faced with different types of problems the internal channels of communication among these agencies may not be the most appropriate ones, nor may the agencies themselves. Indeed, there may be no present agency charged with monitoring for a given set of future problems. Even if an agency does engage in such monitoring, it may be unclear who has responsibility for assessing and communicating whether or not a problem merits further attention on any agency's agenda. Internal communications may need major revision.

What about problem overload? Any available organizational slack could be more than consumed in one of several ways. If problems are unfamiliar or seemingly more complex, it may take longer to agree on their definition and to devise an acceptable response; other problems would have to be placed "on hold." Furthermore, if Platt (1969) is correct, the emerging challenge is not simply one of different kinds of problems but of more problems occurring concurrently.

Coping with a certain type of problem in foreign affairs has become part of the mission or goals of particular foreign policy organizations. The difficulty arises when no agency regards a certain problem as falling within the definition of its primary mission or goals. The real possibility exists that the present array of organizational goals of the various American foreign policy bureaucracies are such that any meaningful attention to some potential problems of the future is, in effect, unlikely.

CONCLUSIONS

The Iran-*contra* affair discussed at the opening of this essay provides the basis for several concluding observations. First, the problem may represent a kind of transition case from the classical political-military confrontations of the Cold War to those of a different nature which the United States may face increasingly in the future. In certain respects some of the old, familiar features were present, particularly with respect to the Central American dimension of the issue, in which opposing military forces received backing from their respective superpower. In other ways, as has been noted, the problem appears different. Some actors were not national governments (e.g., the groups in Lebanon holding American hostages); some actors are not allied with either side in the Cold War (e.g., Iran); and repeatedly the outcomes were dependent on third parties with whom the United States has complex, interdependent relationships (e.g., Israel, Costa Rica, Honduras). Moreover, the dynamics of the case involve some issues that have little to do directly with Soviet-American rivalry (e.g., the Iran-Iraq War, the Palestinian desire for a homeland).

Second, the episode dramatically illustrates what can happen to problem definition when the government cannot agree on goals and objectives. Releasing the hostages, aiding the *contras,* and improving relations with Iran became competing objectives. The difficulty was complicated by disagreement on cause and effect. (For example, could Iran cause the hostages to be released?)

Third, the case highlights the dependent relationship between the president and the bureaucracies. The Tower Commission (Tower, Muskie, and Scowcroft, 1987:89) begins its recommendations by noting the source of foreign policy innovation and the source of resistance to change:

> The policy innovation and creativity of the President encounters a natural resistance from the executing departments. . . . Circumventing the departments, perhaps by using the National Security Advisor or the NSC Staff to execute policy, robs the President of the experience and capacity resident in the departments. The President must act largely through them, but the agency heads must ensure that they execute the President's policies in an expeditious and effective manner.

Here we see in stark terms the dilemma this essay explores. Bureaucracies can resist change, and can fail to see new problems, and can fail to implement policy effectively for the reasons that have been reviewed. But if in frustration a president tends to ignore them and conduct policy without their assistance, he can make serious errors.

It can be argued that the picture sketched in this essay exaggerates the constraints and difficulties in problem management and response in foreign policymaking. The author hopes so, but perhaps more than hope is needed to make certain that the interaction of new situations and old organizational routines does not obstruct the recognition and definition of problems that need to get on the American national agenda as well as on the agenda of other governments and world actors. The avoidance of these pitfalls in part entails modifying organizational capabilities to meet the requirements of foreign policy in the 1990s and beyond.

Some might be tempted initially to regard substitution or replacement as the approach. The government, it could be argued, should shift from an East-West framework to one focused on North-South conflicts; from agencies concerned with military capability to those working on economic capability; from crisis management to long-range planning. All indications are that such attempts to "redistribute" responses would be most inadequate and inappropriate. Few careful observers would claim that many of the older type of problems have been resolved or have faded away. The U.S. government must still attend to such problems. Even though various sources seek to dramatize presently emerging issues, relatively few responsible individuals or groups claim to have a clear and certain vision of what the total array of future foreign policy problems will be. Thus, a greater sensitivity to the unusual in international affairs and in the international environment appears to be a watchword for monitoring, rather than locking on a given alternative domain of new problems.

Going beyond the heightened attention to various forms of activity, those responsible for foreign policy—and the conduct of government generally—may need to invest more in the exploration of new forms of social organization for collective problem recognition and management. McNeill (1963) argues that civilizations began to emerge when people developed primitive administrative and bureaucratic skills. If we are to avert an unpleasant future, we should devote significantly more resources to the design of new forms of collective problem recognition and management.

NOTES

1. For a social psychological study of the mistaken belief in events and their anticipated effect, see Festinger, Riecken, and Schachter (1956). In organizational theory, Thompson (1967) has defined activities done on the basis of collective beliefs about cause and effect relationships as an organization's core technology—regardless of whether the organization's collective beliefs are correct or not. Misperception in international politics has been a major concern of Jervis (1976).

2. The task of mobilizing support is well documented in the case of the Marshall Plan by Jones (1955), for the Truman Doctrine by Gaddis (1972), and for NSC-68 by Hammond (1962).

3. This difficulty in problem recognition is illustrated by the "loss" in the system of cues that might have alerted U.S. policymakers to the Pearl Harbor attack (see Wohlstetter, 1962) and by the failure to consider intelligence about the location of German *Panzer* divisions prior to the beginning of Operation Market-Garden in 1944 (see Ryan, 1974).

4. It is possible to construct some plausible organizational parallels to the Pool and Kessler (1969) statements about selective perception of individuals. Consider these examples: (a) an organization pays more attention to information pertaining to itself or its mission; (b) an organization pays less attention to—or seeks to deny or to alter—information that contradicts its objectives or that challenges its prior behavior.

5. See Keohane and Nye (1975) for a discussion of problems they believe need prompt attention if adverse effects are to be avoided sometime between 2001 and 2020.

REFERENCES

Festinger, Leon, Riecken, Henry W., and Schachter, Stanley (1956). *When Prophecy Fails.* Minneapolis: University of Minnesota Press.

Gaddis, John Lewis (1972). *The United States and the Origins of the Cold War.* New York: Columbia University Press.

Hammond, Paul Y. (1962). "NSC-68: Prologue to Rearmament." Pp. 267–378 in W. R. Schilling, Paul Y. Hammond, and Glenn H. Snyder, *Strategy, Politics, and Defense Budgets.* New York: Columbia University Press.

Hermann, Charles F. (1979). "Why New Foreign Policy Challenges Might Not be Met." Pp. 269–292 in Charles W. Kegley, Jr., and Pat McGowan (eds.), *Challenges to America.* Beverly Hills, Calif.: Sage.

Hoffmann, Stanley (1968). *Gulliver's Troubles, or the Setting of American Foreign Policy.* New York: McGraw-Hill.

Jervis, Robert (1976). *Perception and Misperception in International Politics.* Princeton, N.J.: Princeton University Press.

Jones, Joseph N. (1955). *The Fifteen Weeks.* New York: Harcourt, Brace and World.

Keohane, Robert O., and Nye, Joseph S. (1975). "Organizing for Global Environmental and Resource Interdependence." Pp. 43–64 in *Appendices for Commission on the Organization of the Government for the Conduct of Foreign Policy,* Vol. 1, Appendix B. Washington, D.C.: U.S. Government Printing Office.

Kissinger, Henry A. (1966). "Domestic Structure and Foreign Policy," *Daedalus,* 95 (2):503–529.

McNeill, William (1963). *The Rise of the West.* New York: Mentor.

Mesarovic, Mihajlo, and Pestel, Eduard (1974). *Mankind at the Turning Point.* New York: Dutton.
Ogburn, Charlton (1961). "The Flow of Policy-Making in the Department of State." Pp. 229–244 in James N. Rosenau (ed.), *International Politics and Foreign Policy.* First edition. New York: Free Press.
Paige, Glenn D. (1968). *The Korean Decision.* New York: Free Press.
Platt, John (1969). "What We Must Do." *Science,* 166 (November 28):1115–1120.
Pool, Ithiel de Sola, and Kessler, Allen (1969). "The Kaiser, the Tsar and the Computer." Pp. 664–678 in James N. Rosenau (ed.), *International Politics and Foreign Policy.* Second edition. New York: Free Press.
Rostow, Walt W. (1978). *Getting From Here to There.* New York: McGraw-Hill.
Ryan, Cornelius (1974). *A Bridge Too Far.* New York: Simon and Schuster.
Schell, Jonathan (1982). *The Fate of the Earth.* New York: Knopf.
Snyder, Richard C., Bruck, H. W., and Sapin, Burton (1962). *Foreign Policy Decision-Making.* New York: Free Press.
Tagiuri, Renato (1969). "Person Perception." Pp. 395–449 in Gardner Lindzey and Elliot Aronson (eds.), *Handbook of Social Psychology,* Vol. 3. Reading, Mass.: Addison-Wesley.
Tajfel, Henri (1969). "Social and Cultural Factors in Perception." Pp. 305–394 in Gardner Lindzey and Elliot Aronson (eds.), *Handbook of Social Psychology,* Vol. 3. Reading, Mass.: Addison-Wesley.
Thompson, James (1967). *Organizations in Action.* New York: McGraw-Hill.
Tower, John, Muskie, Edmund, and Scowcroft, Brent (1987). *The Tower Commission.* New York: Bantam/Times Book.
Wohlstetter, Roberta (1962). *Pearl Harbor: Warning and Decision.* Stanford, Calif.: Stanford University Press.

20. THE ROLE OF LEADERS AND LEADERSHIP IN THE MAKING OF AMERICAN FOREIGN POLICY

Margaret G. Hermann

When we think about the leaders who have helped shape American foreign policy in the twentieth century, names like Woodrow Wilson, Harry Truman, Franklin Roosevelt, Henry Kissinger, John Foster Dulles, Cyrus Vance, J. William Fulbright, Richard Helms, Clark Clifford, Douglas MacArthur, Robert McNamara, and George Marshall come to mind. Among these people are presidents, secretaries of state and defense, directors of the CIA, presidential advisers, senators, and generals. All were part of the foreign policy machinery of the United States; all led groups and organizations that have an input into American foreign policy decisions. Why do we remember these leaders? What is it about the quality of their leadership and their personalities that links their names to American foreign policy? In this chapter we will explore the aspects of leadership that are likely to influence the way foreign policy is made and the resulting policy itself. We will discover what it is about our political leaders we need to learn to determine how they will affect American foreign policy.

THE LEADERSHIP DILEMMA

Let us consider four images of leadership. The first might be called the "pied piper of Hamelin" image. Like the pied piper who led the rats out of Hamelin, this type of leader sets goals and directions for his followers and with promises charms them into following him. The leader is in charge of what happens and how it happens.

A second image is that of the leader as salesperson. Leadership involves being sensitive to what people want and offering to help them get it. Responsiveness to people's needs and desires is important, as is being able to persuade people that you can help them. As Harry Truman (see Neustadt, 1960:10) noted: "The principal power that the President has is to bring people in and try to persuade them to do what they ought to do without persuasion."

A third image focuses on the leader as a puppet. In this image of leadership, the leader is given direction and strength by his followers, who pull the strings and make him move. The leader is the agent of the group, reflecting the goals of the group and working in its behalf.

The fire-fighting view of leadership provides a fourth image. In this image leadership occurs in response to what is happening in the environment. The environment provides demands, constraints, and choices to which the leader must react.

The dilemma of American leadership today is that we expect our political leaders to exhibit all four of these images. We want strong leaders who have vision but who at the same time are responsive to our wishes, able to persuade us of their convictions, and be able to deal with the problems facing the country. As Cronin (1980:3–22) has observed about the presidency, we want a decent and just leader who is also decisive and guileful, a leader with programmatic ideas who is also pragmatic, an innovative and inventive leader who is also responsive to the majority's wishes, an open and sharing leader who is also courageous and independent, as well as a symbolic, ceremonial leader who is also a tough manager. There is little recognition of the contradictions inherent in our expectations and images. In effect, we seek superheroes.

How can we make our expectations more realistic? One way is to consider the many different types of political leadership there are. Leadership involves more than one kind of behavior; it is an umbrella concept that has within it a number of different variables. Figure 1 suggests the ingredients in leadership. To understand leadership we need to know something about: (1) the leader's personality and background; (2) what groups and individuals the leader is accountable to (that is, who the leader leads) and what they are like; (3) the nature of the relationship between the leader and those he or she leads; (4) the context or setting in which the leadership is taking place; and (5) what happens when the leader and those led interact in a specific situation. What kind of leadership we have depends on the nature and combination of these five ingredients. As in a recipe for food, these basic ingredients can be combined in different ways to produce a variety of results.

In examining the relationship between leadership and the formulation of American foreign policy, an important initial consideration is who the leaders are we should be studying. The positions that appear to afford their occupants an opportunity to influence American foreign policy and that provide for the exercise of control over others are president, secretary of state, secretary of

Figure 1. The Ingredients of Leadership.

Context or Setting

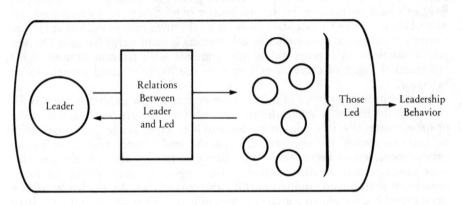

defense, director of the Central Intelligence Agency, presidential adviser for national security affairs (at least since the Kennedy administration), chair of the Joint Chiefs of Staff, and, in some instances, chair of a foreign policy-related congressional committee. As this list suggests, the concept of "leader" is relative, since the president also has authority over the other leaders with the exception of the chairs of congressional committees. With the exception of the latter, these leaders are appointed by the president and are accountable to him. For purposes of the present discussion, however, we will use as examples individuals who have held any of the seven roles listed above.

Having established which leaders can affect American foreign policy, let us examine the various ingredients of leadership, in order to see why certain people have more of an impact on foreign policy than others, and the nature of that leadership.

LEADER CHARACTERISTICS

What is the leader like? Specifically, what characteristics may influence leaders' proposals in the foreign policy arena? A search of writings by students of American foreign policy suggests six kinds of characteristics are important to learn about leaders. We want to know: (1) what their worldview is, (2) what their political style is like, (3) what motivates them to have the position they do, (4) whether they are interested in and have any training in foreign affairs, (5) what the foreign policy climate was like when the leader was starting out his or her political career, and (6) how the leader was socialized into his or her present position. Worldview, political style, and motivation tell us something about the leader's personality; the other characteristics give information about the leader's previous experiences and background.

View of the World

The most direct linkage between what a leader is like and American foreign policy behavior is through the leader's view of the world. View of the world shapes how the leader interprets the international environment and America's place in that environment. It helps the leader chart or map the foreign policy terrain in which the United States is operating, as he or she perceives that terrain to be. A worldview implies certain goals and strategies. For example, Reagan's push to increase the defense budget in his first term in office grew out of his belief that the United States was losing the arms race to the Soviet Union. Carter's belief in the importance of confronting human rights issues led him to urge reductions in foreign aid to governments with flagrant human rights violations. In each of these cases a view of the world affected foreign policy behavior.

Another important piece of information concerns how *important* the world-view is to the leader. Is the leader so persuaded of the particular worldview he or she espouses that it is a dominant force of life, acting as a lens through which all external events are interpreted, or is the leader more responsive to the environment, letting events shape and change certain beliefs? A leader's world-view can have a more direct influence on American foreign policy the more resistant it is to outside influences. Like the crusader of old, the leader with a strong worldview seeks to convince others of his or her position, and is likely to see most international activity as relevant to the cause. Leaders whose world-views are less firmly entrenched are more pragmatic. The nature of the situation will generally determine how firmly—and whether—such leaders press their case. An astute observer of American foreign policy (Stoessinger, 1985) has argued that this is a critical dimension in assessing the effectiveness of those responsible for making American foreign policy in the twentieth century, and that recent American presidents and secretaries of state can be divided into "crusaders" and "pragmatists."

Political Style

A leader's political style also can influence a government's foreign policy. The influence, however, is more indirect than that of worldview. Political style has an effect by shaping how the government responds to foreign policy problems. Political style here refers to the techniques the leader prefers to use in dealing with other governments, that is, the particular activities the leader favors when it comes to interacting with other governments. For example, does the leader, like Kissinger, emphasize personal diplomacy and face-to-face meetings with world leaders? Or, as with Dulles, is the emphasis on political rhetoric and propaganda? Is there a flair for the dramatic like that Nixon showed when he opened relations with China? Is there a willingness to work with leaders of other governments in solving problems, or is the tendency to "go it alone"? Is there an interest, like that Johnson had, in wanting to see information firsthand—to talk, for example, to the ship captains in the Gulf of Tonkin off Vietnam—or is the leader content, as Nixon was, to examine summaries of events based on staff interpretation? Is secrecy essential? Each of these questions focuses on an element of political style.

The style characteristics of a leader can have the effect of limiting the choices of behavior available to those under the leader. Political style limits choice in at least two ways. First, there is a tendency on the part of subordinates, particularly at the highest levels of government, to cater to the stylistic preferences of the leader in order to keep open access to him. Thus, for example, it is said (see Safire, 1982) that because Reagan preferred information presented in a visual format, the bureaucracy geared up to produce material in a movie or television context. Here emphasis is given to one type of material, with its advantages and disadvantages, to the exclusion of other sources of information.

The second way in which political style can limit choice results from what Bennis (1973) calls the *doppelgänger* effect. Political leaders tend to surround themselves with people who are their doubles or doppelgangers—people with similar stylistic preferences or complementary styles. In effect, the leader selects advisers and staff with whom he feels "comfortable" and "compatible." As observed about President Nixon and his special assistant for national security affairs, Henry Kissinger, both acted as if "centralized authority was a prerequisite for flexibility; both men were critical of ad hoc styles of decision making . . . [and both] were distrustful of bureaucracies" (Eldridge, 1976: 20). Through his doubles, the leader's style permeates the bureaucracy.

Motivation for Position

What are the leader's reasons for seeking a leadership position? Among the motives attributed to political leaders are the need for power, a cause (a problem they want to see addressed, a philosophy they want adopted, a crisis), a sense of obligation, the need for approval and esteem from others, the challenge of the position, the need for status and recognition, and the need to compensate for personal problems (see Burns, 1978; Hermann, 1977; Knutson, 1973; Lasswell, 1948). These motives have implications for what political leaders will do. Barber (1965) has found that different kinds of motives lead to different kinds of political behavior. He identified four types of political leaders, based on motivation: the advertiser, spectator, reluctant, and lawmaker. The advertiser is interested in status and recognition and uses the political arena as a forum for self-advancement; the spectator is motivated by the need for approval and becomes a cue-taker and consensus seeker in the political process; the reluctant, drawn into the political arena out of a sense of obligation, becomes involved with moral and ethical issues and matters of principle; and the lawmaker is challenged by the position and becomes actively involved in initiating legislation and solving problems.

Barber (1977, 1983) has classified twentieth century presidents according to these motive patterns: advertisers—Woodrow Wilson, Herbert Hoover, Lyndon Johnson, and Richard Nixon; spectators—William Howard Taft, Warren Harding, and Ronald Reagan; reluctants—Calvin Coolidge and Dwight Eisenhower; and lawmakers—Franklin Roosevelt, Harry Truman, John Kennedy, and Jimmy Carter. Motives suggest what the focus of attention is likely to be in the foreign policy arena. Thus, Walker (1983) has found that these motive patterns relate to different strategies in foreign policy; for example, the advertiser tends to use the bully strategy in dealing with other countries, the spectator appeasement.

Interest and Training in Foreign Affairs

In considerations of foreign policy, ascertaining any leader's interest and training in foreign affairs is critical to knowing how involved they will become in foreign policy issues and the extent of the repertoire of feasible behaviors they will bring to dealing with foreign policy problems. Presidents, in particular, have differed in their interest in foreign policy. Franklin Roosevelt and John Kennedy were so interested in foreign affairs that they became, in effect, their own secretaries of state. Such a president "closely involves himself in major problems, sets high policy standards, intrudes upon routine, and engages heavily in diplomatic negotiations" (Koenig, 1981: 222). Not much will happen in the foreign policy arena that such a president will not try to control. At the other extreme are presidents whose interest in foreign policy issues is not all consuming and who are willing to delegate much of the responsibility to others. Eisenhower and Ford are examples of presidents who appear to have granted much of the authority for foreign policy-making to their secretaries of state, Dulles and Kissinger. Former Senator Fulbright is quoted as saying: "Secretary Dulles seemed at times to be exercising those 'delicate, plenary and exclusive powers' which are supposed to be vested in the President" (Koenig, 1981: 223). Although both Eisenhower and his aides indicated that major decisions were not made without consultation and prior approval, the question arises where policy originated. With the highly interested president, policies and ideas are likely to be generated by his staff, whereas with the less intensely interested president, policies and ideas probably originate outside the White House.

Because intense interest in foreign affairs on the part of the president generally leads to concentration on foreign policy problems, it can have several pitfalls. The first is that foreign problems and policies can become internalized—the leader identifies with the policy and problem to such an extent that they are no longer just issues of American foreign policy but personal concerns. The leader's sense of self becomes tied to the success or failure of personal policies. The leader tries to repeat foreign policy successes but can experience severe stress when policies are failing (Hermann, 1979). Vietnam became such a stressful issue for Johnson; release of hostages became a similar issue for Carter and Reagan. Such stress makes leaders more rigid, less likely to consider the consequences of their actions, more willing to make decisions quickly, more likely to rely on close associates for information and advice, and more likely to see the present in terms of the past (see George, 1980; Hermann, 1979; Janis, 1972). In effect, the leader focuses more on searching for support than on dealing with the situation, thus avoiding facing the full ramifications of the problem.

A second pitfall centers around the president or leader becoming so involved in what is happening that he loses perspective. Information is sought from sources "on the scene" without being filtered or set into context through bureaucratic exchange. Thus, the president may talk with persons involved in what is going on as it is happening, as Lyndon Johnson did with the harried U.S. ambassador to the Dominican Republic whose embassy was under siege, and act on this information. Often the leader's reaction and subsequent actions are more extreme than the situation warrants because he or she gets caught up in the event.

Training in foreign affairs can temper interest in foreign affairs. Training here refers to the amount of time individuals have spent dealing with foreign policy issues and problems in previous jobs before assuming their leadership position. In the latter part of the twentieth century, most American presidents have had little foreign policy experience at the time they assumed office. To compensate for this lack of experience these presidents have tended to choose secretaries of state or national security advisers with previous experience and expertise. Experience provides the leader with an idea of what will and will not work and with what protocol and precedent dictate. With little experience or training in foreign affairs, leaders may be unduly influenced by experts. Moreover, their view of the world and political style are more likely to affect what they propose, since they have little other background on which to rely (see Hermann, 1980).

Examination of the Kennedy presidency offers an example of the effects of lack of experience. With Kennedy we note the difference between his handling of the Bay of Pigs situation in the early months of his administration and the Cuban missile crisis a year later. Accounts of the Bay of Pigs decision (George, 1980; Janis, 1972; Sorensen, 1965) suggest that Kennedy was somewhat overwhelmed by the expert opinion around him; some of the important voices giving him advice, such as CIA Director Allen Dulles, were carryovers from the Eisenhower administration and considered expert on Cuba and Castro. George (1980:211) has commented:

The lessons [Kennedy] and his close associates had drawn from his inept management of the policymaking group in the Bay of Pigs case were quickly put to use in improvising a quite different approach to crisis decisionmaking when they were suddenly confronted in October 1962 by Khrushchev's deployment of missiles into Cuba.

Kennedy understood better in the fall of 1962 than in the spring of 1961 the realities of the Cuban situation and the nature of the personnel in his own administration.

Table 1 suggests how interest and training in foreign affairs interrelate in determining the leader's involvement and focus on foreign policy issues. When interest is low the leader tends to delegate. The choice of who is given authority will depend on the extent of the leader's experience—the leader with more experience will seek out persons with foreign policy outlooks and experiences similar to his own. The leader with less experience will tend to choose those with a reputation in the foreign policy arena, but with little control for similarity of outlook. When the leader's interest is high, he insists on being part of the foreign policy-making process. With training the leader tends to focus on what is happening in the particular situation. The leader with less experience will base his decisions more on his own predilections (views of the world, political style, motives) than on nuances in the situation.

Effects of Political Socialization

American leaders do not come "full-blown from the head of Zeus." In many ways they are the product of their experience and the times in which they live. Stewart (1977) has argued that even birth order helps mold our leaders' political skills. According to Stewart's data, first-born sons and only children who are given authority early over others and generally present a "take charge" or parentlike demeanor are more likely to be elected president during periods in American history of international and domestic crisis when the people want someone to tell them what to do. Franklin Roosevelt, who was an only child, is an example. It is younger sons who have had to learn from early childhood the

Table 1. Effects of Interest and Training in Foreign Affairs

| | | Extent of Interest in Foreign Affairs | |
		Low	High
Extent of Training in Foreign Affairs	Low	Will rely on experts for advice; will probably delegate foreign policymaking to others.	Will want to be involved in foreign policymaking; leader's view of world and political style will dominate policy proposals.
	High	Will rely on historical precedents in making foreign policy; will choose foreign policy advisers to delegate responsibilities to whose interests and experiences match leader's.	Will want to be involved in all facets of foreign policymaking; will want to personally interact with other world leaders; will be interested in the particulars of foreign policy situations and problems.

political tools of persuasion, coalition building, and consensus formation in order to get their way in the family who have become president during times of relative peace and consolidation, when the people want leaders who are responsive to their wishes. Andrew Jackson, a third-born son who was elected president at the beginning of a period of domestic consolidation, is an example of a younger son president.

What kinds of backgrounds have our leaders had that might affect their foreign policy positions? One piece of background information that has proven relevant to studying foreign policymakers in other countries is travel and study abroad (see, for example, Welsh, 1977). Has the leader had many encounters with other cultures, enough to build an understanding of what these other peoples are like? Were these experiences primarily in one part of the world or were they more general? We note that General Douglas MacArthur, who was central in shaping American policy during the reconstruction of Japan, took an extensive tour of the Far East during his mid-twenties. MacArthur (1964: 32) observed:

> [This trip] was without a doubt the most important factor of preparation in my entire life. . . . It was crystal clear to me that the future and, indeed, the very existence of America, were irrevocably entwined with Asia and its island outposts. It was to be sixteen years before I returned to the Far East, but always was its mystic hold upon me.

Barber (1977) has indicated that another important piece of background information is learning about the first political position a leader has held. The experiences enabling the leader to gain and hold this first position often shape political style and worldview. A leader will fall back on future occasions on the rhetoric and practices which helped him or her succeed the first time. Moreover, early experiences, because they are first, are often more vivid and given extra significance in memory. Reagan's views on Communism appear to have been shaped by his first political position, president of the Screen Actors Guild. As he observed in an interview with Barrett (1980: 19–20):

> [I was] unaware that certain labor unions had been infiltrated by the American Communist Party. I was unbelieving until they made their big effort in a jurisdictional strike to gain control of the picture business. Then I discovered firsthand the cynicism, the brutality, the complete lack of morality of their positions and the cold-bloodedness of their attempt, at any cost, to gain control of that industry. . . . [Communists] have one course and one course only. They are dedicated to the belief that they are going to take over the world.

In addition to our own experiences, we are also products of our times. What was going on in the United States and the world when the leader was growing up, seeking his or her first job, and assuming responsibility? What were the events and ideas shaping young people during the time the leader was moving from adolescence through early adulthood? Surveying America's future leaders, Broder (1981:11) has commented:

> America is changing hands. In the 1980s the custody of the nation's leadership will be transferred from the World War II veterans, who have held sway for a generation, to a new set of men and women. These newcomers . . . are the products of a set of experiences different from those which shaped the dominant American

personalities of the past quarter-century. They do not carry the memories or the scars of the Great Depression. They were not part of the victory over totalitarianism in Italy, Germany, and Japan. The next ones who will take power . . . were shaped in a different time. Theirs has been a time of affluence and inflation, of extraordinary education advance, and of wrenching social change and domestic discord. . . . [T]heir wars were fought in Korea and Vietnam, and if fewer of them returned as casualties, none returned as victors.

Broder's observations suggest the common generational experiences that can have an effect on those who become leaders. If not imbued themselves with the ideas that have shaped their generation, leaders will have to deal with these ideas to stay in power.

LEADERS' CONSTITUENCIES

Leaders are leaders because they have followers—people who have granted them authority and to whom they are accountable: their constituents. Political leaders often have more than one constituency for whom they are providing leadership. To understand the relationship between leadership and American foreign policy, we need to recognize who the leader's various constituencies are. What do they want the leader to do or help them to do? What images do they hold of the leader? In learning about a political leader's constituencies, we can begin to see to whom the leader is responding and why, to ascertain the degree of support the leader is likely to have for various kinds of activities and from whom, and to determine the degree of confidence, authority, and esteem invested in the leader.

Let us consider the constituencies the president must deal with. To be effective in shaping foreign policy, presidents must work with the people who elected them, the Congress, the agencies and departments of the executive branch of government, their own staffs and cabinet, and foreign leaders. What kinds of expectations and images do these various groups have of the president?

If foreign policy becomes an important campaign issue for the presidency, there is an expectation on the part of the public that something will happen. In the elections of both Eisenhower in 1952 and Nixon in 1968, getting out of an unpopular war was an important campaign issue, and the public wanted action. Special interest groups within the public can also have foreign policy expectations that presidents must consider in dealing with specific foreign policy problems. We note the so-called Jewish lobby that becomes quite active when questions of Israel are under consideration. At times there can be a ground swell of public opinion for or against a particular policy that demands attention—the increased public dissatisfaction with the Vietnam War in the late 1960s and the concern for a freeze on the level of nuclear arms in the 1980s are examples. Most of the time, though, the American public is something like the crowd at a football game who cheer when they approve of what is going on and boo when they disapprove or want more action. Like these spectators, the American public's response to foreign policy issues is generally more emotional than rational, felt but not always carefully thought through. And the response is highly time-specific, changing as the situation changes. By such responses the public appears to indicate what the outer boundaries are on what a president can do in the foreign policy arena at a particular point in time. The fickleness of the public, however, enables the president to consider molding public opinion. Sorensen (1963), a Kennedy speechwriter, has observed that the president can use public opinion as a sword as well as a compass.

Turning to Congress as a constituent, we note that in most instances Congress enacts what the president proposes with regard to foreign policy. As the old adage goes, "the president proposes and the Congress disposes." But since Watergate and the Vietnam War, this process has not been as automatic as it once was. In fact, since the mid-1970s an adversarial relationship has developed between Congress and the president. Representatives are asking to be told the facts and to be convinced why a particular foreign policy activity is appropriate. They are interested in exercising more influence over foreign policy than they perceive they have had in the past. As former Senator Fulbright (1979) observed, representatives want to advise the president on broad policy directions. They seem intent on moving congressional relations with the president away from those characteristic of an "imperial presidency" (Schlesinger, 1973) toward those found in a "tethered presidency" (Franck, 1981).

The image that representatives have of the president is determined by several factors: the amount of attention the president pays to winning their support, the president's popularity with the people, and the president's popularity with foreign leaders. Koenig (1981) suggests that representatives are more responsive to a president who becomes involved in gaining their support for policies—in courting their favor. On foreign policy issues this courting often must cut across party lines. For example, Carter's problems with Congress were often attributed to his aloofness in dealing with the Senate and the House (Cronin, 1980). Congress also responds like a barometer to the president's popularity at home and abroad. Members of Congress become more assertive and less supportive of the president's policies when his popularity is low, particularly if it is an election year.

When we examine the expectations and images of the president that are held in departments and agencies of the executive branch, we assume that there will be a similarity between the president's view of foreign policy and those held within the bureaucracy. Such is not necessarily the case, however; presidents come and go, and many are only in office for four years. Career bureaucrats, on the other hand, expect to spend their professional lives in a particular department, bureau, or agency. Their loyalty is to their organization and not to the president. There is often a resistance on the part of career bureaucrats to policies they perceive are not in the best interests of the United States. Moreover, each department tends to define problems from its own perspective and to seek support for options that further its view of what American foreign policy should be.

The image career bureaucrats have of the president varies with the president's skill at involving such officials in the foreign policy–making process. Conflict tends to arise when departments and agencies think they are being bypassed. But as a Kennedy aide observed, it is much easier to give an order than to try to win cooperation (Cronin, 1980: 233).

Among the president's various constituencies, the group most likely to share his views on foreign policy are his staff and cabinet appointees. All owe their positions to the president and serve at his request. Cabinet appointees, how-

276 Margaret G. Hermann

ever, can quickly become swept up in departmental issues and constrained by the fact that they are accountable to Congress as well as to the president:

> Every power a cabinet officer exercises is derived from some Act of Congress; every penny he or she expends must be appropriated by the Congress; every new statutory change the Cabinet officer desires must be submitted to the Congress and defended there. A Cabinet officer's every act is subject to oversight by one or more regular or special Congressional Committees. . . . (Patterson, 1976: 17–18)

Thus, cabinet members often feel themselves caught in a tug-of-war between the wishes of their departments, the Congress, and the president. Generally the images cabinet members have of the president are more positive the more latitude they are given to perform their functions and the more support they receive from the president for their initiatives. By such behavior the president helps to eliminate one of the tugs on them and to reduce the pressure they feel themselves under.

Of his many constituents, the president's staff are usually the most supportive—loyalty is a prerequisite for the job. Moreover, many staff members are chosen because they have served the president well in previous positions—in political roles or on the campaign trail. The key presidential staff position in the foreign policy arena since the Kennedy administration has become the adviser for national security affairs. McGeorge Bundy, W. W. Rostow, Henry Kissinger, and Zbigniew Brzezinski are among those who have held this role since the Kennedy administration. Because of the difficulty in controlling their other constituencies, presidents have increasingly turned to their national security affairs advisers and to these advisers' staffs for the development of foreign policy and oversight of the foreign policy-making process. Information on foreign policy issues is filtered from the various departments and agencies through the adviser for national security affairs; thus he or she can shape the expectations of the president and, in turn, the image others hold of the foreign policy-making skills of the president. How much influence the national security adviser has in shaping what the president knows about a particular foreign policy problem is vividly portrayed in the Tower Commission Report on the Iran-*contra* scandal during the Reagan administration. One of the indictments of this foreign policy process was that "the national security adviser failed in his responsibility to see that an orderly process was observed" (Tower, Muskie, and Scowcroft, 1987: xviii); that is, the national security adviser failed to act as an "honest broker." He failed to see that "issues are presented clearly to the president; that all reasonable options, together with an analysis of their disadvantages and risks, are brought to his attention; and that the views of the President's other principal advisers are accurately conveyed" (Tower, Muskie, and Scowcroft, 1987: 10).

One last constituency is important in considering American foreign policy: foreign leaders. To be effective in international relations, the president must convince foreign leaders as well as American policymakers that a particular course of action is appropriate. Moreover, foreign leaders often have certain expectations concerning the president's behavior. Leaders of countries allied with the United States—for example, leaders of NATO countries—expect to be consulted before the United States endorses an action that has implications for their countries. Soviet leaders have expectations regarding what Americans will do in foreign policy, as do leaders of Third World countries. Foreign leaders' images of the president are built on how well he meets these expectations. They are interested in how much they can count on the American president and how predictable his behavior is.

Moreover, coming full circle, how the president conducts himself with foreign leaders has implications for how the American public will view the president. The American people want their leader to appear to be in charge and to be having some influence in his interactions with foreign leaders. Thus, they observe his trips abroad, his White House meetings with foreign dignitaries, and his communications with foreign leaders with interest. Judgments about how effective the president is emerge from these observations, as do the seeds of discontent. Ascertaining the American public's view on the president's skill in dealing with foreign leaders provides insight into how satisfied it is likely to be with the president.

LEADERS' RELATIONS WITH CONSTITUENCIES

How does a leader like the president relate to the constituencies we have just described, in order that at least some of their expectations are met and that his own worldview has a chance of becoming part of American foreign policy? How does he mobilize these constituencies to deal effectively with foreign policy issues? In effect, the president is faced with building relationships that foster convergence, or at least minimize the conflict, among these groups to whom he is accountable. Eric Jonsson, a former mayor of Dallas, has likened this process to "walking on a moving belt while juggling," with people throwing things at one and with an end of the belt on fire (quoted in Kotter and Lawrence, 1974: 175).The president becomes involved in what Thompson (1967) has called the coalignment process; he works on maintaining a "fit" ("match," "congruence," "compatibility") between the expectations and needs of his various constituencies, his own goals and interests, and the proposed solutions to the problems the country faces. How effective the president is in achieving this fit depends on how well he carries out certain functions or activities, that is, how well he (1) builds networks and coalitions, (2) sets the agenda and shapes policy, (3) inspires enthusiasm, (4) shapes and maintains an image, (5) selects and develops an effective staff, (6) gathers information, and (7) accomplishes tasks (solves problems). Or, in other words, how good a consensus builder, policy advocate, motivator, advertiser, recruiter, listener, and manager is he?

Neustadt (1960) defined the major tools of the president as those of persuasion and bargaining. These are, indeed, the tools of the *consensus-building function* of the presidency. Consensus building involves arranging compromises among people or groups with disparate points of view as well as building support for a particular policy among people and groups previously uncommitted. Consensus building requires being sensitive to what people want and how much they want it. And consensus building requires being willing to "twist arms" as well as "butter up" people. Generally it is done behind the scenes, and thus is as likely to occur in a summit conference or international negotiation as in Congress or in the State Department. Carter's personal diplomacy with Egyptian and Israeli leaders in hammering out a peace settlement, for example, involved much consensus building (see Quandt, 1986). Consensus building often involves promises to one side or the other in order to encourage them to compromise or change their position. One negative outcome of the consensus-building process can be that the leader promises too much and cannot deliver. To remain credible the leader needs to rely on rewards that can be delivered or that are, at least, perceived as within his or her power to deliver.

To ensure that their own ideas about American foreign policy influence and shape government actions, presidents become *policy advocates* for issues they perceive are particularly important. In effect, presidents work on setting the agenda for these issues and work to shape policy. As one of Reagan's aides has observed: "The whole issue of running the Presidency in the modern age is control of the agenda" (Blumenthal, 1981: 110). Like Reagan with his firm stand on the need for increased defense spending, Carter with his advocacy of the Panama Canal treaties, and Kennedy championing a nuclear test ban treaty, the president turns into a sales representative for a particular foreign policy position and lobbies both the Congress and the people for support. Such policy advocacy can also extend to the international arena and involve making specific proposals to the United Nations and other international organizations or to another country. Carter's advocacy of human rights throughout the world is an example of such behavior. Being a policy advocate, however, does not mean automatic success, and presidents often have to settle for compromise. The classic pitfall of the policy advocate is an unwillingness to give even an inch and an urge to stake one's political reputation on the outcome. This is a situation ripe for disaster, as Woodrow Wilson experienced when he was unwilling to compromise with Congress in 1919 on the proposed Versailles treaty, and saw U.S. entry into the League of Nations go down in defeat.

Journalist James Reston has proposed that the White House is the "pulpit of the nation and the president the chaplain." The *motivator function* grows out of this perception of the presidency. In serving as motivator, the president provides inspiration for the people, builds morale, and gives the nation a sense of mission. For example, Franklin Roosevelt with his "fireside chats" provided inspiration to the American people. He was able to arouse confidence in the listener and a sense of pride in the country as well as hope for the future. Nixon's flair for the dramatic, as seen in his trip to China and his enthusiastic support of Kissinger's shuttle diplomacy in the Middle East, as well as Carter's unabashed pleasure in the Camp David accords between Israel and Egypt also captured the imagination of the people and made them proud of what their country was doing in the world. In performing the function of motivator, however, the president must beware of the fleeting quality of inspiration and learn not to count on what was said or done to inspire for long. Motivation is in constant demand.

Because many constituents of the president know him only indirectly, through others' eyes or through the media, presidents' relationships with their followers are often based on the image that results. *Shaping and tailoring that image* so that it represents what the president wants to convey, and matches the needs and expectations of the constituents, can become a preoccupation of presidents. They try to arrange for opportunities to present themselves in the best light or to accentuate their leadership skills—they take advantage of the six o'clock news and photo sessions (see Smoller, 1986). And the foreign policy arena often presents the president with settings valuable for persuading people of one's good intentions. For example, summit conferences provide such image-making events and are used to improve the president's image. Presidents seek press secretaries (or their equivalents) and public opinion specialists to guide these activities. However, the image-making function of the presidency raises serious problems:

- How does a public leader find just the right word or right way to say no more and no less than he means to say—bearing in mind that anything he says may topple governments and may involve innocent lives?
- How does that leader speak the right phrase, in the right way, under the right conditions, to suit the accuracies and contingencies of the moment when he is discussing questions of policy, so that he does not stir a thousand misinterpretations and leave the wrong connotations or impression?
- How does he reach the immediate audience and how does he communicate with the millions of others who are out there listening from afar? (Windt, 1982: 107).

Theodore Roosevelt once remarked that the best executive was one who had sense enough to pick good men to do what he wanted and the self-restraint to keep from meddling with them while they did it. Presidents themselves cannot do everything required of them. They must delegate some responsibilities; thus the importance of the *recruiter function* in leadership. The trick for any leader is to pick people to whom he or she is willing to delegate responsibility. This task becomes all the more important in the foreign policy area because the president often knows less about foreign issues and problems initially than he does about domestic affairs. It is helpful at the outset, at least, to have some individuals around with experience or knowledge in the foreign policy arena. Thus, presidents have selected people like Kissinger and Brzezinski, both academic experts in international relations, to become their advisers for national security affairs, and have sought skilled secretaries of state like Vance and Shultz, who had previous foreign policy-making experience.

In addition to selecting skilled people, the recruiting activity involves using one's appointees effectively. Some presidents (Eisenhower with Dulles, Nixon with Kissinger) have delegated authority and depended on the secretary of state or national security adviser to act as an intermediary for them with the bureaucracy and other countries. Other presidents (Kennedy with Rusk) have preferred a more collegial relationship, with the president involved in day-to-day policy-making using the secretary of state as a source of, and a sounding board for, ideas.

One problem that may arise as a result of the recruitment of highly qualified individuals is a difference of opinion or competition for power between them. In the foreign policy arena such a rivalry has at times developed between the secretary of state and the president's adviser for national security affairs. For example, a difference of perspective on the nature of U.S.-Soviet relations between Secretary of State Vance and National Security Adviser Brzezinski during Carter's administration led to much behind-the-scenes maneuvering for the president's ear. Until the Soviet invasion of Afghanistan, Carter tolerated the clashing perspectives and the vigorous debate within the government over the nature of American policy toward the Soviet Union (see Rosati, 1987). Most presidents, however, have been unable to tolerate for long such open conflict within their inner circle, and have eventually given more authority to either the secretary of state or the national security adviser. The choice of which one gets more authority depends on the president's political style and on the similarity of worldviews between the president and the occupants of these positions. Because the president retains more control over foreign policy-making if his national security adviser is predominant, the power of the national security adviser has since Kennedy's presidency increased.

In order to know what his various constituencies want, to begin to anticipate problems, and to cope with constituents' expectations, the president learns to monitor the environment in which he is operating—to be aware of his constituents' views of what he is doing and advocating. The president becomes a *listener*, reaching out "as widely as he can for every scrap of fact, opinion, gossip, bearing on his interests and relationships [as leader]. . . . He becomes his own director of his own central intelligence" (Neustadt, 1960: 154). The very act of showing interest in learning about constituents' wants and opinions can improve rapport. There is an increased sense of importance and efficacy among the constituents from whom information is sought. In effect, in the information-gathering process the president keeps in close touch with his various constituents while increasing their sense of participation in policy-making. The president increases the constituents' stake in the policy process and, in turn, in the resulting policy.

The policy process is not over when a decision is made. There is also the need to implement the policy, to see it carried out. Presidents, therefore, also have to function as *managers* to see that things get done. They have to oversee and push the bureaucracy to ensure that policies are translated into actions. This function can be particularly frustrating for a president, because it must coexist with the need to be making other decisions. Kennedy's frustration during the Cuban missile crisis at discovering that the U.S. missiles he had earlier ordered out of Turkey were still there and could become a quid pro quo for the removal of the Soviet missiles from Cuba is a case in point. Some attention must be paid to monitoring what is happening after a presidential decision is made. However, foreign policy decisions are difficult to monitor, because what happens often occurs in another country and often requires an initial action on the part of the leadership of the other country before anything can start. Like the childhood game where a word is whispered around a circle and checked at the end to see if it is anything like what was started at the beginning, a foreign policy decision is passed through various departments, bureaus, military commands, embassies, and even at times clandestine personnel that need to operate on it. And, like the usual result of the game, the decision may change somewhat in form if not substance before it is implemented—if, indeed, it is implemented at all.

We have described seven different functions a president can perform in working on foreign policy. It is important to note that presidents do not necessarily perform all seven functions equally or emphasize all seven functions equally. Indeed, the characteristics of the president and the nature of the various constituencies that the particular president is accountable to often help to determine the emphasis and how well any are performed. For example, the president with a fixed worldview who is relatively insensitive to other's opinions may focus more activity on policy advocacy than the president whose view is less fixed and, thus, more open to the input of others. The latter type of president may find the consensus-building function more palatable. Part of the stress presidents can experience results when there is an incompatibility between the functions they as presidents feel comfortable performing and the desires and expectations of their important constituencies. Lyndon Johnson's interest and skills in consensus building included much behind-the-scenes activity, which led the public to perceive him as a "wheeler-dealer" and to become suspicious of the nature of the private promises he was making. People believed he was not telling them the truth about what was happening in Vietnam. Johnson was never able to understand this reaction, since backroom political bargaining was a way of life for him, and, particularly as his troubles with the public over Vietnam mounted, he lashed out at those people he thought were responsible for his problems—the press, liberals, and intellectuals.

THE CONTEXT OF LEADERSHIP

What leadership functions are relevant as well as what constituents are likely to be expecting is in large part determined by the situation of the moment. What kind of foreign policy problem is the leadership of the country facing? For example, are leaders such as the president faced with an international crisis (a war, the seizure of hostages, an embargo of Middle East oil), the need to replace an ambassador, an attempt by Congress to reassert itself in the foreign policy arena, or discontent among the people about a particular foreign policy issue? In each of these instances the president would need to emphasize different functions to deal effectively with the problem. Showing that he has a possible solution to the problem or has a way of working on the problem (policy advocacy) is important for a president during times of international crisis. Groups turn to the president for guidance. Selection of an ambassador involves the recruiting function and the need to choose someone who will both serve the president's interests and work well with the leadership of the country to which he or she will be assigned. The selection can also involve patronage and reward to someone for past service. Building a working coalition in Congress or acting as a consensus builder is needed when Congress poses threats to the president's programs. When the public becomes overly disgruntled with a particular policy (or the lack of a particular policy), the president can benefit by becoming a motivator, trying to show why the country needs to do what it is doing but also listening to the leaders of the disaffected groups and seeking to mold their opinions.

Whether presidents pick up the cues from the situation and fit their behavior to the context depends on their personalities and backgrounds. Worldview, political style, training in foreign affairs, and how their earliest political successes and failures have structured their behavior will affect their malleability.

Two other types of situations that presidents face merit comment. One is the honeymoon period following an election; the other is the election itself. Every president appears to enjoy a period early in his term, generally within the first 100 days of taking office, when both Congress and the people lend their support and hold back criticism. Bipartisanship runs strong in the Congress and an air of expectancy and optimism pervades the country. Even foreign leaders will often refrain from criticism. Within this period, presidents, if organized, can shape what happens in foreign policy more than at any other time during their presidency. They have the opportunity to set the foreign policy agenda for their administration. The opposite, however, is true of election periods. With politicians nowadays starting to run for the presidency several years before an election, politics becomes an important part of most presidential policy-making by the end of the third year of a president's term, and may be pivotal at the midterm elections if public support for the president has declined. Unless forced by international events, presidents become careful at election times (whether the midterm or presidential election) not to embroil themselves in foreign policy debates that might prove politically costly.

Presidents, like other political leaders, must also be attuned to the general tenor of the times in which they are operating (see Hermann, 1986). Is the period one of relatively little change, turmoil, or crisis, or one of rapid change, much turbulence, and many crises? Different styles of leadership are required as times move from the relatively peaceful to the more turbulent. Jackson and Rosberg (1984) have likened the differences in leadership to what happens to the commander of a ship in a storm as opposed to in calm waters. When the sea is calm the commander is involved in political navigation, guiding and steering the country toward its goals; in a storm the commander is engaged in political seamanship, trying to keep the country and government afloat with some stability and order. In turbulent times constituents become more demanding, coordination among activities and groups becomes more difficult, and the president's legitimacy and position are often under attack.

Another aspect of the times that can haunt presidents is whether the period is one in which resources are plentiful or scarce. As one observer of presidents (Wrightsman, 1982) has commented, it requires different political style and motivation to lead a government when things must be continuously cut back than when one has the luxury of starting new programs and of going in new directions. As resources become scarcer, competition among constituents can become exaggerated, as can criticism of the leader. The president always appears to be favoring one side over another, whether or not such is indeed the case. The values of equality and "fair play" can develop into rallying cries for groups of constituents. Leaders, in effect, are "damned if they do and damned if they don't." As the United States becomes increasingly a debtor nation in the world, presidents will face the hard choices involved in reducing the debt while trying to minimize the cost to their various constituencies. The "Buy American" slogans that have already begun to appear, and the wrangles with Japanese leaders over import quotas that continue, are harbingers of what presidents will have to cope with.

SUMMARY

To understand the relevance of leadership to the examination of American foreign policy, we have argued that it is important to learn not only what the leaders involved are like but also what the expectations are of those they lead, how the leaders relate to their various constituents, and the nature of the current situation. Leadership can change as these ingredients change, with consequences for foreign policy. We have indicated the kinds of personality characteristics and experiences of American foreign policy leaders that can influence foreign policy decisions as well as the expectations that various players in the foreign policy-making process are likely to have of their leader. Moreover, we have suggested the kinds of functions a leader, particularly a president, will have to perform to meet what is expected of him. The situation helps determine which foreign policy leaders and which constituencies are relevant. American foreign policy results from the interaction of the particular president with his characteristics, and the relevant constituencies, with their expectations. In effect, American foreign policy is made by people, and what those people are like helps shape what happens.

REFERENCES

Barber, James David (1983). "President Reagan's Character: An Assessment," pp. 494–500 in Charles W. Kegley, Jr., and Eugene R. Wittkopf (eds.), *Perspectives on American Foreign Policy*. New York: St. Martin's Press.
Barber, James David (1977). *The Presidential Character*. Englewood Cliffs, N.J.: Prentice-Hall.
Barber, James David (1965). *The Lawmakers*. New Haven, Conn.: Yale University Press.
Barrett, Laurence I. (1980). "Meet the Real Ronald Reagan," *Time*, October 20.
Bennis, Warren (1973). "The Doppelganger Effect," *Newsweek*, September 17, 13.
Blumenthal, Sidney (1981). "Marketing the President," *New York Times Magazine*, September 13, 110.
Broder, David S. (1981). *Changing of the Guard: Power and Leadership in America*. New York: Penguin.
Burns, James MacGregor (1978). *Leadership*. New York: Harper & Row.
Cronin, Thomas E. (1980). *The State of the Presidency*, 2nd ed. Boston: Little, Brown.
Eldridge, A. F. (1976). "The Crisis of Authority: The President, Kissinger, and Congress (1969–1974)." Paper presented at the meeting of the International Studies Association, Toronto, March.
Franck, T. M. (1981). *The Tethered Presidency: Congressional Restraint on Executive Power*. New York: New York University Press.
Fulbright, J. William (1979). "The Legislator as Educator," *Foreign Affairs*, 57, 719–732.
George, Alexander L. (1980). *Presidential Decisionmaking in Foreign Policy: The Effective Use of Information and Advice*. Boulder, Colo.: Westview Press.
Hermann, Margaret G. (1986). "Ingredients of Leadership," pp. 167–192 in Margaret G. Hermann (ed.), *Political Psychology*. San Francisco: Jossey-Bass.
Hermann, Margaret G. (1980). "Explaining Foreign Policy Behavior Using the Personal Characteristics of Political Leaders," *International Studies Quarterly*, 24, 7–46.
Hermann, Margaret G. (1979). "Indicators of Stress in Policymakers during Foreign Policy Crises," *Political Psychology*, 1, 27–46.
Hermann, Margaret G. (ed.) (1977). *A Psychological Examination of Political Leaders*. New York: Free Press.
Jackson, R. H., and Rosberg, C. G. (1984). "Personal Rule: Theory and Practice in Africa," *Comparative Politics*, 16, 421–442.
Janis, Irving L. (1972). *Victims of Groupthink*. Boston: Houghton Mifflin.
Knutson, Jeanne N. (1973). "Personality in the Study of Politics," in Jeanne N. Knutson (ed.), *Handbook of Political Psychology*. San Francisco: Jossey-Bass.
Koenig, Louis W. (1981). *The Chief Executive*. 4th ed. New York: Harcourt Brace Jovanovich.
Kotter, J. P., and Lawrence, P. R. (1974). *Mayors in Action: Five Approaches to Urban Governance*. New York: Wiley.
Lasswell, Harold D. (1948). *Power and Personality*. New York: Viking Penguin.
MacArthur, Douglas (1964). *Reminiscences*. New York: McGraw-Hill.
Neustadt, Richard (1960). *Presidential Power*. New York: Wiley.
Patterson, Bradley H., Jr. (1976). *The President's Cabinet: Issues and Questions*. Washington, D.C.: American Society for Public Administration.
Quandt, William B. (1986). *Camp David: Peacemaking and Politics*. Washington, D.C.: The Brookings Institution.
Rosati, Jerel A. (1987). *The Carter Administration's Quest for Global Community: Beliefs and Their Impact on Behavior*. Columbia, S. C.: University of South Carolina Press.
Safire, William (1982). "Is Castro Convertible?" *Columbus Citizen Journal*, April 27, 6.
Schlesinger, Arthur M., Jr. (1973). *The Imperial Presidency*. Boston: Houghton Mifflin.
Smoller, Fred (1986). "The Six O'Clock Presidency: Patterns of Network News Coverage," *Presidential Studies Quarterly*, 16, 31–49.

Sorensen, Theodore C. (1965). *Kennedy*. New York: Harper & Row.

Sorensen, Theodore C. (1963). *Decision Making in the White House*. New York: Columbia University Press.

Stewart, Lewis H. (1977). "Birth Order and Political Leadership," pp. 206–236 in Margaret G. Hermann (ed.), *A Psychological Examination of Political Leaders*. New York: Free Press.

Stoessinger, John E. (1985). *Crusaders and Pragmatists: Movers of Modern American Foreign Policy*. New York: Norton.

Thompson, J. (1967). *Organizations in Action*. New York: McGraw-Hill.

Tower, John, Muskie, Edmund, and Scowcroft, Brent (1987). *The Tower Commission Report*. New York: New York Times and Bantam Books.

Walker, Stephen G. (1983). "The Motivational Foundations of Political Belief Systems: A Re-Analysis of the Operational Code Construct," *International Studies Quarterly*, 27, 179–202.

Walker, Stephen G. (1977). "The Interface between Beliefs and Behavior: Henry A. Kissinger's Operational Code and the Vietnam War," *Journal of Conflict Resolution*, 21, 129–168.

Welsh, William A. (1977). "Effect of Career and Party Affiliation on Revolutionary Behavior among Latin American Political Elites," pp. 276–308 in Margaret G. Hermann (ed.), *A Psychological Examination of Political Leaders*. New York: Free Press.

Windt, Theodore (1982). *Presidential Rhetoric: 1961 to the Present*. 3rd ed. Dubuque, Iowa: Kendall/Hunt.

Wrightsman, Lawrence S. (1982). "The Social Psychology of U.S. Presidential Effectiveness." Robert I. Watson Memorial Lecture, University of New Hampshire, April 13.

ABOUT THE EDITORS AND CONTRIBUTORS

Gordon Adams is director of the Defense Budget Project of the Center on Budget and Policy Priorities. He is author of *The Politics of Defense Contracting: The Iron Triangle* (1982) and a frequent contributor to *The Nation, Bulletin of the Atomic Scientists,* and *Mother Jones.*

Mitchell Bard is a foreign policy analyst at the University of California, Irvine. He has published in *Public Opinion* and the *Presidential Studies Quarterly.*

Ryan J. Barilleaux is assistant professor of political science at Miami University. He formerly was an aide to Senator J. Bennett Johnson. He is author of *The President and Foreign Affairs: Evaluation, Performance, and Power* (1985) and has published in a number of professional journals.

Duncan L. Clarke is professor of international relations at The American University. He is author of *Politics of Arms Control: The Role and Effectiveness of the U.S. Arms Control and Disarmament Agency* (1979) and editor of *Decisionmaking for Arms Limitation: Assessments and Prospects* (1983).

Thomas E. Cronin is McHugh Professor of American Institutions and Leadership at The Colorado College. He is author or coauthor of several books on American government and the American presidency, including *The State of The Presidency* (1980) and *Government by The People* (1987). He was honored by the American Political Science Association in 1986 with the Charles E. Merriam Award for the person whose writings and career made a significant contribution to the art of government.

I. M. Destler is a Senior Fellow at the Institute for International Economics. He was formerly Senior Associate at the Carnegie Endowment for International Peace and the Brookings Institution. His books include *Presidents, Bureaucrats, and Foreign Policy: The Politics of Organizational Reform* (1974) and *American Trade Politics: System Under Stress* (1986).

William A. Dorman is professor of journalism at California State University, Sacramento, and an associate of the Center for Study of War, Peace and the News Media at New York University. He is coauthor of the forthcoming book *U.S. Press and Iran: Foreign Policy and the Journalism of Deference,* and has published in the *Bulletin of the Atomic Scientists, World Policy Journal,* and elsewhere.

Theodore Draper is author of *Present History* (1983) as well as a number of other works dealing with U.S. Communism, nuclear weapons, Cuba, U.S. policy in Vietnam, Israel, and world politics. He has been a fellow of the Institute for Advanced Study at Princeton, N.J.

Leslie H. Gelb is the national security correspondent of *The New York Times.* Author of *The Irony of Vietnam: The System Worked* (1979), which won the 1980 Woodrow Wilson Award for the best book published on government, politics, or international affairs, Gelb directed the Pentagon Papers project for the U.S. Department of Defense and served as Director of Politico-Military Affairs in the Department of State.

Alexander L. George is Graham H. Stuart Professor of International Relations at Stanford University. Among his many articles and books are *Woodrow Wilson and Colonel House: A Personality Study* (1964); *Deterrence in*

American Foreign Policy: Theory and Practice (1974), which won the Bancroft Prize in 1975; and *Force and Statecraft: Diplomatic Problems of Our Time* (1983). George served as president of the International Studies Association in 1973–1974.

Fen Osler Hampson is assistant professor in the Norman Patterson School of International Affairs at Carleton University. He is author of *Forming Economic Policy: The Case of Energy in Canada and Mexico* (1986) and coeditor of *Securing Europe's Future* (1986). He has been a Fellow at the Kennedy School of Government at Harvard University and a member of its project "On Avoiding Nuclear War."

Charles F. Hermann is professor of political science and Director of the Mershon Center at The Ohio State University. He is the coauthor of *Why Nations Act* (1978) and has edited *International Crises* (1972) and co-edited *New Directions in the Study of Foreign Policy* (1987); in addition, he has published articles in the *Journal of Conflict Resolution, International Studies Quarterly,* and elsewhere.

Margaret G. Hermann is a Research Scientist at the Mershon Center, The Ohio State University. She is the coauthor of *Describing Foreign Policy Behavior* (1982) and editor of *A Psychological Examination of Political Leaders* (1977) and *Political Psychology* (1986), and has published articles in the *International Studies Quarterly, Political Psychology, American Political Science Review,* and elsewhere.

Ole R. Holsti is George V. Allen Professor of International Affairs at Duke University. He is author of *Crisis Escalation War* (1972) and *Content Analysis for the Social Sciences and Humanities* (1969) and coauthor of *American Leadership in World Affairs* (1984). His articles have appeared in the leading scholarly journals, and he served as president of the International Studies Association in 1979–1980.

David C. Jones is a career military officer and General (ret.) in the U.S. Army. He served on the Joint Chiefs of Staff under four presidents and secretaries of defense and was its chairman in the Carter and Reagan administrations.

Charles W. Kegley, Jr. is Pearce Professor of International Politics and Director of the Byrnes International Center at the University of South Carolina. He has coauthored *World Politics: Trend and Transformation* (1985) and coedited *The Nuclear Reader: Strategy, Weapons, War* (1985) (both with Eugene R. Wittkopf) and *New Directions in the Study of Foreign Policy* (1987). His articles have appeared in the *International Studies Quarterly, Journal of Politics, Journal of Peace Research,* and elsewhere.

Stephen D. Krasner is professor of political science at Stanford University, where he is chairman of the Department of Political Science and editor of the journal *International Organization.* His many publications include *Structural Conflict: The Third World Against Global Liberalism* (1985).

Anthony Lake is Five College Professor of International Relations at Mount Holyoke College. He was director of policy planning in the U.S. Department of State during the Carter administration. He is author of *Third World Radical Regimes: U.S. Policy Under Reagan and Carter* (1985) and (with I.M. Destler and Leslie H. Gelb) *Our Own Worst Enemy: The Unmaking of American Foreign Policy* (1984).

Steven E. Miller teaches defense studies in the Department of Political Science at the Massachusetts Institute of Technology. He is coeditor of the journal *International Security* and has edited a number of books on national security policy, including *The Star Wars Controversy* (1986) and *Conventional Forces and American Defense Policy* (1986).

William B. Quandt is a senior fellow in the Foreign Policy Program at the Brookings Institution. From 1977 to 1979 he was on the staff of the National Security Council with special responsibility for the Middle East. His latest book is *Camp David: Peacemaking and Politics* (1986).

John E. Rielly is president of the Chicago Council on Foreign Relations and editor of the Council's quadrennial reports on *American Public Opinion and U.S. Foreign Policy.*

James N. Rosenau is professor in the School of International Relations at the University of Southern California, where he is Director of the Institute for Transnational Studies. Among his many publications, he has authored *The Scientific Study of Foreign Policy* (1981), coauthored *American Leadership in World Affairs* (1984), and coedited *New Directions in the Study of Foreign Policy* (1987). He served as president of the International Studies Association in 1984–1985.

Arthur M. Schlesinger, Jr. is Albert Schweitzer Professor in the Humanities at the City University of New York. He has published many authoritative essays and books, among which is *A Thousand Days: JFK in the White House* (1966), for which he won the Pulitzer Prize. His most recent book is *The Cycles of American History* (1986).

James C. Thomson, Jr. is professor in the College of Communications at Boston University and formerly Curator, The Nieman Foundation for Journalism at Harvard University. He has published *Sentimental Imperialist: The American Experience in East Asia* (1981).

Eugene R. Wittkopf is professor of political science at Louisiana State University and has published (with Charles W. Kegley) *American Foreign Policy: Pattern and Process* (1987), *The Global Agenda: Issues and Perspectives* (1988), and *Perspectives on American Foreign Policy* (1983). His articles have appeared in the *American Political Science Review, International Studies Quarterly, Social Science Quarterly,* and elsewhere.

ACKNOWLEDGMENTS (continued)

"The President and the Management of Foreign Policy-Making: Styles and Models" by Alexander L. George. Revised and adapted especially for this book from *Presidential Decisionmaking in Foreign Policy: The Effective Use of Information and Advice* (Boulder, Colorado: Westview Press, 1980). Copyright © 1980 by Alexander L. George.

"The Presidency and the Imperial Temptation" by Arthur Schlesinger, Jr. The article is copyrighted by the author and reprinted from *The New Republic* (March 16, 1987).

"Reagan's Junta: The Institutional Sources of the Iran-*Contra* Affair" by Theodore Draper. The article is copyrighted by the author and reprinted from *The New York Review of Books* (January 29, 1987).

"Why State Can't Lead" by Duncan L. Clarke. Reprinted with permission from *Foreign Policy* 66 (Spring 1987). Copyright 1987 by the Carnegie Endowment for International Peace.

"President, Congress, and American Foreign Policy" by Thomas E. Cronin. This article was written especially for this book.

"Politics Over Promise: Domestic Impediments to Arms Control" by Steven E. Miller. Reprinted from *International Security,* Volume 8, No. 4 by permission of The MIT Press, Cambridge, Massachusetts and Steven E. Miller. Copyright © 1984.

"The President, 'Intermestic' Issues, and the Risks of Political Leadership" by Ryan J. Barilleaux. Reprinted with permission of The Center For The Study of the Presidency, publisher of *Presidential Studies Quarterly.*

"What's Wrong With Our Defense Establishment" by David C. Jones. Copyright ©1982 by The New York Times Company. Reprinted by permission.

"How Could Vietnam Happen? An Autopsy", by James C. Thomson, Jr. Copyright © by James C. Thomson, Jr. Reprinted with permission.

"Are Bureaucracies Important? A Re-examination of Accounts of the Cuban Missile Crisis" by Stephen Krasner. Reprinted with permission from *Foreign Policy* 7 (Summer 1972). Copyright 1972 by the Carnegie Endowment for International Peace.

"The Divided Decision-Maker: American Domestic Politics and the Cuban Crises" by Fen Osler Hampson. Reprinted from *International Security,* Volume 9, No. 3 by permission of The MIT Press, Cambridge, Massachusetts, and Fen Osler Hampson. Copyright © 1985.

"New Foreign Policy Problems and Old Bureaucratic Organizations" by Charles F. Hermann. This article was written especially for this book.

"The Role of Leaders and Leadership in the Making of American Foreign Policy" by Margaret G. Hermann. This article was written especially for th's book. Support for writing this article was received from the Leadership Development Program of the Mershon Center at Ohio State University. The article benefited from the exchange of ideas on leadership with members of the Mershon Faculty Leadership Seminar—in particular, Virgil Blanke, Lila Carol, Luvern Cunningham, Charles Hermann, Richard Herrmann, David Lampton, Thoman Milburn, Philip Stewart, and Robert Woyach.